D1603049

COINS OF ENGLAND

AND
THE UNITED KINGDOM

28th Edition

Edited by
Stephen Mitchell and Brian Reeds

adapted, with additional material, from catalogues originally compiled by H. A. *and* P. J. Seaby

London

A Catalogue of the Coins of Great Britain
and Ireland
first published 1929

Standard Catalogue of British Coins
Coins of England and the United Kingdom
28th edition, 1993

© B.A. Seaby Ltd.
7 Davies Street
London W1Y 1LL

Typeset by Data Layout Ltd, 136 Tooley Street, London
Printed and bound by Biddles of Guildford and Kings Lynn

ISBN 1 85264 025 1

FRONT COVER Charles I Bristol Mint half crown chosen to commemorate the celebration of the 350th anniversary of the outbreak of the Civil War.
Photo by Courtesy of the National Museum of Wales.

CONTENTS

PREFACE

Over twenty years ago we prepared the text for the first issue of *Coins of England and the United Kingdom* as the first volume of Seaby's *Standard Catalogue of British Coins*, which itself had been an adaptation and improvement upon our *Standard Catalogue of the Coins of Great Britain and Ireland*, first published in 1945. Over the years the text has been subject to considerable change, the most important being in 1978 when the first of the current series of revised editions was published in a format consistent with our other catalogues on Greek, Roman and Byzantine coins.

For the collector the principal improvements may be seen in the steady increase of detailed information; in values being stated in more than one grade of preservation; in the constant improvement and revision of the text to take into account new coins found each year, and to keep abreast of current numismatic research.

We do not try to lead the market or consciously to anticipate demand for any particular series of coins; we try to reflect the market, taking note of fixed and auction prices during the year. As only few of the coins herein actually turn up in any one year, our aim, as far as possible, is to present to the collector our opinion of what he may reasonably expect to pay for a particular coin.

The catalogue, then, is primarily intended for the collector, but it will also be found to be a compact general handbook for the archaeologist, museum curator and amateur coin finder and, for that matter, any person who has a coin to identify and who wishes to know its approximate value. This is not a catalogue of coins held for sale. It is a guide to the current values of all the coins of the realm.

We would like to acknowledge the help we have received from a number of collectors and specialists. We value the comments and suggestions of those who use this catalogue and we would particularly like to thank all those who have contributed in the past. For the 1993 edition particular thanks are due to David Fletcher for his work on the Decimal Section, to Graham Dyer of the Royal Mint who has provided many of the photographs for that section, and to Robert Van Arsdell for providing us with photographs of Celtic Coins. Andrew Burnett, keeper of Coins at the British Museum, has made helpful comments on the Celtic and Roman Sections.

INTRODUCTION

Arrangement

The arrangement of this catalogue is not completely uniform, but generally it is divided into metals (gold, silver, copper, etc) under each reign, then into coinages, denominations and varieties. In the Celtic section the uninscribed coins are listed before the dynastic coins; under Charles II all the hammered coins precede the milled coinage; the reign of George III is divided into coins issued up to 1816 and the new coinage from 1816 to the end of the reign; and under Elizabeth II the decimal issues are separated from the £.s.d. coinages.

Every major coin type is listed though not every variety. We have endeavoured to give rather more coverage to the varieties of relatively common coins, such as the pence of Edward I, II and III, than to the very much rarer coins of, for instance, King Offa of Mercia.

Values

The values given represent the range of retail prices at which coins are being offered for sale at the time of going to press and **not** the price which a dealer will pay for those coins. These prices are based on our knowledge of the numismatic market, the current demand for particular coins, recent auction sale prices and, in those cases where certain coins have not appeared for sale for some years, our estimation of what they would be likely to sell at today, bearing in mind their rarity and appeal in relation to somewhat similar coins where a current value is known. Values are given for two grades of preservation from the Roman period onwards and three grades of preservation for most coins of the 17th to the 20th century. In the Celtic Section the price quoted is for the condition in which the coin usually appears.

Collectors normally require coins in the best condition they can afford and, except in the case of a really rare coin, a piece that is considerably worn is not wanted and has little value. The values given in the catalogue are for the exact state of preservation stated at the head of each column; and bearing in mind that a score of identical coins in varying states of wear could be lined up in descending order from mint condition (FDC, *fleur de coin)*, through very fine (VF) to *poor* state, it will be realized that only in certain instances will the values given apply to particular coins. A `fine' (F) coin may be worth anything between one quarter and a half of the price quoted for a `very fine' (VF), on the other hand a piece in really mint condition will be valued substantially higher than the price quoted for `extremely fine' (EF). The designation BV has been adopted for coins whose value on the market has yet to exceed its bullion value.

We emphasize again that the purpose of this catalogue is to give a general value for a particular class of coin in a specified state of preservation, and also to give the collector an idea of the range and value of coins in the English series. The value of any particular piece depends on three things:

Its exact design, legend, mintmark or date.

Its exact state of preservation; this is of prime importance.

The demand for it in the market at any given time.

Some minor varieties are much scarcer than others, and, as the number of coins issued varies considerably from year to year, coins of certain dates and mintmarks are rarer and of more value than other pieces of similar type. The prices given for any type are for the commonest variety, mintmark or date of that type.

A BEGINNER'S GUIDE TO COIN COLLECTING

The Scope

Coin collecting is a fascinating recreation. It requires little physical exertion and only as much mental effort as one wishes to give at any time. Numismatics has vast scope and boundless ramifications and byways. It encompasses not only things historical and geographical, but also touches on economics, metallurgy, heraldry, literature, the fine arts, politics, military history and many other disciplines. This catalogue is solely concerned with British coinage, but from the start the beginner should appreciate that the coinage of our own nation may be seen as a small but important part of the whole gamut of world currency.

The first coins, made of electrum, a natural alloy of gold and silver, were issued in western Asia Minor about the middle of the seventh century B.C. Over the next century or so coinage of gold and silver spread across the Aegean to mainland Greece, southwards to the eastern Mediterranean lands and eventually westward to the Adriatic cities and the Greek colonies in southern Italy, Sicily and beyond. The coins of the Greeks are noted for their beautiful, sometimes exquisite craftsmanship, with many of the coin types depicting the patron deities of their cities. Coins of Philip II of Macedon (359-336 B.C.), father of Alexander the Great, circulated amongst the Celtic peoples of the Danubian basin and were widely copied through central Europe and by the Gauls in France. Gold Gaulish staters were reaching Britain around the beginning of the first century B.C. and the earliest gold to be struck in the island must have been produced shortly afterwards.

The coins of the Romans cover some seven centuries and comprise an enormous number of different types current throughout a major part of the civilized world from Spain to Syria and from the Rhine in the north to the Sudan in the south. The Roman province of Britain was part of this vast empire for four hundred years and innumerable Roman coins have been recovered from sites in this country, most being made of brass or bronze. Many are quite inexpensive.

Following the revival of commerce after the Dark Ages, coinage in Western Europe was virtually restricted to silver until the thirteenth century, though gold was still being minted at Byzantium and in the Islamic world. In the Middle Ages many European cities had their own distinctive coinage,and money was issued not only by the kings but also by many lesser nobles, bishops and abbots. From the time of the later Crusades gold returned to the west, and the artistic developments of the Renaissance brought improved portraiture and new minting techniques.

Large silver crown-size thalers were first minted at Joachimsthal in Bohemia early in the sixteenth century. With substantial shipments of silver coming to Europe from the mines of Spanish America over the next couple of centuries a fine series of larger coins was issued by the European states and cities.

Both Germany and Italy became unified nation states during the nineteenth century but balancing the reduction in European minting authorities were the new coins of the independent states of South and Central America. Over the past quarter century many new nations have established their independence and their coinage provides a large field for the collector of modern coins.

It can be seen that the scope for the collector is truly vast, but besides the general run of official coinage there is also the large series of token coins—small change unofficially produced to supplement the inadequate supply of authorized currency. These tokens were issued by merchants, innkeepers and manufacturers in many towns and villages in the 17th, 18th and 19th centuries and many collectors specialize in their local issues.

Some coins have designs of a commemorative nature; an example being the Royal Wedding crown, but there are also large numbers of commemorative medals which, though never intended for use as coinage, are sometimes confused with coins, being metal objects of a similar shape and sometimes a similar size to coins. This is another interesting field for collectors as these medals may have excellent portraits of famous men or women, or they may commemorate important events or scientific discoveries. Other metallic objects of coin-like appearance may be reckoning counters, advertising tickets, various other tickets and passes, and items such as brass coin weights.

Minting processes

From the time of the earliest Greek coins to about the middle of the 16th century coins were made by hand. The method of manufacture was simple. The obverse and reverse designs were engraved or punched into the prepared ends of two bars of iron, shaped or tapered to the diameter of the required coin. The obverse die, known as the *pile,* was usually spiked to facilitate its being anchored firmly into a block of wood or metal. The reverse die, the *trussel,* was held by hand or grasped by tongs.

The coin was struck by placing a metal blank between the two dies and striking the trussel with a hammer. Thus, all coinage struck by this method is known as 'hammered money'. Some dies are known to have been hinged to ensure exact register between the upper and lower die. Usually a 'pair of dies' consisted of one obverse die (normally the more difficult to make) and two reverse dies. This was because the shaft of iron bearing the reverse design eventually split under the constant hammering; two reverse dies usually being needed to last out the life of the obverse die.

Some time toward the middle of the 16th century, experiments, first in Germany and later in France, resulted in the manufacture of coins by machinery.

The term 'milled' which is applied to all machine-made coins comes from the type of machinery used, the mill and screw press. With this machinery the obverse die was fixed and the reverse die brought into contact with the blank by heavy vertical pressure applied by a screw or worm-drive connected to a cross bar with heavy weights at each end. These weights usually had long leather thongs attached which allowed a more powerful force to be applied by the operators who revolved the arms of the press. New blanks were placed on the lower die and struck coins were removed by hand. The screw press brought more pressure to bear on the blanks and this pressure was evenly applied.

Various attempts were made during the reigns of Elizabeth I and Charles I to introduce this type of machinery with its vastly superior products. Unfortunately problems associated with the manufacture of blanks to a uniform weight greatly reduced the rate of striking and the hand manufacture of coins continued until the Restoration, when Charles II brought to London from Holland the Roettiers brothers and their improved screw press.

The first English coins made for circulation by this new method were the silver crowns of 1662, which bore an inscription on the edge, DECVS ET TVTAMEN, 'an ornament and a safeguard', a reference to the fact that the new coins could not be clipped, a crime made easier by the thin and often badly struck hammered coins.

The mill and screw press was used until new steam powered machinery made by Boulton and Watt was installed in the new mint on Tower Hill. This machinery had been used most successfully by Boulton to strike the 'cartwheel' two- and one -penny pieces of 1797 and many other coins, including 'overstriking' Spanish eight real pieces into Bank of England `dollars`, the old Mint presses not being able to exert sufficient power to do this. This new machinery was first used at the Mint to strike the `new coinage' halfcrowns of 1816, and it operated at a far greater speed than the old type of mill and screw presses and achieved a greater sharpness of design.

The modern coining presses by Horden, Mason and Edwards, now operating at the new mint at Llantrisant, are capable of striking at a rate of up to 300 coins a minute.

Condition

One of the more difficult problems for the beginner is to assess accurately the condition of a coin. A common fault among collectors is to overgrade and, consequently, overvalue their coins.

Most dealers will gladly spare a few minutes to help new collectors. Many dealers issue price lists with illustrations, enabling collectors to see exactly what the coins look like and how they have been graded.

Coins cannot always be graded according to precise rules. Hammered coins often look weak or worn on the high parts of the portrait and the tops of the letters; this can be due to weak striking or worn dies and is not always attributable to wear through long use in circulation. Milled coins usually leave the mint sharply struck so that genuine wear is easier to detect. However a x 5 or x 10 magnifying glass is essential, especially when grading coins of Edward VII and George V where the relief is very low on the portraits and some skill is required to distinguish between an uncirculated coin and one in EF condition.

The condition or grade of preservation of a coin is usually of greater importance than its rarity. By this we mean that a common coin in superb condition is often more desirable and more highly priced than a rarity in poor condition. Few coins that have been pierced or mounted as a piece of jewellry have an interest to collectors.

One must also be on the lookout for coins that have been 'plugged', i.e. that have been pierced at some time and have had the hole filled in, sometimes with the missing design or letters re-engraved.

Badly cleaned coins will often display a complexity of fine interlaced lines and such coins have a greatly reduced value. It is also known for coins to be tooled or re-engraved on the high parts of the hair, in order to 'increase' the grade of coin and its value. In general it is better to have a slightly more worn coin than a better example with such damage.

Cleaning coins

Speaking generally, *don't* clean coins. More coins are ruined by injudicious cleaning than through any other cause, and a badly cleaned coin loses much of its value. A nicely toned piece is usually considered desirable. Really dirty gold and silver can, however, be carefully washed in soap and water. Copper coins should never be cleaned or washed, they may be lightly brushed with a brush that is not too harsh.

Buying and selling coins

Exchanging coins with other collectors, searching around the antique shops, telling your relatives and friends that you are interested in coins, or even trying to find your own with a metal detector, are all ways of adding to your collection. However, the time will come for the serious collector to acquire specific coins or requires advice on the authenticity or value of a coin.

At this point an expert is needed, and the services of a reputable coin dealer are necessary. There are now a large number of coin dealers in the U.K., many of whom belong to the B.N.T.A. or the I.A.P.N. (the national and international trade associations) and a glance through the `yellow pages' under 'coin dealer' or 'numismatist' will often provide local information. Many dealers publish their own lists of coins. Studying these lists is a good way for a collector to learn about coins and to classify and catalogue their own collections.

We have been publishing the Standard Catalogue of Coins of England and the UK since 1929. It serves as a price guide for all coin collectors. We also publish books on many aspects of English, Greek, Roman and Byzantine coins and on British tokens. These books serve as a valuable source of information for coin collectors. Our books are available from our premises at 7 Davies Street or your local bookseller. W. H. Smith stock the Seaby Standard Catalogue.

Numismatic Clubs and Societies

There are well over one hundred societies and clubs in the British Isles, a number of which form a part of the social and cultural activities of scholastic or commercial industrial concerns. For details and addresses see page 362.

Useful suggestions

Security and insurance. The careful collector should not keep valuable coins at home unless they are insured and have adequate protection. Local police and insurance companies will give advice on what precautions may be necessary.

Most insurance companies will accept a valuation based on the Standard Catalogue. It is usually `possible to have the amount added to a householder's contents policy. A `Fire, Burglary and Theft' policy will cover loss only from the assured's address, but an `All Risks' policy will usually cover accidental damage and loss anywhere within the U.K.

Coins deposited with a bank or placed in a safe-deposit box will usually attract a lower insurance premium.

Keeping a record. All collectors are advised to have an up-to-date record of their collection, and, if possible, photographs of the more important and more easily identifiable coins. This should be kept in a separate place from the collection, so that a list and photographs can be given to the police should loss occur. Note the price paid, from whom purchased, the date of acquisition and the condition.

Storage and handling. New collectors should get into the habit of handling coins by the edge. This is especially important as far as highly polished proof coins are concerned.

Collectors may initially keep their coins in paper or plastic envelopes housed in boxes, albums or special containers. Many collectors will eventually wish to own a hardwood coin cabinet in which the collection can be properly arranged and displayed. If a home-made cabinet is being constructed avoid oak and cedar wood; mahogany, walnut and rosewood are ideal. It is important that coins are not kept in a humid atmosphere; especial care must be taken with copper and bronze coins which are very susceptible to damp or condensation which may result in a green verdigris forming on them.

From beginner to numismatist

The new collector can best advance to becoming an experienced numismatist by examining as many coins as possible, noting their distinctive features and by learning to use the many books of reference that are available. It will be an advantage to join a local numismatic society, as this will provide an opportunity for meeting other enthusiasts and obtaining advice from more knowledge able collectors. Most societies have a varied programme of lectures, exhibitions and occasional auctions of members' duplicates.

Those who become members of one or both of the national societies, the Royal Numismatic Society and the British Numismatic Society, can be sure of receiving an annual journal containing authoritative papers.

Many museums have coin collections available for study and a number of museum curators are qualified numismatists.

SOME COIN DENOMINATIONS

Gold

Angel	Eighty pence (6s. 8d.) from 1464; later 7s. 6d., 8s., 10s. and 11s.
Angelet or 1/2 Angel	Forty pence (3s. 4d.) from 1464, later 3s. 9d., 4s., 5s., 5s. 6d.
Aureus	Roman currency unit (originally 1/60th lb), discontinued A.D. 324.
Britain Crown	Five shillings, 1604-12; 5s. 6d. (66d.) 1612-19.
Broad	Twenty shillings, Cromwell, 1656.
Crown	Five shillings, from 1544 (and see below and Britain crown above).
Crown of the Rose	Four shillings and 6 pence, 1526.
Crown of the Double Rose	Five shillings, 1526-44.
Florin (Double Leopard)	Six shillings, Edward III.
George Noble	Eighty pence (6s. 8d.) 1526.
Gold `Penny'	Twenty to twenty-four pence, Henry III.
Guinea	Pound (20s.) in 1663, then rising to 30s. in 1694 before falling to 21s. 6d., 1698-1717; 21s., 1717-1813.
Halfcrown	Thirty pence, 1526 intermittently to 1612; 2s. 9d. (33d.), 1612 19.
Helm (Quarter Florin)	Eighteen pence, Edward III.
Laurel	Twenty shillings, 1619-25.
Leopard (Half florin)	Three shillings, Edward III.
Noble	Eighty pence (6s. 8d., or half mark), 1344-1464.
Pound	Twenty shillings, 1592-1600 (see also Unite, Laurel, Broad, Guinea and Sovereign).
Quarter Angel	Two shillings, 1544-7 and later 2s. 6d.
Rose Noble (Ryal)	Ten shillings, 1464-70.
Rose-Ryal	Thirty shillings, 1604-24.
Ryal	Ten shillings, Edward IV and Henry VII; fifteen shillings

	under Mary and Elizabeth I (see also Spur Ryal).
Solidus	Roman currency unit (1/72nd lb) from A.D. 312; the `s' of the *£.s.d.*
Sovereign	Twenty shillings or pound, 1489-1526 (22s. 6d., 1526-44), 1544-53, 1603 -04 and from 1817 (see also Pound, Unite, Laurel, Broad and Guinea, and Fine Sovereign below).
`Fine' Sovereign	Thirty shillings, 1550-96 (see also Rose-Ryal).
Spur-Ryal	Fifteen shillings, 1605-12; 16s. 6d., 1612-25.
Stater	Name commonly given to the standard Celtic gold coin.
Third guinea	Seven shillings, 1797-1813.
Thistle Crown	Four shillings, 1604-12; 4s. 5d., 1612-19.
Thrymsa	Early Anglo-Saxon version of the late Roman tremissis (one-third solidus).
Triple Unite	Three pounds, Charles I (Shrewsbury and Oxford only, 1642-4).
Unite	Twenty shillings, 1604-12 and 1625-62; 22s., 1612-19.

Silver (and Cupro-Nickel)

Antoninianus	Roman, originally 1 1/2 denarii in A.D. 214 (later debased to bronze).
Argenteus	Roman, a revived denarius.
Crown	Five shillings, 1551-1965.
Denarius	Roman, originally 10 then 16 asses (25 to the aureus), later debased: the `d' of the *£.s.d.*
Farthing	Quarter penny, 1279-1553.
Florin	Two shillings, from 1849-1967.
Groat	Four pence, 1279-*c. 1305 and 1351-1662 (Halfgroat from 1351).* `Britannia' groat, 1836-55 (and 1888 for Colonial use only). See also Maundy.
Halfcrown	Thirty pence (2s. 6d.), 1551-1967.
Halfpenny	Intermittently, *c. 890-c. 970, c. 1108, short cross and, more* generally, 1279-1660.
Maundy money	Four, three, two and one penny, from 1660.
New pence	Decimal coinage: 50p from 1969, 25p. (crown) 1972 and 1977, 80, 81, 10p. and 5p. from 1968. `New' removed in 1982.
Quinarius	Roman, half denarius or 8 asses; later debased.
Penny (*pl. pence)*	Standard unit of currency from c. 775/780 A.D.
Sceat	Early Anglo-Saxon, small, thick penny.
Shilling	Twelve pence, 1548-1966.
Siliqua	Roman, 1/24th solidus.
Sixpence	From 1551-1967.
Testern (Portcullis money)	One, two, four and eight testerns for use in the Indies (and equal to the Spanish 1, 2, 4 and 8 reales); 1600 only.
Testoon	Shilling, Henry VII and VIII.
Threefarthings	Elizabeth I, 1561-82.
Threehalfpence	Elizabeth I, 1561-82, and for Colonial use, 1834-62.
Threepence	From 1551-1944 (then see Maundy).
Twenty pence	Decimal coinage from 1982.

Copper, Bronze, Tin, Nickel-Brass, etc.

As	Roman, an early unit of currency; reduced in size and equal to 1/16th denarius in Imperial times.
Centenionalis	Roman, replaced the depleted follis in A.D. 346.
Dupondius	Roman, brass two asses or one-eighth of a denarius.
Farthing	Quarter penny: Harrington, Lennox, Richmond, Maltravers and `rose' farthings, 1613-49; regal issues, 1672-1956 (tin, 1684-92).
Follis	Roman, silver-washed bronze coin, 1/5th argenteus, introduced *c. A.D. 290, later debased.*
Half Farthing	Victoria, 1839-56 (and for Colonial use 1828-37).
Halfpenny	From 1672 to 1967 (tin, 1685-92).
New Pence	Decimal coinage; 2p., 1p. and 1/2p. from 1971. `New' removed from 1982.
Penny	From 1797 to 1967 (previously a silver coin).
Pound	Decimal coin from 1983.
Quadrans	Roman, quarter as or 1/64th denarius.
Quarter Farthing	For Colonial use only, 1839-53.
Semis	Roman, half as or 1/32nd denarius.
Sestertius	Roman, brass four asses or quarter denarius.
Third Farthing	For Colonial use only, 1827-1913.
Threepence	Nickelbrass, 1937-67.
Twopence	George III, `Cartwheel' issue, 1797 only.

SOME NUMISMATIC TERMS EXPLAINED

Obverse	That side of the coin which normally shows the monarch's head or name.
Reverse	The side opposite to the obverse.
Blank	The coin as a blank piece of metal, i.e. before it is struck.
Flan	The whole piece of metal after striking.
Type	The main, central design.
Legend	The inscription.
Field	That flat part of the coin between the main design and the inscription or edge.
Exergue	That part of the coin below the main design, usually separated by a horizontal line, and normally occupied *by the date.*
Die	The block of metal, with design cut into it, which actually impresses the coin blank with the design.
Die variety	Coin showing slight variation of design.
Mule	A coin with the current type on one side and the previous (and usually obsolete) type on the other side, or a piece struck from two dies that are not normally used together.
Graining	The crenellations around the edge of the coin, commonly known as `milling'.
Proof	Carefully struck coin from special dies with a mirror-like or matt surface. (In this country `Proof' is *not* a term used to describe the state of preservation, but the method of striking.)

| Hammered | Refers to the old craft method of striking a coin between dies hammered by hand. |
| Milled | Coins struck by dies worked in a coining press. |

ABBREVIATIONS

Archb.	Archbishop	*mm.*	*mintmark*
Bp.	Bishop	mon.	monogram
cuir.	cuirassed	*O., obv.*	obverse
d.	penny, pence	p.	new penny, pence
diad.	diademed	pl	plume
dr.	draped	quat.	quatrefoil
ex.	exergue	qtr.	quarter
grs.	grains	rad.	radiate
hd.	head	R., *rev.*	reverse
i.c.	inner circle	r.	right
illus.	illustration	s.	shillings
l.	left	var.	variety
laur.	laureate	wt.	weight

CONDITIONS OF A COIN

The grade of preservation in order of merit as generally used in England.

Proof	Carefully struck coin from special dies with a mirror - like or matt surface.
FDC	*Fleur-de-coin.* Flawless, unused, without any wear, scratches or marks. Usually only applied to proofs.
Unc.	*Uncirculated.* A coin in new condition as issued by the Mint but, owing to modern mass-production methods of manufacture and storage, not necessarily perfect.
EF	*Extremely Fine.* A coin that shows little sign of having been in circulation, but which may exhibit slight surface marks or faint wear on very close inspection.
VF	*Very Fine.* Some wear on the raised surfaces; a coin that has had only limited circulation.
F	*Fine.* Considerable signs of wear on the raised surfaces, or design weak through faulty striking.
	Fair. A coin that is worn, but which has the inscriptions and main features of the design still distinguishable, or a piece that is very weakly struck.
	Poor. A very worn coin, of no value as a collector's piece unless extremely rare.

EXAMPLES OF CONDITION GRADING

EXTREMELY FINE

VERY FINE

FINE

FAIR

Edward III groat   *George II halfcrown*   *Victoria halfcrown*

BRITISH MINTS

LEGEND

Anglo Saxon and Norman, including Angevin mints. (to 1279) •

Edwardian and later mints. (after 1279) ○

Mints operating in both periods. ◉

Charles 1 and Civil War mints. ✳

CELTIC COINAGE

PERIOD OF BELGIC MIGRATION

The earliest uninscribed coins found in Britain were made in Gaul and brought to this country by trade and by the migration of Belgic peoples from the continent (Gallo-Belgic issues A to F). The earliest may date from some time late in the second century B.C., coinciding with Germanic tribes pushing westward across the Rhine and ending with refugees fleeing from the Roman legions of Julius Caesar. Certain of these coins became the prototypes for the first gold staters struck in Britain, their designs being ultimately derived from the gold staters (M) of Philip II, King of Macedonia (359-336 B.C.).

The following list is based on the 1975 edition of R. P. Mack, *The Coinage of Ancient Britain,* which now incorporates the classification for the coins published by D. F. Allen, *The Origins of Coinage in Britain: A Reappraisal,* and from information kindly supplied by H. R. Mossop, Esq.

The new `V' reference in this series equates to R. D. Van Arsdell, *Celtic Coinage of Britain,* in which are listed many more varieties and sub-varieties than are included here.

M	1	3	5	7

Gold Gallo-Belgic Issues £*

1 Gallo-Belgic A. (Ambiani), *c.* 125-100 B.C. *Stater.* Good copy of Macedonian stater, large flan. Laureate hd. of Apollo to l. or r. R̟. Horse to l. or r. *M. 1, 3; V. 10, 12* 950

2 — *Quarter stater.* As last. *M. 2, 4; V. 15, 20* 350

3 — B. (Ambiani), *c.* 115 B.C. *Stater.* Somewhat similar to 1, but small flan and 'defaced' *obv.* die, some with lyre shape between horse's legs on *rev. M. 5, 7; V. 30, 33* 400

4 — — *Quarter stater.* As last. *M. 6, 8; V. 35, 37* 275

5 — C. (Ambiani), *c.* 100-70 B.C. *Stater.* Disintegrated face and horse. *M. 26; V. 44* 325

6 — D. c. 80 B.C. *Quarter stater.* Portions of Apollo head. R. A mixture of stars, crescents, pellets, zig-zag lines; often referred to as 'Geometric' types. (See also British 'O', *S. 49.*) *M. 37, 39, 41, 41a, 42; V. 65/7/9/146* 100

7 — E. (Ambiani), *c.* 57-45 B.C. *Stater.* Blank obv. R. Disjointed curved horse, pellet below. *M. 27; V. 52, 54* 225

8 — F. (Suessiones), *c.* 50 B.C. *Stater.* Disintegrated head and horse to r. *M. 34a; V. 85* 250

*The prices quoted throughout this Celtic Coinage Section are for the condition in which the coin usually appears.

£*

9   — Xc. *c.* 80 B.C. *Stater.* Blank except for VE monogram at edge of coin, R.
     S below horse to r. *M. 82; V. 87-1*   425
10 — — *Quarter stater.* Similar, but horse to l. *M. 83; V. 355*............................   250
11 — Xd. *c.* 50 B.C. *Quarter stater.* Head l. of good style, horned serpent
     behind ear. R. Horse l. *M. 79; V. 78*   500

12   13

18

Armorican (Channel Isles and N.W. Gaul), *c.* 75-50 B.C   £*
12 *Stater* Class I. Head r. R. Horse, boar below, remains of driver with
     Victory above, lash ends in one or two loops, or 'gate'..   45
13 Class II. Head r. R. Horse, boar below, remains of Victory only, lash ends
     in small cross of four pellets   40
14 Class III. Head r., anchor-shaped nose. R. Somewhat similar to Class I.............   45
15 Class IV. Head r. R. Horse with reins, lyre shape below, driver holds
     vertical pole, lash ends in three prongs..   50
16 Class V. Head r. R. Similar to last, lash ends in long cross with four pellets......   50
17 Class VI. Head r. R. Horse, boar below, lash ends in 'ladder'   60
18 *Quarter stater* Similar types to above ....*from*   85

Celtic Coins Struck In Britain
Uninscribed gold staters
19 A. Westerham type, *c.* 95-65 B.C. As 5, but horse more disjointed. *M. 28,
     29; V. 200, 202*..   325

19   20   21   22

£*

20 B. Chute type, *c*. 85-55 B.C. Similar but crab-like figure below horse.
   M. 32; V. 1205 150
21 C. Yarmouth (I.O.W.) type, *c*. 80-70 B.C. Crude variety of 5. *M. 31; V.
   1220* 600
22 D. Cheriton type, *c*. 80-70 B.C. Variety of 20 with large crescent face.
   M. 33; V. 1215 475
23 E. Waldingfield type, *c*. 90-70 B.C. Annulet and pellet below horse. *M.48,
   V. 1462* .... *Extremely rare*
24 F. Clacton type 1, *c*. 90-70 B.C. Similar to Westerham type but rosette
   below horse to l. *M. 47; V. 1458* 425

24 25 26 28

25 G. Clacton type 2. Similar, but horse r., with pellet, or pellet with two
   curved lines below. *M. 46, 46a; V. 30, 1455* 350
26 H. North East Coast type, *c*. 75-30 B.C. Variety of 5, pellet or rosette
   below horse to r. *M. 50, 50a, 51, 51a; V. 800* 300
27 I. — — Similar, horse l., pellet, rosette or star with curved rays below.
   M. 52-57; V. 804, 805, 807 375
28 J. Norfolk wolf type, *c*. 65-45 B.C. R. Crude wolf to r. or l. *M. 49, 49a,
   49b; V. 610* 600

30 30A 31

29 Ka. Coritani, South Ferriby type, *c*. 30 B.C.-A.D. 10. Crude wreath. R.
   Disjointed horse l., rectangular compartment enclosing four pellets above.
   M. 447-448; V. 825, 829 350
30 Kb. — — Similar, but star or rosette below horse. *M. 449-450a; V. 809,
   811, 815, 817* 300
30A — — — Trefoil with central rosette of seven pellets. R. Similar to last.
   M. 450a; V. 821. In auction 1985 $5500. (this coin)....................*Extremely rare*

Uninscribed gold staters *continued*   £*

31 L. Whaddon Chase type, *c*. 45-20 B.C. R. Spirited horse r. of new style,
    various symbols below. *M. 133-138a, 139a; V. 1470-6, 1485/7/91/93*   350
32 — *O*. Plain. R. Horse r., with ring ornament below or behind. *M. 140-
    143; V. 1498-1505*   325
33 Lx. North Thames group, *c*. 40-20 B.C. *O*. Blank apart from reversed SS.
    R. Similar to last. *M. 146; V. 1509*   .... *Extremely rare*
34 Ly. North Kent group, *c*. 45-20 B.C. *O*. Blank. R. Horse l. or r., numerous
    ring ornaments in field. *M. 293, 294; V. 14 2, 157*............................   400
35 Lz. Weald group, *c*. 35-20 B.C. *O*. Blank. R. Horse l., panel below. *M. 84,
    292; V. 150, 144*..   600
36 Lz. *O*. Blank with some traces of Apollo head. R. Horse r., large wheel
    ornament below. *M. 144-145; V. 1507*   425

                34   35   37

37 M. Wonersh type. *c*. 35-20 B.C. Crossed wreath design with crescents back
    to back in centre. R. Spiral above horse, wheel below. *M. 148; V. 1520.*   425

                    38   39

38 Na. Iceni, *c*. 30 B.C.-A.D. 10. Double crescent design. R. Horse r. *M. 397,
    399; V. 620*..   475
39 Nb. — Trefoil on cross design. R. Similar to last. *M. 401-403a; V. 626*   475
40 Nc. — Cross of pellets. R. Similar to last. *M. 400; V. 624*................................   600

                41   42

£*

41 Qa. British 'Remic' type, *c*. 45-25 B.C. Crude laureate head. R. Triple-
tailed horse, wheel below. *M. 58, 60, 61; V. 210-14* 350

42 Qb. — Similar, but *obv*. blank. *M. 59, 62; V. 216, 1526* 250

43 R. Dobunni, *c*. 30 B.C.-A.D. 10. Similar, but branch emblem or ear of
corn on *obv*. *M. 374; V. 1005* 600

Uninscribed quarter Staters

44   45   46

43A F. Clacton type. *O*. Plain, traces of pattern. R. Ornamental cross with
pellets. *M. 35; V. 1460* 350

44 Lx. N. Thames group, *c*. 40-20 B.C. Floral pattern on wreath. R. horse l.
or r. *M. 76, 151, 270-271; V. 234, 1608, 1623, 1688* 200

45 Ly. N. Kent group, *c*. 45-20 B.C. *O*. Blank. R. Horse r. *M. 78, 284-285;
V. 158/163/170* 200

46 Lz. Weald group, *c* . 35-20 B.C. Spiral design on wreath. R. Horse l. or r.
M. 77, 80-81; V. 250, 254, 366 200

47 — — *O*. Blank. R. Horse l., panel below. *M. 85; V. 151* 250

48 N. Iceni, *c*. 30 B.C.-A.D. 10. Floral pattern. R. Horse r . *M. 404; V. 628* 200

49   50   51

49 O. Geometric type, Sussex group, *c*. 80-60 B.C. Unintelligible patterns
(some blank on *obv*.). *M. 40, 43-45; V. 143, 1425/27/29* 75

50 P. Kentish group, *c*. 65- 45 B.C. *O*. Blank. R. Trophy design. *M. 36, 38;
V. 145-7* 175

51 Qc. British 'Remic' type, *c*. 40-20 B.C. Head or wreath pattern, R. Triple-
tailed horse, l. or r. *M. 63-67, 69-75; V. 220-32, 36, 42-6, 56, 1015* 225

52 R. Dobunni, *c*. 30 B.C.-A.D. 10. *O*. Blank. R. Somewhat as last. *M. 68;
V. 1010* 275

Uninscribed silver

53   55   56   58

Uninscribed silver *continued*

52A	North Thames group. Head l. with headband (or diadem) and flowing hair. R. New style horse of Whaddon Chase type l. (See *S. 31a*). *M. —; V. 80/1* ....*Extremely rare*	£*
52B	— — Similar. R. Pegasos. *M. —; V. —*	200
53	L x . Head l. or r. R. Horse l. or r. *M. 280, 435, 436, 438, 441; V. 80, 1546, 1549, 1555*	125
54	— — Head l. R. Goat r., with long horns. *M. 437; V. 1552*	140
55	— — Two horses or two beasts. *M. 442, 443, 445; V. 474, 1626, 1948*	150
56	— — Star of four rays or wreath pattern. R. Horse or uncertain animal r. *M. 272a, 414, 439; V. 164, 679, 1543*	125
56A	— — Hd. r. with corded hair and headband. R. Horse l., leaf (?) below, ornaments in field. (Somewhat similar to *S. 77*.) *M. —* ....*Extremely rare*	
56B	— — *Half unit*. Cruciform pattern with ornaments in angles. R. Horse l., ear of corn between legs, crescent and pellets above. *M. —*	250
56C	— — *Quarter unit* (minim). Cross pattern. R. Two-tailed horse	75
57	L z . South Thames group. Wreath or head of serpent. R. Horse *M. 446B* (*Allen L 28-10*)	125
58	— — Helmeted head r. R. Horse. *M. 89; V. 264*	200
58A	— — Facing hd. of Celtic god with horns, wheel between. R. Triple-tailed horse. l., ornaments in field. *M. —* (May be Gaulish) ....*Extremely rare*	
58B	— — Two swans (or cranes), boar and eel (?) below. R. Reindeer l., boar on hindquarters. *M. —* (May be Gaulish)	*Unique*
59	— — *Quarter unit* (3 1/2-4 grains). Similar to 58. *M. 90-91; V. 268-70*	150

      60   61   61A

60	Durotriges, *c.* 60 B.C.-A.D. 20. Size and type of Westerham staters (nos. 19 and 81). *M. 317; V. 1235* Quality of Æ varies, price for good Æ	60
61	— Size and type of Sussex Geometric type (no. 49 above). *M. 319; V. 1242/ 49*	50
61A	— ‛Starfish’ design. R. ‛Geometric’ pattern. *M. 320; V. 1270*	90
62	— Very thin flans, *c.* 55 B.C. Crude hd. of lines and pellets. R. Horse similar. *M. 321; V. 1280*	150
63	Dobunni, *c.* 30 B.C.-A.D. 10. Head r., with recognisable face. R. Triple-tailed horse l. or r. *M. 374a, b, 375, 376, 378; V. 1558, 1020, 1042*	100
64	— Very crude head. R. Similar to last. *M. 378a-384d; V. 1035, 37, 45, 49, 74, 75, 78, 85, 95*	75
65	— *Quarter unit*. As last. *M. 384c; V. 1080* ....*Extremely rare*	

                          63   64

66 69 72

£*

66 Coritani, *c.* 50 B.C.-A.D. 10. I. Prototype issue of good style and execution. Boar r., with rosette and ring ornaments. R. Horse. *M. 405, 405a, b, 406, 451; V. 855, 57, 60, 64* 135
67 — — *Half unit.* Similar. *M. 406a, 451a; V. 862/6* 115
68 — II. South Ferriby type. Vestiges of boar on *obv.* R. Horse. *M. 410, 452, 453; V. 875/7* 90
69 — — *O.* Plain. R. Horse. *M. 453a, 454; V. 884/7* 60
70 — — *Half unit.* Similar. *M. 455-456; V. 879/89* 50
71 — — *Quarter unit.* Similar. *M. 456a; V. 881* 65

74 77 82

72 Iceni, *c.* 10 B.C.-A.D. 60. Boar r. R. Horse r. *M. 407-409; V. 655/7/9* 50
73 — *Half unit.* Similar. *M. 411; V. 661* 60
74 — Head r. R. Horse. *M. 412-413e; V. 665, 790, 792, 794* 80
74A — Similar, but inverted ear of corn between legs of horse on *rev.* M. — *(413 variety)* 200
75 — Double crescent and wreath pattern. R. Horse. *M. 414-415, 440; V. 675/79/1611* 30
76 — *Half unit.* Similar. *M. 417a; V. 683* 70
76A — — Three crescents back to back. R. Horse r. *M. 417; V. 681* 80

Uninscribed bronze
77 Lx. North Thames group. Head l. with braided hair. R. Horse l. *M. 273, 274, see also M. 281; V. 1615, 1646* 70
78 — — Horned pegasus l. R. Pegasus l. *M. 446; V. 1629* .... *Extremely rare*
79 — — Other types............ *from* 150
80 Ly. North. Kent group. Boar. R. Horse. *M. 295-296; V. 154* 125
81 Durotriges, *c.* A.D. 20-50. Debased form of Æ stater (no. 60). *M. 318; V. 1290* 30
82 — Cast coins, *c.* A.D. 50-70. As illustration. *M. 322-370; V. 1322-70* 60

Potin (bronze with very high tin content)

83   84

£*

83 Thames and South, *c.* 1st century B.C. Cast. Class I. Crude head. R. Lines
    representing bull. (Allen, types A-L.) *M. 9-22a; V. 104, 106, 108, 112, 114,*
    115, 117, 119, 120, 122, 123, 125, 127, 129, 131, 133   35
84 Kent and N. Thames, *c.* mid. 1st century A.D. Cast. Class II. Smaller flan,
    large central pellet. (*Allen* types M-P.) *M. 23-25; V. 135-9*   75
84A Thurrock (Essex) 100-90 B.C. Cast, better style Apollo head L. R charging bull
    r. V.A. 1402-42   75

CELTIC DYNASTIC ISSUES

The Celtic dynastic issues are among the most interesting and varied of all British coins.
Soemthing is known about some of the issuers from Julius Caesar's *Commentaries* and other
sources—chiefly the kings of the Atrebates, Regni and Catuvellauni—while many are issues of
kings quite unknown to history bearing legends which defy interpretation.

Roman influence in coinage design is particularly noticeable in the reign of Cunobelin, but the
Icenian revolt of A.D. 61, in which Colchester and London were sacked with the massacre of
over 70,000 Romans, resulted in the termination of British Celtic coinage which previously had
been allowed to circulate along with Roman coins. The dates given for the various rulers are, in
most cases, very approximate. Staters and quarter staters are gold coins of varying quality.
Bronze coins in poor condition are worth very much less than the values given. All coins, even
good specimens, are worth less if they lack clear legends, are struck off-centre or have striking
cracks.

SOUTHERN BRITAIN

Atrebates and Regni. *Berks., Hants., Surrey and Sussex*
85 **Commius** *c.* 35-20 B.C. *Stater.* Portions of laureate hd. r. R. COMMIOS
    around triple tailed hor se r. *M. 92; V. 350*   2500
    Copied from the 'Remic' type QA(*no. 41*), *this is the first inscribed British coin.*

85   86   88

86 **Tincommius,** *c.* 20 B.C.-A.D. 5. Celtic style. *Stater.* Similar, but TINC
    COMMI F, or TIN DV around horse. *M. 93, 94; V. 362, 363*   850
87 — *Quarter stater.* TINCOM, zig-zag ornament below. R. Horse l. *M. 95;*
    V. 365   500
88 Classical style. *Stater.* TINC or COM ·.F on tablet. R. Horseman with
    javelin. *M. 96, 98, 100; V. 375, 376, 385*   800
89 — *Quarter stater.* TINC on a tablet, C above, A or B below. R. Medusa
    hd. facing. *M. 97; V. 378*   550
90 — — *O.* As 88. R. Horse l. or r. *M. 99, 101-104; V. 379, 387-90*   275
91 — *Silver.* Head r., TINCOM. R. Eagle facing. *M. 105; V. 397*   225

£*

91A   — — Head l. R. Bull charging l., TINC. *M. 106; V. 396* 150

92   — — Facing hd. with ornate hair. R. As last. *M. —; V. 370* 100

92A   — — Laureate head l. R. Boar charging l., pentagram, TINCO in field.
    V. 396 150

92B   — — Similar, but head r., C (?) behind. R. Bull charging r. *M. —; V. 381* 150

92C   — — — TINCOMMIVS. R. Horse l. *M. 131b; V. 473*. (Listed in Mack
    under Verica.) 175

93   — — TINC. R. Animal prancing l. *M. 106a; V. 382* 175

93A   — Victory r., TIN. R. CO.F. within wreath. *M. —* 150

93B   — — TINC in angles of four rays, pellets in centre. R. Lion on hippocamp
    l. *M. —; V. 372* 120

93C   — — Five pointed star, pellet in centre. R. Boy on a dolphin r., TIN below.
    M. —; V. 371 75

94   — Silver quarter unit. C F within two interlinked squares. R. Dog to r.,
    TINC. *M. 118; V. 383* ....*Extremely rare*

94A   — — Tablet contains CoF. R. Medusa hd. 375

89   95

95   **Eppillus,** *c.* A.D. 5-1 0 (see also under Cantii). *Quarter stater.* Stars above
    and below CALLEV *(Silchester).* R. EPPI over hound r. *M. 107; V.407* 175

96   98   99

95A   — EPPILLV ·. COMM ·. F ·. around crescent. R. Horse r., star above and
    below. *M. —; V. 409* 325

96   *Silver.* EPP over eagle. R. REX crescent CALLE. *M. 108; V. 415* 65

96A   — Bearded hd. r. in wreath, no legend. R. Boar r., EPPI COM or EPPI F
    CO. *M. —; V. 416* 80

96C   — Quarter unit. Crook-ended cross, pellets in angles. R. Horse r., EPP;
    V. 421 ....*Extremely rare*

96D   — — Bull's hd. facing. R. Ram (?)r., dividing EPPI CO. *M. —; V. 422* 100

96E   *Bronze* Floral design of 8 petals surrounded by 4 crescents and 4 annulets.
    R . Hound r., EPPI above, COM F below ....*Extremely rare*

97   Verica, *c.* A.D. 10-40. *Stater.* Group I. COM .· F on tablet. R. VIR below
    horseman r. *M. 109, 110; V. 460/1* 500

98   — II. Similar but title REX added. *M. 121; V. 500* 450

99   — III. Vineleaf between VI-RI. R. Horseman r. *M. 125; V. 520* 600

100   *Quarter stater* I. COM · F etc. R. Horse VIR etc. *M. 111-114; V. 465-8* 200

101   — II. VERIC COM ·. F in two lines. R. Horse r., REX below. *M. 122; V. 501* . 225

102   — III. Vineleaf, VERI below. R. Horseman as no. 97. *M. 124; V. 525* 300

103   — — Head or seated figure. R. Horseman r. *M. 126-127; V. 526/7* 325

Atrebates and Regni *continued*   £*
104   *Silver* I. Crescents, COM ˙. F. R. Boar. *M. 115; V. 470*..............................   70
104A — — — R. Eagle l. VIR. *M. —; V. 471*..   70
104B — — VIRIC across field, ornaments above and below. R. Pegasus r., star
      design below (12.2 grs) ....*Extremely rare*

105   — II. Name around circles. R. Lion r. *M. 123; V. 505*...................................   80
106   — III. Horseman with spear. R. Horseman with shield. *M. 128; V. 530*   100
107   — — Seated figure. R. Two cornucopiae. *M. 129; V. 531*   70
108   — — Head r. R. Seated or standing figure. *M. 130-131; V. 532/3*   100
108A — — Head r. R. Eagle. *M. 131a; V. 534*   150
108B — — Bull dividing VERICA REX. R. Stg. fig. with head on a standard,
      COMM F. *M. — ; V. 506*   120
109   *Silver quarter unit* I. *O.* Various. R. Animal. *M. 116-117; 119-120e;*
      V. 480/2/4, 510/11, 552   70
109A — — VIR in box. R. Boar's hd. r., CF. *M. —; cf. V. 564*   140
109B — Sphinx C.F. R. Dog or wolf curled head to tail. VERI; *V. 557*   140
109C Eagle r. VERCA COMMI F. R. Wine krater. *M. —; V. 563*   130
110   — III. C ˙. F in wreath. R. Head r., VERI. *M. 132; V. 551*   60
111A — IV. VIR/VAR on tablet. R. Pegasus r., CO below. *M. —; V. 551*.............   90
111B — — VERICA around bucranium. R. Tomb, or altar, C.F. *M. —; V. 552*......   100
111C — — `Maltese cross' design, pellets in angles. R. Hand grasping trident,
      VER REX; *V. 487* (now attributed to Eppillus)   175
111D — Two cornucopiae. R. Eagle. *M.; V. 555*   100
111E Acorn pattern r. R. RVER CA, hippocamp; *V. 556*   100
111F Interlinked C's or crescents, standard between dividing CR at top. R.
      Hippocamp, VERICA. *M. —*...   100
111G Human headed Sphinx, VERIC. R. Hd. r., SCF(?). *M. —*   100
111H Helmeted bust r. in Roman style. R. Horse r., CF between legs. *M. —,*
      V. 558..   100
112   **Epaticcus**, *c.* A.D. 25-35. *Stater*. TASCI ˙. F, ear of wheat. R. EPATICCV,
      horseman r. *M. 262; V. 575*   1250

113   *Silver* Head of Hercules r., EPATI. R. Eagle stg. on snake. *M. 263; V. 580* ...   45
114   — Victory seated r. R. Boar. *M. 263a; V. 581*...   75
114A — EPATI in panel. R. Lion r. *M. —; V. 583*.............................*Extremely rare*
115   Silver quarter unit. *O.* EPATI. R. Boar's head (?), TA below. *M. 264;*
      V. 585..   100

£*

116 — Lion (?) r., EPA. R. TA in centre of double lozenge. *M.* —........................... *Rare*
117 Caratacus, *c.* A.D. 35-40. *Silver.* As 113, CARA. *M. 265; V. 593* 350
The above two rulers were brother and son of Cunobelin (see Catuvellauni), but their coins appear in the same area as Verica's.
117A *Silver quarter unit* CARA around pellet in circle. R. Pegasus r., no legend. *M. —; V. 595* 150

Cantii *Kent*

118 **Dubnovellaunus** *c.* 15-1 B.C. *(See also under Trinovantes.) Stater. O.*Blank. R. Horse r., DVBNOVELLAVNOS or DVBNOVI. *M. 282-283; V. 169/76* 550
119 *Silver* Griffin r. or horned animal. R. Horse l. or seated figure. *M. 286-287; V. 171/8* 250
119A — Triangular or cruciform design. R. Horse r.; *cf. V. 164* 250
120 — Head l. R. Pegasus. *M. 288; V. 165* 250
121 *Bronze* Boar. R. Eagle, horseman or horse. *M. 289, 291, 291a, V. 173, 180/1* 125
122 — Animal. R. Horse or lion l., DVBN on tablet below. *M. 290; V. 166* 125

117   117A   118

123 **Vosenos**, *c.* A.D. 5. *Stater. O.* Blank. R. Serpent below horse. *M. 297; V. 184* .... *Extremely rare*
124 *Quarter stater*, Similar. VOSII below horse. *M. 298; V. 185* 450
125 *Silver.* Griffin and horse. R. Horse, retrograde legend. *M. 299a; V. 186*........... 350
126 *Bronze.* Boar l. R. Horse l., SA below. *M. 299; V. 187* 250

124   128

127 **Eppillus**, *c.* A.D. 10-25. *(See also under Atrebates.) Stater.*COM ˙. F in wreath. R. Horseman l., EPPILLVS. *M. 300; V. 430* .... ·900
128 — Victory in wreath. R. Horseman r. Illustrated above. *M. 301; V. 431* 1500
129 *Quarter stater.* EPPIL/COM ˙. F. R. Pegasus. *M. 302; V. 435* 200
130 — EPPI a round wreath, or COM ˙. F. R. Horse. *M. 303-304; V. 436/7* 225
31 *Silver.* Head r. or l. R. Lion or horseman. *M. 305-306; V. 417/41* 125
132 — Diademed head l. or r., IOVIR. R. Victory or capricorn. *M. 307-308a; V. 442/3* 200*
133 *Bronze.* Head l. R. Victory holding wreath. *M. 311; V. 452* 125
134 — Cruciform ornament or bull. R. Eagle. *M. 309-310; V. 450/1* 125
135 — Bearded head l. R. Horse r. *M. 312; V. 453* 125

130   131

Cantii *continued*   £*

136 **Amminus,** *c.* A.D. 15? *Silver*. Plant. R. Pegasus r. *M. 313; V. 192* 400

137 — A within wreath. R. Capricorn r. *M. 314; V. 194* 225

138 *Silver quarter unit.* A within curved lines. R. Bird. *M. 316; V. 561* 150

139 *Bronze.* Head r. R. Capricorn r. *M. 315; V. 195* 140

139A 'B' within octagonal pattern. R. Bird. *M.*—.. *Extremely rare*

Unattributed coins of the Cantii

140 *Silver quarter unit* Horseman. R. Seated figure wearing belt and holding
     spear or staff. *M. 316e; V. 153* .... *Extremely rare*

141 *Bronze.* Boar or head. R. Lion to r. or l. *M. 316a, c; V. 154* 125

143 — *O.* Uncertain. R. Ring ornaments. *M. 316d; V. 154* .... *Extremely rare*

144 *Bronze quarter unit.* Quatrefoil pattern. R. Horse r. *M. 316f; V. 154* 125

         136   145   148

Durotriges *W. Hants., Dorset, Somerset and S. Wilts*

145 **Crab.** *Silver.* CRAB in angles of cross. R. Eagle. *M. 371; V. 1285* 450

146 *Silver quarter unit.* CRAB on tablet. R. Star shape. *M. 372; V. 1286* 350

NORTH THAMES

Trinovantes *Essex and counties to the West*

         150   152   154

148 **Addedomaros,** *c.* 15-1 B.C. *Stater.* Crossed wreath or spiral. R. Horse,
     wheel or cornucopiae below. *M. 266-267; V. 1605/20* 500

149 — Double crescent ornament. R. Horse, branch below. *M. 268; V. 1635* 700

150 *Quarter stater.* Similar, but rectangle or wheel below horse. *M. 269;*
     V. 1638 650

[Note. For uninscribed bronze, sometimes attributed to Addedomaros, see
S. 77 (M. 273/274; V. 1646).]

151 **Diras?,** *c.* A.D. 1? *Stater. O.*Blank. R. DIRAS and snake (?) over horse,
     wheel below. *M. 279; V. 162* .... *Extremely rare*

152 **Dubnovellaunus** *c.* A.D. 1-10. *(See also under Cantii.) Stater.* Wreath
     design. R. Horse l., branch below. *M. 275; V. 1650* 550

153 *Quarter stater.* Similar. *M. 276; V. 1660* 275

154 *Bronze.* Head r. or l. R. Horse l. or r. *M. 277-278, see also M. 281; V. 1665,*
     1667, 1669 60

£*

155 — Without legend but associated with the Trinovantes. Head or boar. R. Horse or horseman. *M. 280a, b, d*.. 100

Catuvellauni *N. Thames, Herts., Beds., spreading East and South*

157

Tasciovanus, *c.* 20 B.C.-A.D. 10, and associated coins

157 *Stater.* Crescents in wreath. R. TASCIAV and bucranium over horse. *M. 149-150; V. 1680/2* 650

158 — Similar, sometimes with VER *(Verulamium).* R. Horseman r., TASC. *M. 154-156; V. 1730/2/4* 600

159 — Similar, but T, or V and T. R. Similar to last. *M. 157; V. 1790* 700

160 — As 157. R. Horse, CAMV monogram *(Camulodunum). M. 186; V. 1684* 800

161 — TASCIOV / RICON in panel. R. Horseman l. *M. 184; V. 1780* 1100

162 — TASCIO in panel. R. Horseman r., SEGO. *M. 194; V. 1845* 1100

163 *Quarter stater.* Wreath, TASCI or VERO. R. Horse, TAS or TASC. *M. 152-153; V. 1690/2* 275

164 — *O.* As 160. R. CAMVL mon. over horse. *M. 187; V. 1694* 275

165 — *O.* As 161, omitting RICON. R. Pegasus l. *M. 185; V. 1786* 275

166 — *O.* As 162. R. Horse l. omitting SEGO. *M. 195; V. 1848* 275

167 *Silver.* Bearded head l. R. Horseman r., TASCIO . *M. 158; V. 1745* 200

168 — Pegasus l., TAS . R. Griffin r., within circle of pellets. *M. 159; V. 1790* 200

169 — Eagle stg. l., TASCIA. R. Griffin r., *M. 160; V. 1792* 200

170 —VER in beaded circle. R. Horse r., TASCIA. *M. 161; V. 1699* 160

171 — — R. Naked horseman, no legend. *M. 162; V. 1747* 160

172   175   178

172 — Laureate hd. r., TASCIA. R. Bull butting l. *M. 163; V. 1794* 185

173 — Cruciform ornament, VERL. R. Boar, r. TAS *M. 164; V. 1796* 185

173A — Saltire over cross within square, serpentine design around. R. Similar to last. *M. —*... 275

174 — TASC in panel. R. Pegasus l. *M. 165; V. 1798* 150

175 — — R. Horseman l. carrying a long shield. *M. 166; V. 1800* 150

176 — SEGO on panel. R. Horseman. *M. 196; V. 1851* 300

177 — DIAS / C / O. R. Horse, VIR (?) below. *M. 188; V. 1877* 300

178 *Bronze.* Two heads in profile, one bearded. R. Ram l., TASC . *M. 167; V. 1705* 75

179 — Bearded head r. R. Horse l., VIIR, VER or TAS. *M. 168-169; V. 1707-9* 75

180 — Head r., TASC. R. Pegasus l., VER. *M. 170; V. 1711* 75

£*

181 *Bronze* — — TAS ANDO. R. Horse r. *M. 170a; V. 1873a* .... *Unique*
182 — Head r., TAS. R. Horseman r., VER. *M. 171; V. 1750* 70
183 — VERLAMIO between rays of star-shaped ornament. R. Bull l. *M. 172; V. 1808* 70

185   190   191

184 — Similar, without legend. R. Sphinx l., legend SEGO? *M. 173; V. 1855* 70
185 — Similar. R. Bull r. *M. 174; V. 1810* 70
186 — Similar. R. Horse l., TASCI. *M. 175; V. 1812* 70
187 — Head r., TASC. . . R. Horse r. in double circle. *M. 175a; V. 1873* .... *Extremely rare*
188 — Laureate hd. r., TASCIO. R. Lion r., TASCIO. *M. 176; V. 1814* 70
189 — Head r. R. Figure std. l., VER below. *M. 177; V. 1816* 75
190 — — TASCIAVA. R. Pegasus l., TAS. *M. 178; V. 1818 (double bronze denomination* ....*Extremely rare*
191 — Cruciform ornament of crescents and scrolls. R. Boar r., VER. *M. 179; V. 1713* 90
192 — Laureate head r. R. Horse l., VIR. *M. 180; V. 1820* 75
193 — Raised band across centre, VER or VERL below, uncertain objects above. R. Horse grazing r. *M. 183a; V. 1717* 100
194 — RVII above lion r. within wide beaded circle. R. Eagle looking l., sometimes reading RVE. *M. 189; V. 1890* 120
195 — Bearded head r., RVIIS. R. Horseman r., VIR. *M. 190; V. 1892* 80
196 — RVIIS on panel. R. Animal l. *M. 191; V. 1895* 90
197 — Head r., TASC DIAS. R. Centaur r. playing double pipe, or sometimes horses. *M. 192; V. 1882* 90
198 *Bronze half denomination.* Lion? r. R. Sphinx l. *M. 181; V. 1824* 150
199 — Bearded head l. or r., VER. R. Goat or boar r. *M. 182-183; V. 1715, 1826* 100
200 — Head l. R. Animal l. with curved tail. *M. 183b, c; V. 1822* 100
201 — Annulet within square with curved sides. R. Eagle l., RVII. *M. 193;*

196   202   203

V. 1903 90
202 *Andoc, c. A.D . 5-15. Stater.* Crossed wreath design. R. Horse r., AND. *M. 197; V. 1860* 1250
203 *Quarter stater.* Crossed wreaths, ANDO. R. Horse l. *M. 198; V. 1863* 325
204 *Silver.* Bearded head l. in looped circle. R. Pegasus l., ANDOC. *M. 199; V. 1868* 300
205 *Bronze.* Head r., ANDOCO. R. Horse r., AND. *M. 200; V. 1871* 150

205 207 208

£*

206 *Bronze half denomination.* Head l. R. Horse r., A between legs, branch in exergue. *M. —* 175

207 **Cunobelin** *(Shakespeare's Cymbeline). c.* A.D. 10-40. *Stater.* CAMVL on panel. R. Leaf above two horses galloping l., CVNOBELIN on curved panel below. *M. 201; V. 1910* 1300

208 — Ear of corn dividing CA MV. R. Horse prancing r., CVNO below. *M. 203, 206, 210-213. V. 2010/25/1925/31/33/2020* Varying in style, from— 500

209 — Similar, but horse l. *M. 208; V. 2029* 1000

210 *Quarter stater.* Simi lar to 207. *M. 202; V. 1913* 400

211 — Similar to 208. *M. 204, 209; V. 1927, 2015* 250

212 — Similar to 208 but CAM CVN on *obv. M. 205; V. 2017* 375

213 *Silver.* Two bull headed snakes inter twined. R. Horse l. , CVNO. *M. 214; V. 1947* 175

214 — Head l., CAMVL before. R. CVNO beneath Victory std. r. *M. 215; V. 2045* 75

215 — CVNO BELI in two panels. R. CVN below horseman galloping r. (legends sometimes retrograde). *M. 216, 217; V. 1951/3* 125

216 — Two leaves dividing CVN. R. CAM below horseman galloping r. *M. 218; V. 2047* 150

217 — Flower dividing CA MV. R. CVNO below horse r. *M. 219; V. 2049* 150

218 — CVNO on panel. R. CAMV on panel below griffin. *M. 234; V. 2051* 125

219 — CAMVL on panel. R. CVNO below centaur l. carrying palm. *M. 234a; V. 1918* 125

219A CAMVL on panel. R. Figure seated l. holding wine amphora, CVNOBE. *M. —* 150

219B — Plant, CVNOBELINVS (see no. 136 Amminus). R. Hercules stg. r. holding club and thunderbolt, dividing CA MV. *M. —* 225

219C — Laur. hd. r., CVNOBELINVS. R. Pegasus springing l., CAMV below. *M. —* 225

220 — CVNO on panel. R. TASC F below Pegasus r. *M. 235; V. 2053* 175

221 — Head r., CVNOBELINI. R. TASCIO below horse r. *M. 236; V. 2055* 250

212 221 225

222 — Winged bust r., CVNO. R. Sphinx std. l., TASCIO. *M. 237; V. 2057* 75

223 — Draped female figure r., TASCIIOVAN. R. Figure std. r. playing lyre, tree behind. *M. 238; V. 2059* 175

224 — Male figure stg. dividing CV NO. R. Female std. side saddle on animal, TASCIIOVA. *M. 239; V. 2061* 175

224A — Laur. hd. r., CVNOBELINVS. R. Victory r., TASCIO[VAN . . .] 175

Cunobelin Silver *continued*   £*

225 — Figure r. carrying dead animal, CVNOBELINVS. R. Figure stg.
     holding bow, dog at side, TASCIIOVANI. *M. 240; V. 2063* 200
226 — CVNO on panel, horn above, two dolphins below. R. Figure stg. r.,
     altar behind. *M. 241a; V. 2065* 225
227 — CVNO on panel. R. Fig. walking r., CV N. *M. 254; V. 2067* 200
228 — — R. Animal springing l. *M. 255; V. 1949* 260
229 — CVN in centre of wreath. R. CAM below dog or she-wolf stg. r. *M. 256;*
     V. 2069 260
230 — CVNO, animal l. R. CA below figure std. r. holding caduceus. *M. 258;*
     V. 2071 375
231 — SOLIDV in centre of looped circle. R. Standing figure l., CVNO. *M.*
     259; V. 2073 400
232 *Bronze*. Head l., CVNO. R. Boar l., branch above. *M. 220; V. 1969* 60
233 — CVNOB ELINI in two panels. R. Victory std. l., TASC ·. F. *M. 221;*
     V. 1971 60
234 — Winged animal l., CAM below. R. CVN before Victory stg. l. *M. 222a;*
     V. 1973 60
235 — Bearded head facing. R. Similar to no. 232. *M. 223; V. 1963* 85
236 — Ram-headed animal coiled up within double ornamental circle. R.
     CAM below animal. *M. 224; V. 1965* 100
237 — Winged animal r., CAMV. R. CVN below horse galloping r. *M. 225;*
     V. 2081 70
238 — Bearded head l., CAMV. R. CVN or CVNO below horse l. *M. 226, 229,*
     V. 2085/2131 65
239 — Laureate head r., CVNO. R. CVN below bull butting l. *M. 227; V. 2083* ... 100
240 — Crude head r., CVN. R. Figure stg. l., CVN. *M. 228; V. 2135* 65
241 — CAMVL / ODVNO in two panels. R. CVNO beneath sphinx crouching
     l. *M. 230; V. 1977* 70

242   245   251

242 — Winged beast springing l., CAMV. R. Victory stg. r. divides CV NO.
     M. 231; V. 1979 80
243 — Victory walking r. R. CVN below, horseman r. *M. 232; V. 1981* 80
244 — Beardless head l., CAM. R. CVNO below eagle. *M. 233; V. 2087* 80
245 — Laureate he ad l., CVNOBELINI. R. Centaur r., TASCIOVANI ·F.
     M. 242; V. 2089 60
246 — Helmeted bust r. R. TASCIIOVANII above, sow stg. r., F below.
     M. 243; V. 2091 60
247 — Horseman galloping r. holding dart and shield, CVNOB. R. Warrior
     stg. l., TASCIIOVANTIS. *M. 244; V. 2093* 50
248 — Helmeted bust l., CVNOBII. R. TASC . FIL below boar l. std. on
     haunches. *M. 245; V. 1983* 110
249 — Bare head r., CVNOBELINVS REX. R. TASC below bull butting r.
     M. 246; V. 2095 75

£*

250 *Bronze* Bare head l., CVNO. R. TASC below bull stg. r. *M. 247; V. 1985* 100
251 — Winged head l., CVNOBELIN. R. Metal worker std. r. holding
hammer, working on a vase, TASCIO behind. *M. 248; V. 2097* 50
252 — Pegasus springing r., CVNO. R. Victory r., sacrificing bull, TASCI. *M.
249; V. 2099* 50
253 — CVNO on panel within wreath. R. CAMV below horse, full faced,
prancing r. *M. 250; V. 2101* 85

254   255

254 — Bearded head of Jupiter Ammon l., CVNOBELIN. R. CAM
below horseman galloping r. *M. 251; V. 2103* 80
255 — Janus head, CVNO below. R. CAMV on panel below, sow std. r.
beneath a tree. *M. 252; V. 2105* 100
256 — Bearded head of Jupiter Ammon r., CVNOB. R. CAM on panel below
lion crouched r. *M. 253; V. 2107* 90
257 — Sphinx r., CVNO. R. Fig. stg. l. divides CA M. *M. 260; V. 2109* 125
258 — Animal stg. r. R. CVN below horseman r. *M. 261; V. 1987* 150
259 *Bronze half denomination.* Animal l. looking back. R. CVN below horse l.
M. 233a; V. 1967 200

S.W. MIDLANDS

Dobunni *Glos., Here., Mon., Som., Wilts. and Worcs.*
260 **Anted.** *Stater.* Ear of corn. R. ANTED or ANTEDRIG over triple-tailed
horse r. *M. 385-386; V. 1062/6* 750

261 *Silver.* Crude head r., as 64. R. AN TED over horse l. *M. 387; V. 1082* 200
262 **Eisu.** *Stater.* Similar to 260 but EISV or EISVRIG. *M. 388; V. 1105* 1350
263 *Silver.* Similar to 261 but EISV. *M. 389; V. 1110* 150
264 **Inam.** (or Inara). *Stater.* Similar to 260 but INAM (or INARA). *M. 390;
V. 1140* .... *Extremely rare*

265   267

265 **Catti.** *Stater.* Similar to 260 but CATTI. *M. 391; V. 1130* 850
266 **Comux.** *Stater.* Similar to 260 but COMVX outwardly. *M. 392; V. 1092* 1000
267 **Corio.** *Stater.* Similar to 260 but CORIO. *M. 393; V. 1035* 925
268 *Quarter stater.* COR in centre. R. Horse r. without legend. *M. 394; V. 1039* 1250

Dobunni *continued*

269   270

		£*
269	**Bodvoc.** *Stater.* BODVOC across field. R. As last. *M. 395; V. 1052*................	1200
270	*Silver.* Head l., BODVOC. R. As last. *M. 396; V. 1057*	200

EASTERN ENGLAND

Iceni *Cambs., Norfolk and Suffolk c.*A.D. 10-61

272   273   279

271	**Duro.** *Silver.* Boar. R. Horse r., CAN(s) above, DVRO below. *M. 434; V. 663*	500
272	**Anted.** *Stater.* Triple crescent design. R. ANTED in two monograms below horse. *M. 418; V. 705*	1600
273	*Silver.* Two crescents back to back. R. ANTED as last. *M. 419-421; V. 710/11/15*	30
274	*Silver half unit.* Similar to last. *M. 422; V. 720*	40
275	**Ecen.** *Silver.* As 273. R. Open headed horse r., ECEN below. *M. 424 V. 730*	35
276	*Silver half unit.* Similar, but legends read ECE, EC, or ECN. *M. 431; V. 736* ...	50
277	**Ed.** *Silver.* Similar to 275 but ED (also, E, EI and EDN) below horse. *M. 423, 425b; V. 734/40*	100
278	**Ece.** *Silver.* As 273. R. Stepping horse r., ECE below. *M. 425a; V. 761*	50
279	— Similar, but 'Y' headed horse r., ECE below. *M. 426-427; V. 762/4*	40
280	— Similar, but horse l. *M. 428; V. 766*	40
281	**Saenu.** *Silver.* As 273. R. 'Y' headed horse r., SAENV below. *M. 433; V. 770*	125
282	**Aesu.** *Silver.* As 273. R. As last, AESV. *M. 432; V. 775*	200

283

£*

283 **Prasutagus,** Client King of the Iceni under Claudius; husband of Boudicca.
Silver. Head of good style l. SUB RII PRASTO. R. Rearing horse r.,
ESICO FECIT. *M. 434a; V. 780* 950
*The attribution by H. Mossop of these rare coins to King Prasutagus has
been made after a study of the legends on the ten known specimens and is
published in 'Britannia', X. 1979.*

Coritani (usually known as 'Corieltauvi') *Lincs., Yorks. and E. Midlands c.* A.D. 10-61

284 **Iat Iso.** *Silver.* IAT ISO (retrograde) on tablet, rosettes above and below.
R. Horse r., E above. *M. 416; V. 998* 500

285 **Ale Sca.** *Silver.* Boar r., ALE below. R. Hor se, SCA below. *M. 469; V. 996* ... 300

291   294

286 **Aun Cost.** *Stater.* Crude wreath type. R. Disjointed horse l., AVN COST.
M. 457; V. 910 750

287 *Silver. O.* Blank or crude wreath design. R. AVN above horse l. *M. 458;
V. 914* 150

288 *Silver half unit.* Similar. *Vide M. p. 166; V. 918* 200

289 **Esup Asu.** *Stater.* As 286 but IISVP ASV. *M. 456b; V. 920* 1100

290 *Silver.* Similar. *M. 456c; V. 924* 200

291 **Vep Corf.** *Stater.* As 286. R. Disjointed horse, VEP CORF. *M. 459, 460;
V. 930* 475

292 *Silver.* Similar. *M. 460b, 464; V. 934, 50* 175

293 *Silver half unit.* Similar. *M. 464a; V. 938* 125

294 — Similar but VEPOC (M)ES, pellets below horse. *M. —; V. 955* 150

295 *Silver half unit.* Similar. *M. —; V. 958* 200

296 **Vep.** *Stater. O.* Blank. R. VEP.*M. 460a; V. 905* 1100

297 *Silver.* As 286 or blank. R. VEP only. *M. —; V. 965* 150

298 *Silver half unit.* Similar. *M. 464b; V. 967* 125

299 **Dumno Tigir Seno.** *Stater.* DVMN (OC)? across wreath. R. Horse l.,
TIGIR SENO. *M. 461; V. 972* 1000

300 *Silver. O.* DVMNO(C)? R. Horse r., legend as last. *M. 462; V. 974* 350

297   299

Coritani *continued*

300   301

£*

301 **Volisios Dumnocoveros.** *Stater.* VOLI / SIOS in two lines. R. Horse,
     DVMNOCOVEROS across crude wreath. *M. 463; V. 978* 750
302 *Silver.* As last. *M. 463a; V. 978 or 80* 300
303 *Silver half unit.* As last but DVMNOCO. *M. 465; V. 984* 250
304 **Volisios Dumnovellaunos.** *Stater.* As 301. R. Horse, DVMNOVELAV
     NOS. *M. 466; V. 988* 850

305

305 *Silver half unit.* As last but DVMNOVE. *M. 467; V. 992* 175
306 **Volisios Cartivel.** *Silver half unit.* As 301. R. Horse, CARTIVEL. *M. 468;*
     V. 994 200

ROMAN BRITAIN

From the middle of the first century A.D. until the early part of the fifth century, Britannia was a province of the vast Roman Empire—a single state encompassing the whole of the Mediterranean basin. In common with other western provinces, no local coinage was officially produced in Britain during this period (unlike the Eastern part of the Empire where hundreds of towns were permitted to issue muncipal currency) until the latter part of the third century. It was, therefore, the regular Imperial coinage produced mainly at Rome until the mid-third century, that supplied the currency requirements of the province, and no representative collection of British coins is complete without some examples of these important issues.

Although Britain was on the fringe of the Roman World, and never entirely subdued by the legions, a surprisingly large number of coin types allude to events in the province—usually frontier wars in the north. In the closing years of the third century, the usurper Carausius established two mints in Britain; one in London, the other not yet certainly identified (either Camulodunum: Colchester or Clausentum: Bitterne, Southampton). After the defeat of the rebellion London became an official Roman mint, with a substantial output of billon coinage until its closure, by Constantine the Great, in A.D. 325. Other coins were produced unofficially in Britain at various times: soon after the conquest (copies of bronze coins of Claudius, etc.), in the troubled times of the early 270s (copies of Claudius II and the Tetrici, i.e., 'Barbarous radiates') and the final years of the occupation (mostly imitated from the bronze coinage of Constantius II—'soldier spearing fallen horseman' type).'

The Roman legions were withdrawn to the Continent by Honorius in A.D. 411, and this date can be taken to be the formal end of Roman Britain, although a Romano-British civil administration continued to operate for some time afterward until disrupted by the Teutonic invasions.

For general information on Roman coinage see *Roman Coins and their Values* by D. R. Sear and *Roman Coins* by J. P. C. Kent; for more detailed works consult *Roman Imperial Coinage*, the British Museum Catalogues of Roman coins, *Roman Silver Coins* (5 vols.), the first four by H. A. Seaby and Vol. V by Dr C. E. King, and *The Coinage of Roman Britain* by G. Askew (2nd edition).

An invaluable companion volume for anyone studying Roman coinage is J. Melville Jones, *A Dictionary of Ancient Roman Coins* while S. W. Stevenson's *A Dictionary of Roman Coins* is also useful.

THE REPUBLIC

Only a few representative examples are listed. Many Republican coins circulated well into the Imperial period and found their way to Britain where they are often found in many early hoards.

	F £	VF £
451 C. Naevius Balbus, moneyer, 79 B.C. *Æ denarius*. Diad. hd. of Venus r. R.Victory in triga r.	15	30
452 C. Calpurnius Piso, moneyer, 67 B.C. *Æ denarius*. Head of Apollo r. R. Horseman galloping r.	15	35

452   454

453 **Julius Caesar**, dictator, †44 B.C. Made two expeditions to Britain in 55 and 54 B.C. *Æ denarius*. Laur. head r. R. Venus stg. l.	130	325
454 *Æ denarius*. Elephant stg. r. R. Sacrifical implements	90	200
455 **Mark Antony**, triumvir, †30 B.C. *Æ denarius*. Galley r. R. Legionary eagle between two standards	35	80

Known for all Legions from I (PRI*mus*) *to XXIII, though only the following are known to have served in Britain during the Roman occupation—II Augusta, VI Victrix, IX Hispania, XIV Gemina Martia Victrix and XX Valeria Victrix.*

THE EMPIRE

456   461

		F	VF
		£	£
456	**Augustus,** 27 B.C.-A.D. 14. Æ *denarius.* R. Caius and Lucius Caesars	25	65
457	Æ. R. The altar of Lugdunum	30	65
458	**Divus Augustus Pater,** commemorative issue. Æ *as.* R. PROVIDENT S . C. Altar	25	65
459	**Livia,** wife of Augustus. Æ *dupondius.* R. Legend around S. C	65	200
460	**Agrippa,** general and statesman, †12 B.C. Æ *as.* R. Neptune stg. 1.	35	85
461	**Tiberius,** A.D. 14-37. Æ *denarius.* R. Livia seated r.	40	85
	This coin is often referred to as the 'Tribute Penny' of the Bible.		
462	**Drusus,** son of Tiberius, †A.D. 23. Æ *as.* R. Legend around S. C	45	110
46	**Nero Claudius Drusus,** father of Claudius, †9 B.C. Æ *sestertius.* R. Claudius seated amidst arms	110	350
464	**Antonia,** mother of Claudius, †A.D. 37. Æ *dupondius.* R. Claudius stg.l.	65	150
465	**Germanicus,** father of Caligula, †A.D. 19. Æ *as.* R. Legend around S. C.	45	120
466	**Agrippina Senior,** wife of Germanicus, †A.D. 33. Æ *sestertius.* R. Two mules drawing covered carriage	150	500
467	**Caligula,** 37-41. Æ *as.* R. VESTA. Vesta seated l.	65	150
468	**Claudius,** 41-54. Invaded Britain A.D. 43. Æ *aureus.* R. DE BRITANN on triumphal arch	500	2500

468   473

469	Æ *denarius.* Similar	250	750
470	Æ *didrachm* of Caesarea. R. DE BRITANNIS below Emperor in quadriga r.	110	350
471	Æ *sestertius.* R. SPES AVGVSTA S. C. Spes walking l., of barbarous style, struck in Britain	65	220
472	Æ *dupondius.* R. CERES AVGVSTA S. C. Ceres seated l., of barbarous style, struck in Britain	45	95
473	Æ *as.* R. S . C. Minerva brandishing javelin r., of barbarous style, struck in Britain	35	85
474	**Nero,** 54-68. Æ *denarius.* R. SALVS. Salus seated l.	65	150
475	Æ *as.* R. S . C. Victory flying l.	35	95
476	**Galba,** 68-69. Æ *denarius.* R. DIVA AVGVSTA. Livia stg. l.	65	180

		F £	VF £
477	**Otho,** 69. Æ *denarius.* R. SECVRITAS P . R. Securitas stg. l.	110	350
478	**Vitellius,** 69. Æ *denarius.* R. XV. VIR SACR. FAC. Tripod with dolphin	100	250

479   482

479	**Vespasian,** 69-79. Commanded one of the legions in the Claudian invasion of Britain. Æ *denarius.* R. ANNONA AVG. Annona seated l.	25	55
480	Æ *as.* R. PROVIDENT. S. C. Large altar	35	75
481	**Titus,** 79-81. Æ *denarius.* R. FORTVNA AVGVST. Fortuna stg. l.	45	85
482	**Domitian,** 81-96. Æ *denarius.* R. IMP . XI. COS . XI . CENS . P . P . P. Minerva fighting	35	50
483	Æ *dupondius.* R. VIRTVTI AVGVSTI. S . C. Virtus stg. r.	20	50
484	**Nerva,** 96-98. Æ *denarius.* R. CONCORDIA EXERCITVVM. Clasped hands	25	65

485   489

485	**Trajan,** 98-117. Æ *denarius.* R. P . M . TR . P . COS . III . P . P. Victory standing r. on prow	35	65
486	Æ *sestertius.* R. S . P . Q . R . OPTIMO PRINCIPI. S . C. Fortuna stg l.	40	110
487	**Hadrian,** 117-138. Visited Britain *c.* A.D. 122 and constructed his famous wall from the Tyne to the Solway. Æ *denarius.* R. FIDES PVBLICA. Fides stg. r.	25	65
488	Æ *sestertius.* R. ADVENTVI AVG . BRITANNIAE. S . C. Emperor and Britannia sacrificing over altar	*Extremely rare*	
489	— R. BRITANNIA. S . C. Britannia seated l.	*Extremely rare*	
490	— R. EXERC. BRITANNI. S . C. Emperor on horseback addressing soldiers	*Extremely rare*	
491	Æ *as.* R. PONT. MAX . TR . POT . COS . III . BRITANNIA. S . C. Britannia seated l.	120	330

		F	VF
		£	£
492	**Sabina,** wife of Hadrian, Æ *denarius*. R. CONCORDIA AVG. Concordia seated l.	25	65
493	**Aelius Caesar,** 136-138. Æ *as*. R. TR . POT . COS . II . S . C. Fortuna stg. l.	35	95
494	**Antoninus Pius,** 138-161. His generals in Britain pushed the Roman frontier forward to the Forth-Clyde line (the Antonine Wall). *N aureus*. R. IMPERATOR II . BRITAN. Victory stg. on globe	550	1250
495	Æ *denarius*. R. AEQVITAS AVG. Aequitas stg. l.	10	25

491   496

496	Æ *sestertius*. R. B RITANNIA. S . C. Britannia seated l. on rocks	350	1000
497	— R. IMPERATOR II . BRITAN. S . C. Victory stg. on globe	150	450
498	Æ *as*. R. Victory l. holding shield inscribed BRI. TAN	75	225
499	— R. BRITANNIA COS . III . S . C. Britannia seated l.	45	135
	This coin was very possibly struck at a temporary travelling mint in Britain.		
500	**Faustina Senior,** wife of Antoninus Pius, Æ *denarius*. R. AVGVSTA. Ceres stg. r.	25	55
501	Æ *sestertius*. R. IVNO S . C. Juno stg. l.	35	85
502	**Marcus Aurelius,** 161-180. Æ *denarius*. R. COS III. Jupiter seated l.	25	65
503	Æ *sestertius*. R. IMP . VI . COS . III. S . C. Roma seated l.	85	200

504   510   515

	F £	VF £
504 **Faustina Junior,** wife of Marcus Aurelius. *Æ denarius*. R. IVNONI REGINAE. Juno and peacock	15	35
505 *Æ as*. R. DIANA LVCIF . S . C. Diana stg. l.	20	45
506 **Lucius Verus,** 161-169. *Æ denarius*. R. CONCORD . AVG . COS . II. Concordia seated l.	20	50
507 **Lucilla,** wife of Lucius Verus. *Æ dupondius*. R. SALVS S . C. Salus stg. l.	20	55
508 **Commodus,** 177-192. There was considerable military activity in northern Britain in the early part of his reign. *Æ denarius*. R. MARTI VLTORI AVG. M ars stg. l.	15	45
509 *Æ sestertius*. R. BRITT . etc. Britannia stg., holding sword and wreath	*Extremely*	*rare*
510 — R. VICT . BRIT . etc. Victory seated r., inscribing shield	75	225
511 **Crispina,** wife of Commodus, *Æ as*. R. IVNO LVCINA S . C. Juno stg. l	18	55
512 **Pertinax,** 193. One time governor of Britain, under Commodus. *Æ denarius*. R. LAETITIA TEMPOR COS . II. Laetitia stg. l.............	250	500
513 **Didius Julianus,** 193. *Æ sestertius*. R. CONCORD MILITS . C. Concordia stg. l..	250	600
514 **Clodius Albinus,** 195-197. Proclaimed emperor while governor of Britain. *Æ denarius*. R. MINER . PACIF . COS . II. Minerva stg. l. ..	55	150
515 **Septimius Severus,** 193-211. Campaigned in Britain with his sons Caracalla and Geta; died at York. *A aureus*. R. VICTORIAE BRIT. Victory l., holding wreath and palm..	850	2500
516 *Æ denarius*. R. Similar..	25	70
517 — R. Similar, but Victory seated l.	35	75
518 — R. Similar, but Victory stg. beside palm tree	40	85
519 — R. VIRT . AVG. Roma stg. l.	15	40

520   528

520 *Æ sestertius*. R. VICTORIAE BRITTANNICAE S.C. Two Victories affixing shield to palm tree, two captives below	450	1200
521 *Æ dupondius*. R. Similar, but Victory inscribing shield on palm tree ..	85	250
522 *Æ as*. R. Similar, Victory stg. r. holding vexillum	85	250
524 **Julia Domna,** wife of Septimius Severus. *Æ denarius*. R. PIETAS PVBLICA. Pietas stg. l..	20	50
525 **Caracalla,** 198-217. Personally led the campaign of A.D. 210. *A aureus*. R. VICTORIAE BRIT. Victory seated l., holding shield...	850	2500

		F £	*VF* £
526	*N quinarius*. R. VICTORIAE BRIT. Victory advancing l., holding wreath and palm	1100	3000
527	*R denarius*. R. MARTI PACATORI. Mars stg. l................................	12	30
528	— R. VICTORIAE BRIT. Victory advancing l., holding wreath and palm.	25	65
529	— R. VICTORIAE BRIT. Victory advancing r., holding trophy	30	70
530	*Æ sestertius*. R. VICT . BRIT . P . M . TR . P . XIII . COS . III . P . P . S . C. Victory stg. r., erecting trophy	200	450
531	— R. VICT . BRIT . etc. Victory inscribing shield on tree..................	200	450
532	— R. VICTORIAE BRITTANNICAE. S . C. Two Victories erecting shield on tree..	250	500
533	*Æ dupondius*. R. VICTORIAE BRITTANNICAE. S . C. Victory seated l., on shields	45	130
534	**Plautilla,** wife of Caracalla. *R denarius*. R. PIETAS AVGG. Pietas stg. r.	20	50
535	**Geta,** 209-212. *R denarius*. R. PONTIF . COS . II. Genius stg. l.	20	50
536	— R. VICTORIAE BRIT. Victory advancing r., holding wreath and palm	35	80
537	*Æ sestertius*. R. VICTORIAE BRITTANNICAE. S . C. Victory seated r., inscribing shield	250	500

537   541

538	— R. VICTORIAE BRITTANNICAE. S . C. Victory standing r., erecting trophy; Britannia stg. facing with hands tied..........................	250	500
538A	Billon tetradrachm of Alexandria, Egypt. R. NEIKH . KATA . BPET . Victory flying l.	300	700
539	**Macrinus,** 217-218. *R denarius*. R. SALVS P VBLICA. Salus seated l., feeding snake	30	75
540	**Diadumenian Caesar,** 217-218. *R denarius*. R. PRINC IVVENTVTIS. Diadumenian holding sceptre	80	200
541	**Elagabalus,** 218-222. *R denarius*. R. FIDES MIL ITVM. Fides stg. l., head r., holding standards	12	35
542	**Julia Paula,** wife of Elagabalus. *R denarius*. R. CONCORDIA. Concordia seated l.	40	90
543	**Aquilia Severa,** wife of Elagabalus. *R denarius*. R. CONCORDIA. Concordia stg. l..	65	140
544	**Julia Soaemias,** mother of Elagabalus. *R denarius*. R. VENVS CAELESTIS. Venus stg. l.	30	65
545	**Julia Maesa,** grandmother of Elagabalus. *R denarius*. R. IVNO. Juno stg. l.	18	40

546 550

		F £	VF £
546	**Severus Alexander,** 222-235. Æ *denarius.* R. PAX AVG. Pax advancing l.	12	25
547	Æ *sestertius.* R. FIDES MILITVM. S . C. Fides stg l.	15	35
548	**Orbiana,** wife of Severus Alexander. Æ *denarius.* R. CONCORDIA AVGG. Concordia seated l.	65	150
549	**Julia Mamaea,** mother of Severus Alexander. Æ *denarius.* R. VENVS VICTRIX. Venus stg. l.	20	45
550	**Maximinus I,** 235-238. Æ *denarius.* R. PAX AVGVSTI. Pax stg. l.	20	45
551	Æ *sestertius.* R. VICTORIA AVG. S . C. Victory advancing r.	30	85
552	**Maximus Caesar,** 235-238. Æ *sestertius.* R. PRINCIPI IVVENTVTIS. S . C. Maximus stg. l.	45	120
553	**Balbinus,** 238. Æ *denarius.* R. VICTORIA AVGG. Victory stg. l.	90	200
554	**Pupienus,** 238. Æ *denarius.* R. PAX PVBLICA. Pax seated l.	90	200
555	**Gordian III** 238-244. Æ *denarius.* R. SALVS AVGVSTI. Salus stg. r. feeding serpent	12	25
556	Æ *antoninianus.* R. ORIENS AVG . Sol stg. l.	15	25
557	Æ *sestertius.* R. AEQVITAS AVG. S . C. Aequitas stg. l.	20	45

558 563

		F £	VF £
558	**Philip I,** 244-249. Æ *antoninianus.* R. ROMAE AETERNAE. Roma seated l.	12	25
559	Æ *sestertius.* R. SECVRIT. ORBIS S . C. Securitas seated l.	25	45
560	**Otacilia Severa,** wife of Philip I. Æ *antoninianus.* R. PIETAS AVGV-STAE. Pietas stg. l.	15	35
561	**Philip II,** 247-249. Æ *antoninianus.* R. AETERNIT . IMPER. Sol advancing l.	20	45
562	**Trajan Decius,** 249-251. Æ *antoninianus.* R. DACIA. Dacia stg. l.	20	45
563	**Herennia Etruscilla,** wife of Trajan Decius. Æ *antoninianus.* R. PVDICITIA AVG. Pudicitia stg. l.	10	25
564	**Herennius Etruscus Caesar,** 251. Æ *antoninianus.* R. SPES PVBLICA. Spes advancing l.	30	65

		F £	VF £
565	**Hostilian Caesar,** 251. Æ *antoninianus.* R. PIETAS AVGVSTORVM. Sacrificial implements................	35	80
566	**Trebonianus Gallus,** 251-253. Æ *antoninianus.* R. LIBERTAS AVGG. Libertas stg. l........................	12	30
567	**Volusian,** 251-253. Æ *antoninianus.* R. CONCORDIA AVGG. Concordia seated l..................	8	22
568	**Aemilian,** 252-253. Æ *antoninianus.* R. PACI AVG. Pax stg. l.............	45	95
569	**Valerian I,** 253-260. Billon *antoninianus.* R. VICTORIA AVGG. Victory stg. l........................	8	20

270   576

		F £	VF £
570	**Gallienus,** 253-268. Æ *antoninianus.* R. DIANAE CONS . AVG. Antelope........................	10	20
571	**Salonina,** wife of Gallienus. Æ *antoninianus.* R. PIETAS AVG. Pietas stg. l............................	6	18
572	**Valerian II Caesar,** 253-255. Billon antoninianus. R. PIETAS AVGG. Sacrificial implements........................	12	30
573	**Saloninus Caesar,** 259. Billon *antoninianus.* R. SPES PVBLICA. Spes advancing l........................	7	20
574	**Macrianus,** usurper in the East, 260-261. Billon *antoninianus.* R. SOL. INVICTO. Sol stg. l........................	30	80
575	**Quietus,** usurper in the East, 260-261. Billon *antoninianus.* R. ROMAE AETERNAE. Roma seated l........................	30	80
576	**Postumus,** usurper in the West, 259-268. Æ *antoninianus.* R. MONETA AVG. Moneta stg. l........................	15	40
577	**Laelianus,** usurper in the West, 268. Æ *antoninianus.* R. VICTORIA AVG. Victory advancing r........................	85	220
578	**Marius,** usurper in the West, 268. Æ *antoninianus.* R. VICTORIA AVG. Victory advancing r........................	30	70
579	**Victorinus,** usurper in the West, 268-270. *N aureus.* R. LEG . XX . VAL . VICTRIX. Boar l........................	3500	10000
580	Æ *antoninianus.* R. SALVS LVS AVG. Salus stg. l........................	8	20
581	**Claudius II Gothicus,** 268-270. Æ *antoninianus.* R. MARTI PACIF. Mars advancing l........................	8	20
582	**Tetricus I,** usurper in the West, 270-273. Æ *antoninianus.* LAETITIA AVG. Laetitia stg. l........................	8	20
583	**Tetricus II Caesar,** usurper in the West, 270-273. Æ *antoninianus.* R. SPES AVGG. Spes advancing l........................	8	20

	584A	584B	584C		

		F	VF
		£	£
584	**Barbarous radiates.** British and Continental copies of Æ *antoniniani*, mostly of Claudius II (A), Tetricus I (B) and Tetricus II (C)	5	10
585	**Quintillus,** 270. Æ *antoninianus.* R. FIDES MILIT. Fides stg. l.	18	50
586	**Aurelian,** 270-275. Æ *antoninianus.* R. SECVRIT . AVG. Securitas stg. l.	8	25

	587		596

587	**Severina,** wife of Aurelian. Æ *antoninianus.* R. PROVIDEN . DEOR. Fides and Sol stg.	15	45
588	**Tacitus,** 275-276. Æ *antoninianus.* R. CLEMENTIA TEMP. Clementia stg. l.	12	30
589	**Florianus,** 276. Æ *antoninianus.* R. SALVS AVG. Salus stg. l.	30	80
590	**Probus,** 276-282. Æ *antoninianus.* R. ABVNDANTIA AVG. Abundantia stg. r.	10	25
591	**Carus,** 282-283. Æ *antoninianus.* R. PAX EXERCITI. Pax stg. l.	12	35
592	**Numerian,** 283-284. Æ *antoninianus.* R. ORIENS AVG. Sol advancing l.	12	35
593	**Carinus,** 283-285. Æ *antoninianus.* R. AETERNIT. AVG. Aeternitas stg. l.	10	30
594	**Diocletian,** 284-305, London mint reopened *c*. 297. Æ *argenteus.* R. VIRTVS MILITVM. Tetrarchs sacrificing before camp gate	80	220
595	Æ *antoninianus.* R. CLEMENTIA TEMP. Diocletian and Jupiter stg.....	8	25
596	Æ *follis.* R. GENIO POPVLI ROMANI. Genius stg. l., LON (London) mm.	15	45

	597		600

Diocletian *continued*

		F	VF
		£	£
597	Æ *follis*. R. Similar, no *mm*. (London)	12	40
598	— R. Similar, other *mms*.	10	35
599	**Maximianus,** 286-310. Æ *argenteus*. R. VIRTVS MILITVM. Tetrarchs sacrificing before camp gate	65	180
600	Æ *antoninianus*. R. SALVS AVGG. Salus stg. l.	8	20
601	Æ *follis*. R. GENIO POPVLI ROMANI. Genius stg. l., LON. *mm*.	10	30
602	— R. Similar, no *mm*.	7	?4
603	**Carausius,** commander of the Roman Channel fleet, who took power in Britain and Northern Gau l, 287-293. *London mint*. *Aʋ aureus*. R. PAX AVG. Pax stg. l., no *mm*.	7500	17500

604   623

604	Æ *denarius*. R. RENOVAT ROMANO. Wolf and Twins.	550	1500
605	Æ *antoninianus*. R. ADVENTVS AVG. Emperor riding l.	55	160
606	— R . COHR . PRAEF. Four standards	70	200
607	— R . COMES AVG. Victory stg. l.	25	70
608	— R. CONCORD . EXERCI. Four standards	40	120
609	— R. CONCORDIA MILI TVM. Clasped hands	40	120
610	— R. CONSERVAT . AVG. Sol stg. l.	55	160
611	— R. FELICIT . TEMP. Felicitas stg. l.	25	70
612	— R. FIDES MILITVM. Fides stg. l.	55	160
613	— R. FORTVNA AVG. Fortuna stg. l.	20	55
614	— R. GENIVS AVG. Genius stg. l.	55	160
615	— R. GERMANICVS MAX . V. Trophy between captives	130	360
616	— R. LAETITIA AVG. Laetitia stg. l.	20	55
617	— R. LEG . II . AVG. Capricorn l.	55	160
618	— R. LEG XX . V . V. Boar r.	65	175
619	— R. MARS VLTOR. Mars walking r.	55	160
620	— R. MONETA AVG. Moneta stg. l.	20	55
621	— R. ORIENS AVG. Sol walking r.	25	70
622	— R. PACATOR ORBIS. Bust of Sol r.	95	280
623	— R. PAX AVG. Pax stg. l.	16	50
624	— R. PIAETAS AVG. Pietas sacrificing at altar	25	70
625	— R. SALVS AVG. Salus feeding serpent	20	55
626	— R. SECVRIT . PERP. Securitas stg. l.	25	70
627	— R. VICTORIA AVG. Victory walking r.	25	70

628 643

		F £	VF £
628	Æ *antoninianus*. Struck in the name of Diocletian. R. PAX AVGGG. Pax stg. l.	20	60
629	Æ *antoninianus*. Struck in the name of Maximianus. R. PROVIDENTIA AVG. Providentia stg. l.	20	60
630	*Colchester or Clausentum (C) mint. Æ denarius.* R. CONCORDIA MILITVM. Clasped hands	350	1000
631	Æ *antoninianus*. R. ABVNDANTIA AVG. Abundantia stg. l.	25	70
632	— R. APOLINI CON . AV. Griffin walking r.	90	240
633	— R. CONCORDIA AVGGG. Two emperors stg.	110	320
634	— R. CONSTANT. AVG. Nude male stg. r.	55	160
635	— R. EXPECTATE VENI. Britannia stg. r.	90	240
636	— R. FELICITAS AVG. Galley	40	120
637	— R. GENIO BRITANNI. Genius stg. l.	120	340
638	— R. HILARITA S AVG. Hilaritas stg. l.	20	55
639	— R. IOVI CONSERV. Jupiter stg. l.	25	70
640	— R. LEG. I. MIN. Ram stg. r.	55	160
641	— R. LIBERALITAS AVG. Carausius seated with subordinates	70	200
642	— R. PAX AVG. Pax stg. l.	20	55
643	— R. PROVID . AVG. Providentia stg. l.	20	60
644	— R. RENOVAT . ROMA. She-wolf suckling Romulus and Remus	65	175
645	— R. RESTIT . SAECVL. Carausius and Victory s tg.	65	175
646	— R. ROMAE AETER. Roma seated l.	28	72
647	— R. SAECVLARES AVG. Lion walking r.	55	160
648	— R. SOLI INVICTE. Sol in quadriga	55	168
649	— R. SPES PVBLICA. Spes walking r.	20	60
650	— R. TEMP . FELICIT. Felicitas stg. l.	20	60
651	— R. VIRTVS AVG. Mars stg. r.	20	55
651A	Æ *antoninianus*. Struck in the name of Diocletian. R. PAX AVGGG. Pax stg. l.	20	60
652	Æ *antoninianus*. Struck in the name of Maximianus. R. PAX AVGGG. Pax stg. l.	20	60

653 662

		F £	*VF* £
653	**Carausius, Diocletian and Maximianus.** Æ *antoninianus.* Struck by Carausius. CARAVSIVS ET FRATRES SVI. Jugate busts of three emperors l. R. PAX AVGGG. Pax stg. l.	600	1750
654	**Allectus,** chief minister and murderer of Carausius, 293-296. *London mint. N aureus.* R. PAX AVG. Pax stg. l.	7500	20000
655	Æ *antoninianus.* R. AEQVITAS AVG. Aequitas stg. l.	25	65
656	— R. COMES AVG. Minerva stg. l.	25	65
657	— R. FORTVNA AVG. Fortuna seated l.	55	160
658	— R. HILARITAS AVG. Hilaritas stg. l.	20	60
659	— R. LAETITIA AVG. Laetitia stg. l.	28	70
660	— R. LEG . II. Lion walking l.	150	4
661	— R. ORIENS AVG. Sol stg. l.	60	175
662	— R. PAX AVG. Pax stg. l.	30	70
663	— R. PIETAS AVG. Pietas stg. l.	25	65
664	— R. PROVIDENTIA AVG. Providentia stg. l.	40	80
665	— R. SAECVLI FELICITAS. Emperor stg. r.	65	15
666	— R. SALVS AVG. Salus feeding serpent	25	65
667	— R. SPES PVPLICA. Spes holding flower	25	60
668	— R. TEMPORVM FELICI. Felicitas stg. l.	25	60
669	— R. VICTORIA AVG. Victory stg. r.	25	60
670	— R. VIRTVS AVG. Mars stg. r.	25	65
671	Æ *quinarius.* R. VIRTVS AVG. Galley	25	65
672	*Colchester or Clausentum (C) mint.* Æ *antoninianus.* R. ABVND . AVG. Abundantia stg. l.	30	70
673	— R. ADVENTVS AVG. Emperor riding l.	90	220
674	— R. DIANAE REDVCI. Diana leading stag	70	180
675	— R. FELICITAS SAECVLI. Felicitas stg. l.	70	180
676	— R. FIDES EXERCITVS. Four standards	65	150
677	— R. IOVI CONSERVATORI. Jupiter stg. l.	70	180

678   681

678	— R. MONETA AVG. Moneta stg. l.	30	85
679	— R. PAX AVG. Pax stg. l.	28	70
680	— R. ROMAE AETERN. Roma in temple	75	200
681	Æ *quinarius.* R. LAETITIA AVG. Galley	30	70
682	— R. VIRTVS AVG. Galley	40	100

683   698

	F	VF
	£	£

683 **Constantius I, Chlorus, Caesar** 293-305. Augustus 305-306, campaigned in Britain and died at York. Æ follis. R. GENIO POPVLI ROMANI. Genius stg. l., no *mm.* .... | 9 | 28

684 *Æ follis.* R. MEMORIA FELIX. Eagles beside altar. PLN. *mm.* .... | 8 | 25

685 *Æ radiate.* R. CONCORDIA MILITVM. Constantius and Jupiter stg.... | 7 | 20

686 **Galerius,** Caesar 293-305, Augustus 305-311. *Æ follis.* R. GENIO IMPERATORIS. Genius stg. l. .... | 5 | 12

687 — R. GENIO POPVLI ROMANI. Genius stg. l., no *mm.* .... | 6 | 16

688 **Galeria Valeria,** wife of Galerius. *Æ follis.* R. VENERI VICTRICI. Venus stg. l. .... | 45 | 100

689 **Severus II,** 306-307. *Æ follis.* R. FIDES MILITVM. Fides seated l..... | 25 | 70

690 *Æ follis.* R. GENIO POPVLI ROMANI. Genius stg. l., no *mm.* .... | 28 | 75

691 *Æ radiate.* R. CONCORDIA MILITVM. Severus and Jupiter stg. .... | 20 | 55

692 **Maximinus II,** 309-313. *Æ follis.* R. GENIO AVGVSTI. Genius stg. l. | 8 | 25

693 — R. GENIO POP . ROM. Genius stg. l., PLN. *mm.*........................... | 7 | 20

694 **Maxentius,** 306-312, *Æ follis.* R. CONSERV . VRB SVAE. Roma in temple... | 12 | 35

695 **Licinius I,** 308-324. *Æ follis.* R. GENIO POP . ROM. Genius stg. l., PLN . *mm.* .... | 8 | 25

696 *Æ 3.* R. SOLI INVICTO COMITI . Sol stg. l. .... | 6 | 15

697 **Licinius II Caesar,** 317-324. Æ 3. R. PROVIDENTIAE CAESS. Camp gate.. | 8 | 20

698 **Constantine I, the Great,** 307-337. Came to power in Britain following his father's death at York. London mint closed 325. *Æ follis.* R. COMITI AVGG NN Sol stg. l., PLN *mm.*... | 15 | 35

699 *Æ 3.* R. BEATA TRANQVILLITAS. Altar. PLON *mm.* .... | 10 | 20

700 *Æ 3.* R. VOT . XX. in wreath.. | 5 | 10

701   702

701 **Commemorative issues,** Æ 3/4, commencing A.D. 330. Bust of Roma. R. She-wolf suckling Romulus and Remus .... | 5 | 12

702 *Æ 3/4.* Bust of Constantinopolis. R. Victory stg. l. .... | 5 | 12

703 **Fausta,** wife of Constantine. *Æ 3.* R. SPES REIPVBLICAE. Fausta stg. | 18 | 50

704 — R. Similar. PLON *mm.*.. | 55 | 135

		F	VF
		£	£
705	**Helena,** mother of Constantine. Æ 3. R. SECVRITAS REIPVBLICE. Helena st g. l.	10	25
706	— R. Similar. PLON *mm.*	35	100

707   714

707	**Theodora,** second wife of Constantius I, struck after her death. Æ 4. R. PIETAS ROMANA. Pietas holding child	8	30
708	**Crispus Caesar,** 317-326. Æ 3. R. CAESARVM NOSTRORVM VOT . V. Wreath	6	20
709	— R. PROVIDENTIAE CAESS. Camp gate. PLON *mm.*	8	22
710	**Delmatius Caesar,** 335-337. Æ 3. R. GLORIA EXERCITVS. Two soldiers stg.	15	40
711	**Hanniballianus Rex,** 335-337. Æ 4. R. SECVRITAS PVBLICA. Euphrates reclining	100	250
712	**Constantine II Caesar,** 317-337. Æ 3. R. BEAT . TRANQLITAS. Altar. PLON *mm.*	10	25
713	Æ 3/4. R. GLORIA EXERCITVS. Two soldiers stg.	7	20
714	**Constans,** 337-350. Visited Britain in 343. Æ *centenionalis.* R. FEL . TEMP . REPARATIO. Constans stg. on galley	8	30

715   723   733   741

715	**Constantius II,** 337-361. Æ *centenionalis.* R. FEL . TEMP . REPARATIO. Soldier spearing fallen horseman	8	30
716	Æ 3. R. PROVIDENTIAE CAESS. Camp gate. PLON *mm.*	30	60
717	**Magnentius,** usurper in the West, 350-353. Æ *centenionalis.* R. VICTOR IAE DD . NN . AVG . ET CAE. Two Victories	30	80

	F	*VF*
	£	£

718 **Decentius Caesar,** usurper in the West, 351-353. Æ *centenionalis.* R. VICTORIAE DD . NN . AVG . ET . CAE . Two Victories 20 50

719 **Constantius Gallus Caesar,** 351-354. Æ *centenionalis.* R. FEL . TEMP REPARATIO. Soldier spearing fallen horseman 8 22

720 **Julian II,** 360-363. *R siliqua.* R. VOT . X . MVLT . XX with wreath... 25 55

721 Æ 3. R Similar 10 20

722 **Jovian,** 363-364. Æ 3. R. VOT . V . within wreath 25 55

723 **Valentinian I,** 364-375. Æ 3. R. SECVRITAS REIPVBLICAE. Victory advancing l. 4 10

724 **Valens,** 364-378. *R siliqua.* R. VRBS ROMA. Roma seated l. 20 45

725 Æ 3. R. GLORIA ROMANORVM. Valens dragging captive 4 10

726 **Gratian,** 367-383. *R siliqua.* R. VRBS ROMA. Roma seated l. 25 55

727 Æ 3. R. CONCORDIA AVGGG. Constantinopolis seated l................... 7 18

728 **Valentinian II,** 375-392. *R siliqua.* R. VICTORIA AVGGG. Victory advancing l. 30 65

729 Æ 2. R. GLO RIA ROMANORVM. Valentinian stg. on galley 9 22

730 Æ 4. R. SALVS REIPVBLICAE. Victory advancing l........................... 3 10

731 **Theodosius I,** 379-395. Æ 2. R. GLORIA ROMANORVM. Theodosius stg. on galley 12 30

732 Æ 4. R. SALVS REIPVBLICAE. Victory advancing l.......................... 5 15

733 **Magnus Maximus,** usurper in the West, 383-388, proclaimed emperor by the Roman army in Britain, *N solidus.* R. VICTORIA AVGG. Two emperors seated. Victory between them; AVGO B *mm.* (London) 2750 8000

734 *R siliqua.* R. VICTORIA AVGG. Victory advancing l. AVGPS *mm.* (London)... 225 600

735 — R. VIRTVS ROMANORVM. Roma seated l. 25 66

736 **Flavius Victor,** usurper in the West, 387-388. Æ 4. R. SPES ROMA-NORVM. Camp gate... 55 80

737 **Eugenius,** usurper in the West, 392-394. *R siliqua.* R. VIRTVS ROMA-NORVM. Roma seated l. 90 250

738 **Arcadius,** 383-408. Æ 2. R. GLORIA ROMANORVM. Arcadius stg. r. 9 22

739 **Honorius,** 393-423, during whose reign the so-called 'Roman withdrawal' from Britain took place. *R siliqua.* R. VIRTVS ROMANORVM. Roma seated l... 25 65

740 Æ 3. R. VIRTVS EXERCITI. Honorius stg. r...................................... 7 20

741 **Constantine III,** usurper in the West, proclaimed emperor in Britain, 407-411. *R siliqua.* R. VICTORIA AVGGGG. Roma seated l. 100 300

742 **Valentinian III,** 425-455, Æ 4. R. VOT . PVB. Camp gate.................. 18 50

NOTES

ANGLO-SAXON EARLY PERIOD, *c.* 600-*c.* 775

The withdrawal of Roman forces from Britain early in the 5th century A.D. and the gradual decline of central administration resulted in a rapid deterioration of the money supply. The arrival of Teutonic raiders and settlers hastened the decay of urban commercial life and it was probably not until late in the 6th century that renewed political, cultural and commercial links with the kingdom of the Merovingian Franks led to the appearance of small quantities of Merovingian gold *tremisses* (one-third solidus) in England. A purse containing such pieces was found in the Sutton Hoo ship-burial. Native Anglo-Saxon gold *thrymsas* were minted from about the 630s, initially in the style of their continental prototpyes or copied from obsolete Roman coinage and later being made in pure Anglo-Saxon style. By the middle of the 7th century the gold coinage was being increasingly debased with silver, and gold had been superseded entirely by about 675.

These silver coins, contemporary with the *deniers or denarii* of the Merovingian Franks, are the first English pennies, though they are commonly known today as *sceattas* (a term more correctly translated as 'treasure' or 'wealth'). They provide important material for the student of Anglo-Saxon art.

Though the earliest sceattas are a transition from the gold thrymsa coinage, coins of new style were soon developed which were also copied by the Frisians of the Low Countries. Early coins appear to have a standard weight of 20 grains (1.29 gms) and are of good silver content, though the quality deteriorates early in the 8th century. These coins exist in a large number of varied types, and as well as the official issues there are mules and other varieties which are probably contemporary imitations. Many of the sceattas were issued during the reign of Aethelbald of Mercia, but as few bear inscriptions it is only in recent years that research has permitted their correct dating and the attribution of certain types to specific areas. Some silver sceats of groups II and III and most types of groups IV to X were issued during the period (A.D. 716-757) when Aethelbald, King of Mercia, was overlord of the southern English. In Northumbria very debased sceattas or *stycas* continued to be issued until the middle of the ninth century. Though a definitive classification has not yet been developed, the arrangement given below follows the latest work on the series: this list is not exhaustive.

The reference '*B.M.C.*' is to the type given in *British Museum Catalogue: Anglo-Saxon Coins*, and *not* the item number.

North, J. J. *English Hammered Coinage*, Vol. 1, *c.* 650-1272 (1980).
Metcalf, D. M. 'A stylistic analysis of the `porcupine' sceattas'. *Num. Chron.*, 7th ser., Vol. VI (1966).
Rigold, S. E. 'The two primary series of sceattas', *B.N.J.*, xxx (1960).
Sutherland, C. H. V. *Anglo-Saxon Gold Coinage in the light of the Crondall Hoard* (1948).

ᚠᚪᚦᚻᚱᚪ·ᚷᚹᚾᚻᛁ◊ᚷᛃᛤᚣᛁᛏᛒᛗᚪᚱᛉᚻᚩᚠᚪᚳᚪ

f u th o r k . z w h n i j ih p x s t b e m l ng d œ a Æ ea y
Early Anglo-Saxon Runes

GOLD

A. Anglo-Merovingian types

751   **Thrymsa** (*c.* 1.32 gms). Name and portrait of Bishop Leudard (chaplain to Q. Bertha of Kent). R. Cross. *N. 1* ....*Unique*

752   *Canterbury.* Bust r., moneyer's name. R. Cross, mint name. *N. 2*   *Extremely rare*

753   762   763

753   No mint name. Bust l. R. Cross. *N. 3-5, 7* ....*Extremely rare*
754   Bust r. R. Cross. *N. 6-9, 12*..*Extremely rare*
755   Cross both sides. *N. 10* ....*Extremely rare*
756   Bust r. R. Cross, runic letters, *N. 11* ....*Extremely rare*

B. **Roman derivatives**

		F	*VF*
		£	£
757	**Solidus.** Bust r. copied from 4th cent. solidus. R. Various. *N. 13, 14*	*Extremely rare*	
758	— Runic inscription on reverse. *N. 15*	*Extremely rare*	
759	**Thrymsa.** Radiate bust. r. R. Clasped hands. *N. 16*	*Extremely rare*	
760	Bust r., hands r aised to cross. R. Camp gate. *N. 17*	1250	2500
761	Helmeted bust r. R. Cross, runic inscription. *N. 18*	—	6500
762	Diad. bust r. R. 'Standard', TOV / XX in centre. *N. 19. M.*	—	3250
763	— Sim ilar. R. Victory protecting 'two emperors'. *N. 20*	1250	2500

C. **'London' and derived issues**

764   765   767

764	**Thrymsa.** Facing bust, no legend. R. Greek cross, LONDVNIV. *N. 21* ...	*Extremely rare*	
765	Head r. or l. R. Plain cross, legend jumbled. *N. 22-24*	*Extremely rare*	

D. **'Witmen' group**

766	**Thrymsa.** Bust r. with trident centre. R. Cross with forked limbs, moneyer's name. *N. 25*	*Extremely rare*	
767	— Similar, but blundered legend on reverse, *N. 25 var*	1500	3000
768	— R. Cross potent. *N. 26*	1500	3000

E. **'York' group**

769   771   772

769	**Thrymsa.** Three crosses with geometric squared design below. R. Small cross. *N. 27*	*Extremely rare*	

F. **'Regal' coinages**

770	**Solidus** (4.12 gms). Diad.. bust r., moneyer's name around. R. Cross potent on steps. *N. 28*	*Extremely rare*	
771	**Thrymsa.** Diad. bust r., AVDVARLD REGES. R. Orb with cross, moneyer's name. *N. 29*	2000	4000
772	Diad. bust l., moneyer's name around. R. Cross and pellets, legend of Xs. *N. 30*	*Extremely rare*	
773	Diad. bust r. R. Cross bootonee, PADA in runes. *N. 31*	1000	2250

| | *F* | *VF* |
| | £ | £ |

Miscellaneous issues

774 **Thrymsa.** Crude bust r. R. Standing figure with arms outstretched. *N. 33* *Extremely rare*

775 Crude bust or head r. R. Various. *N. 35, 38* .... *Extremely rare*

776 Forked cross both sides, and other types. *N. 36, 37, 39* .... *Extremely rare*

SILVER

I. **Transitional types struck in silver,** by thrymsa moneyers, *c.* 675-690

         779   780   781

777 **Sceat.** *Kentish.* As 773, diad. bust r. R. *Pada* in runes across field. *N. 152* 600 1250

778 — Obv. Similar. R. Cross on steps. *B.M.C. type 2* .... *Extremely rare*

778A As 763. R. Victory over two emperors. *B.M.C. 1* .... *Extremely rare*

779 — Diad. bust r., TNC to r. R. Cross with annulet in each angle, *Pada* in
     runes in legend. *B.M.C. 3* 550 1100

780 — 'Varimundus'. As 761, helmeted bust r. with sceptre. R. Cross pattee,
     TmVNVmVC, etc. *Rigold VB, 4-9* 650 1350

II. **Primary Sceattas,** *c.* 690-725

         783   785   786

781 Series A, *Kentish.* Radiate bust r., usually of good style, TIC to r. R.
     'Standard'. *B.M.C. 2a* 65 150

782 Series B, *Kentish.* Diad. bust r. R. Bird above cross on steps. *B.M.C. 26* . 100 225

783 — Diad. head r. within serpent-circle or bust r. R. Bird above cross and
     two annulets, serpent-circle around. *B.M.C. 27a* 60 125

784 — (Bz.) Diad. head r. of poorer style. R. Bird and cross larger and cruder.
     B.M.C. 27b (see also 791) 85 200

785 Series C, *East Anglian (?) Runic.* Radiate bust r. somewhat as 781. *Epa*
     (etc.) in runes to r. R. Neat 'Standard' type. *B.M.C. 2b; Rigold R1* (see
     also 832, and for Frisian copies nos. 839 and 840) 60 100

786 *Early 'porcupines'.* Porcupine-like figure, body with annulet at one end,
     triangle at other. R. 'Standard' with four pellets around central annulet.
     Metcalf D 45 90

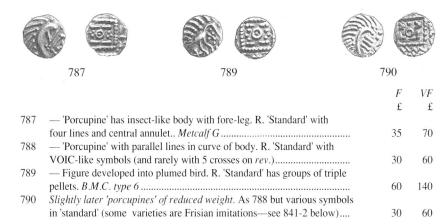

787   789   790

	F £	VF £
787 — 'Porcupine' has insect-like body with fore-leg. R. 'Standard' with four lines and central annulet.. *Metcalf G*	35	70
788 — 'Porcupine' with parallel lines in curve of body. R. 'Standard' with VOIC-like symbols (and rarely with 5 crosses on *rev*.)	30	60
789 — Figure developed into plumed bird. R. 'Standard' has groups of triple pellets. *B.M.C. type 6*	60	140
790 *Slightly later 'porcupines' of reduced weight.* As 788 but various symbols in 'standard' (some varieties are Frisian imitations—see 841-2 below)....	30	60

III. **'Mercian' types,** *c.* 705-730. More than one mint, possibly including London; the fineness dropping from good silver to under .500.

791   792   793

791	Derivative of 784, but bird and cross larger and cruder, no serpent circles. *B.M.C. 27b*	75	175
792	Two heads face-to-face, cross with trident base between. R. Four birds clockwise around cross. *B.M.C. 37*	100	250
793	Man holding two crosses. R. Bird and branch. *B.M.C. 23b*	110	225
794	Diad. bust r. with bird or cross. R. Hound and tree. *B.M.C. 42*	150	400
795	Diad. bust r. with chalice. R. Man standing with cross and bird. *B.M.C. 20*	100	225
796	Diad. bust r. with cross. R. Wolf curled head to tail. *B.M.C. 32a*	100	250
797	— Similar, but wolf-headed serpent	125	275
798	— Similar, but wolf-serpent within torque. *B.M.C. 32b*	125	275
799	— Similar, but wolf's head r. or l. with long tongue. *B.M.C. 33*	175	400
800	— Obv. Similar. R. Celtic cross or shield. *B.M.C. 34*	125	275

IV. **Types of similar style or finess,** *of uncertain political attribution*

800	A Kneeling archer r., tree behind. R. Bird on branch r., head turned l. *B.M.C.* —	*Extremely rare*	
801	As 791, but cross before head. R. Large and small bird. *B.M.C. 36*	200	400
802	Bust r., lettering around or with cable border. R. Bird r. in torque. *B.M.C. 38*	175	350
803	Bust l. within cable border. R. Man with two crosses. *B.M.C. 21*	200	400
804	Facing bust. R. Interlaced cruciform pattern. *B.M.C. 52*	325	700

797   805   806

		F	VF
V. South Wessex types, *c.* 725-750. Found predominantly in excavations at Hamwic (Southampton)		£	£
805	Scutiform design (shield with bosses). R. Bird and branch as 794. *B.M.C.* *type 39*	120	200
806	Jewel-head, roundels around. R. Bird and branch. *B.M.C. 49*	125	250
807	Scutiform design. R. Wolf-head whorl. *B.M.C. 48*	125	250

VI. South Saxon types, *c.* 720-750

808	Diad. bust r. cross before. R. 'Standard'. *B.M.C. 3a*	125	250
809	— Similar but crude style and of very base silver	80	150

808   815   816

VII. 'Dragon' types, *c.* 725-735?

		F	VF
810	Two standing figures, long cross between. R. Monster looking back to r. or l. *B.M.C. type 41b*	150	300
811	One standing figure, cross either side. R. As last. *B.M.C. 23a and 40*	175	350
812	Four interlaced shields. R. As last. *B.M.C. 43*	175	350
813	Bust r., cross before. R. As last. *N. 114*	*Extremely rare*	
814	Wolf's head facing. R. As last. *N. 122*	350	700
815	Wolf and twins. R. Bird in vine. *B.M.C. 7*	200	400
816	Diad. bust r. + LEV. R. 'Porcupine' l. *B.M.C. 9*	200	425
817	Facing head. R. Fantastic animal r. or l. *N. 143-146*	250	625

VIII. 'London issue' *of around .400 silver content or less, c.* 740-750

818	Diad. bust r., LVNDONIA (sometimes blundered). R. Man holding two long crosses. *B.M.C. type 12*	250	600
819	— Obv. As last. R. 'Porcupine' to l. *B.M.C. 12/15*	300	650
820	— Obv. As last. R. Seated figure r. holding sceptre. *B.M.C. 13*	—	750
821	— Obv. As last but bust l. R. Scutiform design. *B.M.C. 14*	300	600
822	Diad. bust r. with cross, no legend. R. As 818. *B.M.C. 15a*	150	300
823	— As last. R. Man standing with branch and cross, or two branches. *B.M.C. 15b*	150	350
824	Diad. bust r. with floral scroll. R. As last	150	350
825	— As last. R. Man with two crosses. *B.M.C. 16*	120	275
826	As 813 but bust l. *B.M.C. 17*	135	325
827	Diad. bust r. with cross. R. Man standing with cross and bird. *B.M.C. 18*	150	300

		F	*VF*
		£	£
828	Diad. bust l. with cross. R. As last. *B.M.C. 19*	140	325
829	Victory standing with wreath. R. Man with two crosses. *B.M.C. 22*	250	550

818   831

IX. **'Wolf-head whorl'** *types, mostly of about .300 silver or less, c.* 740-750

830	Man standing holding two crosses. R. Wolf-head whorl. *B.M.C. 23e*	85	200
831	Sphinx or female centaur with outstretched wings. R. As above. *B.M.C. 47*	110	225
	See also No. 807.		

832

X. **East Anglian types,** *of about .500 silver or less, c.* 735-750. Struck to a standard of 15 grs./0.97 gm. or less

832	Crude radiate bust l. or r., *Epa, Wigraed,* or *Spi*, etc., in runes. R. 'Standard'. *Rigold R2* (compare with 785)	75	135
832A	Crude bust r. R. Porcupine modified into profile 1/2 moon face	200	350
833	— Similar. R. Cross with each limb ending in annulet. *Rigold R2Z, N. 160*	110	250
833A	Saltire in square. R. Cross ending in annulets. *B.M.C. 51*	75	150
834	Bird r. looking back. R. 'Standard' with four annulets in saltire. *B.M.C. 46*	125	225
835	'Standard' both sides. *N. 55-57*	150	325
836	Fantastic bird r. or l. R. Fantastic quadruped l. or r. *B.M.C. 44*	100	250
836A	— As above *rev.* on both sides	100	225
836B	— Hd. r. R. As 836 *obv.*	150	350
836C	— Quadruped r. R. Spiral	150	250

836   837   839

XI. **Late sceattas,** *on a restored silver standard, c.* 750-775. These probably include some specimens of 830 and 831 and the following types:

837	'Porcupine'. R. *Aethili/raed* in runes in two lines. *B.M.C. 4*	350	650
838	'Porcupine'. R. Small cross, S E D E in angles. *N. 47* ....*Extremely rare*		

XII. **Frisian sceattas,** *c.* 700-750. A number of large sceatta hoards have been found in the Netherlands and Lower Rhine area. Some of the coins are now known to have been minted in Frisia but some also circulated in England

839	Crude radiate bust l. or r., as 832, sometimes crude runes. R. Plain cross with pellets or annulets in angles. *Rigold R3. B.M.C. 2c*	25	65
839A	Helmeted head r. R. Cross with annulets	60	150

		F	VF
		£	£
840	'Standard'. R. Cross and pellets. *B.M.C. 50*...	40	100
840A	Very crude facing bust. R. Similar..	50	100
841	'Porcupine' with III, XII or XIII in curve. R. 'Standard'. *Metcalf A, B & C*	25	60
842	'Porcupine' has a triangle attached to curve or an outline of pellets. *Metcalf E & F*...	30	65

843   844

		F	VF
843	Facing 'Wodan' head. R. Monster. *B.M.C. 31*	100	225
843A	Similar but 'Standard' on *rev.*	175	350
844	— Similar. R. Two men with staves or long cross. *B.M.C. 30a & b*........	125	250
844A	Good style bust l.; runic inscription. R. Annulet cross and pellets	—	300

XIII. Uncertain issues

847

846	**Ealdfrith** (? possibly sub-king of Lindsey, *c.* 790). Now considered to be Northumbria (see 846 below)		
847	**Beonna,** King of East Anglia, *c.* 758. Æ sceat. Pellet in centre, Runic inscription. R. EFE in Roman characters around saltire cross	400	800
847A	— Similar. R. Name in Runic	650	1250
847B	— Similar. R. Interlace pattern	*Extremely rare*	

44

KINGS OF NORTHUMBRIA

In the North a series of silver sceats was struck with the king's name on the obverse and a fantastic animal on the reverse. Towards the end of the eighth century the coinage degenerated to one of base silver and finally to copper or brass; from the second reign of Aethelred I the design becomes standardised with the king's name retained on the obverse but with the moneyer's name on the reverse and in the centre of both sides a cross, pellet or rosette., etc. A parallel series of ecclesiastical coins was struck by the Archbishops of York.

The coinage continued until the conquest of Northumbria by the Danes and the defeat of Osbert in 867, almost a century after introduction of the broad silver penny in Southern England.

846	**Aldfrith** (685-705). *Æ sceat.* Pellet in annulet. R. Fantastic animal l. with trifid tail	600	1250
852	**Eadberht** (737-758). *Æ sceat.* Small cross. R. Fantastic quadruped to l. or r.	175	400
	Aethelwald Moll (759-765). See Archbishop Ecgberht of York		

853   859   861

		F	VF
		£	£
853	**Alcred** (765-774). *Æ sceat.* As 852	350	800
854	**Aethelred I,** first reign (774-779). *Æ sceat.* As last	350	800
855	**Aelfwald I** (779-788). *Æ sceat.* As last	400	950
856	— — Small cross. R. With name of moneyer CVDBEVRT	375	900
857	**Aethelred I,** second reign (789-796). *Æ sceat.* Similar. R. SCT CVD (St. Cuthbert), shrine	*Extremely rare*	
858	— Small cross. R. With moneyer's name	200	450
	The last and the rest of the sceats, except where otherwise stated, have on the obv. the king's name,and on the rev. the moneyer's name: in the centre on both sides is a cross, a pellet, a rosette, etc. During the following reign the silver sceat becomes debased and later issues are only brass or copper.		
859	**Eanred** (810-c. 854). Base *Æ sceat*	30	70
859A	— *Æ penny.* Bust r. R. Cross, part moline part crosslet	*Unique*	
860	— *Æ sceat*	20	45
861	**Aethelred II,** first reign (c. 854-858). *Æ sceat*	20	50
862	— R. Quadruped	200	600
863	**Redwulf** (c. 858). *Æ sceat.*	45	100
864	**Aethelred II,** second reign (c. 858-c. 862). *Æ sceat,* mainly of the moneyer EARDWVLF	20	45
865	**Osbert** (c. 862-867). *Æ sceat*	70	150
	Coins with blundered legends are worth less than those with normal readings, and to this series have been relegated those coins previously attributed to Eardwulf and Aelfwald II.		

ARCHBISHOPS OF YORK

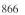

866   868

866 **Ecgberht** (732 or 734-766). Æ *sceat*, with king Eadberht. As illustration, or
holds cross and crozier 275 600
866A — — with Aethelwald Moll. Cross each side .... *Extremely rare*
867 — — with Alchred. Cross each side. .... *Extremely rare*
868 **Eanbald II** (796-*c*. 830). Æ *sceat*. R. With name of moneyer 65 165
869 — Æ *sceat*, as last 40 120

	F	VF

870   871

	£	£
870 **Wigmund** (837-854). Gold *solidus*. Facing bust. R. Cross in wreath		*Unique*
871 — Æ *sceat*, various	35	65
872 **Wulfhere** (854-900). Æ *sceat*	85	150

ANGLO-SAXON MIDDLE PERIOD, *c.* 780-973

In the kingdom of the Franks a reformed coinage of good quality *deniers* struck on broad flans had been introduced by Pepin in 755 and continued by his son Charlemagne and his descendants. A new coinage of *pennies* of similar size and weighing about 20 grains (1.3 gms) was introduced into England, probably by Offa, the powerful king of Mercia, about 755/780, though early pennies also exist of two little known kings of Kent, Heaberht and Ecgberht, of about the same period.

The silver penny (*Lat.* 'denarius', hence the *d.* of our £ *s. d.*) remained virtually the sole denomination of English coinage for almost five centuries, with the rare exception of occasional gold coins and somewhat less rare silver halfpence. The penny reached a weight of 24 grains, i.e., a 'pennyweight' during the reign of Aelfred the Great. Silver pennies of this period normally bear the ruler's name, though not always his portrait, and the name of the moneyer responsible for their manufacture.

Pennies were issued by various rulers of the Heptarchy for the kingdoms of Kent, Mercia, East Anglia and Wessex (and possibly Anglian Northumbria), by the Danish settlers in the Danelaw and the Hiberno-Norse kings of York, and also by the Archbishops of Canterbury and a Bishop of London. Under Eadgar, who became the sole ruler of England, a uniform coinage was instituted throughout the country, and it was he who set the pattern for the 'reformed' coinage of the later Anglo-Saxon and Norman period.

Halfpence were issued by most rulers from Alfred to Eadgar between 871-973 for S. England, and although all are rare today, it is probable that reasonable quantities were made.

Nos. 873-1387 are all silver pennies except where stated.

NB. Many pennies of the early part of this period have chipped flans and prices should be reduced accordingly.

KINGS OF KENT

		F £	VF £
873	**Heaberht** (*c.* 765). Monogram for REX. R. Five annulets, each containing a pellet, joined to form a cross		*Unique*
874	**Ecgberht** (*c.* 780). Similar. R. Varied *from*	1350	3500
875	**Eadberht Praen** (796-798). As illustration. R. Varied	1350	3500

875   877

876	**Cuthred** (798-807). *Canterbury.* Various types without portrait ....*from*	425	1000
877	— As illustration	475	1200

878   879

878	**Anonymous** (*c.* 822-823). *Canterbury.* As illustration	650	1650
879	**Baldred** (*c.* 823-825). *Canterbury.* Head or bust r. R. Varied	1000	2500

	F £	VF £
880 — Cross each side	750	2000
881 *Rochester*. Diademed bust r. R. Varied	1000	2500

ARCHBISHOPS OF CANTERBURY

882   885

887

882	**Jaenberht** (765-792). His name around central ornament or cross and wedges. R. OFFA REX in two lines	1250	2750
883	— His name in three lines. R. OFFA REX between the limbs of Celtic cross	1750	4000
884	**Aethelheard** (el. 792, cons. 793, d. 805). With Offa as overlord. First issue (792-793), with title *Pontifex*	1250	3250
885	— Second issue (793-796), with title *Archiepiscopus*	1200	3000
886	— With Coenwulf as overlord. Third issue (796-805)	1150	2750
886a	— Alone, as last. R. Moneyer, cross with pellets etc	—	3000
887	**Wulfred** (805-832). group I (805-*c*. 810). As illustration. R. Crosslet, alpha-omega	700	2500
888	— Group II (*c*. 810). As last. R. DOROVERNIA C monogram	600	1450
889	— Group III (pre- 823). Bust extends to edge of coin. R. As last	550	1200
890	— Groups IV and V (*c*. 822-823). Anonymous under Ecgberht. Moneyer's name in place of the Archbishop's. R. DOROBERNIA CIVITAS in three or five lines	575	1400
891	— Group VI (*c*. 823-825). Baldred type. Crude portrait. R. DRVR CITS in two lines	600	2100
892	— Group VII (*c*. 832). Second monogram (Ecgberht) type. Crude portrait r., PLFRED. R. DORIB C. Monogram as 1035	600	2100

893   894

893	**Ceolnoth** (833-870). Group I with name CIALNOD. Tonsured bust facing. R. Varied *from*	275	750
894	— Group II. Similar but CEOLNOD. R. Types of Aethelwulf of Wessex	300	600
895	— Group III. Diad. bust r. R. Moneyer's name in and between lunettes	400	900

896

		F £	VF £
896	**Aethered** (870-889). Bust r. R. As illustration or with long crosswith lozenge panel...	1750	4500

898

897	— Cross pattee. R. ELF / STAN...		*Unique*
898	**Plegmund** (890-914). DORO in circle. R. As illustration above, various moneyers..*from*	350	850
899	— Similar, but title EPISC, and XDF in centre	550	1300
900	— Small cross pattee. R. Somewhat as last	300	750
901	— Crosses moline and pommee on *obv*..	550	1300

KINGS OF MERCIA

Until 825 Canterbury was the principal mint of the Kings of Mercia and some moneyers also struck coins for the Kings of Kent and Archbishops of Canterbury.

GOLD

902   903

902	**Offa** (757-796). Gold *dinar*. Copy of Arabic dinar of Caliph Al Mansur, dated 157 A.H. (A.D. 774), with OFFA REX added on *rev*......................	*Unique*
903	Gold *penny*. Bust r., moneyer's name. R. Standing figure, moneyer's name	*Unique*

SILVER

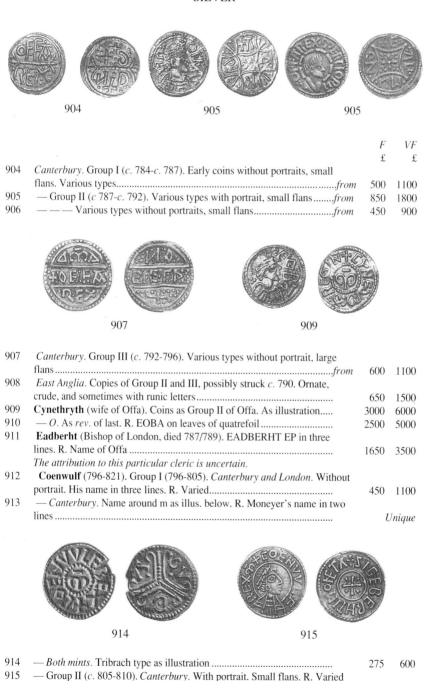

904   905   905

907   909

		F £	VF £
904	*Canterbury*. Group I (*c*. 784-*c*. 787). Early coins without portraits, small flans. Various types...*from*	500	1100
905	— Group II (*c* 787-*c*. 792). Various types with portrait, small flans........*from*	850	1800
906	— — — Various types without portraits, small flans.............................*from*	450	900
907	*Canterbury*. Group III (*c*. 792-796). Various types without portrait, large flans...*from*	600	1100
908	*East Anglia*. Copies of Group II and III, possibly struck *c*. 790. Ornate, crude, and sometimes with runic letters..	650	1500
909	**Cynethryth** (wife of Offa). Coins as Group II of Offa. As illustration.....	3000	6000
910	— *O*. As *rev*. of last. R. EOBA on leaves of quatrefoil	2500	5000
911	**Eadberht** (Bishop of London, died 787/789). EADBERHT EP in three lines. R. Name of Offa	1650	3500
	The attribution to this particular cleric is uncertain.		
912	**Coenwulf** (796-821). Group I (796-805). *Canterbury and London.* Without portrait. His name in three lines. R. Varied..	450	1100
913	— *Canterbury.* Name around m as illus. below. R. Moneyer's name in two lines		*Unique*

914   915

| 914 | — *Both mints.* Tribrach type as illustration .... | 275 | 600 |
| 915 | — Group II (*c*. 805-810). *Canterbury.* With portrait. Small flans. R. Varied but usually cross and wedges .... | 400 | 900 |

		F	VF
		£	£
916	— Groups III and IV (*c.* 810-820). *Canterbury.* Similar but larger flans. R. Varied	350	750
917	— *Rochester.* Large diad. bust of coarse style. R. Varied. (Moneyers: Dun, Ealhstan)	475	1100
918	— *London.* With portrait generally of Roman style. R. Crosslet	450	1000
919	— *E. Anglia.* Crude diad. bust r. R. Moneyer's name LVL on leaves in arms of cross	450	1050
920	— — *O.* as last. R. Various types ....*from*	400	900

921   929

921	**Ceolwulf I** (821-823). *Canterbury.* Group I. Bust r. R. Varied. (Moneyers: Oba, Sigestef)	575	1350
922	— — Group II. Crosslet. R. Varied	500	1250
923	— — Group III. Tall cross with MERCIOR Ū. R. Crosslet. SIGESTEF DOROBERNIA		*Unique*
924	— *Rochester.* Group I. Bust r. R. Varied	500	1250
925	— — Group IIA. As last but head r.	550	1350
926	— — Group IIB. Ecclesiastical issue by Bp. of Rochester. With mint name, DOROBREBIA, but no moneyer		*Extremely rare*
927	— *East Anglia.* Crude style and lettering with barbarous portrait. R. Varied	500	1250
928	**Beornwulf** (823-825). Bust r. R. Moneyer's name in three lines	1200	3250
929	— R. Cross crosslet in centre	1000	2500
930	Crude copy of 928 but moneyer's name in two lines with crosses between.		*Extremely rare*

931   933

931	**Ludica** (825-827). Bust r. R. Moneyer's name in three lines as 928		*Extremely rare*
932	— Similar. R. Moneyer's name around cross crosslet in centre, as 929....		*Extremely rare*
933	**Wiglaf,** first reign (827-829). Crude head r. R. Crosslet	1750	4500

934

		F	VF
		£	£
934	Second reign (830-840). Cross and pellets. R. Moneyer's name in and between lunettes of pellets	1350	3750

935

935	**Berhtwulf** (840-852). Various types with bust...*from*	700	1650
936	— Cross potent over saltire. R. Cross potent	750	1850
937	Berhtwulf with Aethelwulf of Wessex. As before. R. IAETHELWLF REX. cross pommee over cross pattee		*Unique*
938	**Burgred** (852-874). *B.M.C. type A.* Bust r. R. Moneyer's name in and between lunettes..	70	150
939	— — B. Similar but lunettes broken in centre of curve.............................	100	210

938	939	940	941	

940	— — C. Similar but lunettes broken in angles	100	200
941	— — D. Similar but legend divided by two lines with a crook at each end	90	160
942	— — E. As last, but m above and below	350	900
943	**Ceolwulf II** (874-*c.* 880). Bust r. R. Two emperors seated. Victory above.		*Unique*

944

944	— R. Moneyer's name in angles of long cross with lozenge centre.........	3000	7500

946   948   950

	F £	VF £

Beonna (*c*. 760). See no. 847

946   **Aethelberht** (d. 794). As illustration .... *Only 3 known*

947   **Eadwald** (*c*. 798). King's name in three lines. R. Moneyer's name in
quatrefoil or around cross.. 1350 | 3250

948   **Aethelstan I** (*c*. 825-840). Bust r. or l. R. Crosslet or star .... 750 | 2000

949   Bust r. R. Moneyer's name in three or four lines..................................... 750 | 2000

950   Alpha or A. R. Varied .... 350 | 775

951   *O*. and *rev*. Cross with or without wedges or pellets in angles .... 350 | 850

952   — Similar, with king's name both sides .... 500 | 1250

952A Name around ship in centre. R. Moneyer Eadgar, pellets in centre.
(Possibly the earliest of his coins.).. *Extremely rare*

953   954

953   **Aethelweard** (*c*. 840-*c*. 855), A. Omega or cross and crescents. R. Cross
with pellets or wedges... 550 | 1350

954   **Edmund** (855-870). Alpha or A. R. Cross with pellets or wedges .... 325 | 600

955   — *O*. Varied. R. Similar... 325 | 600

*For the St. Edmund coins and the Danish issues struck in East Anglia bearing the name of Aethelred
I of Wessex, see Danish East Anglia.*

VIKING COINAGES

Danish East Anglia, *c.* 885-915

956   957

		F £	VF £
956	**Aethelstan II** (878-890), originally named Guthrum? Cross pattee. R. Moneyer's name in two lines	1000	2500
957	**Oswald** (unknown except from his coins). Alpha or A. R. Cross pattee..		*rare*
958	— Copy of Carolinigian 'temple' type. R Cross and pellets		*Unique fragment*
959	**Aethelred I.** As last, with name of Aethelred I of Wessex. R. As last, or cross-crosslet		*Extremely rare*
960	**St. Edmund,** memorial coinage, Æ *penny,* type as illus. below, various legends of good style	75	125
961	— Similar, but barbarous or semi-barbarous legends	70	110
962	*Halfpenny.* Similar	400	1000

961   963

963	**St. Martin of Lincoln.** As illustration	1500	3750
964	**Alfred.** (Viking imitations, usually of very barbarous workmanship.) Bust r. R. *Londonia* monogram	550	1500
965	— Similar, but *Lincolla* monogram		*Extremely rare*

966   970

966	— Small cross, as Alfred group II (*Br. 6*), various legends, some read REX DORO .... *from*	200	425
967	— Similar. R. 'St. Edmund type' A in centre	500	1500
968	— Two emperors seated. R. As 964. (Previously attributed to Halfdene.)		*Unique*
969	*Halfpenny.* As 964 and 965 .... *from*	500	1500
970	— As 966	450	1350

	F	VF
	£	£

Danelaw, *c.* **898-915**

971   **Alfred** (Imitations). ELFRED between ORSNA and FORDA. R. Moneyer's name in two lines (occasionally divided by horizontal long cross)   250   650

972   — *Halfpenny.* Similar, of very crude appearance ....   *Extremely rare*

971   975

973   **Alfred/Plegmund.** *Obv.* ELFRED REX PLEGN.....................................   *Extremely rare*
974   **Plegmund.** Danish copy of 900   300   750
975   **Earl Sihtric.** Type as 971. SCELDFOR between GVNDI BERTVS. R SITRIC COMES in two lines...   *Extremely rare*

Viking Coinage of York?

References are to 'The Classification of Northumbrian Viking Coins in the Cuerdale hoard', by C. S. S. Lyon and B. H. I. H. Stewart, in Numismatic Chronicle, 1964, p. 281 ff.

976   **Siefred.** C. SIEFRE DIIS REX in two lines. R. EBRAICE CIVITAS (or contractions), small cross. *L. & S. Ia, Ie, Ii*...   200   550
977   — Cross on steps between. R. As last. *L. & S. If, Ij*   275   750
978   — Long cross. R. As last. *L. & S. Ik*..   *Extremely rare*
979   SIEFREDVS REX, cross crosslet within legend. R. As last. *L. & S. Ih*...   130   325
980   SIEVERT REX, cross crosslet to edge of coin. R. As last. *L. & S. Ic, Ig, Im*   130   325
981   — Cross on steps between. R. As last. *L. & S. Il*....................................   240   650
982   — Patriarchal cross. R. DNS DS REX, small cross. *L. & S. Va*..............   150   400
983   — — R. MIRABILIA FECIT, small cross. *L. & S. VIb*...........................   185   50
984   REX, at ends of cross crosslet. R. SIEFREDVS, small cross. *L. & S. IIIa, b*   140   385
985   — Long cross. R. As last. *L. & S. IIIc*   120   325
986   *Halfpenny.* Types as 977, *L. & S. Ib;* 980, *Ic;* and 983, *VIb* ....   *Extremely rare*

980   984   993

987   **Cnut.** CNVT REX, cross crosslet to edge of coin. R. EBRAICE CIVITAS, small cross. *L. & S. Io, Iq*   70   150
988   — — R. CVNNETTI, small cross. *L. & S. IIc*   80   175

		F	VF
		£	£
989	— Long cross. R. EBRAICE CIVITAS, small cross. *L. & S. Id, In, Ir*	65	120
990	— — R. CVNNETTI, small cross. *L. & S. IIa, IId*	65	120
991	— Patriarchal cross. R. EBRAICE CIVITAS, small cross. *L. & S. Ip, Is*	65	120
992	— — R.—*Karolus* monogram in centre. *L. & S . It*	400	1000
993	— — R. CVNNETTI, small cross. *L. & S. IIb, IIe*	65	110
994	*Halfpenny.* Types as 987, *L. & S. Iq;* 989, *Id;* 991, *Is;* 992, *Iu;* 993, *IIb and e* ....*from*	400	850
995	As 992, but CVNNET TI around *Karolus* monogram. *L. & S. IIf*	400	875

995   998   1000

996	**Cnut and/or Siefred.** CNVT REX, patriarchal cross. R. SIEFREDVS, small cross. *L. & S. IIId*	110	235
997	— — R. DNS DS REX, small cross. *L. & S. Vc*	150	325
998	— — R. MIRABILIA FECIT. *L. & S. VId*	140	200
999	EBRAICE C, patriarchal cross. R. DNS DS REX, small cross. *L. & S. Vb*	120	250
1000	— — R. MIRABILIA FECIT. *L. & S. VIc*	140	275
1001	DNS DS REX in two lines. R. ALVALDVS, small cross. *L. & S. IVa*	—	1500
1002	DNS DS O REX, similar. R. MIRABILIA FECIT. *L. & S. VIa*	250	550
1003	*Halfpenny.* As last. *L. & S. VIa*	*Extremely rare*	
1004	**'Cnut'.** Name blundered around cross pattée with extended limbs. R. QVENTOVICI around small cross. *L. & S. VII*	300	600
1005	*Halfpenny.* Similar. *L. & S. VII*	450	1000
	Possibly not Northumbrian; the reverse copied from the Carolingian coins of Quentovic, N. France.		

York, early tenth century issues

1006	**St. Peter coinage.** Early issues. SCI PETRI MO in two lines. R. Cross pattee	175	400
1007	— similar. R. 'Karolus' monogram	*Extremely rare*	
1008	*Halfpenny.* Similar. R. Cross pattee	1000	2250

1002   1006   1009

1009	**Regnald** (blundered types). RAIENALT, head to l. or r. R. EARICE CT, 'Karolus' monogram	1250	3000

		F	*VF*
		£	£
1010	— Open hand. R. Similar	1000	2500
1011	— Hammer. R. Bow and arrow	1250	3000
1012	— Similar. R. Sword	*Extremely rare*	

English Coins of the Hiberno-Norse Vikings

Early period, *c.* **919-925**

1013	**Sihtric** (921-927). SITRIC REX, sword. R. Cross or T	1500	3750

1015   1016

1014	**St. Peter coinage.** Late issues SCI PETRI MO, sword and hammer. R. EBORACEI, cross and pellets	350	850
1015	— Similar. R. Voided hammer	450	1000
1016	— Similar. R. Solid hammer	700	1600

St. Peter coins with blundered legends are rather cheaper.
NB. *Modern coins of this type are sold at the Jorvic Centre, York . They have a larger flan.*

Later period, 939-954 (after the battle of Brunanburh). Mostly struck at York.

1017	**Anlaf Guthfrithsson,** 939-941. Flower type. Small cross, ANLAF REX TO D. R. Flower above moneyer's name	2500	6000
1018	**Olaf Guthfrithsson.** Circumscription type, with small cross each side, ANLAF CVNVNC, M in field on reverse (*Derby*)	2500	6000
1018A	— Two line type. ONLAF REX. Large letter both sides (*Lincoln?*)	2000	5000

1019   1020

1019	— Raven type. As illustration, ANLAF CVNVNC	2000	5000
1020	**Olaf Sihtricsson,** first reign, 941-944. Triquetra type. As illus., CVNVNC. R. Danish standard	2000	5000
1021	— Circumscription type (a). Small cross each side, CVNVNC	2000	5000
1022	— Cross moline type, CVNVN C. R. Small cross	*Extremely rare*	
1023	— Two line type. Small cross. R. ONLAF REX. R. Name in two lines	2000	5000
1024	**Regnald Guthfrithsson,** 943-944. Triquetra type. As 1020. REGNALD CVNVNC	3000	7500
1025	— Cross moline type. As 1022, but REGNALD CVNVNC	2500	6000
1026	**Sihtric Sihtricsson,** *c.* 942. Triquetra type. As 1020, SITRIC CVNVNC	*Unique*	

1025   1030

		F	VF
		£	£
1027	— Circumscription type. Small cross each side..		*Unique*
1028	**Eric Blood-axe,** first reign, 948. Two line type. Small cross, ERICVC REX A; ERIC REX AL; or ERIC REX EFOR. R. Name in two lines...............	2500	6000
1029	**Olaf Sihtricsson,** second reign, 948-952. Circumscription type (b). Small cross each side. ONLAF REX	2750	6500
1029A	— Flower type. small cross ANLAF REX R. Flower above moneyer's name	2500	6000
1029B	— Two line type. Small cross, ONLAF REX. R. Moneyer's name in two lines	2000	5000
1030	**Eric Blood-axe,** second reign, 952-954. Sword type. ERIC REX in two lines, sword between. R. Small cross..	2750	6500

KINGS OF WESSEX
Later, KINGS OF ALL ENGLAND
All are silver pennies unless otherwise stated

BEORHTRIC, 786—802
Beorhtric was dependent on Offa of Mercia and married a daughter of Offa.

1031

1031	As illustration	*Extremely rare*
1032	Alpha and omega in centre. R. Omega in centre.......................................	*Extremely rare*

ECGBERHT, 802—839
King of Wessex only, 802-825; then also of Kent, Sussex, Surrey, Essex and East Anglia, 825—839, and of Mercia also, 829-830.

1033	*Canterbury.* Group I. Diad. hd. r. within inner circle. R. Various............*from*	1450	3500
1034	— II. Non-portrait types. R. Various ....*from*	750	2250

1035

		F £	VF £
1035	— III. Bust r. breaking inner circle. R. DORIB C	1100	2500
1036	*London.* Cross potent. R. LVN / DONIA / CIVIT....................................		*Unique*
1037	— — R. REDMVND MONE around TA..	1500	4250
1038	*Rochester,* royal mint. Non-portrait types with king's name ECGBEO RHT..*from*	1150	3250
1039	— — Portrait types, ECGBEORHT..*from*	1350	4000
1040	*Rochester,* bishop's mint. Bust r. R. SCS ANDREAS (APOSTOLVS)....	1450	4600
1041	*Winchester.* SAXON monogram or SAXONIORVM in three lines. R. Cross	1150	3250

AETHELWULF, 839—858

Son of Ecgberht; sub-King of Essex, Kent, Surrey and Sussex, 825-839; King of all southern England, 839-855; King of Essex, Kent and Sussex only, 855-858. No coins are known of his son Aethelbald who ruled over Wessex proper, 855-860.

1042   1044

1042	*Canterbury.* Phase I (839-*c.* 843). Head within inner circle. R. Various. *Br. 3*	225	600
1043	— — Larger bust breaking inner circle. R. A. *Br. 1 and 2*	225	600
1044	— — Cross and wedges. R. SAXONIORVM in three lines in centre. *BR. 10*	225	550
1045	— — Similar, but OCCINDENTALIVM in place of moneyer. *Br. 11*	225	750
1046	— Phase II (*c.* 843-848?). Cross and wedges. R. Various, but chiefly a form of cross or a large A. *Br. 4*	225	500
1047	— — New portrait, somewhat as 1043. R. As last. *Br. 7*	225	500
1048	— — Smaller portrait. R. As last, with *Chi/Rho* monogram. *Br. 7*	250	500
1049	— Phase III (*c.* 848/851-*c.* 855). DORIB in centre. R. CANT mon. *Br. 5*	225	500
1050	— — CANT mon. R. CAN M in angles of cross. *Br. 6*	250	500

1049 1051

	F £	VF £
1051 — Phase IV (*c.* 855-859). Type as Aethelberht. New neat style bust R. Large voided long cross. *Br. 8*	225	425
1052 *Winchester.* SAXON mon. R. Cross and wedges. *Br. 9*	350	750

AETHELBERHT, 858-865/866

Son of Aethelwulf; sub-King of Kent, Essex and Sussex, 858-860; King of all southern England, 860-865/6.

1053 As illustration below	200	400
1054 *O.* Similar, R. Cross fleury over quatrefoil	700	1500

1053

AETHELRED I, 865/866-871

Son of Aethelwulf; succeeded his brother Aethelberht.

1055 As illustration	250	700
1056 Similar, but moneyer's name in four lines	600	1500

For another coin with the name Aethelred see 959 under Viking coinages.

1055

Brother and successor to Aethelred, Alfred had to contend with invading Danish armies for much of his reign. In 878 he and Guthrum the Dane divided the country, with Alfred holding all England south and west of Watling Street. Alfred occupied London in 886.

		F £	VF £

Types with portraits

1057	Bust r. R. As Aethelred I. *Br. 1 (name often* AELBRED)	300	650
1058	— R. Long cross with lozenge centre, as 9544, *Br. 5*	1500	4000
1059	— R. Two seated figures, as 943. *Br. 2*		*Unique*
1060	— R. As Archbp. Aethered; cross within large quatrefoil. *Br. 3*		*Unique*

1057   1061   1062

1061	*London.* Bust. r. R. LONDONIA monogram..	600	1400
	Copies made in tin at the Wembley Exhibition are common		
1062	— R. Similar, but with moneyer's name added	750	1600
1063	— *Halfpenny.* Bust r. R. LONDONIA monogram as 1061	900	2500
1064	*Gloucester.* R. Æ GLEAPA in angles of three limbed cross		*Unique*

Types without portraits

| 1065 | King's name on limbs of cross, trefoils in angles. R. Moneyer's name in quatrefoil. *Br. 4.* .... | | *Unique* |

1066   1069

1066	Cross pattée. R. Moneyer's name in two lines. *Br. 6*	175	350
1067	— As last, but neater style, as Edw, the Elder	185	375
1068	— *Halfpenny.* As 1066..	650	1650
1069	*Canterbury.* As last but DORO added on *obv. Br. 6a*..............................	250	550

For other pieces bearing the name of Alfred see under the Viking coinages.

1070	*Exeter?* King name in four lines. R. EXA vertical	—	5000
1071	*Winchester?* Similar to last, but PIN..		*Extremely rare*
1072	'Offering penny'. Very large and heavy. AELFRED REX SAXORVM in four lines. R. ELIMO in two lines i.e. (*Elimosina*, alms)		*Extremely rare*

Edward, the son of Alfred, aided by his sister Aethelflaed `Lady of the Mericians', annexed all England south of the Humber and built many new fortified boroughs to protect the kingdom.

	F £	VF £

1074

Rare types

		F	VF
1073	*Br. 1. Bath?* R. BA	*Extremely rare*	
1074	— 2. *Canterbury.* Cross moline in pommee. R. Moneyer's name.............	800	2000
1075	— 3. *Chester?* Small cross. R. Minster..	825	2500
1076	— 4. — Small cross. R. Moneyer's name in single line	700	1800
1077	— 5. — R. Two stars	950	2250

1078   1082

		F	VF
1078	— 6. — R. Flower above central line, name below	900	2500
1079	— 7. — R. Floral design with name across field	900	2400
1080	— 8. — R. Bird holding twig..	*Extremely rare*	
1081	— 9. — R. Hand of Providence	1500	3000
1082	— 10. — R. City gate of Roman style	*Extremely rare*	
1083	— 11. — R. Anglo-Saxon burg	900	2000

Ordinary types

1084   1087

		F	VF
1084	. *Br. 12.* Bust l. R. Moneyer's name in two lines ....*from*	400	900
1085	— — As last, but in *gold*		*Unique*
1086	— 12a. Similar, but bust r. of crude style	350	1250
1087	— 13. Small cross. R. Similar (to 1084)...	140	260
1088	*Halfpenny.* Similar to last..		2000

Aethelstan, the eldest son of Eadward, decreed that money should be coined only in a borough, that every borough should have one moneyer and that some of the more important boroughs should have more than one moneyer.

1089   1093

1094

		F £	VF £
1089	**Main issues.** Small cross. R. Moneyer's name in two lines	225	450
1090	Diad. bust r. R. As last	650	1500
1091	— R. Small cross	550	1350
1092	Small cross both sides	185	400
1093	— Similar, but mint name added	200	450
1094	Crowned bust r. As illustration. R. Small cross	450	1000
1095	— Similar, but mint name added	400	850
1096	**Local Issues.** *N. Mercian mints.* Star between two pellets. R. As 1089	550	1250
1097	— Small cross. R. Floral ornaments above and below moneyer's name	550	1250
1098	— Rosette of pellets each side	275	550

1100   1104

		F	VF
1099	— Small cross one side, rosette on the other side	300	650
1100	*N.E. mints.* Small cross. R. Tower over moneyer's name	550	1500
	1101 Similar, but mint name added	750	1750
1102	— Bust in high relief r. or l. R. Small cross	500	1150
1103	— Bust r. in high relief. R. Cross-crosslet	500	1150
1104	'Helmeted' bust r. R. As last	600	1500
1104A	Halfpenny, small cross. R. Moneyer's name in two lines	*Extremely rare*	

Eadmund, the brother of Aethelstan, extended his realm over the Norse kingdom of York.

1105   1107

		£	£
1105	Small cross or rosette. R. Moneyer's name in two lines with crosses or rosettes between ....*from*	160	350
1106	Crowned bust r. R. Small cross..	300	750
1107	Similar, but with mint name..	400	950
1108	Small cross either side, or rosette on one side	200	425
1109	Cross of five pellets. R. Moneyer' s name in two lines	225	475
1110	Small cross. R. Flower above name	900	2000
1111	'Helmeted' bust r. R. Cross-crosslet	750	1750
1112	*Halfpenny.* As 1105 ....*from*	800	1750

1112

EADRED, 946-955
Eadred was another of the sons of Eadward. He lost the kingdom of York to Eric Bloodaxe.

1113   1115

1113	As illustration. R. Moneyer's name in two lines..	135	275
1114	— Similar, but mint name after REX..	300	750
1115	Crowned bust r. As illustration	350	700
1116	— R. Similar, with mint name added..	400	950

	F	VF
	£	£
1117 Rosette. R. As 1113	125	250
1118 Small cross. R. Rosette	135	285
1119 — R. Flower enclosing moneyer's name. *B.M.C. II*	*Extremely rare*	
1120 *Halfpenny.* Similar to 1113	750	1500

HOWEL DDA, d. 949-950

Grandson of Rhodri Mawr, Howel succeeded to the kingdom of Dyfed *c.* 904, to Seisyllog *c.* 920 and became King of Gwynedd and all Wales, 942.

1121

1121   HOPÆL REX, small cross or rosette. R. Moneyer's name in two lines...   *Unique*

EADWIG, 955-959

Elder son of Eadmund, Eadwig lost Mercia and Northumbria to his brother Eadgar in 957.

1122   1123

1122 *Br. 1.* Type as illustration	200	400
1123 — — Similar, but mint name in place of crosses	350	1000
1123A— Similar to 1122, but star in place of cross on *obv.*	*Unique*	
1124 — 2. As 1122, but moneyer's name in one line	600	2200
1125 — 3. Similar. R. Floral design	675	2250
1126 — 4. Similar. R. Rosette or small cross	250	550
1127 — 5. Bust r. R. Small cross	*Extremely rare*	

1128

1128 *Halfpenny.* Small cross. R. Flower above moneyer's name	*Unique*	
1128A— Similar. R. PIN (Winchester) across field	*Extremely rare*	

King in Mercia and Northumbria from 957; King of all England 959-975.

It is now possible on the basis of the lettering to divide up the majority of Eadgar's coins into issues from the following regions: N.E. England, N.W. England, York, East Anglia, Midlands, S.E. England, Southern England, and S.W. England. (*See* 'Anglo-Saxon Coins', ed. R. H. M. Dolley.)

1129 1135

		F £	VF £
1129	*Br I*. Small cross. R. Moneyer's name in two lines, crosses between, trefoils top and bottom	100	185
1130	— — R. Similar, but rosettes top and bottom (a N.W. variety)	100	210
1131	— — R. Similar, but annulets between	150	300
1132	— — R. Similar, but mint name between (a late N.W. type)	125	325
1133	— 2. — R. Floral design	750	2000
1134	— 4. Small cross either side	110	250
1135	— — Similar, with mint name	225	475
1136	— — Rosette either side	150	275
1137	— — Similar, with mint name	225	475
1138	— 5. Large bust to r. R. Small cross	400	900
1139	— — Similar, with mint name	600	1300
1140	*Halfpenny*. (8 1/2 grains.) *Br. 3*. Small cross. R. Flower above name	*Extremely rare*	
1140A	— — R. Mint name around cross (Chichester)	*Unique*	
1140B	— Bust r. R. `Londonia' monogram		4500

For Eadgar `reform' issues see overleaf

ANGLO-SAXON LATE PERIOD

In 973 Eadgar introduced a new coinage. A royal portrait now became a regular feature and the reverses normally have a cruciform pattern with the name of the mint in addition to that of the moneyer. Most fortified towns of burghal status were allowed a mint, the number of moneyers varying according to their size and importance: some royal manors also had a mint and some moneyers were allowed to certain ecclesiastical authorities. In all some seventy mints were active about the middle of the 11th century (see list of mints pp. 65-67).

The control of the currency was retained firmly in the hands of the central government, unlike the situation in France and the Empire where feudal barons and bishops controlled their own coinage. Coinage types were changed at intervals to enable the Exchequer to raise revenue from new dies and periodic demonetization of old coin types helped to maintain the currency in a good state. No halfpence were minted during this period. During the latter part of this era, full pennies were sheared into `halfpennies' and `farthings'. They are far rarer than later `cut' coins.

	F	VF
	£	£

EADGAR, 959-975 *continued*

1141

1141	**Penny**. Type 6. Small bust l. R. Small cross, name of moneyer and mint.	500	950

EDWARD THE MARTYR, 975-978

Son of Eadgar and Aethelflaed, Eadward was murdered at Corfe, reputedly on the orders of his stepmother Aelfthryth.

1142

1142	Type as illustration above	650	1250

He was the son of Eadgar and Aelfthryth. His reign was greatly disturbed by incursions of D a n i s h fleets and armies which massive payments of money failed to curb. He was known as 'The Unready', from UNREDE, meaning 'without counsel', ie. he was without good advice.

1143   1144

		F £	VF £
1143	First small cross type. Style of 1142, usually backless dress, 3 pellets in front, *Br. 1; B.M.C. I*	350	800
1144	First Hand type. Bust r., no sceptre. R. Hand of Providence. *Br. 2; B.M.C. IIa*	90	180
1145	— Similar, but bust to l. *B.M.C. IIb*	375	850

1146   1147

1146	Second Hand type, with sceptre. *B.M.C. IId*	90	175
1147	Benediction type. *O.* As last. R. Hand giving Benediction. *B.M.C. IIf*	400	900

1148   1151

1148	CRVX type. *Br. 3; B.M.C. IIIa*	70	130
1149	— Lightweight issue. Small flan, sceptre slants into drapery	90	200
1150	Intermediate small cross type. Somewhat as 1143, no pellets, similar bust to CRVX type (1148) but no sceptre	500	1250
1151	Long cross type. *Br. 5; B.M.C. IVa*	70	125

1152

		V	VF
		£	£
1152	Helmet type. *Br. 4; B.M.C. VIII*	75	135
1153	— — Similar, but struck in **gold**		*Unique*
1154	Last small cross type. As 1143, but different style	70	115
1154A	Similar, but bust r.	200	500

1154

1156

1155	— Similar, but bust to edge of coin. *B.M.C. Id*	250	550
1156	Agnus Dei type. *Br. 6; B.M.C. X*		*Extremely rare*

CNUT, 1016-1035

Son of Swegn Forkbeard, King of Denmark, Cnut was acclaimed King by the Danish fleet in England in 1014 but was forced to leave. He returned in 1015 and in 1016 agreed on a division of the country with Eadmund Ironsides, the son of Aethelred. No coins of Eadmund are known and on his death in November 1016 Cnut secured all England, marrying Emma of Normandy, widow of Aethelred.

Main types

1157   1158   1159   1160

	F	VF
	£	£
1157 Quatrefoil type. *BR. 2; B.M.C. VIII*	85	145
1158 Helmet type. *Br. 3; B.M.C. XIV*	80	130
1159 Short cross type. *BR. 4; B.M.C. XVI*	75	125
1159A — Similar, but with banner in place of sceptre..........................	250	500
1160 Jewel cross type. *Br. 6; B.M.C. XX*. Type as 1163	500	1100

This type is now considered to be a posthumus issue struck under the auspices of his widow, Aelgifu Emma.

HAROLD I, 1035-1040

Harold, the son of Cnut and Aelgifu of Northampton, initially acted as regent for his half-brother Harthacnut on Cnut's death, was then recognised as King in Mercia and the north, and King throughout England in 1037.

1163   1165

1163 Jewel cross type, as illustration. *Br. 1; B.M.C. 1*	155	335
1164 Long cross and trefoils type. *Br. 2; B.M.C. V*	160	350
1165 — Similar, but fleur de lis in place of trefoils. *B.M.C. Vc*	150	325

HARTHACNUT, 1035-1042

He was heir to Cnut but lost the throne to his half-brother Harold owing to his absence in Denmark. On Harold's death he recovered his English realm.

1167   1168

1166 **Early period, 1036.** Jewel cross type, as 1163; bust l. *Br. 1; B.M.C. I*....	750	1600
1167 — Similar, but bust r. *B.M.C. Ia*	700	1500
1168 **Restoration, 1040-1042.** Arm and sceptre type, with name Harthacnut. *Br. 2; B.M.C. II*	700	1500
1169 — Similar, but with name 'Cnut'...	450	850

1169   1170

	F £	VF £
1170 **Danish types,** of various designs, some of English type mostly struck at Lund, Denmark (now Sweden) ....*from*	175	375

EDWARD THE CONFESSOR, 1042-1066

Edward was the son of Aethelred II and Emma of Normandy. A number of new mints were opened during his reign.

1171   1173

1171	PACX type, cross extends to edge of coin. *Br. 4; B.M.C. IVa*	150	325
1172	— Similar, but cross ends at legend. *B.M.C. IV*.......................................	150	325
1173	Radiate type. *Br. 2; B.M.C. I*..	80	140

1174   1175

1174	Trefoil quadrilateral type. *Br. 1; B.M.C. III*...	75	135
1175	Short cross type, small flans. *Br. 3; B.M.C. II*	70	120

1176   1179

1176	Expanding cross type; light issue (18 grs.). *Br. 5; B.M.C. V*	80	135

	F	VF
	£	£
1177 — — Heavy issue (27 grs.).......................................	75	140
1178 — — Similar, but struck in **gold**..............................		*Unique*
1179 Helmet type. *Br. 6; B.M.C. VII*	70	120
1180 — — Similar but bust l.	350	900

1181

1182

| 1181 Sovereign type. *Br. 7; B.M.C. IX* .... | 95 | 165 |
| 1182 Hammer cross type. *Br. 8; B.M.C. XI* .... | 75 | 130 |

1183

1184

| 1183 Facing bust type. *Br. 9; B.M.C. XIII* .... | 70 | 125 |
| 1184 Pyramids type. *Br. 10; B.M.C. XV* .... | 90 | 160 |

1185

| 1185 Large facing bust with sceptre. R. Similar.............................. | 950 | 2000 |

Most York coins of this reign have an annulet in one quarter of the reverse.

Harold was the son of Godwin Earl of Wessex. He was the brother-in-law of Edward the Confessor and was recognised as King on Edward's death. He defeated and killed Harald of Norway who invaded the north, but was himself defeated and killed at the Battle of Hastings by William of Normandy.

1186   1187

		F	VF
		£	£
1186	Bust l. with sceptre. R. PAX across centre of *rev. B.M.C. I*	300	575
1187	Similar, but without sceptre. *B.M.C. Ia*	325	700
1188	Bust r. with sceptre	600	1250

ANGLO-SAXON, NORMAN AND EARLY PLANTAGENET MINTS

In Anglo-Saxon times coins were struck at a large number of towns. The place of mintage is normally given on all coins from the last quarter of the 10th century onwards, and generally the name of the person responsible (e.g. BRVNIC ON LVND). Below we give a list of the mints, showing the reigns (Baronial of Stephen's reign omitted), of which coins have been found. After the town names we give one or two of the spellings as found on the coins, although often they appear in an abbreviated or extended form. On the coins the Anglo-Saxon and Norman *w* is like a Þ or Γ and the *th* is Đ. We have abbreviated the kings' names, etc.:

Alf	—	Alfred the Great	Wi	—	William I
EE	—	Edward the Elder	Wii	—	William II
A'stan	—	Aethelstan	He	—	Henry I
EM	—	Edward the Martyr	ST	—	Stephen (regular issues)
Ae	—	Aethelred II	M	—	Matilda
Cn	—	Cnut	HA	—	Henry of Anjou
Hi	—	Harold I	WG	—	William of Gloucester
Htr	—	Harthacnut	T	—	'Tealby' coinage
ECfr	—	Edward the Confessor	SC	—	Short cross coinage
Hii	—	Harold II	LC	—	Long cross coinage

Abergavenny (FANI), Wi.
Axbridge (ACXEPO, AGEPOR) Ae, Cn, Ht.
Aylesbury (AEGEL) Ae, Cn, ECfr.
Barnstaple (BEARDA, BARDI), Edwig, Ae-Hi, ECfr, Wi, He.
Bath (BADAN) EE-Edmund, Edwig-ECfr, Wi, He, St.
Bedford (BEDANF, BEDEF) Edwig-T.
Bedwyn (BEDE C IN) ECfr, Wi.
Berkeley (BEORC) ECfr, Wi.
Bramber ? (BRAN) St.
Bridport (B RIPVT, BRIDI) A'stan, Ae, Cn, Ht, ECfr, Wi.
Bristol (BRICSTO) Ae-T, M. HA, LC.
Bruton (BRIVT) Ae-Cn, ECfr.
Buckingham (BVCIN) EM-Hi, ECfr.
Bury St. Edmunds (EDMVN, SEDM, SANTEA) A'stan?, ECfr, Wi, He-LC.
Cadbury CADANB) Ae, Cn.
Caistor (CASTR) EM, Ae, Cn.
Cambridge (GRANTE) Edgar-Wii.
Canterbury (DORO, CAENT, CANTOR, CANT C AR) Alf, A'stan, Edgar-LC.
Cardiff (CAIRDI, CARDI, CARITI) Wi, He, St, M.
Carlisle (CAR, CARDI, EDEN) He-LC.
Castle Gotha ? (GEOĐA, IOĐA) Ae-Ht.
Castle Rising (RISINGE) St.
Chester (LEIGECES, LEGECE, CESTRE) A'stan, Edgar-T.
Chichester (CISSAN CIV, CICES, CICST) A'stan, Edgar-St, SC.
Chippenham ? (CIPEN) St.
Christchurch, see Twynham.
Cissbury (SIĐEST) Ae, Cn.
Colchester (COLEAC, COLECES) Ae-Hi, ECfr-T.
Crewkerne (CRVCERN) Ae, Cn.
Cricklade (CROCGL, CRIC, CREC) Ae-Wii.
Derby (DEOR, DIORBI, DERBI) A'stan, Edgar-ECfr, Wi-St.
Dorchester (DORCE, DORECES) Ae-ECfr, Wi-He, WG.
Dover (DOFER) A'stan, Edgar-St.
Droitwich (PICC, PICNEH) ECfr. Hii.
Dunwich (DVNE) St.
Durham (DVRE DVRHAN) Wi, St-LC.
Exeter (EAXANC, EXEC, XECST) Alf, A'stan, Edwig-LC.
Eye (EI, EIE) St.
Frome ? (FRO) Cn-ECfr.
Gloucester (GLEA C EC, GLE C , G C) Alf, A'stan, Edgar-St, HA, T, LC.
Guildford (GILDEF) EM-Cn, Ht-Wii.

Hastings (HAESTIN) Ae-St.
Hedon, near Hull (HEDVN) St.
Hereford (HEREFOR) A'stan, Ae-St, HA, T, LC.
Hertford (HEORTF) A'stan, Edwig-Hi, ECfr, Wi, Wii.
Horncastle ? (HORN) EM, Ae.
Horndon ? (HORNIDVNE) ECfr.
Huntingdon (HVNTEN) Edwig-St.
Hythe (HIÐEN) ECfr, Wi, Wii.
Ilchester (IVELCE, GIFELCST, GIVELC) Edgar, E M-He, T, LC.
Ipswich (GIPES C IC) Edgar-SC.
Kings Lynn (LENN, LENE) SC.
Langport (LANCPOR) A'stan, Cn, Hi, ECfr.
Launceston (LANSTF, SANCTI STEFANI) Ae, Wi, Wii, St. T.
Leicester (LIGER, LIHER, LEHRE) A'stan, Edgar-T.
Lewes (LAEPES) A'stan, Edgar-T.
Lichfield (LIHFL) SC.
Lincoln (LINCOLNE, NICOLE) Edgar-LC.
London (LVNDENE) Alf-LC.
Louth ? (LVD) Ae.
Lydford (LYDAN) EM-Hi, ECfr.
Lympne (LIMEN) A'stan, Edgar-Cn.
Maldon (MAELDVN, MAELI) A'stan, Ae-Hi, ECfr, Wii.
Malmesbury (MALD, MEALDMES) Ae-Wii, HA.
Marlborough (MAERLEB) Wi, Wii.
Milbourne Port (MYLE) Ae, Cn.
Newark (NEPIR, NIPOR) Edwig, Eadgar, Ae, Cn.
Newcastle (NEWEC, NIVCA) St, T, LC.
Newport (NIPAN, NIPEP) Edgar, ECfr.
Northampton (HAMTVN, NORHANT) Edwig, Edgar-Wi, He-LC.
Norwich (NORPIC) A'stan-LC.
Nottingham (SNOTINC) A'stan, Ae-St.
Oxford (OXNAFOR, OXENEF) A'stan, Edmund, Edred, Edgar-St, M, T-LC.
Pembroke (PAN, PAIN) He-T.
Pershore (PERESC) ECfr.
Peterborough (MEDE, BVR) Ae, Cn, Wi.
Petherton (PEÐÐR) ECfr.
Pevensey (PEFNESE, PEVEN) Wi, Wii, St.
Reading (READIN) ECfr.
Rhuddlan (RVDILI, RVLA) Wi, SC.
Rochester (ROFEC) A'stan, Edgar-He, SC.
Romney (RVME, RVMNE) Ae-Hi, ECfr-He.
Rye (RIE) St.
Salisbury (SAEREB, SALEB) Ae-ECfr, Wi- T.
Sandwich (SANPIC) ECfr, Wi-St.
Shaftesbury (SCEFTESB, SCEFITI) A'stan, Ae-St.
Shrewsbury (SCROBES, SALOP) A'stan, Edgar-LC.
Southampton (HAMWIC, HAMTVN) A'stan, Edwig-Cn.
Southwark (SVDGE, SVD C EEORC) Ae-St.
Stafford (STAFF, STAEF) A'stan, Ae-Hi, ECfr, Wi, Wii, St, T.
Stamford (STANFOR) Edgar-St.
Steyning (STAENIG) Cn-Wii.
Sudbury (SVDBI, SVB) Ae, Cn, ECfr, Wi- St.
Swansea (SWENSEI) HA?
Tamworth (TOMPEARÐGE, TAMPRÐ) A'stan, Edwig-Hi, ECfr, Wi-St.
Taunton (TANTVNE) Ae, Cn, Ht-St.
Thetford (ÐEOTFOR,, TETFOR) Edgar-T.
Torksey (TORC, TVRC) EM-Cn.
Totnes (DARENT VRB, TOTANES, TOTNESE) A'stan, Edwig-Cn, Wii.
Twynham, now Christchurch (TPIN, TVEHAM) Wi, He.
Wallingford (PELING, PALLIG) A'stan, Edgar-He, T, LC.
Wareham (PERHAM) A'stan, Ae, Cn, Ht-St, M, WG.
Warminster (PORIME) Ae-Hi, ECfr.
Warwick (PAERING, PERPIC) A'stan, Edgar-St.
Watchet (PECEDPORT, PICEDI) Ae-ECfr, Wi-St.
Wilton (PILTVNE) Edgar-LC.

Winchcombe (PINCELE, PINCL) Edgar-Cn, Ht-Wi.
Winchester (PINTONIA, PINCEST) Alf-A'stan, Edwig -LC.
Worcester (PIHRAC, PIHREC) Ae-Hi, ECfr-Sc.
York (EBORACI, EOFERPIC) A'stan, Edmund, Edgar-LC.

The location of the following is uncertain.
AESTHE *(? Hastings)* Ae.
BRYGIN *(? Bridgnorth,* but die-links with NIPAN and with *Shaftesbury)* Ae.
DERNE, DYR (E. Anglian mint) ECfr.
DEVITVN *(? Welsh Marches* or *St. Davids)* Wi.
EANBYRIG, Cn.
MAINT, Wi.
ORSNAFORDA *(? Horsforth or Orford)* Alf.
WEARDBYRIG *(? Warborough)* A'stan, Edgar.

EDWARDIAN AND LATER MINTS

London, Tower: Edw. I-GEO. III.
London, Tower Hill: Geo. III-Eliz. II.
London, Durham House: Hen. VIII (posth.)-Edw. VI.
Ashby de la Zouche: Chas. I.
Aberystwyth: Chas. I.
Aberystwyth: -Furnace: Chas. I.
Bridgnorth: Chas. I.
Berwick-on-Tweed: Edw. I-Edw. III.
Birmingham, Heaton: Vic., Geo. V.
Birmingham, King's Norton: Geo. V.
Birmingham, Soho: Geo. III.
Bombay, India (branch mint): Geo. V.
Bristol: Ed w. I, Edw. IV, Hen. VI rest., Hen. VIII-Edw. VI, Chas. I, Wm. III.
Bury St. Edmunds: Edw. I-Edw. III.
Calais: Edw. III-Hen. IV, Hen. VI.
Canterbury: Edw. I-Edw. III, Edw. IV, Hen. VII-Edw. VI.
Carlisle: Chas. I.
Chester: Edw. I, C has. I, Wm. III.
Colchester: Chas. I.
Coventry: Edw. IV.
Durham: Edw. I-Edw. IV, Rich. III-Hen. VIII.
Exeter: Edw. I, Chas. I, Wm. III.
Hartlebury Castle, Worcs.: Chas. I.
Kingston-upon-Hull: Edw. I.
Lincoln: Edw. I.
Llantrisant: Eliz. II (decimal coinage).
Melbourne, Australia (branch mint): Vic.-Geo. V.
Newark: Chas. I.
Newcastle-upon-Tyne: Edw. I.
Norwich: Edw. IV, Wm. III.
Ottowa, Canada (branch mint): Edw. VII-Geo. V.
Oxford: Chas I.
Perth, Australia (branch mint): Vic.-Geo. V.
Pontefract: Chas. I.
Pretoria, South Africa (branch mint): Geo. V.
Reading: Edw. III.
Scarborough: Chas. I.
Shrewsbury: Chas. I.
Southwark: Hen. VIII-Edw. VI.
Sydney, Australia (branch mint): Vic.-Geo. V.
Tournai, Belgium: Hen. VIII.
Truro: Chas. I.
Welsh Marches: Chas I
Worcester: Chas I.
York: Edw. I, Edw. III-Edw. IV, Rich. III-Edw. VI, Chas. I, Wm. III.

NORMAN KINGS

There were no major changes in the coinages following the Norman conquest. The controls and periodic changes of the type made in the previous reigns were continued. Nearly seventy mints were operating during the reign of William I; these had been reduced to about fifty-five by the middle of the 12th century and, under Henry II, first to thirty and later to eleven. By the second half of the 13th century the issue of coinage had been centralized at London and Canterbury, with the exception of two ecclesiastical mints. Of the thirteen types with the name PILLEMVS, PILLELM, etc. (William), the first eight have been attributed to the Conqueror and the remaining five to his son William Rufus. Cut 'halfpennies' and 'farthings' were still made in this period and are scarce until the later issues of Henry I and Stephen.

From William I to Edward II inclusive all are silver pennies unless otherwise stated.

WILLIAM I, 1066-1087

William Duke of Normandy was the cousin of Edward the Confessor. After securing the throne of

1250	1251
1252	1253
1254	1255

England he had to suppress several rebellions.

No.	Description		
1250	*Penny.* Profile left type. *Br. I*	145	350
1251	Bonnet type. *Br. II*	120	210
1252	Canopy type. *Br. III*	150	360
1253	Two sceptres type. *Br. IV*	135	280
1254	Two stars type. *Br. V*	100	175
1255	Sword type. *Br. VI*	160	365

	F £	VF £
1256 Profile right type. *Br VII*	250	500
1257 PAXS type. *Br. VIII*	85	130

WILLIAM II, 1087-1100

William Rufus was the second son of William I, his elder brother Robert succeeded to the Dukedom of Normandy. He was killed while hunting in the New Forest.

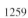

1258 *Penny*. Profile type. *Br. 1*	225	500
1259 Cross in quatrefoil type. *Br. 2*	225	475

1260 Cross voided type. *Br. 3*	225	475
1261 Cross pattée and fleury type. *Br. 4*	250	575

1262 Cross fleury and piles type. *Br. 5*	350	650

Fifteen types were minted during this reign. In 1108 provision was made for minting round halfpence again, none having been struck since the time of Eadgar, but relatively few can have been made. The standard of coinage manufacture was now beginning to deteriorate badly. Many genuine coins were being cut to see if they were plated counterfeits and there was a reluctance by the public to accept such damaged pieces. About 1108-9 an extraordinary decision was taken to order the official mutilation of all new coins by snicking the edges, thus ensuring that cut coins had to be accepted. Pennies of types VII to XII (Nos. 1268-1273) usually have a cut in the flan that sometimes penetrated over a third of the way across the coin.

At Christmas 1124 the famous `Assize of the Moneyers' was held at Winchester when all the moneyers in England were called to account for their activities and a number are said to have been mutilated for issuing coins of inferior quality.

Note. Academic opinion is now agreed that the order of types II to XI is in doubt. A new chronology for these types was published in Spinks' *Numismatic Circular,* Sept. 1990. We have put the new proposed dates against the original types in our text. The principal changes are: type III precedes type II, and types VII to XI now have the following order: IX, VIII, VII, XI, X. We have revised the dates for each type in accordance with current opinions and research.

	1263		1263A	

		F	VF
		£	£
1263	**Penny.** *Br. I.* Annulets type (1101-2)	300	750
1263A	— II. Profile l. R. Cross fleury (1102-3)	300	650

	1264		1265

| 1264 | — III. PAX type (1103-4).. | 350 | 750 |
| 1265 | — IV. Facing bust. R. Five annulets and four piles (1104-5).................... | 400 | 900 |

	1266		1267

| 1266 | — V. — R. Voided cross with fleur in each angle (1105-6) .... | 500 | 1100 |
| 1267 | — VI. Pointing bust and stars type (1106-7)... | 900 | 1850 |

1268

	F	VF
	£	£
1268 — VII. Facing bust. R. Quatrefoil with piles (1108-9)	250	500

<table>
<tr><td>1269</td><td></td></tr>
<tr><td>1270</td><td></td></tr>
</table>

1269   1270

1269	*Br.* VIII. Large bust l. R. Cross with annulet in each angle (1109-10)	600	1450
1270	— IX. Facing bust. R. Cross in quatrefoil (1107-8)	450	1000

1271   1272

1271	— X. Small facing bust in circle. R. Cross fleury (1114-19)	200	450
1272	— XI. Very large bust l. R. 'Double inscription' around small cross pattee (1110-14)	600	1100

1273   1274

1273	— XII. Small bust l. R. Cross with annulet in each angle (1119-20)	350	750
1274	— XIII. Star in lozenge fleury type (1120-2)	250	550

1275   1276

		F	VF
		£	£
1275	— XIV. Pellets in quatrefoil type (1122-4)	120	275
1276	— XV. Quadrilateral on cross fleury type (1125-36)	100	225

*Full flan pieces with good legends may be worth more than the price stated.

1277

1277*	*Halfpenny.* Facing head. R. Cross potent with pellets in angles	2000	4000
1277A	— As above R. Similar to penny die of type IX		*Unique*

*A number of specimens have appeared lately in new finds.

STEPHEN, 1135-1154
and the Civil War and Anarchy, 1138-1153

Stephen of Blois, Count of Boulogne and a nephew of Henry I, hastily crossed the Channel on his uncle's death and secured the throne for himself, despite Henry's wishes that his daughter Matilda should succeed him. She was the widow of the German emperor Henry V, and was then married to Geoffrey, Count of Anjou. Two years later Matilda arrived in England to claim the throne, supported by her half-brother Robert of Gloucester. During the protracted civil war that ensued Matilda and later her son, Henry of Anjou, set up an alternative court at Bristol and held much of the west of England, striking coins at mints under their control. Many irregular coins were struck during this troubled period, some by barons in their own name. Particularly curious are the coins from the Midlands and E. Anglia which have Stephen's head defaced, now believed to have been issued during the Interdict of 1148. In 1153, following the death of Stephen's son, Eustace, a treaty between the two factions allowed for the succession of Matilda's son Henry and a uniform coinage was once more established throughout the kingdom. *B.M.C.*— British Museum Catalogue: *Norman Kings,* 2 vols. (1916). *M.*—Mack, R. P., 'Stephen and the Anarchy 1135-54', *BNJ, XXXV* (1966), pp. 38-112.

STEPHEN
Regular regal issues

1278   1280

	F £	VF £

1278 **Penny.** Cross moline (Watford) type. Bust r., with sceptre. R. Cross moline with lis in angles. *B.M.C. I; M. 3-42* 90 200
1279 — Similar, but obv. reads PERERIC or PERERICM. *M. 43-50* 350 800
1280 Voided cross type. Facing bust with sceptre. R. Voided cross pattee with mullets in angles. *East and South-east mints only. B.M.C. II; M. 53-66*... 150 350

1281

1282

1281 Cross fleury type. Bust l. with sceptre. R. Cross fleury with trefoils in angles. *East and South-east mints only. B.M.C. VI; M. 77-99* 350 800
1282 Cross pommee (Awbridge) type. Bust half-left with sceptre. R. Voided cross pommee with lis in angles. *B.M.C. VII; M. 99z-135b* 150 325
For B.M.C. types III, IV & V, see 1300-1302.

Local and irregular issues of the Civil War

A. Coins struck from erased or defaced dies (interdict of 1148)

1283

1288

1283 As 1278, with king's bust defaced with long cross. *East Anglian Mints. M. 137-147* 400 950
1284 — Similar, but king's bust defaced with small cross. *Nottingham. M. 149* 400 800
1285 — Similar, but sceptre defaced with bar or cross. *Nottingham, Lincoln and Stamford. M. 148 and 150-154* 300 800
1286 — Similar, but king's name erased. *Nottingham. M. 157* 500 1000
1286A— Other defacements .... *Extremely rare*

B. South-Eastern variant
1287 As 1278, but king holds mace instead of sceptre. *Canterbury. M. 158* ..... *Extremely rare*

C. Eastern variants
1288 As 1278, but roundels in centre or on limbs of cross or in angles. *Suffolk mints. M. 159-168* 600 1200
1288A As 1278, but star before sceptre and annulets at tips of *fleurs on reverse. Suffolk mints. M. 188* 1000 2500

	F £	VF £

1289 As 1278, but thick plain cross with pellet at end of limbs, lis in angles. *Lincoln. M. 169-173*................ 600 1200

1290 — Similar, but thick plain cross superimposed on cross moline. *M. 174* . *Extremely rare*

1290A As 1278. R. Quadrilateral over voided cross. *M. 17 6*....................... *Extremely rare*

1290B As 1278. R. Long cross to edge of coin, fleurs outwards in angles. *Lincoln. M. 186-187*......................... *Extremely rare*

D. Southern variants

1291 As 1278, but with large rosette of pellets at end of obverse legend. *M. 184-185* .... *Extremely rare*

1292 — Similar, but star at end of obverse legend. *M. 187y*....................... *Extremely rare*

1293 Crowned bust r. or l. with rosette of pellets before face in place of sceptre. R. As 1280, but plain instead of voided cross. *M. 181-183*................... *Extremely rare*

1291   1295

1295 As 1278, but usually collar of annulets. R. Voided cross moline with annulet at centre. *Southampton. M. 207-212* 600 1500

E. Midland variants

1296

1296 As 1278, but cross moline on reverse has fleured extensions into legend. *Leicester. M. 177-178* 1000 2500

1297 As 1278 but crude work. R. Voided cross with lis outwards in angles. *Tutbury. M. 179* .... *Extremely rare*

1298 Somewhat similar. R. Voided cross with martlets in angles. *Derby. M. 175* 1200 3000

1298   1300

	F	VF
	£	£
1299 As 1278. R. Plain cross with T-cross in each angle. *M. 180*		*Extremely rare*
1300 Facing bust with three annulets on crown. R. Cross pattee, fleurs inwards in angles. *Northampton or Huntingdon (?). B.M.C. III; M.67-71*	1200	3000

1301   1302

1301 Facing bust with three fleurs on crown. R. Lozenge fleury, annulets in angles. *Lincoln or Nottingham. B.M.C. IV; M. 72-75*	1250	3250
1302 Bust half-right with sceptre. R. Lozenge with pellet centre, fleurs inwards in angles. *Leicester. B.M.C. V; M. 76*	1250	3250
1303 **Robert,** Earl of Leicester(?). As 1280, but reading ROBERTVS. *M. 269*	*Extremely rare*	

F. North-east and Scottish border variants

1304 As 1278, but star before sceptre and annulets at tips of fleurs on reverse. *M. 188*	1000	2500
1305 As 1278, but a voided cross extending to outer circle of reverse. *M. 189-192*	*Extremely rare*	
1306 As 1278, but crude style, with Stephen's name. *M. 276-279 and 281-282*	700	1750
1307 — Similar. R. Cross crosslet with cross-pattée and crescent in angles. *M. 288*	*Extremely rare*	
1308 David I (K. of Scotland). As 1305, but with name DAVID REX. *M. 280*	1500	
1309 **Henry** (Earl of Northumberland, son of K. David). hENRIC ERL. As 1278. *M. 283-285*	1200	3000
1310 — Similar. R. Cross fleury. *M. 286-287*	1000	2500
1311 — As 1307, but with name NENCI : COM on obverse. *M. 289*	1200	2750

G. 'Ornamented' series. *So-called 'York Group' but probably minted in Northern France*

| 1312 As 1278, with obverse inscription NSEPEFETI, STEFINEI or RODBDS. R. WISÐ. GNETA, etc., with o rnament(s) in legend (sometimes retrograde). *M. 215-216 and 227* .... | *Extremely rare* | |

1313   1315

| 1313 Flag type. As 1278, but king holds lance with pennant, star to r. R. As 1278, mostly with four ornaments in legend. *M. 217* .... | 1250 | 2500 |
| 1313A— Similar, but with eight ornaments in reverse inscription. *M. 217* .... | 1250 | 2500 |

		F	VF
		£	£

1314   As 1278, but STIEN and ornaments, sceptre is topped by pellet in lozenge.
R. Cross fleury over plain cross, ornaments in place of inscription.
M. 218 .... *Extremely rare*

1314A King stg. facing, holding sceptre and long standard with triple-tailed
pennon. R. Cross pattee, crescents and quatrefoi ls in angles, pellets
around, ornaments in legend .... *Unique*

1315   **Stephen and Queen Matilda.** Two standing figures holding sceptre, as
illustration. R. Ornaments in place of inscription. *M. 220* 2500   5000

1316   1320

1316   **Eustace.** EVSTACIVS, knight stg. r. holding sword. R. Cross in quatrefoil,
EBORACI EDTS (or EBORACI TDEFL). *M. 221-222* .... *Extremely rare*

1317   — Similar, but ThOMHS FILIuS VIF. *M. 223* .... *Extremely rare*

1318   — Similar, but mixed letters and ornaments in rev. legend. *M. 224* 1500

1319   [EVSTA] CII . FII . IOANIS, lion passant r, collonnade (or key?) below.
R. Cross moline with cross-headed sceptres in angles, mixed letters and
ornaments in legend. *M. 225* .... *Unique*

1320   Lion rampant r., looped object below, EISTAOhIVS. R. Cross fleury with
lis in angles, mostly, ornaments in legend. *M. 226* 1400   3250

1321   **Rodbert.** Knight on horse r., RODBERTVS IESTV (?). R. As 1314. *M.
228* .... *Extremely rare*

1321   1322

1322   **Bishop Henry.** Crowned bust r., crozier and star to r., HENRICVS EPC.
R. Somewhat as last, STEPhANVS REX. *M. 229* .... *Extremely rare*

H. Uncertain issues

1323   Crowned bust r. with sceptre, -NEΓ:. R. Cross pattée with annulets in
angles (as Hen. I type XIII). *M. 272* .... *Extremely rare*

1324   Crowned facing bust with sceptre, star to r. (as Hen. I type XIV). R. As
last. *M. 274Extr* .... *Extremely rare*

1325   Other types .... *Extremely rare*

1326   1331

1326 **Matilda,** Dowager Empress, Countess of Anjou (in England 1139-1148).
As 1278, but cruder style, MATILDI IMP. etc. *M. 230-240* 750 1750
1326A Obv. similar. R. Cross pattee over cross fleury (Cardiff hoard) 750 1750
1326B Similar, but triple pellets or plumes at end of cross (Cardiff hoard) .... *Extremely rare*
1327 **Duke Henry,** son of Matilda and Geoffrey of Anjou, Duke of Normandy
from 1150 (in England 1147-1149-1150 and 1153-1154). As 1278 but
hENRICVS, etc. *M. 241-245* 2250 5000
1327A As 1295 but hENRIC. *M. 246* .... *Extremely rare*
1327B As 1326B, but hENNENNVS R, etc .... *Extremely rare*
1328 Obverse as 1278. R. Cross crosslet in quatrefoil. *M. 254* .... *Extremely rare*
1329 Crowned bust r. with sceptre. R. Cross fleury over quadrilateral fleury.
M. 248-253 .... 2250 4500
1330 Crowned facing bust, star each side. R. Cross botonnée over a quadrilateral pommée. *M. 255-258* 2250 5000
1331 Obverse as 1330. R. Voided cross botonnee over a quadrilateral pommée.
M. 259-261 .... 2250 5000
1332 **William,** Earl of Gloucester (succeeded his father, Earl Robert, in 1147).
Type as Henry of Anjou, no. 1329. *M. 262* 5500
1333 Type as Henry of Anjou, no. 1330. *M. 263* .... *Unique*
1334 Type as Henry of Anjou, no. 1331. *M. 264-268* 2500 5500
1335 **Brian Fitzcount,** Lord of Wallingford (?). Type as Henry of Anjou, no.
1330. *M. 270* .... *Unique*
1336 **Patrick,** Earl of Salisbury (?). Helmeted bust r. holding sword, star behind.
R. As Henry of Anjou, no. 1329. *M. 271* .... *Extremely rare*

PLANTAGENET KINGS
HENRY II, 1154-1189

Cross-and-crosslets ('Tealby') Coinage, 1158-1180
Coins of Stephen's last type continued to be minted until 1158. Then a new coinage bearing Henry's name replaced the currency of the previous reign which contained a high proportion of irregular and sub-standard pennies. The new Cross and Crosslets issue is more commonly referred to as the 'Tealby' coinage, as over 5000 of these pennies were discovered at Tealby, Lincolnshire, in 1807. Thirty mints were employed in this re-coinage, but once the re-minting had been completed not more than a dozen mints were kept open. The issue remained virtually unchanged for twenty-two years apart from minor variations in the king's portrait. The coins tend to be poorly struck.

Cut coins occur with varying degrees of frequency during this issue, according to the type and local area.

1337A   B   C

Penny

		F	VF
1337	Class A. No hair	35	130
1338	— B. Similar but mantle varies	40	140
1339	— C. Decorated collar, curl of hair	35	130

D   E   F

		F	VF
1340	— D. Decoration continues along shoulder	40	140
1341	— E. Similar bust, but shoulder not decorated	45	150
1342	— F. Hair in long ringlet to r. of bust	45	150

NB. The price quoted for coins in the above section allows for the usual poor quality strike.

Mints and classes of the Cross-and-Crosslets coinage
Approximate dates for the various classes are as follows:
A 1158-1161, B and C 1161-1165, D 1165-1168, E 1168-1170 and F 1170-1180.

Bedford	A - - - - -	Ilchester	A B C D - F	Pembroke	A - - - - -
Bristol	A B C D E F	Ipswich	- B C D E F	Salisbury	A - - - - -
Bury St. Edmunds	A B C D E F	Launceston	A - - - - -	Shrewsbury	A - - - - -
Canterbury	A B C D E F	Leicester	A - - - - -	Stafford	A - C - - -
Carlisle	A - C D E F	Lewes	- - - - ? F	Thetford	A - C D - F
Chester	A - - D - -	Lincoln	A B C D E F	Wallingford	A - - - - -
Colchester	A - C - E -	London	A B C D E F	Wilton	A - - - - -
Durham	A B C - - -	Newcastle	A - C D E F	Winchester	A - C D ? -
Exeter	A B C D - -	Northampton	A - C ? - -	York	A - C D - -
Gloucester	A - - - - -	Norwich	A B C D - F		
Hereford	A - C - - -	Oxford	A - - D E -		

86

'Short Cross' coinage of Henry II (1180-1189)

In 1180 a coinage of new type, known as the Short Cross coinage, replaced the Tealby issue. The new coinage is remarkable in that it covers not only the latter part of the reign of Henry II, but also the reigns of his sons Richard and John and his grandson Henry III, and the entire issue bears the name 'hЄNRICVS'. There are no English coins with names of Richard or John. The Short Cross coins can be divided chronologically into various classes: eleven mints were operating under Henry II and tables of mints, moneyers and classes are given for each reign.

Cut coins continue and although less common than after 1247, they are still up to ten times commoner than during the Anglo-Saxon period.

1a   1b   1c

		F	VF
		£	£
1343	Class 1a. Narrow face, square E, and C, round M	150	375
1343a	1a* Bust of 1a, but round C and Є, square M...	165	400
1344	— 1b. Curls usually 2 to l., 5 to r., round Є and C, square M, stop before REX on most coins	35	75
1345	— 1c. First evidence of degradation, more curls to r. than to l., no stop in *obv.* legend on some coins	30	70

Mints, moneyers, and classes for Henry II

London: Aimer (1a, b, c), Alain (1a, b, c), Alain V (1a, b), Alward (1b), Davi (1b, c), FIL Aimer (1a, b), Gilebert (1c), Godard (1b), Henri (1a, b), Henri Pi (1a, b), Iefrei or Gefrei (1a, b, c), Iohan (1a, b), Osber (1b), Pieres (1a, b, c), Pieres M . (1a, b), Randul (1a, b), Raul (1b, c), Reinald (1b), Willelm (1a, b, c) .... *from* 30
Carlisle: Alain (1b, c) .... *from* 70
Exeter: Asketil (1a, b), Iordan (1a, b), Osber (1a, b), Raul (1b), Ricard (1b, c), Roger (1b) .... *from* 60
Lincoln: Edmund (1b, c), Girard (1b), Hugo (1b), Lefwine (1b, c), Rodbert (1b), Walter (1b), Will . D.F. (1b), Willelm (1b, c)... *from* 55
Northampton: Filipe (1a, b), Hugo (1a, b), Raul (1a, b, c), Reinald (1a, b), Simund (1b), Walter (1a, b, c), Willelm (1a, b)... *from* 60
Norwich: Reinald (1b, c), Willelm (1b) .... *from* 60
(Current research may indicate that these coins are of the Northampton mint).
Oxford: Asketil (1b), Iefrei (1b), Owein (1b), Ricard (1b, c), Rodbert (1b), RODBT F. B. (1b), Sagar (1b)... *from* 75
Wilton: Osber (1a, b), Rodbert (1a, b)... *from* 65
Winchester: Adam (1b, c), Clement (1a, b), Gocelm (1a, b, c), Henri (1a), Osber (1a, b), Reinier (1b), Ricard (1b), Rodbert (1a, b) .... *from* 30
Worcester: Edrich (1b), Godwine (1b, c), Osber (1b) .... *from* 75
York: Alain (1a, b), Efrard (1a, b, c), Gerard (1b), Hugo (1b, c), Hunfrei (1a, b), Isac (1a, b), Turkil (1a, b, c), Willelm (1a, b) .... *from* 30

Pennies of Short Cross type continued to be issued throughout the reign, all bearing the name hЄNRICVS. The coins of class 4, which have very crude portraits, continued to be issued in the early years of the next reign. The only coins bearing Richard's name are from his territories of Aquitaine and Poitou in western France.

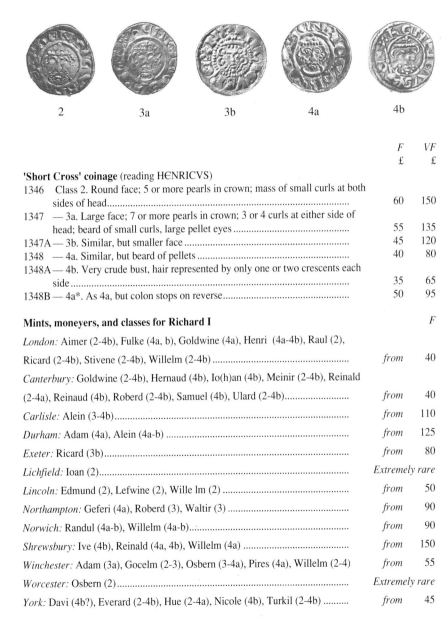

2	3a	3b	4a	4b

	F £	VF £

'Short Cross' coinage (reading HЄNRICVS)

		F £	VF £
1346	Class 2. Round face; 5 or more pearls in crown; mass of small curls at both sides of head......................	60	150
1347	— 3a. Large face; 7 or more pearls in crown; 3 or 4 curls at either side of head; beard of small curls, large pellet eyes	55	135
1347A	— 3b. Similar, but smaller face	45	120
1348	— 4a. Similar, but beard of pellets	40	80
1348A	— 4b. Very crude bust, hair represented by only one or two crescents each side	35	65
1348B	— 4a*. As 4a, but colon stops on reverse................................	50	95

Mints, moneyers, and classes for Richard I

	F
London: Aimer (2-4b), Fulke (4a, b), Goldwine (4a), Henri (4a-4b), Raul (2), Ricard (2-4b), Stivene (2-4b), Willelm (2-4b)	*from* 40
Canterbury: Goldwine (2-4b), Hernaud (4b), Io(h)an (4b), Meinir (2-4b), Reinald (2-4a), Reinaud (4b), Roberd (2-4b), Samuel (4b), Ulard (2-4b)........................	*from* 40
Carlisle: Alein (3-4b)....................................	*from* 110
Durham: Adam (4a), Alein (4a-b)	*from* 125
Exeter: Ricard (3b)......................................	*from* 80
Lichfield: Ioan (2)..	*Extremely rare*
Lincoln: Edmund (2), Lefwine (2), Wille lm (2)	*from* 50
Northampton: Geferi (4a), Roberd (3), Waltir (3)	*from* 90
Norwich: Randul (4a-b), Willelm (4a-b)............................	*from* 90
Shrewsbury: Ive (4b), Reinald (4a, 4b), Willelm (4a)	*from* 150
Winchester: Adam (3a), Gocelm (2-3), Osbern (3-4a), Pires (4a), Willelm (2-4)	*from* 55
Worcester: Osbern (2)................................	*Extremely rare*
York: Davi (4b?), Everard (2-4b), Hue (2-4a), Nicole (4b), Turkil (2-4b)	*from* 45

'Short Cross' coinage *continued.* All with name hƐNRICVS

The Short Cross coins of class 4 will have continued during the early years of John's reign, but in 1205 a re-coinage was initiated and new Short Cross coins of better style replaced the older issues. Coins of classes 5a and 5b were issued in the re-coinage in which sixteen mints were employed. Only ten of these mints were still working by the end of class 5. The only coins to bear John's name are the pennies, halfpence and farthings issues for Ireland.

| 4c | 5a | 5b | 5c | 6a1 | 6a2 |

	F	VF
	£	£
1349 Class 4c. Somewhat as 4b, but letter S is reversed	40	90
1350 — 5a. New coinage of neat style and execution; realistic face; 5 or more pearls to crown; letter S is reversed; *mm* cross pommée	30	65
1350A — — with ornamented letters..	35	110
1350B — 5a/5b or 5b/5a mules..	45	100
1351 — 5b. Similar, but S normal and *mm* reverts to cross pattée....................	25	60
1352 — 5c. Similar, but letter X composed of 4 strokes in the form of a St. Andrew's cross	30	65
1353 — 6a1. Coarser style; letter X composed of 2 wedges in the form of a St. Andrew's cross	25	55
1353A — 6a2. Similar, but letter X has arms at right angles and with rounded ends	25	55

Mints, moneyers and classes for John

		F
London: Abel (5c-6a), Adam (5b-c), Arnaud (5b), Beneit (5b-c), Fulke (4c-5a), Henri (4c-5b), Ilger (5b-6a), Iohan (5b), Rauf (5c-6a), Rener (5b-c), Ricard (4c-5b), Ricard B (5b-c), Ricar d T (5b), Walter (5c-6a), Willelm (4c-5c), Willelm B (5b-c), Willelm L (5b-c), Willelm T (5b-c)	*from*	25
Bury St. Edmunds: Fulke (5b-c)	*from*	50
Canterbury: Arnaud (5a-c), Coldwine (4c-5c), (H)ernaud (5a-c), Hue (4c-5c), Io(h)an (4c-5c), Iohan B (5b-c), Iohan M (5b-c), Rauf (Vc?), Roberd (4c-5c), Samuel (4c-5c), Simon (5a or c), Simun (4c-5b)	*from*	25
Carlisle: Tomas (5b)	*from*	90
Chichester: Pieres (5b), Rauf (5a-b), Simon (5a- b), Willelm (5b)	*from*	50
Durham: Pieres (4c-6a)...	*from*	70
Exeter: Gilebert (5a-b), Iohan (5a-b), Ricard (5a-b)...	*from*	45
Ipswich: Alisandre (5b, c), Iohan (5b-c)	*from*	50
Kings Lynn: Iohan (5b), Nicole (5b), Willelm (5b)	*from*	135
Lincoln: Alain (5a), Andreu (5a-c), Hue (5b-c), Iohan (5a), Rauf (5a-b), Ricard (5a), Tomas (5a, b)...	*from*	40
Northampton: Adam (5b-c), Randul (4c), Roberd (5b), Roberd T (5b)	*from*	45

		F
		£
Norwich: Gifrei (5a-c), Iohan (5a-c), Renald (5a), Renaud (5a-c)	*from*	45
Oxford: Ailwine (5b), Henri (5 b), Miles (5b)	*from*	50
Rhuddlan: An irregular issue probably struck during this reign. Halli, Henricus, Tomas, Simond..	*from*	90
Rochester: Alisandre (5b), Hunfrei (5b)	*from*	100
Winchester: Adam (5a-c), An dreu (5b-c), Bartelme (5b-c), Henri (5a), Iohan (5a-c), Lukas (5b, c), Miles (5a-c), Rauf (5b-c), Ricard (5a, b)	*from*	30
York: Davi (4c-5b), Nicole (4c-5c), Renaud (5b), Tomas (5b)............................	*from*	35

HENRY III, 1216-72

'Short Cross' coinage *continued* (1216-47)

The Short Cross coinage continued for a further thirty years during which time the style of portraiture and workmanship deteriorated. By the 1220s minting had been concentrated at London and Canterbury, one exception being the mint of the Abbot of Bury St. Edmunds.

Halfpenny and farthing dies are recorded early in this issue; a few halfpennies and now two farthings have been discovered. See nos 1357 D-E.

| 6b | 6c | 7 early | 7 middle | 7 late |

	F	*VF*
	£	£

'Short Cross' coinage, 1216-47

1354	Class 6b. Very tall lettering; early coins have a head similar to 6 a, but later issues have a long thin face..	15	40
1355	— 6c. Pointed face	15	40
1355A	— — Ornamental lettering	40	110
1355B	— 6x. Large face, two curls each side of hd., pellet on chin, letter X only by sceptre	100	200
1355C	— 6d. Tall, straight-sided letters, pellet on crossbar of N on most coins .	15	25
1356	— 7. No stops between words in rev. legend; no neck	15	35

| 8a | 8b1 | 8b2 | 8b3 |

1357	— 8a. New style; *mm* cross pattee; letter X curule shaped......................	*Extremely rare*	
1357A	— 8b1. Similar; *mm* cross pommee	20	75
1357B	— 8b2. Cruder version; wedge-shaped letter X......................................	20	75
1357C	— 8b3. Very crude version; letter X is cross pommée	20	75

1357D	1357E

	F
	£
1357D **'Short Cross' coinage.** (*c.* 1221-30). Cl. 7. Halfpenny. hЄNRICVS REX. R. TER.RI ON LUND or ELIS ON LUND (London)	*Extremely rare*
1357E —— Farthing. Similar. R. TERRI ON LUND	*Extremely rare*

Mints, moneyers, and classes for Henry III 'Short Cross' coinage

London: Abel (6b-7), Adam (7), (H)elis (7), Giffrei (7), Ilger (6b-7), Ledulf (7), Nichole (7-8), Rau(l)f (6b-7), Ricard (7), Terri (7), Walter (6b-6c)	*from*	15
Bury St. Edmunds: Io(h)an (7-8), Norman (7), Rauf (6b-7), Simund (7), Willelm (7)	*from*	30
Canterbury: Arnold (6x), Henri (6b-7), Hiun (6b-7), Iun (7), Io(h)an (6b-8), Ioan Chic (7), Ioan F. R. (7), Nicole (7-8), Norman (7), Osmund (7), Roberd (6b), Robert (7), Robert Vi (7), Roger (6b-7), Roger of R (7), Salemun (6x, 7), Samuel (6b-7), Simon (7), Simun (6b-7), Tomas (6d, 7), Walter (6b-7), Willem (7-8), Willem Ta (7)	*from*	15
Durham: Pieres (7)	*from*	100
Winchester: Henri (6c)	*from*	20
York: Iohan (6c), Peres (6c), Tomas (6c), Wilam (6c)	*from*	120

'Long Cross' coinage (1247-72)
By the middle of Henry's reign the coinage in circulation was in a poor state, being worn and clipped. In 1247 a fresh coinage was ordered, the new pennies having the reverse cross extended to the edge of the coin to help safeguard the coins against clipping. The earliest of these coins have no mint or moneyers' names. A number of provincial mints were opened for producing sufficient of the Long Cross coins, but these were closed again in 1250, only the royal mints of London and Canterbury and the ecclesiastical mints of Durham and Bury St. Edmunds remained open.

In 1257, following the introduction of new gold coinages by the Italian cities of Brindisi (1232), Florence (1252) and Genoa (1253), Henry III issued a gold coinage in England. This was a gold 'Penny' valued at 20 silver pence and twice the weight of the silver penny. The coinage was not a success, being undervalued, and coinage ceased after a few years—few have survived.

Cut halfpennies and farthings are common for this period, with a greater concentration in the early part. They are up to 100 times commoner than in late Anglo-Saxon times.

Without sceptre

	Ia		Ib		

		F	VF
		£	£
1358	Class Ia. hЄNRICVS: RЄX. R. ANGLIЄ TЄRCI	150	350
1359	Ib. hЄNRICVS REX. ANG. R. LIE TЄRCI LON *(London)*, CAN *(Canterbury)* or AED *(Bury St. Edmunds)* ... *from*	45	90
1360	—— I/II mule	45	90

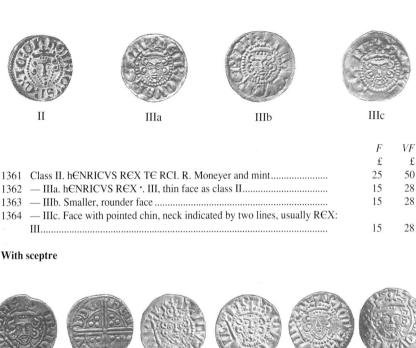

II   IIIa   IIIb   IIIc

		F	VF
		£	£
1361	Class II. hENRICVS REX TE RCI. R. Moneyer and mint......................	25	50
1362	— IIIa. hENRICVS REX ⁘. III, thin face as class II................................	15	28
1363	— IIIb. Smaller, rounder face	15	28
1364	— IIIc. Face with pointed chin, neck indicated by two lines, usually REX: III..	15	28

With sceptre

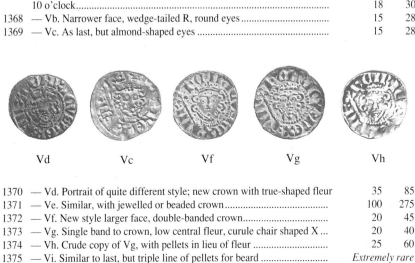

IVa   IVb   Va   Vb   Vc

1365	Class IVa. Similar to last, but with sceptre	60	130
1366	— IVb. Similar, but new crown with half-fleurs and large central fleur..	70	180
1367	— Va. With class IV bust, round eyes, from now on legend begins at 10 o'clock..	18	30
1368	— Vb. Narrower face, wedge-tailed R, round eyes	15	28
1369	— Vc. As last, but almond-shaped eyes	15	28

Vd   Vc   Vf   Vg   Vh

1370	— Vd. Portrait of quite different style; new crown with true-shaped fleur	35	85
1371	— Ve. Similar, with jewelled or beaded crown...	100	275
1372	— Vf. New style larger face, double-banded crown...................................	20	45
1373	— Vg. Single band to crown, low central fleur, curule chair shaped X ...	20	40
1374	— Vh. Crude copy of Vg, with pellets in lieu of fleur	25	60
1375	— Vi. Similar to last, but triple line of pellets for beard	*Extremely rare*	

Vi   1376

| | F | VF |
| | £ | £ |

1376 **Gold penny** of 20d. As illustration.. *Extremely rare*
    A very fine specimen was sold at auction in June 1985 for £65,000.

Mints, Moneyers, and classes for Henry III 'Long Cross' coinage

London: Davi or David (IIIc Vf), Henri (IIIa-Vd, f, g), Ion, Ioh, Iohs or Iohan
(Vc-g), Nicole (Ib/II mule, II-Vc), Renaud (Vg-i), Ricard (IIIc-Vg), Robert (Vg),
Thomas (Vg), Walter (Vc-g), Willem (Vc-g and gold penny)............................ *from* 15

Bristol: Elis (IIIa, b, c), Henri (IIIb) , Iacob (IIIa, b, c), Roger (IIIa, b, c), Walter
(IIIb, c) .... *from* 22

Bury St. Edmunds: Ion or Iohs (II-Va, Vg, h, i), Randulf (Va-f), Renaud (Vg),
    Stephane (Vg) .... *from* 20

Canterbury: Alein (Vg, h), Ambroci (Vg), Gilbert (II-Vd/c mule, Vf, g), Ion, Ioh,
Iohs, or Iohanes (IIIe-Vd, f, g), Nicole or Nichole (Ib/II mule, II-Vh), Ricard
(Vg, h), Robert (Vc-h), Walter (Vc-h), Willem or Willeme (Ib/II mule, II-Vd, f, g) *from* 15

Carlisle: Adam (IIIa, b), Ion (IIIa, b), Robert (IIIa, b), Willem (IIIa, b)............. *from* 55

Durham: Philip (IIIb), Ricard (V, b, c), Roger (Vg), Willem (Vg) .... *from* 65

Exeter: Ion (II-IIIc), Philip (II-IIIc), Robert (II-IIIc), Walter (II-IIIb)............... *from* 40

Gloucester: Ion (II-IIIc), Lucas (II-IIIc), Ricard (II-IIIc), Roger (II-IIIc).......... *from* 25

Hereford: Henri (IIIa, b), Ricard (IIIa, b, c), Roger (IIIa, b, c), Walter (IIIa, b, c) *from* 40

Ilchester: Huge (IIIa, b, c), Ierveis (IIIa, b, c), Randulf (IIIa, b, c), Stephe
(IIIa, b, c)... *from* 60

Lincoln: Ion (II-IIIc), Ricard (II-IIIc), Walter (II-IIIc), Willem (II-IIIc)............. *from* 25

Newcastle: Adam (IIIa, b), Henri (IIIa, b, c), Ion (IIIa, b, c), Roger (IIIa, b, c) .. *from* 22

Northampton: Lucas (II-IIIb), Philip (II-IIIc), Tomas (II-IIIc), Willem (II-IIIc) *from* 25

Norwich: Huge (II-IIIc), Iacob (II-II Ic), Ion (II-IIIc), Willem (II-IIIc) .... *from* 35

Oxford: Adam (II-IIIc), Gefrei (II-IIIc), Henri (II-IIIc), Willem (II-IIIc) .... *from* 35

Shrewsbury: Lorens (IIIa, b, c), Nicole (IIIa, b, c), Peris (IIIa, b, c), Ricard (IIIa,
b, c) .... *from* 45

Wallingford: Alisandre (IIIa, b), Clement (IIIa, b), Ricard (IIIa, b), Robert (IIIa,
b)   .... *from* 35

Wilton: Huge (IIIb, c), Ion (IIIa, b, c), Willem (IIIa, b, c) .... *from* 40

Winchester: Huge (II-IIIc), Iordan (II-IIIc), Nicole (II-IIIc), Willem (II-IIIc) .... *from* 22

York: Alain (II-IIIb), Ieremie (II-IIIb), Ion (II-IIIc), Rener (II-IIIc), Tomas
(IIIb, c) .... *from* 25

'Long Cross' coinage *continued* (1272-79). With name hЄNRICVS
The earliest group of Edward's Long Cross coins are of very crude style and known only of
Durham and Bury St. Edmunds. Then, for the last class of the type, pennies of much improved
style were issued at London, Durham and Bury, but in 1279 the Long Cross coinage was
abandoned and a completely new coinage substituted.

Cut halfpennies and farthings also occur for this issue, and within this context are not
especially rare.

VI   VII

| | F | VF |
	£	£
1377 Class VI. Crude face with new realistic curls, Є and N ligate	15	45
1378 — VII. Similar, but of improved style, usually with Lombardic U	70	125

Mints, moneyers, and classes for Edward I 'Long Cross' coinage ....

		F
London: Phelip (VII), Renaud (VII)	*from*	85
Bury St. Edmunds: Ioce (VII), Ion or Ioh (VI, VII)	*from*	15
Durham: Roberd (VI), Robert (VII)	*from*	175

New Coinage (from 1279).
A major re-coinage was embarked upon in 1279 which introduced new denominations. In
addition to the penny, halfpence and farthings were also minted and, for the first time, a
fourpenny piece called a 'Groat' (from the French *Gros).*

As mint administration was now very much centralized, the practice of including the
moneyer's name in the coinage was abandoned (except for a few years at Bury St. Edmunds).
Several provincial mints assisted with the re-coinage during 1279-81, then minting was again
restricted to London, Canterbury, Durham and Bury.

The provincial mints were again employed for a subsidiary re-coinage in 1299-1302 in order
to remint lightweight coins and the many illegal *esterlings* (foreign copies of the English
pennies) or *Sterlings,* (mainly from the Low Countries), which were usually poorer quality than
the English coins.

1379

| | F | VF |
	£	£
1379 **Groat.** (=4d.; wt. 89 grs.). Type as illustration but several minor varieties	1000	2250

Extant specimens often show traces of having been mounted on the obverse
and gilded on the reverse; unmounted coins are worth more.

1a   1b   1c

	F £	VF £
1380 **Penny.** *London.* Class 1a. Crown with plain band, ЄDW RЄX; Lombardic N on obv.	300	650
1381 — 1b. — ЄD RЄX; no drapery on bust, Roman N	350	750
1382 — Ic. — ЄDW RЄX; Roman N, normal or reversed; small lettering	14	35
1383 — Id. — ЄDW R;—; large lettering and face	12	30

1d(1384)   2a   2b

	F	VF
1384 — — — Annulet below bust (for the Abbot of Reading)	135	325
1385 — 2a. Crown with band shaped to ornaments; large face and short neck similar to 1d; usually broken left petal to central fleur of crown	16	40
1386 — 2b. — tall bust; long neck; N reversed	12	33

3a   3b   3c

	F	VF
1387 — 3a. Crescent-shaped contraction marks; pearls in crown, drapery is foreshortened circle	35	65
1388 — 3b. — — drapery is segment of a circle	25	45
1389 — 3c. — normal crown; drapery in one piece, hollowed in centre	8	25

3e   3f   3g

		F	VF
		£	£
1390	— 3d. — — drapery in two pieces, broad face..	10	30
1391	— 3e. — long narrow face (mostly Northern mints).................................	12	32
1392	— 3f. — broad face, large nose, rougher work, late S first used....................	25	60
1393	— 3g. — small neat bust, narrow face...	9	25

4a   4b   4c   4d   4e

		F	VF
		£	£
1394	— 4a. Comma-shaped contraction mark, late S always used, C and Є open .	10	30
1395	— 4b. Similar, but face and hair shorter	9	25
1396	— 4c. Larger face with more copious hair; unbarred A first used................	9	25
1397	— 4d. Pellet at beginning of *obv.* and/or *rev.*inscription	10	30
1398	— 4e. Three pellets on breast; pellet in *rev.* legend.......................	12	32

5a   5b

1399	— 5a. Well spread coins, pellet on breast, A normally unbarred	35	85
1400	— 5b. Coins more spread, tall lettering, long narrow face, pellet on breast....	35	85

6a   6b   7a   7b

		V	VF
		£	£
1401	— 6a. Smaller coins, initial cross almost plain, crown with wide fleurs.........	90	200
1402	— 6b. Initial cross well pattee; lettering of good style; closed Є (from now on)	50	100
1403	— 7a. Rose on breast; almond-shaped eyes, double barred N........................	50	125

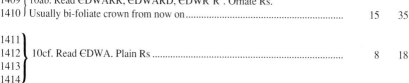

| 8a | 8b | 9a | 9b |

1404	— 7b. — — longer hair, new crown...	50	125
1404A	Type as 7, but no rose	100	225
1405	— 8a. Smaller crown; top-tilted S; longer neck..	25	60
1406	— 8b. Not unlike 9a, but top-tilted S...	25	55
1407	— 9a. Narrow face, flatter crown, star on breast	14	35
1408	— 9b. Small coins; Roman N, normal, un-barred, or usually of pot-hook form; often star or pellet on breast...	10	25

| 10ab | 10cf | 10cf | 10cf |

| 1409 | 10ab. Read ЄDWARR, ЄDWARD, ЄDWR'R'. Ornate Rs. | | |
| 1410 | Usually bi-foliate crown from now on .... | 15 | 35 |

1411			
1412	10cf. Read ЄDWA. Plain Rs	8	18
1413			
1414			

For further classification of Class 10, see 'Sylloge of British Coins, 39, The J. J. North Collection, Edwardian English Silver Coins 1279-1351', Chapter 10, Class 10, c. 1301-10, by C. Wood.

Prices are for full flan, well struck coins.
The prices for the above types are for London. For coins of the following mints (see over page); types are struck in brackets, prices are for the commonest type of each mint.

Berwick Type I   Type II   Type III   Type IV

		F	VF
		£	£
1415	*Berwick-on-T weed.* (Blunt types I-IV) ....*from*	20	60
1416	*Bristol.* (2; 3b; c, d; 3f, g; 9b)..*from*	18	40
1417	*Bury St. Edmunds.* Robert de Hadelie (3c, d, g; 4a, b, c) ....*from*	50	120
1418	— Villa Sci Edmundi (4e; 5b; 6b; 7a; 8a-10f) ....*from*	20	50
1419	*Canterbury.* (2; 3b-g; 4; 5; 7a; 9;10) ....*from*	8	25
1420	*Chester.* (3g; 9b)..*from*	35	70
1421	*Durham.* King's Receiver (9b; 10a, b, e, f).............................*from*	16	35
1422	— Bishop de Insula (2; 3b, c, e, g; 4a) ....*from*	18	40
1423	— Bishop Bec (4b, c, d; 5b; 6b; 7a; 8b; 9; 10b-f) mostly with *mm.* cross		
	moline ....*from*	18	40
1424	— — (4b) cross moline in one angle of *rev.*..................................	130	275
1425	*Exeter.* (9b)...	40	110
1426	*Kingston-upon-Hull.* (9b)..	40	110
1427	*Lincoln.* (3c, d, f, g) ....*from*	16	35
1428	*Newcastle-upon-Tyne.* (3e; 9b; 10)...*from*	20	50
1429	*York.* Royal mint (2; 3b, c, d, f; 9b)..*from*	15	40
1430	— Archbishop's mint (3e, f; 9b). R. Quatrefoil in centre ....*from*	25	70

1431   1433   1436

1431	**Halfpenny,** *London.* Class IIIb. Drapery as segment of circle......................	30	75
1432	—IIIc. Normal drapery as two wedges	30	75
1433	—IIIg. Similar, larger letters, wider crown....................................	25	65
1433A	— — IV c. Comma abbreviation mark, thick waisted s.	30	75
1433B	— — Pellet before LON	35	85
1434	IVe. Usually three pellets on breast, one on *rev.*	40	90
1434A	— VI. Double barred N, small lettering...................................	35	85
1435	— VII. Double barred N, large lettering.............................	32	80
1436	IX. Pot-hook N, usually no star on breast, crown band curved at fleurs	20	55
1437	— X. EDWAR R ANGL DNS hYB, thick waisted letters............................	20	55

The above prices are for London; halfpence of the mints given below were also struck.

1438	*Berwick-on-Tweed.* (Blunt types II and III) ....*from*	60	150
1439	*Bristol.* (IIIc; IIIg)..*from*	50	140

	F	VF
	£	
1440 *Lincoln.* (IIIc)	70	165
1441 *Newcastle.* (IIIe). With single pellet in each angle of *rev.*	135	360
1442 *York.* (IIIb)	60	135

1443   1445   1446

	F	VF
	£	£
1443 **Farthing,** *London.* Class I. Heavy weight (6.65 grains), ЄDWARDVS REX. R. LONDONIЄNSIS, bifoliate crown	25	100
1443A — — trifoliate crown	30	100
1444 — II. Similar, but reversed N's (6.62 grs.)	20	80
1445 — IIIc. As class I, but different bust	20	70
1446 — IIIg. Lighter weight (5.5 grs.) Є R ANGLIЄ, no inner circle on *obv.*	20	70
1446A — IV Reads CIVITAS LONDON, narrow crown	45	120
1446B — V — Wider crown	45	120
1447 — VI+VII. Similar, double barred N, pellet eyes	70	160
1448 VIII. ЄR ANGL DN, closed Є	50	120
1449 — IX. Unbarred Ns	45	110
1450 — X or XI. (Edward II) ЄWARDVS REX A or AN inner circle both sides	20	50

Types 1449 and 1450 often appear on oval flans.

The above prices are for London; farthings of the mints given below were also struck.

1452

	F	VF
1451 *Berwick-on-Tweed.* (Blunt type III)	140	275
1452 *Bristol.* (II, IIIc (heavy), III (light)) *from*	85	185
1453 *Lincoln.* (III)	120	250
1453A *Newcastle* (IIIe), triple pellet in *rev.* quarters *Extremely rare*		
1454 *York.* (II; III) *from*	125	275

For further information see C. Wood 'Syllogue of British Coins, 39, The J. J. North Collection, Edwardian Engilsh Silver Coins 1279-1351'.

The coinage of this reign differs only in minor details from that of Edward I. No groats were issued in the years *c.* 1282-1351.

11a	12	13	14

15a	15b	15c

	F	VF
	£	£
1455 **Penny,** *London.* Class 11a. Broken spear-head or pearl on l. side of crown; long narrow face, straight-sided N	10	30
1456 — 11b. — Є with angular back (till 15b), N with well-marked serifs	10	30
1457 — 11c. — — A of special form	30	65
1458 — 12. Central fleur of crown formed of three wedges	20	45
1459 — 13. Central fleur of crown as Greek double axe	16	40
1460 — 14. Crown with tall central fleur; large smiling face with leering eyes	12	35
1461 — 15a. Small flat crown with both spear-heads usually bent to l.; face of 14	16	40
1462 — 15b. — very similar, but smaller face	16	40
1463 — 15c. — large face, large Є	18	45

The prices of the above types are for London.

Berwick Type V	Type VI	Type VII

	F	VF
1464 *Berwick-on-Tweed.* (Blunt types V, VI and VII) ....*from*	50	95
1465 *Bury St. Edmunds.* (11; 12; 13; 14; 15) ....*from*	16	40
1466 *Canterbury.* (11; 12; 13; 14; 15) ....*from*	16	40
1467 *Durham.* King's Receiver (11a), *mm.* plain cross ....*from*	25	55
1468 — Bishop Bec. (11a), *mm.* cross moline	25	60
1469 — Bishop Kellawe (11; 12; 13), crozier on *rev.* ....*from*	25	55
1470 — Bishop Beaumont (13; 14; 15), *mm.* lion with lis ....*from*	30	70
1471 Sede Vacante (15c); *mm.* plain cross	55	135

1469   1470

	F £	VF £
1472 **Halfpenny** of *London*. ЄDWARDVS REX A(NG)	55	135
1473 — — *Berwick-on-Tweed*. (Blunt type V)	80	200
1474 **Farthing** of *London*. ЄDWARDVS REX (ANG)	65	160
1475 — *Berwick-on-Tweed*. (Blunt type V)	150	—

EDWARD III, 1327-77

During Edward's early years small quantities of silver coin were minted following the standard of the previous two reigns, but in 1335 halfpence and farthings were produced which were well below the .925 Sterling silver standard. In 1344 an impressive gold coinage was introduced comprising the Florin or Double Leopard valued at six shillings, and its half and quarter, the Leopard and the Helm. The design of the Florin was based on the contemporary gold of Philip de Valois of France.

The first gold coinage was not successful and it was replaced later the same year by a heavier coinage, the Noble, valued at 6s. 8d, i.e., 80 pence, half a mark or one third of a pound, together with its fractions. The Noble was lowered in weight in two stages over the next few years, being stabilized at 120 grains in 1351. With the signing of the Treaty of Bretigni in 1360 Edward's title to the Kingdom of France was omitted from the coinage, but it was resumed again in 1369.

In 1344 the silver coinage had been re-established at the old sterling standard, but the penny was reduced in weight to just over 20 grains and in 1351 to 18 grains. Groats were minted again in 1351 and were issued regularly henceforth until the reign of Elizabeth.

Subsequent to the treaty with France which gave England a cross-channel trading base at Calais, a mint was opened there in 1363 for minting gold and silver coins of English type. In addition to coins of the regular English mints, the Abbot of Reading also minted silver pence and a halfpence with a scallop shell badge while coins from Berwick display one or two boars' or bears' heads.

There is evidence of re -use of dies at later periods, e.g. 3rd coinage halfpennies.

Mintmarks

✠	✠	✠	✠	♔	✠	✠	✛
6	1	2	3	74	4	5	7a

1334-51	Cross pattée (6)	1356	Crown (74)
1351-2	Cross 1 (1)	1356-61	Cross 3 (4)
1351-7	Crozier on cross end (76a, *Durham*)	1361-9	Cross potent (5)
1352-3	Cross 1 broken (2)	1369-77	Cross pattée (6)
1354-5	Cross 2 (3)		Plain cross (7a)
			Cross potent and four pellets

The figures in brackets refer to the plate of mintmarks on page 365.

GOLD

Third coinage, 1344-51
First period, 1344

| 1476 | 1477 | 1478 | 1479 |

	F	VF
	£	£

1476 **Florin** or **Double Leopard.** (=6s.; wt. 108 grs.). King enthroned beneath canopy; crowned leopard's head each side. R. Cross in quatrefoil........... *Extremely rare*

1477 **Half-florin** or **Leopard.** Leopard sejant with banner l. R. Somewhat as last... *Extremely rare*

1478 **Quarter-florin** or **Helm.** Helmet on fleured field. R. Floriate cross........ *Extremely rare*

Second period, 1344-46

1479 **Noble** (=6s. 8d., wt. 138 6/13 grs.). King stg. facing in ship with sword and shield. R. L in centre of royal cross in tressure .... *Extremely rare*

1480 **Quarter-noble.** Shield in tressure. R. As last... 1250 2750

Third period, 1346-51

1481 **Noble** (wt. 128 4/7 grs.). As 1479, but Є in centre; large letters 800 1700

1482 **Half-noble.** Similar.. 1250 5000

1483 **Quarter-noble.** As 1480, but Є in centre 250 550

Fourth coinage, 1351-77
Reference: L. A. Lawrence, *The Coinage of Edward III from 1351.*
Pre-treaty period, 1351-61. With French title.

| 1488 | 1498 |

1484 **Noble** (wt. 120 grs.), series B (1351). Open Є and C, Roman M; *mm.* cross 1 (1)... 325 600

1485 — — *rev.* of series A (1351). Round lettering, Lombardic M and N; closed inverted Є in centre 350 675

	F	*VF*
	£	£
1486 C (1351-1352). Closed Є and C, Lombardic M; *mm.* cross 1 (1)	275	500
1487 D (1352-1353). *O.* of series C. R. *Mm.* cross 1 broken (2)	400	700
1488 E (1354-1355). Broken letters, V often has a nick in r. limb; *mm.* cross 2 (3)..	275	500
1489 F (1356). *Mm.* crown (74)	375	650
1490 G (1356-1361). *Mm.* cross 3 (4). Many varieties	250	475
1491 **Half-noble,** B. As noble with *rev.* of series A, but closed Є in centre not inverted..	225	475
1492 C. *O.* as noble. *Rev.* as last	250	500
1493 E. As noble	450	800
1494 G. As noble. Many varieties..	175	375
1495 **Quarter-noble,** B. Pellet below shield. R. Closed Є in centre	135	225
1496 C. *O.* of series B. *Rev.* details as noble..	140	275
1497 E. *O.* as last. *Rev.* details as noble, pellet in centre	160	300
1498 G. *Mm.* cross 3 (4). Many varieties	110	200

Transitional treaty period, 1361. French title omitted, replaced by that of Aquitaine on the noble and (rarely) on the half-noble, but not on the quarter-noble; irregular sized letters; *mm.* cross potent (5).

1499 **Noble.** R. Pellets or annulets at corners of central panel	300	600
1500 **Half-noble.** Similar..	150	350
1501 **Quarter-noble.** Similar. Many varieties	125	250

1499

1500

1503

Treaty period, 1361-69. Omits FRANC, new letters, usually curule-shaped X; *mm.* cross potent(5).

1502 **Noble.** *London.* Saltire or nothing before ЄDWARD..............................	235	500
1503 — Annulet before ЄDWARD (with, rarely, crescent on forecastle)	235	500
1504 *Calais.* C in centre of *rev.*, flag at stern of ship	275	625
1505 — — without flag	275	625

1506   1508

		F	VF
		£	£
1506	**Half-noble.** *London.* Saltire before ЄDWARD	150	300
1507	— Annulet before ЄDWARD	160	320
1508	*Calais.* C in centre of *rev.,* flag at stern of ship	250	575
1509	—— without flag	250	575
1510	**Quarter-noble.** *London.* As 1498. R. Lis in centre	100	200
1511	—— annulet before ЄDWARD	100	200
1512	*Calais.* R. Annulet in centre	125	225
1513	—— cross in circle over shield	135	275
1514	— R. Quatrefoil in centre; cross over shield	150	325
1515	—— crescent over shield	225	500

Post-treaty period, 1369-1377. French title resumed.

		F	VF
1516	**Noble.** *London.* Annulet before ЄD. R. Treaty period die	275	525
1517	——— crescent on forecastle	300	575
1518	—— post-treaty letters. R. Є and pellet in centre	250	500
1519	——— R. Є and saltire in centre	325	600
1520	*Calais.* Flag at stern. R. Є in centre	275	550

1521

		F	VF
1521	—— *Rev.* as 1518, with Є and pellet in centre	235	500
1522	— As 1520, but without flag. R. C in centre	250	575
1523	**Half-noble.** *London. O.* Treaty die. *Rev.* as 1518	*Extremely rare*	
1524	*Calais.* Without AQT, flag at stern. R. Є in centre	325	700
1525	—— R. Treaty die with C in centre	350	725

First coinage, 1327-35 (.925 fineness)

1526	1530	1535	

	F £	VF £
1526 **Penny.** *London.* As Edw. II; class XVd with Lombardic n's	275	650
1527 *Bury St. Edmunds.* Similar	*Extremely rare*	
1528 *Canterbury; mm.* cross pattée with pellet centre	200	450
1529 — — three extra pellets in one quarter	200	475
1530 *Durham.* R. Small crown in centre	400	850
1531 *York.* As 1526, but quatrefoil in centre of *rev.*	175	400
1532 — — — pellet in each quarter of *mm.*	175	400
1533 — — — three extra pellets in one quarter	175	400
1534 — — — Roman N on *obv.*	175	400
1535 *Berwick* (1333-1342, Blunt type VIII). Bear's head in one quarter of *rev.*	250	600
1536 **Halfpenny.** *London.* If struck then indistinguishable from EDWARD II (cf. 1472)	55	135
1537 *Berwick* (Bl. VIII). Bear's head in one or two quarters	50	125
1538 *Farthing. London.* ЄDWARDVS RЄX A*, flat crown	85	175
1539 *Berwick* (Bl. VIII). As 1537	75	175

1537	1540	

Second coinage, 1335-43 (.833 fineness)

	F	VF
1540 **Halfpenny.** *London.* ЄDWARDVS RЄX A(NG)*, rough work, tall crown	20	50
1541 *Reading.* Escallop in one quarter	300	550
1542 **Farthing.** *London.* As halfpenny	50	125

Third or florin coinage, 1344-51. Bust with bushy hair. (.925 fine, 20 grs.)

1543   1555

		F	VF
		£	£
1543	**Penny.** *London.* Class 1. ЄDW, Lombardic n's	13	45
1544	— 2, ЄDWA, n's, but sometimes N's on *rev*...............................	12	35
1545	— 3, ЄDW, N's, sometimes reversed or n's on *rev*............................	12	35
1546	— 4, ЄDW, no stops, reversed N's, but on *rev*. sometimes n's, N's or double-barred N's	12	35
1547	*Canterbury.* ЄDWA, n's..	45	105
1548	— ЄDW, reversed N's..	40	95
1549	*Durham,* Sede Vacante (1345). A, ЄDW R. R. No marks.......................	50	125
1550	— — B, similar, ЄDWAR R	125	275
1551	— Bp. Hatfield. C, similar, but pellet in centre of *rev*....................	75	175
1552	— — — Crozier on *rev*..	75	225
1553	— — — — with pellet in centre of *rev*.	75	225
1554	— — D, ЄDWARDVS RЄX AIn, crozier on *rev*...................................	150	325
1555	*Reading. O.* as 1546. R. Escallop in one quarter..	200	475
1556	*York. O.* as 1546. R. Quatrefoil in centre	30	65
1557	**Halfpenny.** *London.* ЄDWARDVS RЄX(An)	15	35
1558	— — pellet either side of crown sometimes..	25	65
1559	— — saltire either side of crown and in one quarter of *rev*., or pellet in each quarter	25	60
1560	*Reading. O.* Similar. R. Escallop in one quarter	275	500
1561	*Continental imitation.* Mostly reading ЄDWARDIENSIS	18	45
1562	**Farthing.** *London.* ЄDWARDVS REX..	40	100
1562A	*Reading.* As last. R. As halfpenny	*Unique*	

Fourth coinage, 1351-77
Reference: L. A. Lawrence, *The Coinage of Edward III from 1351.*
Pre-treaty period, 1351-61. With French title.

1567

1563	**Groat** (=4d., 72 grs.). *London,* series B (1351). Roman M, open C and Є; *mm.* cross 1..	110	275
1564	— — — crown in each quarter..	*Unique*	
1565	— C (1351-2). Lombardic m, closed C and Є, R with wedge-shaped tail; *mm.* cross 1..	20	60
1566	— D (1352-3). R with normal tail; *mm.* cross 1 or cross 1 broken (2)	25	80
1567	— E (1354-5). Broken letters, V often with nick in r. limb; *mm.* cross 2 (3)	18	50
1568	— — — lis on breast	20	70

1570   1571

		F	VF
		£	£
1569	— F (1356). *Mm.* crown (74)	25	90
1570	— G (1356-61). Usually with annulet in one quarter and sometimes under bust, *mm.* cross 3 (4). Many varieties	20	60
1571	*York,* series D. As London	50	130
1572	— E. As London	40	115

1573   1574

1573	**Halfgroat.** *London,* series B. As groat	50	140
1574	— C. As groat	15	45
1575	— D. As groat	17	50
1576	— E. As groat	15	45
1577	— F. As groat	20	55
1578	— G. As groat	17	50
1579	— — annulet below bust	25	70
1580	*York,* series D. As groat	30	85
1581	— E. As groat	25	65
1582	— — — lis on breast	35	100

1584   1587   1591

1583	**Penny.** *London.* Series A (1351). Round letters, Lombardic m and n, annulet in each quarter; *mm.* cross pattee	60	110
1584	— C. Details as groat, but annulet in each quarter	13	35
1585	— D. Details as groat, but annulet in each quarter	13	35
1586	— E. Sometimes annulet in each quarter	13	35
1587	— F. Details as groat	15	40

	F	VF
	£	£
1588 — G. Details as groat	10	30
1589 — — annulet below bust	15	45
1590 — — saltire in one quarter	25	55
1591 *Durham,* Bp. Hatfield. Series A. As 1583, but extra pellet in each quarter, VIL LA crozier DVRREM	150	350
1592 — C. Details as groat. R. Crozier, CIVITAS DVNЄLMIЄ	30	80
1593 — D — — —	35	85
1594 — E — — —	25	65
1595 — F — C. Crozier, CIVITAS DVRЄMЄ	30	75
1596 — G — —	20	50
1597 — — — — annulet below bust	20	55
1598 — — — — saltire in one quarter	20	55
1599 — — — — annulet on each shoulder	20	55
1600 — — — — trefoil of pellets on breast	25	65
1601 — — — R. Crozier, CIVITAS DVRЄLMIЄ	30	75
1602 *York,* Royal Mint. Series D	30	65
1603 — — E	15	40
1604 — Archb. Thorsby. Series D. R. Quatrefoil in centre	25	55
1605 — — G —	17	40
1606 — — — annulet or saltire on breast	17	40
1607 **Halfpenny.** *London.* Series E. ЄDWARDVS RЄX An	100	250
1608 — G, but with *obv.* of F (*mm.* crown). Annulet in one quarter	—	400
1609 **Farthing.** *London.* Series E. ЄDWARDVS RЄX	150	300
1609A— — Series G. Annulet in one quarter	200	375

Transitional treaty period, 1361. French title omitted, irregular sized letters; *mm.* cross potent (5).

	F	VF
1610 **Groat.** *London.* Annulet each side of crown	120	400
1611 **Halfgroat.** Similar, but only seven arches to tressure	90	22

1611   1612

	F	VF
1612 **Penny,** *London.* Omits RЄX, annulet in two upper qtrs. of *mm*	60	150
1613 *York,* Archb. Thoresby. Similar, but quatrefoil enclosing pellet in centre of *rev.*	40	110
1614 *Durham.* Bp. Hatfield. Similar. R. Crozier, CIVITAS DORЄLMЄ	55	130
1615 **Halfpenny.** Two pellets over *mm.,* ЄDWARDVS RЄX An	75	150

Treaty period, 1361-69. French title omitted, new letters, usually 'Treaty' X; *mm.* cross potent   (5).

	F	VF
1616 **Groat,** *London.* Many varieties	25	90
1617 — Annulet before ЄDWARD	30	100
1618 — Annulet on breast	60	175

1619

		F	VF
		£	£
1619	*Calais.* As last	85	200

1621   1635

1620	**Halfgroat,** *London.* As groat	20	50
1621	— — Annulet before ЄDWARDVS	20	50
1622	— — Annulet on breast	45	120
1623	*Calais.* As last	90	200
1624	**Penny,** *London.* ЄDWARD AnGL R, etc..	15	50
1625	— — — pellet before ЄDWARD	20	60
1626	*Calais.* R. VILLA CALЄ SIE	65	160
1627	*Durham.* R. DIVITAS DVNЄLMIS	50	110
1628	— R. Crozier, CIVITAS DVRЄMЄ	40	100
1629	*York,* Archb. Thoresby. Quatrefoil in centre of *rev.,* ЄDWARDVS DЄI G RЄX An...	35	75
1630	— — — ЄDWARDVS RЄX ANGLI	15	45
1631	— — — — quatrefoil before ЄD and on breast	20	50
1632	— — — — annulet before ЄD..	25	55
1633	— — — ЄDWARD AnGL R DnS HYB...	30	70
1634	**Halfpenny.** ЄDWARDVS RЄX An, pellet stops	25	55
1635	— Pellet before ЄD, annulet stops	25	70
1636	**Farthing.** ЄDWARDVS RЄX, pellet stops...	80	180

Post-treaty period, 1369-77. French title resumed, X like St. Andrew's cross; *mm.* 5, 6, 7a.

1637   1639

1637	**Groat.** Various readings, *mm.* cross pattee..	85	250
1638	— — row of pellets across breast (chain mail)..	165	500
1639	— row of annulets below bust (chain mail); *mm.* cross potent with four pellets	190	600

	F	*VF*
	£	£
1640 **Halfgroat.** Various readings....................................	85	250
1640A— Thin portrait of Richard II......................................		*Rare*
1641 — row of pellets one side of breast (chain mail)	165	525
1642 **Penny,** *London.* No marks on breast............................	40	95
1643 — Pellet or annulet on breast.....................................	50	120
1644 — Cross or quatrefoil on breast	45	110
1645 Durham, Bp. Hatfield. Mm. 7a, CIVITAS DVnOLM, crozier	45	110
1646 — — — — annulet on breast	50	120
1647 — — — — lis on breast	38	95
1648 *York.* Archb. Thoresby or Neville. R. Quatrefoil in centre	25	65
1649 — — — lis on breast	50	105
1650 — — — annulet on breast	30	70
1651 — — — cross on breast...	30	70

1652

| 1652 **Farthing.** ЄDWARD RЄX ANGL, large head without neck .... | 150 | 325 |

There was no significant change in the coinage during this reign. Noteworthy is the first appearance of symbols on the ship's rudder on some of the gold coins. The earlier silver coins have a portrait like that on the coins of Edward III, but the king's head and the style of lettering were altered on the later issues.

Reference: *Silver coinages of Richard II, Henry IV and V.* (B.N.J. 1959-60 and 1963).

Mintmark: cross pattée (6)

1655   1657

GOLD

1653	**Noble,** *London.* With altered *obv.* and/or *rev.* die of Edw. III ....*from*	550	1250
1654	— Lettering as Edw. III, lis over sail	450	1100
1655	— Straight-sided letters, annulet over sail	375	850
1656	— Late issue, fish-tail lettering; no marks, or trefoil by shield	425	950
1657	— — — lis on rudder	575	1250
1658	— — small dumpy lettering; escallop or crescent on rudder and/or trefoil over sail or by shield ....*from*	525	1150

1658   1662

		F	VF
		£	£
1659	*Calais.* Flag at stern, otherwise as 1653.....................................*from*	500	1025
1660	— — as 1655, but quatrefoil over sail	475	1000
1661	— — as 1656; no marks	450	950
1662	— — — lion on rudder	600	1350
1663	— — as 1658	475	1000

1664	1672/3	1673	1677

		F	VF
1664	**Half-noble,** *London*. As 1653..	525	1200
1665	— as 1655	450	1000
1666	— as 1656; lion on rudder...	475	1100
1667	— as 1658; crescent on rudder...	525	1200
1668	*Calais.* Flag at stern, otherwise as 1653...............................	550	1500
1669	— — as 1655; quatrefoil over sail	550	1500
1670	— — as 1656; lion on rudder..	525	1400
1671	— — as 1658, but one var. has saltire behind rudder	700	1600
1672	**Quarter-noble,** *London*. R in centre of *rev*.............................	225	425
1673	— Lis or pellet in centre of *rev*.	185	350
1674	— — *obv*. die of Edw. III altered	240	475
1675	— — escallop over shield	250	500
1676	— — trefoil of annulets over shield......................................	235	450
1677	— — quatrefoil, cross or slipped trefoil over sheild..............*from*	215	425

SILVER

		F	VF
1678	**Groat.** I. Style of Edw. III, F (*i.e. et*) before FRANC, etc.	250	750
1679	II. New lettering, retrograde Z before FRANC, etc.	190	475
1680	III. Bust with bushy hair, 'fishtail' serifs to letters	250	700
1681	IV. New style bust and crown, crescent on breast	1000	2750

1679	1682

		F	VF
		£	£
1682	**Halfgroat.** II. New lettering	200	500
1683	III. As 1680	225	600
1684	— — with *obv.* die of Edw. III (1640A)...	400	850
1685	IV. As 1681, but no crescent...	550	1200
1685A	*Obv.* as Edw. III (1640A). R. As Type IV..		*Rare*
1686	**Penny,** *London.* I Lettering as 1678, RICARDVS REX AnGLIE	175	450
1688	— II. As 1679, Z FRAnC lis on breast..	175	450
1689	— III. As 1680, RICARD REX AnGLIE, fish-tail letters	200	500

1689   1692

1690	*York.* I. Early style, usually with cross or lis on breast, quatrefoil in centre of *rev*..	60	135
1691	— II. New bust and letters, no marks on breast.....................................	55	130
1692	— Local dies. Pellet above each shoulder, cross on breast, REX AnGLIE	35	100
1693	— — — REX DNS EB	45	110
1694	— — — REX AnG FRAnC	45	110
1695	— III. As 1680, REX AnGL Z FRANC (scallop after TAS)..................	75	125
1696	— IV. Very bushy hair, new letters, no crescent. R. R in centre of quatrefoil	225	475
1697	*Durham.* Cross or lis on breast, DVnOLM	250	625

1698   1699   1701   1704

1698	**Halfpenny.** Early style. LONDON, saltire or annulet on breast	60	150
1699	Intermediate style. LOnDOn, no marks on breast	25	65
1700	Type III. Late style. Similar, but fishtail letters	35	85
1700A	Type IV. Short, stubby lettering..	35	85
1701	**Farthing.** Small bust and letters	200	450
1702	— — rose after REX...	225	500
1703	Large head, no bust	250	550
1704	Rose in each angle of *rev.* instead of pellets	450	900

THE HOUSE OF LANCASTER

HENRY IV, 1399-1413

In 1412 the standard weights of the coinage were reduced, the noble by 12 grains and the penny by 3 grains, partly because there was a scarcity of bullion and partly to provide revenue for the king, as Parliament had not renewed the royal subsidies. As in France, the royal arms were altered, three fleur-de-lis taking the place of the four or more lis previously displayed.

Mintmark: cross pattée (6)

GOLD

Heavy coinage, 1399-1412

1707   1705

		F £	VF £
1705	**Noble** (120 grs.), *London.* Old arms with four lis in French quarters; crescent or annulet on rudder	—	6000
1706	— New arms with three lis; crescent, pellet or no marks on rudder	—	6000
1707	*Calais.* Flag at stern, old arms; crown on or to l. of rudder	*Extremely rare*	
1708	— — new arms; crown or star on rudder	—	7500
1709	**Half-noble,** *London.* Old arms	*Extremely rare*	
1710	— new arms	4500	—
1711	*Calais.* New arms	*Extremely rare*	
1712	**Quarter-noble,** *London.* Crescent over old arms	800	1750
1713	— — — new arms	700	1600
1714	*Calais.* New arms. R. *Mm.* crown	900	1900

1708   1710

1715

	F £	VF £

Light coinage, 1412-13

1715 **Noble** (108 grs.). Trefoil, or trefoil and annulet, on side of ship. R. Trefoil
in one quarter 700 1600

1716 **Half-noble.** Similar, but always with annulet... 4000 —

1717

1717 **Quarter-noble.** Trefoils, or trefoils and annulets beside shield, lis above. R.
Lis in centre.. 375 800

SILVER

Heavy coinage, 1399-1412

1718 1722 1723

		F	VF
1718	**Halfgroat** (36 grs.). Star on breast	1000	2500
1718A	— Muled with Edw. III (1640A)		*Rare*
1719	**Penny,** *London.* Similar, early bust with long neck...........................	500	1250
1720	— later bust with shorter neck, no star	500	1250
1721	*York.* Early bust with long neck	300	700
1722	— later bust with broad face, round chin...	300	700
1723	**Halfpenny.** Early small bust..	150	325
1724	Later large bust, with rounded shoulders, annulets by neck	150	325
1725	**Farthing.** Face without neck	400	800

Light coinage, 1412-13

1728   1731   1737

		F	VF
		£	£
1726	**Groat** (60 grs.). I. Pellet to l., annulet to r. of crown; altered die of Richard II	1600	4000
1727	New dies; II. Annulet to l., pellet to r. of crown, 8 or 10 arches to tressure	1350	3250
1728	— III. Similar but 9 arches to tressure	1350	3250
1729	**Halfgroat.** Pellet to l., annulet to r. of crown	*Extremely rare*	
1730	Annulet to l., pellet to r. of crown	650	1500
1731	**Penny,** *London.* Annulet and pellet by crown; trefoil on breast and before CIVI	400	950
1732	— — annulet or slipped trefoil before LON	400	950
1733	— Pellet and annulet by crown	*Unique*	
1734	*York.* Annulet on breast. R. Quatrefoil in centre	350	700
1735	*Durham.* Trefoil on breast, DVnOLM	300	650
1736	**Halfpenny.** Struck from heavy dies	160	325
1737	New dies; annulet either side of crown or none	160	325
1738	**Farthing.** Face, no bust; ?trefoil after REX	475	950

There was no change of importance in the coinage of this reign. There was, however, a considerable development in the use of privy marks which distinguished various issues, except for the last issue of the reign when most marks were removed. The Calais mint, which had closed in 1411, did not re open until early in the next reign.

Mintmarks

Cross pattee (4)   Pierced cross with   Pierced cross (18).
                    pellet centre (20)

GOLD

1744

		F	VF
		£	£
1739	**Noble.** A. Quatrefoil over sail and in second quarter of *rev.* Short broad letters, no other marks	*Extremely rare*	
1740	— B. Ordinary letters; similar, or with annulet on rudder	500	900
1741	— C. Mullet by sword arm, annulet on rudder	450	750
1742	— — — broken annulet on side of ship	300	525
1743	—D. Mullet and annulet by sword arm, trefoil by shield, broken annulet on ship	325	625
1744	— E. Mullet, or mullet and annulet by sword arm, trefoil by shield, pellet by sword point and in one quarter, annulet on side of ship	350	650
1745	— — Similar, but trefoil on ship instead of by shield	400	700
1746	— F. Similar, but no pellet at sword point, trefoil in one quarter	350	700
1747	— G. No marks; annulet stops, except for mullet after first word	625	1150
1748	**Half-noble.** B. As noble; Hen. IV *rev.* die	*Extremely rare*	
1749	— C. Broken annulet on ship, quatrefoil below sail	375	800
1750	— — Mullet over shield, broken annulet on *rev.*	325	650

1750   1756

1751	— F. Similar, but no annulet on ship, usually trefoil by shield	400	850
1752	— F/E. As last, but pellet in 1st and annulet in 2nd quarter	450	1000

		F £	VF £
1753	— G. As noble, but quatrefoil over sail, mullet sometimes omitted after first word of *rev*........................	450	1000
1754	**Quarter-noble.** A. Lis over shield and in centre of *rev*. Short broad letters; quatrefoil and annulet beside shield, stars at corners of centre on rev......	225	425
1755	— C. Ordinary letters; quatrefoil to l., quat. and mullet to r. of shield.....	150	300
1756	— — — annulet to l., mullet to r. of shield	145	280
1757	— F. Ordinary letters; trefoil to l., mullet to r. of shield.........................	175	350
1758	— G. — no marks, except mullet after first word	175	350

SILVER

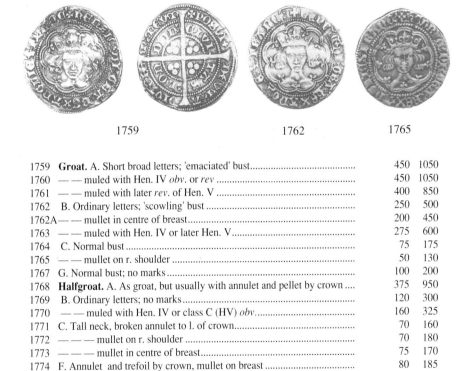

1759   1762   1765

		F	VF
1759	**Groat.** A. Short broad letters; 'emaciated' bust....................................	450	1050
1760	— — muled with Hen. IV *obv.* or *rev*	450	1050
1761	— — muled with later *rev.* of Hen. V	400	850
1762	B. Ordinary letters; 'scowling' bust	250	500
1762A	— — mullet in centre of breast..	200	450
1763	— — muled with Hen. IV or later Hen. V...	275	600
1764	C. Normal bust	75	175
1765	— — mullet on r. shoulder	50	130
1767	G. Normal bust; no marks...	100	200
1768	**Halfgroat.** A. As groat, but usually with annulet and pellet by crown	375	950
1769	B. Ordinary letters; no marks	120	300
1770	— — muled with Hen. IV or class C (HV) *obv*..................................	160	325
1771	C. Tall neck, broken annulet to l. of crown...................................	70	160
1772	— — — mullet on r. shoulder	70	180
1773	— — — mullet in centre of breast..	75	170
1774	F. Annulet and trefoil by crown, mullet on breast	80	185

1773   1774

	V	VF
	£	£
1775 G. New neat bust: no marks	70	180
1776 **Penny.** *London.* A. Letters, bust and marks as 1768	200	580
1777 — B. Altered A *obv.*, with mullet and broken annulet added by crown. R. Ordinary letters	175	425

1778   1791

1778 — C. Tall neck, mullet and broken annulet by crown	20	60
1779 — D. Similar, but whole annulet	25	75
1780 — F. Mullet and trefoil by crown	27	80
1781 — G. New neat bust, no marks, DI GRA	25	75
1782 *Durham.* C. As 1778 but quatrefoil at end of legend	45	135
1783 — D. As 1779	40	125
1784 — G. Similar, but new bust. R. Annulet in one qtr.	50	160
1785 *York.* C. As 1778, but quatrefoil in centre of *rev.*	20	60
1786 — D. Similar, but whole annulet by crown	20	60
1787 — E. As last, but pellet above mullet	40	110
1788 — F. Mullet and trefoil by crown	27	80
1789 — — Trefoil over mullet to l., annulet to r. of crown	35	90
1790 — G. Mullet and trefoil by crown (London dies)	25	70
1791 — — Mullet and lis by crown, annulet in one qtr. (usually local dies and muled with Henry VI)	25	70

1796   1798

1792 **Halfpenny.** A. Emaciated bust, annulets by crown	30	75
1793 — altered dies of Hen. IV	75	200
1794 C. Ordinary bust, broken annulets by crown	20	40
1795 D. Annulets, sometimes broken, by hair........................	20	40
1796 F. Annulet and trefoil by crown	20	45
1797 G. New bust; no marks, usually muled with Henry VI..........	75	175
1798 **Farthing.** G. Small face with neck	150	325

The supply of gold began to dwindle early in the reign, which accounts for the rarity of gold after 1426. The Calais mint was reopened in 1424 and for some years a large amount of coin was struck there. It soon stopped minting gold; the mint was finally closed in 1440. A royal mint at York was opened for a short time in 1423/4.

Marks used to denote various issues become more prominent in this reign and can be used to date coins to within a year or so.

Reference: C. A. Whitton *Heavy Coinage of Henry VI.* (B.N.J. 1938-41).

+	✦	✛	✤	✳	✤	✤
7a	105	18	133	8	9	15

Mintmarks

1422-60	Plain cross (7a, intermittently Lis (105, on gold)	1427-34	Cross patonce (8) Cross fleuree (9)
1422-27	Pierced cross (18)	1434-35	Voided cross (15)
1422-34	Cross pommee (133)	1435-60	Cross fleury (9)
		1460	Lis (105, on *rev.* of some groats)

For Restoration mintmarks see page .134.

GOLD

1799   1805

		F	VF
	Annulet issue, 1422-7	£	£
1799	**Noble.** *London.* Annulet by sword arm, and in one spandrel on *rev.*; trefoil stops on *obv.* with lis after hЄNRIC, annulets on *rev.*, with mullet after IhC	250	480
1800	— Similar, but *obv.* from Henry V die	600	1200
1801	— As 1799, but Flemish imitative coinage	225	425
1802	*Calais.* As 1799, but flag at stern and C in centre of *rev*	425	850
1803	— — with h in centre of *rev.*	375	675
1804	*York.* As London, but with lis over stern	450	800
1805	**Half-noble.** *London.* As 1799	200	350
1806	— Similar, but *obv.* from Henry V die	350	675
1807	*Calais.* As noble, with C in centre of *rev.*	550	1100
1808	— — with h in centre of *rev.*	325	675
1809	**York.** As noble	375	750

	F	VF
	£	£
1810 **Quarter-noble.** *London.* Lis over shield; *mm.* large lis	130	240
1811 — — — trefoil below shield	150	350
1812 — — — pellet below shield	*Extremely rare*	
1813 *Calais.* Three lis over shield; *mm.* large lis	200	400
1814 — Similar but three lis around shield	225	450
1815 — As 1810, but much smaller *mm.*	175	375
1816 *York.* Two lis over shield	225	400

1814   1819

Rosette-mascle issue, 1427-30

1817 **Noble.** *London.* Lis by sword arm and in *rev.* field; stops, rosettes, or rosettes and mascles	525	1150
1818 *Calais.* Similar, with flag at stern	530	1350
1819 **Half-noble.** *London.* Lis in *rev.* field; stops, rosettes and mascles	750	1500
1820 *Calais.* Similar, flag at stern; stops, rosettes	800	1600
1821 **Quarter-noble.** *London.* As 1810; stops, as noble	225	475
1822 — without lis over shield	200	450
1823 *Calais.* Lis over shield, rosettes r. and l., and rosette stops	325	500

Pinecone-mascle issue, 1430-4

1824 **Noble.** *London.* Stops, pinecones and mascles	550	1200
1825 **Half-noble.** *London.* O. Rosette-mascle die. R. As last	*Extremely rare*	
1826 **Quarter-noble.** As 1810, but pinecone and mascle stops	*Unique*	

Leaf-mascle issue, 1434-5

1827 **Noble.** Leaf in waves; stops, saltires with two mascles and one leaf	1500	3000
1828 **Half-noble.** (Fishpool Hoard)	*Unique*	
1829 **Quarter-noble.** As 1810; stops, saltire and mascle; leaf on inner circle of *rev.*	1000	2250

Leaf-trefoil issue, 1435-8

1830 **Noble.** Stops, leaves and trefoils	2000	4500
1830A **Half-noble.** Mule with annulet issue reverse die	*Unique*	
1831 **Quarter-noble.** Similar	*Unique*	

Trefoil issue, 1438-43

1832 **Noble.** Trefoil below shield and in *rev.* legend	1500	3500

Leaf-pellet issue, 1445-54

1833 **Noble.** Annulet, lis and leaf below shield	1500	3500

Cross-pellet issue, 1454-60

1834 **Noble.** Mascle at end of *obv.* legend	*Unique*	

Annulet issue, 1422-7

1835		1836	1840

		F	VF
		£	£
1835	**Groat.** *London.* Annulet in two quarters of *rev.*	20	55
1836	*Calais.* Annulets at neck. R. Similar	20	40
1837	— — no annulets on *rev.*	40	80
1838	*York.* Lis either side of neck. R. As 1835	500	950
1839	**Halfgroat.** *London.* As groat	25	90
1840	*Calais.* As 1836	15	35
1841	— — no annul ets on *rev.*	25	50
1842	— — only one annulet on *rev.* (mule with annulet-trefoil *rev.*)	50	125
1843	*York.* As groat	650	1500
1844	**Penny.** *London.* Annulets in two qtrs.	25	60
1845	*Calais.* Annulets at neck. R. As above	20	40
1846	— — only one annulet on *rev.*	22	60
1847	*York.* As London, but lis at neck	500	950
1848	**Halfpenny.** *London.* As penny	18	40
1849	*Calais.* Similar, but annulets at neck	18	40
1850	*York.* Similar, but lis at neck	350	700
1851	**Farthing.** *London.* As penny, but *mm.* cross pommée	175	350
1852	*Calais.* Similar, but annulets at neck	275	550

1843	1849	1852

Many mules exist which span two or even three issues, dating from the Annulet issue to the Pinecone-mascle issue inclusive, also later on there is adjacent muling.

Annulet-trefoil sub-issue

1854	**Groat.** *Calais,* as 1836 but trefoil to l. of crown.	60	140
1855	**Halfgroat.** *Calais.* Similar, but usually with ann. or ros.-mas. *rev.*	50	125
1856	**Penny.** *Calais.* Similar	60	150
1857	— — only one annulet on *rev*	75	185

Rosette-mascle issue, 1427-30. All with rosettes (early) or rosettes and mascles somewhere in the legends.

		F	VF
		£	£
1858	**Groat.** *London.*	50	100
1859	*Calais*	25	65
1860	— mascle in two spandrels (as illus. 1863)	50	120

1859		1861		1863

1861	**Halfgroat.** *London.*	40	85
1862	*Calais*	20	40
1863	— mascle in two spandrels, as illustrated	35	90
1864	**Penny.** *London.*	60	120
1865	*Calais*	30	60
1866	*York.* Archb. Kemp. Crosses by hair, no rosette	30	70
1867	— — Saltires by hair, no rosette	30	70
1868	— — Mullets by crown	30	70
1869	*Durham,* Bp. Langley. Large star to l. of crown, no rosette, DVNOLMI	60	160
1870	**Halfpenny,** *London*	25	55
1871	*Calais*	20	50
1872	**Farthing,** *London*	110	225
1873	*Calais. Mm.* cross pommee	120	250

1872	1875	1879	1884

Pinecone-mascle issue, 1430-4. All with pinecones and mascles in legends.

1874	**Groat,** *London*	30	70
1875	*Calais*	25	60
1876	**Halfgroat,** *London*	25	60
1877	*Calais*	25	55
1878	**Penny,** *London*	50	100
1879	*Calais*	24	70
1880	*York,* Archb. Kemp. Mullet by crown, quatrefoil in centre of *rev.*	20	55
1881	— — rosette on breast, no quatrefoil	18	50
1882	— — mullet on breast, no quatrefoil	40	90
1883	*Durham,* Bp. Langley. DVNOLMI	60	140
1884	**Halfpenny,** *London*	25	45
1885	*Calais*	25	45

Full flan coins are difficult to find in the smaller denominations.

		F £	VF £
1886	**Farthing,** *London*	100	225
1887	*Calais. Mm.* cross pommee	175	425

Leaf-mascle issue, 1434-5. Usually with a mascle in the legend and a leaf somewhere in the
design.

1888	**Groat.** *London*. Leaf below bust All (?) read NONDON	75	150
1889	— — *rev.* of last or next coinage	40	125
1890	*Calais*. Leaf below bust, and usually below MЄVM	35	110
1891	**Halfgroat.** *London*. Leaf under bust, pellet under TAS and DON..........	30	70
1892	*Calais*. Leaf below bust, and sometimes on *rev.*	32	75
1893	**Penny.** *London*. Leaf on breast, no stops on *rev.*............	35	80
1894	*Calais*. Leaf on breast and below SIЄ....................	40	80
1895	**Halfpenny.** *London*. Leaf on breast and on *rev.*..........	25	60
1896	*Calais*. Leaf on breast and below SIЄ....................	50	110

1892   1897

Leaf-trefoil issue, 1435-8. Mostly with leaves and trefoil of pellets in the legends.

1897	**Groat.** *London*. Leaf on breast	37	95
1898	— without leaf on breast........................	40	120
1899	*Calais*. Leaf on breast	*Extremely rare*	
1900	**Halfgroat.** *London*. Leaf on breast; *mm.* plain cross............	30	85
1901	— *O. mm.* cross fleury; leaf on breast....................	35	90
1902	— — without leaf on breast........................	40	95
1903	**Penny.** *London*. Leaf on breast........................	40	95
1903A	*Calais*. Similar........................	200	500
1904	*Durham,* Bp. Neville. Leaf on breast. R. Rings in centre, no stops, DVПOLM	80	200
1905	**Halfpenny.** *London*. Leaf on breast........................	17	40
1906	— without leaf on breast........................	22	50
1907	**Farthing.** *London*. Leaf on breast; stops, trefoil and saltire on *obv.*	100	325

Trefoil issue, 1438-43. Trefoil of pellets either side of neck and in legend, leaf on breast.

| 1908 | **Groat.** *London*. Sometimes a leaf before LON. .... | 50 | 125 |

1908

	F £	VF £
1909 — Fleurs in spandrels, sometimes extra pellet in two qtrs.	50	135
1910 — Trefoils in place of fleurs at shoulders, none by neck, sometimes extra pellets	40	125
1911 *Calais*	100	350
1911A **Halfgroat.** Similar, but trefoil after DEUM. Mule only with leaf trefoil *obv*.	*Extremely rare*	
1912 **Halfpenny,** *London*	30	70

1912

Trefoil pellet issue, 1443-5
1913 **Groat.** Trefoils by neck, pellets by crown, small leaf on breast; sometimes extra pellet in two quarters...	50	150

Leaf-pellet issue, 1445-54. Leaf on breast, pellet each side of crown, except where stated.
1914 **Groat.** AnGL; extra pellet in two quarters...	35	90
1915 Similar, but AnGLI...	25	75

1915   1927

1916 — — trefoil in *obv.* legend	50	110
1917 Leaf on neck, fleur on breast, often extra pellet in two quarters..............	30	85
1918 As last, but two extra pellets by hair...	75	175
1919 **Halfgroat.** As 1914 *mm.*8..	25	70
1920 Similar, but *mm.* plain cross, some times no leaf on breast, no stops.......	25	80
1921 **Penny.** *London.* Usually extra pellets in two quarters...........................	35	80
1922 — — pellets by crown omitted..	35	80
1923 — — trefoil in legend	40	90
1924 *York,* Archb. Booth. R. Quatrefoil and pellet in centre...........................	24	60
1925 — — two extra pellets by hair (local dies)	20	55
1926 *Durham,* Bp. Neville. Trefoil in *obv.* legend. B. Two rings in centre of cross	100	225
1927 — — Similar, but without trefoil..	100	225
1928 **Halfpenny.** Usually extra pellet in two quarters	20	50
1929 — *mm.* plain cross...	20	50
1930 **Farthing.** As last..	150	325

Unmarked issue, 1453-4
1931 **Groat.** No marks on *obv.;* two extra pellets on *rev.*	200	500
1932 — four extra pellets on *rev.*	350	750
1933 **Halfgroat.** As 1931..	175	400

		F	*VF*
		£	£

Cross-pellet issue, 1454-60

1934 **Groat.** Saltire either side of neck, pellets by crown, leaf and fleur on breast,
extra pellets on *rev.* 85 250

1935 Saltire on neck, no leaf, pellets by crown, usually mullets in legend; extra
pellets on *rev.* 75 175

1936 — Similar, but mascles in place of mullets on *obv.* 85 225

1937 — — pellets by hair instead of by crown 100 300

1938 **Halfgroat.** Saltire on neck, pellets by crown and on *rev.*, mullets in legend 175 400

1939 **Penny.** *London.* Saltire on neck, pellets by crown and on *rev.*, mascle(s), or
mullet and mascle in legend.. 90 250

1940 *York,* Archb. Wm. Booth. Saltires by neck, usually leaf on breast, pellets
by crown. R. Cross in quatrefoil in centre. Illustrated below 40 90

1941 *Durham,* Bp. Laurence Booth. Saltire and B at neck, pellets by crown. R.
Rings in centre 100 250

1942 **Halfpenny.** Saltires by neck, usually two extra pellets on *rev.* 60 125

1943 Similar, but saltire on neck, sometimes mullet after hЄnRIC 50 100

1944 **Farthing.** Saltire on neck, usually pellets by crown and on *rev.*, but known
without either. 150 325

1935   1940   1945

Lis-pellet issue, 1456-60

1945 **Groat.** Lis on neck; pellets by crown. R. Extra pellets............................ 150 325

Full flan coins are difficult to find in the smaller denominations.

THE HOUSE OF YORK

EDWARD IV, First Reign, 1461-70

In order to increase the supply of bullion to the mint the weight of the penny was reduced to 12 grains in 1464, and the current value of the noble was raised to 8s. 4d. Later, in 1465, a new gold coin was issued, the Ryal or 'Rose Noble', weighing 120 grains and having a value of 10s. However, as 6s. 8d. had become the standard professional fee the old noble was missed, and a new coin was issued to take its place, the Angel of 80 grains.

Royal mints were opened at Canterbury and York to help with the re-coinage, and other mints were set up at Bristol, Coventry and Norwich, though they were not open for long.

Reference: C. E. Blunt and C. A Whitton, *The Coinage of Edward IV and Henry VI (Restored)*, B.N.J. 1945-7.

Mintmarks

105	9	7a	33	99	28	74	11

1461-4	Lis (105)	1467-70	Lis (105, York)	
	Cross fleury (9)	1467-8	Crown (74) }	(often
	Plain cross (7a)		Sun (28) }	combined)
1464-5	Rose (33 and 34)	1468-9	Crown (74) }	(sometimes
1464-7	Pall (99, *Canterbury*)		Rose (33) }	combined)
1465-6	Sun (28)	1469-70	Long cross	
1466-7	Crown (74)		fitchee (11) }	often
			Sun (28) }	combined

GOLD

Heavy coinage, 1461-4

		F £	VF £
1946	**Noble** (=6s. 8d., wt. 108 grs.). Normal type, but *obv.* legend commences at top left, lis below shield; *mm.*-/lis	4000	8000
1947	— Quatrefoil below sword arm; *mm.* rose/lis	*Extremely rare*	
1948	— R. Roses in two spandrels; *mm.* rose	*Extremely rare*	
1949	**Quarter-noble**	*Unique*	

1946   1950

Light coinage, 1464-70

1950 **Ryal** or rose-noble (=10s., wt. 120 grs.), *London*. Type as next illus. Large
      fleurs in spandrels; *mm.* 33-74 275   475
1951 — — Small trefoils in spandre ls; *mm.* 74-11 275   475

1952

		F	VF
		£	£
1952	— Flemish imitative coinage (mostly 16th cent. on a large flan)	225	450
1953	*Bristol*. B in waves, large fleurs; *mm.* 28, 74	325	650
1954	— — small fleurs in spandrels; *mm.* 74, 28	350	725
1955	*Coventry*. C in waves; *mm.* sun	650	1400
1956	*Norwich*. N in waves; *mm.* sun, rose?	750	1500
1957	*York*. Є in waves, large fleurs in spandrels, *mm.* 28, 105	325	700
1958	— — small fleurs, *mm.* 105, 28	350	750
1959	**Half-ryal.** *London*. As 1950	250	425
1960	*Bristol*. B in waves; *mm.* 28-28/74	325	750
1961	*Coventry*. C in waves; *mm.* sun	*Extremely rare*	
1962	*Norwich*. N in waves; *mm.* rose	1200	2500

1963   1965

1963	*York*. Є in waves; *mm.* 28, 105, 33/105	225	450
1963	Similar but lis instead of Є in waves (probably York)	*Extremely rare*	
1964	**Quarter-ryal.** Shield in tressure of eight arcs, rose above. R. Somewhat as		
	half ryal; *mm.* 28/33	*Unique?*	
1965	Shield in quatrefoil, R. Є above, rose on l., sun on r.; *mm.* 33/28-74/33 .	175	400
1966	— — sun on l., rose on r.; *mm.* 74-11	190	425

1967   1972

	F £	VF £

1967 **Angel** (=6s. 8d., wt. 80 grs.). St. Michael spearing dragon. R. Ship, rays of sun at masthead, large rose and sun beside mast; *mm.-/33* .... *Extremely rare*

1968 — — small rose and sun at mast; *mm.-/74* .... *Extremely rare*

First reign

1973/4   1978

SILVER

Heavy coinage, 1461-4

1969 **Groat** (60 grs.). Group I, lis on neck, pellets by crown; *mm.* 9, 7a, 105, 9/105 Occasionally EDWARD over HENRIC *mm* 9. 55   150

1970 — Lis on breast, no pellets; *mm.* plain cross, 7a/105............................... 75   200

1971 — — with pellets at crown; *mm.* plain cross 75   200

1972 II, quatrefoils by neck, crescent on breast; *mm.* rose 60   150

1973 III, similar but trefoil on breast; *mm.* rose.. 55   140

1974 — — — eye in *rev.* inner legend, *mm.* rose.. 55   130

1975 — Similar, but no quatrefoils by bust 75   200

1976 — — Similar, but no trefoil on breast 65   165

1977 IV, annulets by neck, eye after TAS; *mm.* rose.. 85   225

1978 **Halfgroat.** I, lis on breast, pellets by crown and extra pellets in two qtrs.; *mm.* 9, 7a 150   450

1979 II, quatrefoils at neck, crescent on breast; *mm.* rose 170   425

1980 III, similar, but trefoil on breast, eye on *rev.; mm.* rose........................... 170   425

1981 — Similar, but no mark on breast 160   400

1982 IV, annulets by neck, sometimes eye on *rev.; mm.* rose 150   375

1983 **Penny** (15 grs.), *London.* I, marks as 1978, but mascle after REX; *mm.* plain cross 150   425

1984 — II, quatrefoils by neck; *mm.* rose... *Extremely rare*

1985

	F	VF
	£	£
1985 — III, similar, but eye after TAS; *mm.* rose	150	350
1986 — IV, annulets by neck; *mm.* rose	200	400
1987 *York,* Archb. Booth. Quatrefoils by bust, voided quatrefoil in centre of *rev.; mm.* rose	120	250
1988 *Durham. O.* of Hen. VI. R. DVnOLIn	160	350
Some of the Durham pennies from local dies may belong to the heavy coinage period, but if so they are indistinguishable from the light coins.		
1989 **Halfpenny.** I, as 1983, but no mascle	100	200
1990 II, quatrefoils by bust; *mm.* rose	60	140
1991 — saltires by bust; *mm.* rose	80	160
1992 III, no marks by bust; *mm.* rose	65	150
1993 IV, annulets by bust; *mm* rose	65	160
1994 **Farthing.** I, as 1989	500	1250

Light coinage, 1464-70. There is a great variety of groats and we give only a selection. Some have pellets in one quarter of the reverse, or trefoils over the crown; early coins have fleurs on the cusps of the tressure, then trefoils or no marks on the cusps, while the late coins have only trefoils.

1995 **Groat** (48 grs.), *London.* Annulets at neck, eye after TAS; *mm.* 33 (struck from heavy dies, IV)	45	120
1996 — — — Similar, but new dies, eye after TAS or DOn	60	130
1997 — Quatrefoils at neck, eye; *mm.* 33 (heavy dies, III)	45	115
1998 — — — Similar, but new dies, eye in *rev.* legend	35	100
1999 — No marks at neck, eye; *mm.* 33	70	150

2000   2002

2000 — Quatrefoils at neck, no eye; *mm.* 33, 74, 28, 74/28, 74/33, 11/28	22	45
2001 — — — rose or quatrefoil on br east; *mm.* 33, 74/28	25	55
2002 — No marks at neck; *mm.* 28, 74, 11/28, 11	25	65
2003 — Trefoils or crosses at neck; *mm.* 11/33, 11/28, 11	25	65

Light coinage, silver, *continued*

		F £	VF £
2004	*Bristol.* B on breast, quatrefoils at neck; *mm.* 28/33, 28, 28/74, 74, 74/28	30	70
2005	— — trefoils at neck; *mm.* 28	30	90
2006	— — no marks at neck; *mm.* 28	50	135
2007	— Without B, quatrefoils at neck; *mm.* 28	45	125

Bristol is variously rendered as BRESTOLL, BRISTOLL, BRESTOW, BRISTOW.

		F £	VF £
2008	*Coventry.* C on breast, quatrefoils at neck, COVETRE; *mm.* 28/33, 28...	50	125
2009	— — Local dies, similar; *mm.* rose	65	175
2010	— — — as last, but no C or quatrefoils	70	225
2011	*Norwich.* n on breast, quatrefoils at neck, nORWIC or nORVIC, *mm.* 28/33, 28	50	125
2012	*York.* Є on breast, quatrefoils at neck, ЄBORACI; *mm.* 28, 105/74, 105, 105/28	30	75
2013	— Similar, but without Є on breast, *mm.* 105	40	120
2014	— Є on breast, trefoils at neck; *mm.* 105/28, 105	30	100
2015	**Halfgroat.** *London.* Annulets by neck (heavy dies); *mm.* 33		*Unique*
2016	— Quatrefoils by neck; *mm.* 33/-, 28/-, 74, 74/28	45	95
2017	— Saltires by neck; *mm.* 74, 74/28	50	100
2018	— Trefoils by neck; *mm.* 74, 74/28, 11/28	45	95
2019	— No marks by neck; *mm.* 11/28	90	180
2020	— *Bristol.* Saltires or crosses by neck; *mm.* 33/28, 28, 74, 74/-	80	210
2021	— Quatrefoils by neck; *mm.* 28/-, 74, 74/-	70	200
2022	— Trefoils by neck; *mm.* 74	95	225
2023	— No marks by neck; *mm.* 74/28	95	225
2024	*Canterbury,* Archb. Bourchier (1464-7). Knot below bust; quatrefoils by neck; *mm.* 99/-, 99, 99/33, 99/28	15	40
2025	— — — quatrefoils omitted *mm.* 99	15	40
2026	— — — saltires by neck; *mm.* 99/-, 99/28	20	45
2026A	— — — trefoils by neck; *mm.* 99	40	90

2027   2030

		F £	VF £
2027	— — — wedges by hair and/or neck; *mm.* 99, 99/33, 99/28	20	60
2028	— — As 2024 or 2025, but no knot	25	70
2029	— Royal mint (1467-9). Quatrefoils by neck; *mm.* 74, 74/-	15	45
2030	— — Saltires by neck; *mm.* 74/-, 74	20	45
2031	— — Trefoils by neck; *mm.* 74, 74/-, 74/28, 33	20	45
2032	— No marks by neck; *mm.* 28	50	125
2033	*Coventry.* Crosses by neck; *mm.* sun		*Unique*
2034	*Norwich.* Saltires by neck; *mm.* sun		*Extremely rare*

	F	VF
	£	£

2035	*York.* Quatrefoils by neck; *mm.* sun, lis , lis/-	60	145
2036	— Saltires by neck; *mm.* lis	50	110
2037	— Trefoils by neck; *mm.* lis, lis/-	50	110
2038	— Є on breast, quatrefoils by neck; *mm.* lis/-	55	115
2039	**Penny** (12 grs.), *London.* Annulets by neck (heavy dies); *mm.* 33	80	180
2040	— Quatrefoils by neck; *mm.* 28, 74	30	60
2041	— Trefoil and quatrefoil by neck; *mm.* 74	35	75
2042	— Saltires by neck; *mm.* 74	35	75
2043	— Trefoils by neck; *mm.* 74, 11	30	60
2044	— No marks by neck; *mm.* 11	*Extremely rare*	
2045	*Bristol.* Crosses, quatrefoils or saltires by neck, BRISTOW; *mm.* crown	85	225
2046	— Quatrefoils by neck; BRI(trefoil)STOLL	100	260
2047	— Trefoil to r. of neck BRISTOLL	125	275
2048	*Canterbury,* Archb. Bourchier. Quatrefoils or saltires by neck, knot on breast; *mm.* pall	70	160
2049	— — Similar, but no marks by neck	80	175
2050	— — As 2048, but no knot	75	170
2051	— — Crosses by neck, no knot	75	170
2052	— Royal mint. Quatrefoils by neck; *mm.* crown	125	300
2053	— *Durham,* King's Receiver (1462-4). Local dies, mostly with rose in centre of *rev.; mm.* 7a, 33	20	60
2054	— Bp. Lawrence Booth (1465-70). B and D by neck, B on *rev.; mm.* 33	22	65
2055	— — Quatrefoil and B by neck; *mm.* 28	27	80
2056	— — B and quatrefoil by neck; *mm.* 74	*Extremely rare*	
2057	— — D and quatrefoil by neck; *mm.* 74	28	85
2058	— — Quatrefoils by neck; *mm.* crown	35	100
2059	— — Trefoils by neck; *mm.* crown	35	100
2060	— Lis by neck; *mm.* crown	35	100
2061	*York,* Sede Vacante (1464-5). Quatrefoils at neck, no quatrefoil in centre of *rev.; mm.* 28, 33	50	125
2062	— Archb. Neville (1465-70). Local dies, G and key by neck, quatrefoil on *rev.; mm.* 33, 7a	35	75

2063   2068

2063	— — London-made dies, similar; *mm.* 28, 105, 11	20	70
2064	— — Similar, but no marks by neck; *mm.* large lis	*Extremely rare*	
2065	— — — Quatrefoils by neck; *mm.* large lis	35	85
2066	— — — Trefoils by neck; *mm.* large lis	40	95
2067	**Halfpenny,** *London.* Saltires by neck; *mm.* 34, 28, 74	50	100
2068	— Trefoils by neck; *mm.* 28, 74, 11	25	55
2069	— No marks by neck; *mm.* 11	*Unique?*	
2070	*Bristol.* Crosses by neck; *mm.* 74	125	275
2071	— Trefoils by neck; *mm.* 74	90	200

	F	VF
	£	£

2072 *Canterbury,* Archb. Bourchier. No marks; *mm.* pall................................. 100 225

2072A——— Trefoils by neck, *mm.* pall... 100 225

2073 — Royal mint. Saltires by neck; *mm.* crown 65 140

2074 —— Trefoils by neck; *mm.* crown... 60 125

2075 *York,* Royal mint. Saltires by neck; *mm.* lis/-, sun/-................................. 65 140

2076 —— Trefoils by neck; *mm.* lis/- 60 125

2077 **Farthing,** *London.* ЄDWARD DI GRA RЄX, no marks at neck,
     mm. 33 .... 400 —

2077A— Trefoils by neck, *mm.* 74... 600 —

Full flan coins are difficult to find in the smaller denominations.

The coinage of this short restoration follows closely that of the previous reign. Only angel gold was issued, the ryal being discontinued. Many of the coins have the king's name reading hЄnRICV—a distinguishing feature.

Mintmarks

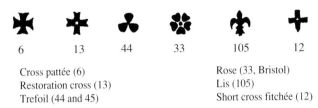

| 6 | 13 | 44 | 33 | 105 | 12 |

Cross pattée (6)
Restoration cross (13)
Trefoil (44 and 45)

Rose (33, Bristol)
Lis (105)
Short cross fitchée (12)

GOLD

2079

		F	VF
		£	£
2078	**Angel,** *London.* As illus. but no B; *mm.* -/6, 13, -/105, none	400	900
2079	*Bristol.* B in waves; *mm.* -/13, none	650	1500
2080	**Half-angel,** *London.* As 2078; *mm.* -/6, -/13, -/105	1400	3000
2081	*Bristol.* B in waves; *mm.* -/13	*Unique*	

SILVER

2082   2084

2082	**Groat,** *London.* Usual type; *mm.* 6, 6/13, 6/105, 13, 13/6, 13/105, 13 /12	125	200
2083	*Bristol.* B on breast; *mm.* 13, 13/33, 13/44, 44, 44/13, 44/33, 44/12	150	325
2084	*York.* Є on breast; *mm.* lis, lis/sun	125	265
2085	**Halfgroat,** *London.* As 2082; *mm.* 13, 13/-	225	500
2086	*York.* Є on breast; *mm.* lis	*Extremely rare*	
2087	**Penny,** *London.* Usual type; *mm.* 6, 13, 12...	300	650

			F	VF
			£	£
2087A	*Bristol.* Similar; *mm.* 12		*Unique?*	
2088	*York.* G and key by neck; *mm.* lis		175	400
2089	**Halfpenny,** *London.* As 2087; *mm.* 12		200	400
2090	*Bristol.* Similar; *mm.* cross		*Unique?*	

EDWARD IV, Second Reign, 1471-83

The Angel and its half were the only gold denominations issued during this reign. The main types and weight standards remained the same as those of the light coinage of Edward's first reign. The use of the 'initial mark' as a mintmark to denote the date of issue was now firmly established.

33	105	12	55	44	55	28	56	17

37	6	18	19	20	31	11	38

Mintmarks

1471-83	Rose (33, *York & Durham*)	1473-7	Cross pattée (6)
	Lis (105, *York*)		Pierced cross 1 (18)
1471	Short cross fitchee (12)	1477-80	Pierced cross and
1471-2	Annulet (large, 55)		pellet (19)
	Trefoil (44)		Pierced cross 2 (18)
	Rose (33, *Bristol*)		Pierced cross, central
1471-3	Pansy (30, *Durham*)		pellet (20)
1472-3	Annulet (small, 55)		Rose (33, *Canterbury*)
	Sun (28, *Bristol*)	1480-3	Heraldic cinquefoil (31)
1473-7	Pellet in annulet (56)		Long cross fitchee
	Cross and four pellets (17)		(11, *Canterbury*)
	Cross in circle (37)		Halved sun and rose (38)?

GOLD

2091   2093

		F	VF
		£	£
2091	**Angel.** *London.* Type as illus.; *mm.* 12, 55, 56, 17, 18, 19, 31	180	375
2092	*Bristol.* B in waves; *mm.* 55	650	1400
2093	**Half-angel.** As illus.; *mm.* 55, cross in circle, 19, 20/19, 31	175	350
2094	King's name and title on *rev.*; *mm.* 12/-	350	650
2095	King's name and the title both sides; *mm.* 55/-	300	550

SILVER

2096	2101

2106

	F £	VF £
2096 **Groat**, *London*. Trefoils on cusps, no marks by bust; *mm.* 12-37	25	70
2097 — — roses by bust; *mm.* 56	35	95
2098 — Fleurs on cusps; no marks by bust; *mm.* 18-20	25	65
2099 — — pellets by bust; *mm.* 18 (2)	60	165
2100 — — rose on breast; *mm.* 31	25	60
2101 *Bristol*. B on breast; *mm.* 33, 33/55, 28/55, 55, 55/-, 28 no marks by bust	60	165
2102 *York*. Є on breast; *mm.* lis	65	175
2103 **Halfgroat**, *London*. As 2096; *mm.* 12-31	30	80
2104 *Bristol*. B on breast; *mm.* 33/12	*Extremely rare*	
2105 *Canterbury* (Royal mint). As 2103; *mm.* 33, 11, 11/31, 31	25	65
2106 — C on breast; *mm.* rose	20	55
2107 — — R. C in centre; *mm.* rose	20	55
2108 — — R. Rose in centre; *mm.* rose	20	60
2109 *York*. No. Є on breast; *mm.* lis	75	200
2110 **Penny**, *London*. No marks by bust; *mm.* 12-31	30	70
2111 *Bristol*. Similar; *mm.* rose	300	—
2112 *Canterbury* (Royal). Similar; *mm.* 33, 11	65	140
2113 — C on breast; *mm.* 33	80	175

2115	2116	2123

2114 *Durham*, Bp. Booth (1471-6). No marks by neck; *mm.* 12, 44	18	60
2115 — — D in centre of *rev.*; B and trefoil by neck; *mm.* 44, 33, 56	18	65
2116 — — — two lis at neck; *mm.* 33	18	60
2117 — — — crosses over crown, and on breast; *mm.* 33	15	55
2118 — — — crosses over crown, V under CIVI; *mm.* 33, 30	20	70
2119 — — — B to l. of crown, V on breast and under CIVI	15	55
2120 — — — As last but crosses at shoulders	15	55
2121 — Sede Vacante (1476). R. D in centre; *mm.* 33	35	125
2122 — Bp. Dudley (1476-83). V to r. of neck; as last	25	80
2123 — — D and V by neck; as last, but *mm.* 31	15	55

Nos. 2117-2123 are from locally-made dies.

2125   2134

		F £	VF £
2124	*York,* Archb. Neville (1471-2). Quatrefoils by neck. R . Quatrefoil; *mm.* 12 (over lis)	90	225
2125	— — Similar, but G and key by neck; *mm.* 12 (over lis)	13	35
2126	— Neville suspended (1472-5). As last, but no quatrefoil in centre of *rev.*	15	37
2126A	— — no marks by bust, similar; *mm.* annulet	90	225
2127	— — No marks by neck, quatrefoil on *rev.*; *mm.* 55, cross in circle, 33..15	40	
2128	— — Similar but Є and rose by neck; *mm.* 33	15	40
2129	— Archb. Neville restored (1475-6). As last, but G and rose	18	45
2130	— — Similar, but G and key by bust	20	50
2131	— Sede Vacante (1476). As 2127, but rose on breast; *mm.* 33	18	45
2132	— Archb. Lawrence Booth (1476-80). B and key by bust, quatrefoil on *rev.; mm.* 33, 31	20	50
2133	— Sede Vacante (1480). Similar, but no quatrefoil on *rev.*; *mm.* 33	15	45
2134	— Archb. Rotherham (1480-3). T and slanting key by neck, quatrefoil on *rev.; mm.* 33	13	40
2135	— — — Similar, but star on breast	150	350
2136	— — — Star on breast and to r. of crown	80	175
2137	**Halfpenny,** *London.* No marks by neck; *mm.* 1 2-31	25	65
2138	— Pellets at neck; *mm.* 18	30	70
2139	*Canterbury* (Royal). C on breast and in centre of *rev.; mm.* rose	70	150
2140	— C on breast only; *mm.* rose	60	130
2141	— Without C either side; *mm.* 11	70	160
2142	*Durham,* Bp. Booth. No marks by neck. R. DERAM, D in centre; *mm.* rose	120	250
2142A	— — Lis either side of neck. R. D or no mark in centre	*Extremely rare*	
2143	— — — Similar, but V to l. of neck	120	250

Full flan coins are very difficult to find in the small denominations.

Mintmark: Halved sun and rose.

The consensus of opinion now favours the last year of Edward IV for the introduction of the halved-sun and rose mintmark, but it is suggested that the earliest coins of Edward V's reign were struck from these Edw. IV dies. The coins are very rare.

GOLD

		F	VF
		£	£
2144	**Angel.** As 2091	700	1750
2145	**Half-angel.** As 2093	*Extremely rare*	

2145   2146

SILVER

2146	**Groat.** As 2098	325	750
2147	**Penny.** As 2110	600	1200
2148	**Halfpenny.** As 2137	300	700

2149

EDWARD V, 1483

On the death of Edward IV, 9th April, 1483, the 12-year-old Prince Edward was placed under the guardianship of his uncle, Richard, Duke of Gloucester, but within eleven weeks Richard usurped the throne and Edward and his younger brother were confined to the Tower and were never seen alive again. The boar's head was a personal badge of Richard, Edward's `Protector'.

Recent research indicates that the mint marks previously thought to be for this reign are now attributable to Edward IV, Edward IV or V, or Richard III.

Mintmarks: Boar's head on *obv.*, halved sun and rose on *rev.*

GOLD

2149	**Angel.** As 2091	*Extremely rare*
2150	**Half-angel.** Similar	*Unique*

SILVER

2151

		F	VF
		£	£
2151	**Groat.** As 2098		Rare
2152	**Halfgroat.** As 2103		Unique
2153	**Penny.** As 2110		Unknown?

RICHARD III, 1483-85

Richard's brief reign was brought to an end on the field of Bosworth. His coinage follows the pattern of the previous reigns. The smaller denominations of the London mint are all rare.

Mintmarks

38	62	63	105	33

Halved sun and rose, 3 styles (38, 39 and another with the sun more solid, see *North*).
Boar's head, narrow (62) wide (63).
Lis (105, *Durham*)
Rose only (33).

GOLD

2154	**Angel.** Reading ЄDWARD but with R and rose by mast; *mm.* sun and rose	Unique
2155	— Similar, but boar's head *mm.* on *obv*	Unique

2156   2158

2156	Reading RICARD or RICAD. R. R and rose by mast; *mm.* various combinations	500	950
2157	— Similar, but R by mast over rose (?)	650	1200
2158	**Half-angel.** R. R and rose by mast; *mm.* boar's head	Extremely rare	

SILVER

2159   2160

		F	VF
		£	£
2159	**Groat,** *London. Mm.* various combinations	225	400
2160	— Pellet below bust	250	450
2161	*York. Mm.* Sun and rose (*obv.*)	350	800
2162	**Halfgroat.** *Mm.* sun and rose on *obv.* only	750	1500
2163	Pellet below bust; *mm.* sun and rose		*Unique*
2164	— *mm.* boar's head (*obv.*)	850	1750
2165	**Penny.** *London. mm.* boar's head (*obv.*)		*Unique*

This was the R. Carlyon-Britton specimen. It was stolen from our premises Feb. 1962.

2168   2169

2166	*York,* Archb. Rotherham. R. Quatrefoil in centre; *mm.* sun and rose........	300	550
2167	— — T and upright key at neck; *mm.* rose	150	350
2168	— — — *mm.* boar's head	175	400
2169	*Durham,* Bp. Sherwood. S on breast. R. D in centre; *mm.* lis..................	125	300
2170	**Halfpenny,** *London. Mm.* sun and rose	325	600
2171	— *Mm.* boar's head..	350	700

Most small denomination coins are short of flan and unevenly struck.

THE HOUSE OF TUDOR

HENRY VII, 1485-1509

For the first four years of his reign Henry's coins differ only in name and mintmark from those of his predecessors, but in 1489 radical changes were made in the coinage. Though the pound sterling had been a denomination of account for centuries, a pound coin had never been minted. Now a magnificent gold pound was issued, and, from the design of the king enthroned in majesty, was called a 'Sovereign'. The reverse had the royal arms set in the centre of a Tudor rose. A few years later the angel was restyled and St. Michael, who is depicted about to thrust Satan into the Pit with a cross-topped lance, is no longer a feathered figure but is clad in armour of Renaissance style. A gold ryal of ten shillings was also minted again for a brief period.

The other major innovation was the introduction of the Shilling in the opening years of the 16th century. It is remarkable for the very fine profile portrait of the King which replaces the representational image of a monarch that had served on the coinage for the past couple of centuries. This new portrait was also used on groats and halfgroats but not on the smaller denominations.

Mintmarks

39	41	40	42	33	11	7a	123
105	76b	31	78	30	91	43	57
	85	94	118	21	33	53	

1485-7	Halved sun and rose (39)	1495-8	Pansy (30)
	Lis upon sun and rose (41)		Tun (123, *Canterbury*)
	Lis upon half rose (40)		Lis (105, *York*)
	Lis-rose dimidiated (42)	1498-9	Crowned leopard's head (91)
	Rose (33, *York*)		Lis issuant from rose (43)
1487	Lis (105)		Tun (123, *Canterbury*)
	Cross fitchy (11)	1499-1502	Anchor (57)
1487-8	Rose (33)	1502-4	Greyhound's head (85)
	Plain cross (7a, *Durham*)		Lis (105, profile issue only)
1488-9	No marks		Martlet (94, *York*)
1489-93	Cinquefoil (31)	1504-5	Cross-crosslet (21)
	Crozier (76b, *Durham*)	1504-9	Martlet (94, York and
1492	Cross fitchy (11, gold only)	1492	Cross fitchy (11, gold only)
1493-5	Escallop (78)		*Canterbury*
	Dragon (118, gold only)		Rose (33, *York* and
	Lis (105, *Canterbury* and *York*		*Canterbury*)
	Tun (123, *Canterbury*)	1505-9	Pheon (53)

GOLD

		F £	*VF* £
2173	**Sovereign** (20s; wt. 240 grs.). Group I. Large figure of king sitting on backless throne. R. Large shield crowned on large Tudor rose. *mm.* 31...		*Unique*
2172	— Group II. Somewhat similar but throne has narrow back, lis in background. R. Large Tudor rose bearing small shield. *mm.* -/11		*Extremely rare*

2174

		F £	*VF* £
2174	— III. King on high-backed very ornamental throne, with grey-hound and dragon on side pillars. R. Shield on Tudor rose; *mm.* 118	5500	13000
2175	IV. Similar but throne with high canopy breaking legend and broad seat, *mm.* 105/118, (also with no *obv.* i.c. *mm.* 105/118, very rare)............................	5000	10500
2176	— Narrow throne with a portcullis below the king's feet (like Henry VIII); *mm.* 105/21, 105/53..	5250	11000
2177	**Double-sovereign** and **Treble-sovereign** from same dies as 2176. These piedforts were probably intended as presentation pieces *mm.* 105/21, 105/53 .*Extremely rare*		

2178

2178	**Ryal** (10s.). As illustration: *mm.* -/11	6500	15000

2181　　　　　　　　　　2183

	F	VF
	£	£

2179　**Angel** (6s. 8d). I. Angel of old type with one foot on dragon. R. PER
　　　CRVCEM. etc., *mm*. 39, 40, (also muled both ways) .... | 275 | 700
2179A— With Irish title, and legend over angel head. *mm*. 33/- .... *Extremely rare*
2180　— — Name altered from RICARD? and h on *rev*. from R. *mm*. 41/39,
　　　41/40, 41/-, 39/? .... | 500 | 1100
2181　II. As 2179, but *mm*. none. 31/-. .... | 250 | 550
2181A II/III mule. *mm*. 31/78, R. PER CRUC or AVTEM TRANS................... | 275 | 575
2182　As 2181. R. IhC AVTEM TRANSIENS etc.; *mm*. none, 31/-................. | 275 | 575
2183　III. New dies, angel with both feet on dragons; (large straight lettering) *mm*.
　　　78-85 except 91 (many mules exist) .... | 200 | 400
2183A— Angel with very small wings. *mm*. 78................................... *Rare*
2184　— — R. IhC AVTEM TRANSIENS, etc.; *mm*. 78 .... | 250 | 550
2185　IV. Small square lettering; *mm*. 85 (also muled with 2183) .... | 200 | 475
2186　— Tall thin lettering; *mm*. 21 (also muled with 2185 *obv*.)............... | 200 | 400
2187　V. Large crook-shaped abbreviation after hENRIC; *mm*. 21 and 53
　　　(combinations and mules exist).. | 175 | 360
2188　**Half-angel or angelet.** I. *Mm*. 39, 41, (old dies RIII altered) .... | 300 | 725
2189　III. Angel with both feet on dragon: *mm*. 30, 57/30, -/85 .... | 225 | 500
2190　IV. Small square lettering; *mm*. 33 .... *Extremely rare*
2191　— *Obv*. as last. R. Tall thin lettering; *mm*. 33/21............................. *Extremely rare*
2192　V. As angel; *mm*. pheon.. | 165 | 350

SILVER

Facing bust issues. Including 'Sovereign' type pennies.

2194　　　　　　　　　　2195

2193　**Groat.** I. Open crown; *mm*. 40 (rose on bust), 39-42 and none (combinations) | 60 | 140
2194　— — crosses or saltires by neck, 41, 40, 105-33 and none (combinations) | 70 | 165
2195　IIa. Large bust with out-turned hair, crown with two plain arches; *mm*.
　　　none, 31, 31/-, 31/78 .... | 40 | 90
2196　— — similar but crosses by neck; *mm*. none, -/105 .... | 50 | 110
2197　— — R . Portcullis over long cross; *mm*. -/lis.. *Extremely rare*

2198   2199   2201

	F	VF
	£	£

*2198 **Groat.** IIIa. Bust as IIa. Crown with two jewelled arches; *mm.* 31, 78 ....45 110

*2198A IIIb. Similar, but new bust with hair turning inwards; *mm.* 78, 30 ....25 55

*2199 IIIc. Bust as IIIb, but crown with one plain and one jewelled arch, new
     realistic hair; *mm.* 30-21 and none...35 60

*2199A IIId. As last, but plainer letters. *mm* 57, 85, 33 and none 35 90

2200   IVa. Wide single arch crown; arch is single or double bar with 4 crockets;
     mm. 85, 85/33, 21...35 75

2201   IVb. — Similar, but arch is double bar with 6 uprights or crockets as
     jewels; *mm.* 85, 21/85, 21 ....30 60
     * *mm.*s muled.

2202   **Halfgroat,** *London.* I. Open crown, tressure unbroken; *mm.* 40/-,
     40/39 (R. III mule) 350 750

2203   — IIIa. Double arched crown, rosettes on tressure; *mm.* 78.................................. *Rare*

2204   — IIIb. Similar, nothing on tressure. R. Lozenge panel in centre; *mm.* lis...........40 100

2205   — — Similar, but also with lis on breast; *mm.* lis...40 100

2206   — IIIc. Unarched crown with tressure broken. R. Lozenge panel in centre;
     mm. lis...25 55

2206A— — — Similar but smaller dies and much smaller lettering..............................25 55

2211   2214

2207   *Canterbury,* Archb. Morton. I. Open crown, crosses by neck. R. M in
     centre; *mm.* tun/- 30 75

2208   — — II. Similar, but double-arched crown; no *mm.* 30 50

2209   III King and Archb. jointly. As l ast but without M; (a) early lettering,
     trefoil stops; *mm.* lis, tun and lis/lis 15 40

2209A *Obv.* as last. R. As 2207; *mm.* lis/- 25 50

2210   — — (b) ornate lettering, rosette stops; *mm.* tun, lis in combinations 15 40

2211   — — (c) — saltire or no stops; *mm.* 123, 123 & 30/123....................................15 40

2212   *York,* Royal mint. (a) Double-arched crown, lis on breast (rarely omitted).
     R. Lozenge panel in centre; *mm.* lis...25 55

2213   — — (b) Similar, but unarched crown, tressure broken, *mm.* lis. 20 45

		F	VF
		£	£
2214	— Archb. Savage. (a) Double-arched crown, keys at neck, no tressure; ornate lette ring; *mm.* martlet	20	45
2215	— — (b) Similar, but fleured tressure, small square lettering; *mm.* 94	20	45
2216	— — (c) As last, but tall thin lettering; *mm.* 94	20	45
2217	— As last but no keys; *mm.* 94	20	50

2221   2226

		F	VF
2218	**Penny.** Old type. London; *mm.* 40/-	300	600
2219	— — — crosses by bust, *mm.* small cross (*obv.*)	*Extremely rare*	
2220	— *Canterbury,* Archb. Morton. Open crown, *mm.* tun/- R. M in centre	*Extremely rare*	
2221	— — King and Archb. jointly, arched crown; *mm.* tun, tun/-	40	100
2222	— *Durham,* Bp. Sherwood. S on breast. R. D in centre; *mm.* 7a/-	75	175
2223	— *York,* Archb. Rotherham. With or without cross on breas t, *mm.* 33/-, T and cross or key at neck. R. H in centre	35	90
2224	— — — T and trefoil at neck. R. Quatrefoil in centre and two extra pellets; *mm.* 41/-	40	100
2225	'Sovereign' type. *London.* Early lettering, no stops, no pillars to throne; no *mm.*	*Extremely rare*	
2226	— — — single pillar on king's right side, trefoil stops; no *mm.* or 31/-	17	60
2227	— — Ornate letters, rosette stops, single pillar; *mm.* lis (can be muled with above)	20	70
2228	— — saltire stops or none, two pillars; *mm.* none, -/30	17	60
2229	— — Similar, but small square lettering; no *mm.*	17	60
2230	— — Similar, but lettering as profile groats two double pillars; *mm.* 21, 53, none (sometimes on one side only)	20	70
2231	— *Durham,* Bp. Sherwood. Crozier to r. of king, throne with one pillar. R. D and S beside shield	25	70
2232	— — Throne with two pillars, no crozier. R. As last	30	80
2233	— — Bp. Fox. Throne with one pillar. R. Mitre above shield, RD or DR at sides, no *mm.*	25	60
2234	— — Similar, but two pillars	25	70
2235	*York,* Archb. Rotherham. Keys below shield; early lettering, trefoil stops, no pillars to throne, no *mm.*	20	55

2231   2233   2235

	F	VF
	£	£
2236 **Penny.** — — — single pillar	25	55
2237 — — — ornate lettering, rosette or no stops, single pillar	25	55
2238 — — — — — — two pillars sometimes with crosses between legs of throne	25	55

2245   2248   2249

2239 **Halfpenny,** *London.* I. Open crown; *mm.* 40, 42..........................	75	150
2240 — — — trefoils at neck; no *mm.*, rose	75	150
2241 — — — crosses at neck; *mm.* 33..	65	135
2242 — II. Double arched crown; *mm.* cinquefoil, none............................	25	60
2243 — — — saltires at neck; no *mm.*	20	55
2244 — III. Crown with single arch, ornate lettering; no *mm.*	25	60
2245 — V. Much smaller portrait; *mm.* pheon, lis, none...................................	35	75
2246 *Canterbury,* Archb. Morton. I. Open crown. R. M in centre	*Extremely rare*	
2247 — — II. Similar, but arched crown, saltires by bust; *mm.* profile eye (82)	*Extremely rare*	
2248 — III. King and Archb. Arched crown; *mm.* 105, none	75	175
2249 *York,* Archb. Savage. Arched crown, key below bust..............................	100	250
2250 **Farthing,** *London.* hЄnRIC DI GRA RЄX (A), arched crown	150	300

*No.s 2239-49 have *mm.* on *obv.* only.

Profile issue

2253

2251 **Testoon** (ls.). Type as groat. hЄnRIC (VS); *mm.* lis	4000	8000
2252 — hЄnRIC VII; *mm.* lis..	4500	9000
2253 — hЄnRIC SЄPTI M; *mm.* lis..	5000	10000

2254   2258

		F £	VF £
2254	**Groat,** *Tentative issue* (contemporary with full-face groats). Double band to crown, hЄnRIC VII; *mm.* none, 105/-, -/105: 105/85, 105, 85, 21	100	220
2255	— — — tressure on *obv.; mm.* 21	2750	5000
2256	— — hЄnRIC (VS); *mm.* 105, -/105, 105/ 85, none..............................	225	550
2257	— — hЄnRIC SЄPTIM; *mm.* -/105	3250	6000
2258	*Regular issue.* Triple band to crown; *mm.* 21, 21 and 53/21, 21/21 and 53, 53 (both *mm.*s may o ccur on some *obv.* and *rev.*)...................................	45	120

2261   2262

2263

2259	**Halfgroat,** *London.* As last; *mm.* 105, 53/105, 105/53, 53......................	50	125
2260	— — no numeral after King's name, no *mm.,* -/lis.................................	*Extremely rare*	
2261	*Canterbury,* King and Archb. As London, but *mm.* 94, 33, 94/33............	35	70
2262	*York,* Archb. Bainbridge. As London, but two keys below shield; *mm.* 94, 33, 33/94...	30	65
2262A	— Similar but no keys; *mm.* 94, 33/94	35	70
2263	— — XB beside shield; *mm.* 33/94	900	—

Henry VIII is held in ill-regard by numismatists as being the author of the debasement of England's gold and silver coinage; but there were also other important numismatic innovations during his reign. For the first sixteen years of the reign of the coinage closely followed the pattern of the previous issues, even to the extent of retaining the portrait of Henry VII on the larger silver coins.

In 1526, in an effort to prevent the drain of gold to continental Europe, the value of English gold was cried up by 10%, the sovereign to 22s. 0d. and the angel to 7s. 4d., and a new coin valued at 4s. 6d.—the Crown of the Rose—was introduced as a competitor to the French *ecu au soleil*. The new crown was not a success and within a few months it was replaced by the Crown of the Double Rose valued at 5 shillings but made of gold of only 22 carat fineness, the first time gold had been minted below the standard 23³/₄ carat. At the same time the sovereign was again revalued to 22s. 6d. and the angel to 7s. 6d., with a new coin, the George Noble, valued at 6s. 8d. (one-third pound).

The royal cyphers on some of the gold crowns and half-crowns combine the initial of Henry with those of his queens: Katherine of Aragon, Anne Boleyn and Jane Seymour. The architect of this coinage reform was the Chancellor, Cardinal Thomas Wolsey, but besides his other changes he had minted at York a groat bearing his initials and cardinal's hat in addition to the other denominations normally authorized for the ecclesiastical mints.

In view of Henry's final break with Rome in 1534, followed by the Act of Supremacy of 1535, it was hardly surprising that the Church's coining privileges in England were finally terminated and the mints of Durham and York (ecclesiastical) were closed.

In 1544, to help finance the king's inordinate extravagances, it was decided to extend the process of debasement. Initially all the 'fine' gold coins were reduced in quality to 23 carat, then in the following year gold was issued of 22 carat and later of 20 carat fineness. Concurrently the silver coins were reduced from the sterling standard fineness of 11 oz. 2 dwt. (i.e. .925 silver) to 9 oz. (.750), and later to 6 oz. (.500) and eventually 4 oz. (.333) fineness. Henry's nickname of 'Old Coppernose' was earned not through his own personal characteristics but by his last poor `silver' coins which soon displayed their two-thirds copper content once they became slightly worn.

Mintmarks

53	69	70	108	33	94	73	11
105	22	23	30	78	15	24	110
52	72a	44	8	65a	114	121	90
36	106	56	S	E	116		

1059-26	Pheon (53)		1509-14	Martlet (94, *York*)
	Castle (69)		1509-23	Radiant star (22, *Durham & York*)
	Castle with H (70, gold)		1513-18	Crowned T
	Portcullis crowned (108)		1514-26	Star (23, *York & Durham*)
	Rose (33, *Canterbury*)			Pansy (30, *York*)
	Martlet (94, *Canterbury*)			Escallop (78, *York*)
	Pomegranate (73, but broader, *Cant.*)			Voided cross (15, *York*)
	Cross fitchée (11, *Cant.*)		1523-26	Spur rowel (24, *Durham*)
	Lis (105, *Canterbury, Durham*)			

GOLD

1526-44	Rose (33)	1526-32	Cross patonce (8, *Cant.*)
	Lis (105)		T (114, *Canterbury*)
	Sunburst 110)		Uncertain mark (121,
	Arrow (52)		*Canterbury*)
	Pheon (53)	1529-44	Radiant star (22, *Durham*)
	Lis (106)	1530-44	Key (90, *York*)
	Star (23, *Durham*)	1533-44	Catherine wheel (3 6,
1526-9	Crescent (72a, *Durham*)		*Canterbury*)
	Trefoil (44 variety,	1544-7	Lis (105 and 106)
	Durham)		Pellet in annulet (56)
	Flower of eight petals and		S (Southwark)
	circle centre (*Durham*)		Є or E (Southwark)
1526-30	Cross (7a, sometimes	1546-7	WS monogram (116, *Bristol*)
	slightly voided, *York*)		
	Acorn (65a, *York*)		

First coinage, 1509-26

		F	VF
		£	£
2264	**Sovereign** (20s.). Similar to last sov. of Hen. VII; *mm.* 108	3000	6500
2264A	**Ryal** (10s.) King in ship holding sword and shield. R. Similar to 1950, *mm.*-/108		*Unique*
2265	**Angel** (6s. 8d.). As Hen. VIII, but hЄnRIC? VIII DI GRA RЄX, etc.; *mm.* 53, 69, 70, 70/69, 108, R. May omit h and rose, or rose only; *mm.* 69, 108	175	350
2266	**Half-angel.** Similar (sometimes without VIII), *mm.* 69, 70, 108/33, 108	160	340

2265

Second coinage, 1526-44

2267

2267	**Sovereign** (22s. 6d.). As 2264, R. single or double tressure *mm.* 110, 105, 105/52..	2500	500
2268	**Angel** (7s. 6d.). As 2265, hЄnRIC VIII D(I) G(RA) R(EX) etc,; *mm.* 110, 105..	250	600
2269	**Half-angel.** Similar; *mm.* 105	400	900

Second coinage gold

2270   2272

	F £	VF £
2270 **George-noble** (6s. 8d.). As illustration; *mm.* rose	2250	5500
2270 — Similar, but more modern ship with three masts, without initials hR. R.		
St. George brandishing sword behind head.		*Unique*
2271 **Half-George-noble.** Similar to 2270		*Unique*
2272 **Crown of the rose** (4s. 6d., 23 ct). As illustration; *mm.* rose	*Extremely rare*	

2279   2285

	F	VF
2273 **Crown of the double-rose** (5s., 22 ct). Double-rose crowned, hK (Henry and Katherine of Aragon) both crowned in field. R. Shield crowned; *mm.* rose	175	350
2274 — hK both sides; *mm.* rose/lis, lis, arrow..	190	350
2275* — hK/hA or hA/hK; *mm.* arrow	200	550
2276* — hR/hK or hI/hR; *mm.* arrow	*Extremely rare*	
2277 — hA (Anne Boleyn); *mm.* arrow	225	575
2278 — hA/hR; *mm.* arrow..	—	2250
2279 — hI (Jane Seymour); *mm.* arrow..	200	425
2280* — hK/hI; *mm.* arrow..	225	650
2281 — hR/hI; *mm.* arrow	225	675
2282 — hR (Rex); *mm.* arrow	200	425
2283 — — but with hIBERIE REX; *mm.* pheon..	400	1000
2284 **Halfcrown.** Similar but king's name henric 8 on *rev.*, no initials; *mm.* rose	170	400
2285 — hK uncrowned on *obv.; mm.* rose	150	375
2286 — hK uncrowned both sides; *mm.* rose/lis, lis, arrow	160	385
2287 — hhI uncrowned both sides; *mm.* arrow	225	500
2288 — hR uncrowned both sides; hIB REX; *mm.* pheon..........................	325	750

*The hK initials may on later coins refer to Katherine Howard (Henry's fifth wife).

Third coinage, 1544-7

2291

		F	VF
		£	£
2289	**Sovereign,** I (20s., Wt. 200 grs., 23 ct.). As illustration but king with larger face and larger design; *mm.* lis	4000	9500
2290	II (20s., wt. 200 or 192 grs., 23, 22 or 20 ct.). *Tower.* As illustration; *mm.* lis, pellet in annulet/lis	1150	3050
2291	— *Southwark.* Similar; *mm.* S, Є/S	1200	2950
2292	— — Similar but Є below shield; *mm.* S/Є	Extremely rare	
2293	— *Bristol.* As London but *mm.* WS/-	2750	5000
2294	**Half-sovereign** (wt. 100 or 96 grs.), *Tower.* As illus.; *mm.* lis, pellet in annulet	175	475
2295	— Similar, but with annulet on inner circle (either or both sides)	200	550
2296	*Southwark. Mm.* S	200	550
2297	— Є below shield; *mm.* S, Є, S/Є, Є/S, (known without sceptre; *mm.* S)	175	500
2298	*Bristol.* Lombardic lettering; *mm.* WS, WS/-	350	900

2294

2303   2304

2299	**Angel** (8s., 23 ct). Annulet by angel's head and on ship, ʜєɴʀɪᴄ' 8; *mm.* lis	175	350
2300	— Similar, but annulet one side only or none	185	375
2301	**Half-angel.** Annulet on ship; *mm.* lis	175	425
2302	— No annulet on ship; *mm.* lis	200	475
2303	— Three annulets on ship; *mm.* lis	250	500
2304	**Quarter-angel** Angel wears armour; *mm.* lis	175	400
2304A	— Angel wears tunic; *mm.* lis	200	450

Third coinage gold

		F £	VF £
2305	**Crown,** *London.* Similar to 2283, but hЄnRIC' 8 ; Lombardic lettering; mm . 56	160	350
2306	— without RVTILAnS; *mm.* 56.	170	375
2307	— — — with annulet on inner circle	180	400
2307A	— King's name omitted. DEI GRA both sides, *mm.* 56	*Extremely rare*	
2308	— *Southwark.* As 2306; *mm.* S, Є, E/S, Є/-, E/Є	225	425
2309	*Bristol.* hЄnRIC VIII. ROSA etc. R. D G, etc.; *mm.*-/WS	165	375
2310	— Similar but hЄnRIC(VS) 8 R. D(EI) G(RA); *mm.* -/WS, WS	165	375
2311	**Halfcrown,** *London.* Similar to 2288; *mm.* 56, 56/-	125	300
2312	— — with annulet on inner circle *mm.* 56	135	310
2313	*Southwark.* As 2311; *mm.* S	160	375
2314	— *O.* hЄnRIC 8 ROSA SIN Є SPIn. R. DЄI GRA, etc.; *mm.* Є	225	600
2315	*Bristol. O.* RVTILAn S, etc. R. hЄnRIC 8; *mm.* WS/-	250	450

For other gold coins in Henry's name see page 156.

SILVER

First coinage, 1509-26

2316   2327

2316	**Groat.** Portrait of Hen. VII. *London mm.* 53, 69, 108	45	110
2317	— *Tournai; mm.* crowned T. R. CIVITAS TORnACЄn*	160	450
2318	**Halfgroat.** Portrait of Hen. VII. London; *mm.* 108, 108/-	90	180
2319	— *Canterbury,* Archb. Warham. POSVI *rev.; mm.* rose	70	180
2320	— — — WA above shield; *mm.* martlet	30	100
2321	— — — WA beside shield; *mm.* cross fitchee	40	120
2322	— — CIVITAS CAnTOR *rev.,* similar; *mm.* 73, 105, 11/105	40	90
2323	— *York,* POSVI *rev.,* Archb. Bainbridge (1508-14). Keys below shield; *mm.* martlet	40	90
2324	— — — XB beside shield no keys; *mm.* martlet	55	125
2325	— — — Archb. Wolsey (1514-30). Keys and cardinal's hat below shield; *mm.* 94, 22	80	170
2326	— — CIVITAS Є BORACI *rev.* Similar; *mm.* 22, 23, 30, 78, 15, 15/78	35	70
2327	— — As last with TW beside shield; *mm.* voided cross	50	120
2327A	— *Tournai.* As 2317	*Unique*	

*Other non-portrait groats and half-groats exist of this mint, captured during an invasion of France in 1513. (Restored to France in 1518.)

2332   2335   2336

		F	VF
		£	£
2328	**Penny,** 'Sovereign' type, *London; mm.* 69, 108 /-	35	75
2329	— *Canterbury.* WA above shield; *mm.* martlet	*Extremely rare*	
2330	— — WA beside shield; *mm.* 73/-	40	80
2331	— *Durham,* Bp. Ruthall (1509-23). TD above shield; *mm.* lis............	30	65
2332	— — TD beside shield; *mm.* lis, radiant star....................................	25	60
2333	— — Bp. Wolsey (1523-9). DW beside shield, cardinal's hat below; spur rowel	90	225
2334	**Halfpenny.** Facing bust, hЄNRIC DI GRA RЄX (AGL). *London; mm.* 69, 108/-	35	75
2335	— *Canterbury.* WA beside bust; *mm.* 73/-, 11	80	175
2336	**Farthing. O.** *Mm.* 108/-, hЄNRIC DI GRA RЄX, a portcullis as type. R. CIVITAS LOnDON, rose in centre of long cross	650	1100

Second coinage, 1526-44

2337   2337 D   2337 E

2337	**Groat.** His own young portrait. *London;* bust r., with heavy jowls; mainly *mm.* rose, Roman letters, both sides, roses in cross ends......................	120	275
2337A	*Obv.* as last. R. Lombardic letters, saltires in cross ends; *mm.* rose	100	225
2337B	Bust as 2337 but Lombardic letters. R. Lombardic letters but roses in cross ends; *mm.* rose..	75	150
2337C	*Obv.* as last. R. As 2337A; *mm.* rose	65	135
2337D	Second bust, Greek profile, longer hair, less heavy jowls; *mm.* rose ...	35	85
2337E	Third bust, stereotyped as ill. 2337 E; *mm.* 33-53 (muling occurs)......	30	70
2338	— — with Irish title HIB; larger flan, saltires in cross ends; *mm.* 53, 105 (also muled), 53/105, 105/53, 105	225	550
2339	— *York,* Archb. Wolsey. TW beside shield, cardinal's hat below; *mm.* voided cross, acorn, muled (both ways)	50	120
2340	— — omits TW; *mm.* voided cross	150	375

Second coinage silver

2342	2343	2348

			F	VF
			£	£
2341	**Halfgroat.** Type as groats, Lombardic lettering both sides. *London;*			
	mm. rose to arrow (*obv.*) or none (sometimes muled)		35	80
2341A	*Obv.* Similar to 2337, *mm.* rose, R Lombardic letters			*Rare*
2342	— — with Irish title HIB; *mm.* pheon		350	800
2343	— *Canterbury*, Archb. Warham (—1532). R. CIVITAS CAΠTOR, WA			
	beside shield; *mm.* 121, 121/-, 121/33, 8, 8/T, T		20	40
2344	— — — nothing by shield; *mm.* 121/-		40	90
2345	— — Archb. Cranmer (1533—). TC beside shield; *mm.* 36, 36/-........		25	60
2346	— *York,* Archb. Wolsey (—1530). R. CIVITAS Є BORACI, TW			
	beside shield, hat below; *mm.* 15/-, 15..		25	70
2347	— — Sede Vacante (1530/1). No marks; *mm.* key		40	90
2348	— — Archb. Lee (1531-44). EL or LE beside shield; *mm.* key...........		25	70

2350	2354	2359

			F	VF
2349	**Penny.** 'Sovereign' type h . D . G . ROSA SIΠЄ SPIΠA, *London;*			
	mm. rose to arrow (*obv.* only)		30	70
2350	— *Canterbury.* WA beside shield; *mm.* 121/-, 8/-, T/-		75	175
2351	— — TC beside shield; *mm.* 36/-		50	135
2352	— *Durham,* Bp. Wolsey (—1529). TW beside shield, hat below; *mm.* 23,			
	23/44, 23/-, 72a/-, 44, 44/-, 72a/44 (muled with 2333 *obv.*, *mm.* 24/44)		20	55
2353	— — Sede Vacante (1529-30). No marks; *mm.* 23/-, 22/-		40	90
2354	— — Bp. Tunstall (1530—). CD beside shield; *mm.* 23, 23/-, 22/-, 22		20	55
2355	— *York.* EL beside shield; *mm.* key/-		80	185
2356	**Halfpenny.** Facing bust, h D G ROSA SIЄ SPIA. *London; mm.* rose to			
	arrow (*obv.* only)...		30	65
2357	— *Canterbury.* WA beside bust; *mm.* 8/-, T/-		50	140
2358	— — TC beside bust; *mm.* 36/-		45	100
2359	— *York.* TW beside bust; *mm.* 15/-, acorn/-		55	125
2360	— — Sede Vacante. Key below bust; *mm.* 15/-		65	125
2361	— — EL or LE beside bust; *mm.* key/-		45	90
2362	**Farthing.** *O.* RVTILANS ROSA, portcullis; *mm.* 33/-, 105/-, 110/-. R.			
	DEO GRACIAS...., long cross with pellet in each angle		600	1050
2363	— — *mm.* arrow/- R. DEO GRACIAS, rose on long cross		*Extremely rare*	
2363A	— *Canterbury.* O. Similar. R. Similar. *mm.* 36/-................................		*Extremely rare*	

Third coinage, 1544-7 (Silver progressively debased. 9oz (.750), 6oz (.500) 4oz (.333).)

2364   2365

		Fair £	Fine £	VF £
2364	**Testoon.** *Tower.* hЄnRIC'. VIII, etc. R. Crowned rose between h and R.POSVI, etc.; *mm.* lis, lis and 56, lis/two lis	100	300	800
2365	— hЄnRIC 8, *mm.* 105 and 56, 105/56, 105 and 56/56, 56	90	275	750
2366	— — annulet on inner circle of rev. or both sides; *mm.* pellet in annulet	110	325	825
2367	*Southwark.* As 2365. R. CIVITAS LOnDOn; *mm.* S, Є, S/Є, Є/S	90	275	750
2368	*Bristol. Mm.*-/WS monogram. (Tower or local dies.)	135	375	950

2384   Bust 1   Bust 2   Bust 3

2369	**Groat.** *Tower.* As ill. above, busts 1, 2, 3; *mm.* lis/-, lis	40	135
2369A	Bust 1, R. As second coinage; i.e. saltires in forks; *mm.* lis	70	185
2370	Bust 2 or 3 annulet on inner circle, both sides or rev. only	65	175
2371	*Southwark.* As 2367, busts 1, 2, 3, 4; no *mm.* or lis/-; S or S and Є or Є in forks	50	150
2372	*Bristol. Mm.*-/WS monogram, Bristol bust and Tower bust 2 or 3	55	160
2373	*Canterbury.* Busts 1, 2, (2 var); no *mm.* 105/-	55	150
2374	*York.* Busts 1 var., 2, 3, no *mm.*	55	140
2375	**Halfgroat.** *Tower.* As 2365, bust 1; *mm.* lis, none	65	150
2376	*Southwark.* As 2367, bust 1; no *mm.*; S or Є and S in forks	*Extremely rare*	
2377	*Bristol. Mm.*-/WS monogram	55	165
2378	*Canterbury.* Bust 1; no *mm.*	45	140
2379	*York.* Bust 1; no *mm.*	55	165
2380	**Penny.** *Tower.* Facing bust; no *mm.* or lis/-	40	110
2381	*Southwark.* Facing bust; *mm.* S/-, Є/-, -/Є	*Extremely rare*	
2382	*Bristol.* Facing bust; no *mm.* (Tower dies or local but truncated at neck)	45	120
2383	*Canterbury.* Facing bust; no *mm.*	45	125
2384	*York.* Facing bust; no *mm.*	45	120
2385	**Halfpenny.** *Tower.* Facing bust; no *mm.* or l is/-, pellet in annulet in *rev.* centre	40	125
2386	*Bristol.* Facing bust; no *mm.*	70	185
2387	*Canterbury.* Facing bust; no *mm.*, (some read H 8)	40	135
2388	*York.* Facing bust; no *mm.*	40	135

These coins were struck during the reign of Edward VI but bear the name and portrait of Henry VIII, except in the case of the half-sovereigns which bear the youthful head of Edward.

Mintmarks

| 56 | 105 | 52 | K | E | 116 |

| 66 | 115 | 33 | 122 | t | 94 |

1547	Annulet and pellet (56)	1549	TC monogram (115, *Bristol*)
1547-8	Lis (105)		Lis (105, *Canterbury*)
1547-9	Arrow (52)		Rose (33, *Canterbury*)
	K		Grapple (122)
	Roman E (*Southwark*)	1549/50	t (*Canterbury*)
	WS monogram (116, *Bristol*)	1550/1	Martlet (94)
1548-9	Bow (66, *Durham House*)		

GOLD

		F	VF
		£	£
2389	**Sovereign** (20 ct), *London*. As no. 2290, but Roman lettering; *mm*. lis	1350	3750
2390	— *Bristol*. Similar but *mm*. WS	1700	4250

2391   2391A

2395

		F	VF
		£	£
2391	**Half-sovereign.** As 2294, but with youthful portrait with sceptre. *Tower*; mm. 52, 105, 94 (various combinations)	225	550
2391A	— Similar but no sceptre; mm. 52, 52/56	250	600
2392	— — — K below shield; mm.-/K, none,. E/-	240	575
2393	— — — grapple below shield; mm. 122, none, 122/-, -/122	250	600
2394	— *Southwark*. Mm. E, E/-, -/E, Є /E. Usually Є or E (sometimes retrograde) below shield (sceptre omitted; mm. -/E)	225	550
2394A	— — — R. As 2296; mm.-/S	225	600
2395	**Crown.** Similar to 2305. *London; mm.* 52, 52/-, -/K, 122, 94, K	300	700
2396	— Similar but transposed legends without numeral; mm. -/arrow	375	775
2396A	— As 2395, but omitting RVTILANS; mm. arrow	Extremely rare	
2396B	Similar, but RVTILANS both sides; mm. arrow	Extremely rare	
2397	— *Southwark*. Similar to 2396; mm. E	Extremely rare	
2398	— — King's name on obv.; mm. E/-, E, -/E	400	800
2399	**Halfcrown.** Similar to 2311. *London; mm.* 52, K/-, 122/-, 94, -/52	250	600
2399A	As last but E over h on rev., mm. 56/52	Extremely rare	
2399B	As 2399 but RUTILANS etc. on both sides; mm. arrow	Extremely rare	
2400	— *Southwark*. Mm. E, E/-, -/E	250	600

SILVER

AR (4oz .333)		Fair	Fine
2401	**Testoon.** *Tower*. As 2365 with lozenge stops one side; -/56, 56	125	425
2402	*Southwark*. As 2367; mm. S/E	140	450

Bust 4   Bust 5   Bust 6

Some of the Bristol testoons, groats and halfgroats with WS monogram were struck after the death of Henry VIII but cannot easily be distinguished from those struck during his reign.

2403	**Groat.** *Tower*. Busts 4, 5, 6 (and, rarely, 2). R. POSVI, etc.; mm. 105-94 and none (frequently muled)	45	150
2404	*Southwark*. Busts 4, 5, 6. R. CIVITAS LONDON; no mm. -/E; lis/-, -/lis, K/E; roses or crescents or S and Є in forks	50	160
2405	*Durham House*. Bust 6. R. REDDE CVIQUE QVOD SVVM EST; mm. bow	110	300
2406	*Bristol*. Mm. WS on rev. Bristol busts A and B, Tower bust 2 and 3	50	185
2407	— — Mm. TC on rev. Similar, Bristol bust B	90	300
2408	*Canterbury*. Busts 5, 6; no mm. or rose/-	45	140
2409	*York*. Busts 4, 5, 6; no mm. or lis/-, -/lis	55	160
2410	**Halfgroat.** Bust 1. *Tower*. POSVI, etc.; mm. 52, 52/-, 52/K , -/K, 52/122, 122, -/122	35	110
2411	— *Southwark*. CIVITAS LONDON; mm. E, -/E, none, 52/E, K/E	30	100

		F	*VF*
		£	£
2412	— *Durham House.* R. REDD, etc.; *mm.* bow, -/bow	250	500
2413	— *Bristol.* Mm. WS on *rev.*	40	120
2414	— — *mm.* TC on *rev.*	60	150

2415

| 2415 | **Halfgroat.** *Canterbury.* No *mm.* or t/-, -/t .... | 30 | 100 |
| 2416 | — *York.* No *mm.*, bust 1 and three quarter facing .... | 40 | 130 |

2422   2418   2427

2417	**Penny.** *Tower.* CIVI TAS LONDON. Facing bust; *mm.* 52/-, -/52, -/K,		
	122/-, -/122, none..	30	100
2418	— — three-quarter bust; no *mm.*	30	100
2419	*Southwark.* As 2417; *mm.* E, -/E..	75	225
2420	*Durham House.* As groat but shorter legend; *mm.* -/bow	135	400
2421	*Bristol.* Facing busts, as 2382 but showing more body, no *mm.*	35	120
2422	*Canterbury.* Similar	30	100
2423	— three-quarters facing bust; no *mm.*...	35	120
2424	*York.* Facing bust; no *mm.*	30	100
2425	— three-quarters facing bust; no *mm.*...	35	120
2426	**Halfpenny.** *Tower.* 52?, none..	40	150
2427	*Canterbury.* No *mm.*, sometimes reads H8	50	140
2428	*York.* No *mm.*	40	130

Coinage in his own name

While base coins continued to be issued bearing the name of Henry VIII, plans were made early in Edward's reign to reform the coinage. As a first step, in 1549, the standard of the gold was raised to 22 carat and 'silver' was increased to 50% silver content. Baser shillings were issued in 1550, but finally, in 1551, it was decided to resume the coinage of some 'fine' gold and a new silver coinage was ordered of 11 oz. 1 dwt. fineness, i.e. almost up to the ancient standard. At the same time four new denominations were added to the coinage—the silver crown, halfcrown, sixpence and threepence. Pennies continued to be struck in base silver.

The first dates on English coinage appear in Roman numerals during this reign;
MDXLVIII=1548; MDXLIX=1549; MDL=1550; MDLI=1551.

66	52	35	115	E	53	122

t	T	111	Y	126	94	91A

92	105	y	97	123	78	26

Mintmarks

1548-9	Bow (66, *Durham House*)	1550	Martlet (94)	
1549	Arrow (52)	1550	Leopard's head (91A)	
	Grapple (122)	1550-1	Lion (92)	
	Rose (35, *Canterbury*)		Lis (105, *Southwark*)	
	TC monogram (115, *Bristol*)		Rose (33)	
	Roman E (*Southwark*)	1551	Yor y (117, *Southwark*)	
	Pheon (53)		Ostrich's head (97, gold only)	
	t or T (*Canterbury*)	1551-3	Tun (123)	
1549-50	Swan (111)		Escallop (78)	
	Roman Y (*Southwark*)	1552-3	Pierced mullet (26, *York*)	
1549-50	6 (126 gold only)			

GOLD

First period, Apr. 1547-Jan. 1549

2429   2431

		F £	VF £
2429	**Half-sovereign** (20 ct). As 2391, but reading EDWARD 6. Tower; *mm.* arrow	400	850
2430	— *Southwark* (Sometimes with E or Є below shield); *mm.* E	350	750
2431	**Crown.** RVTILANS, etc., crowned rose between ER both crown ed. R. EDWARD 6, etc., crowned shield between ER both crowned; *mm.* arrow, E over arrow/-	*Extremely rare*	
2431A	— *Obv.* as last. R. As 2305, *mm.* 52/56	*Extremely rare*	
2432	**Halfcrown.** Similar to 2431, but initials not crowned; *mm.* arrow	*Extremely rare*	

Second period, Jan. 1549-Apr. 1550

2433

		F £	VF £
2433	**Sovereign** (22 ct). As illustration; *mm.* arrow, Y, -/52	1600	3000

2435   2438

		F £	VF £
2434	**Half-sovereign.** Uncrowned bust. *London.* TIMOR etc., MDXLIX on *obv. mm.* arrow	*Extremely rare*	
2435	— — SCVTVM, etc., as illustration; *mm.* arrow, **6,** Y	350	875
2436	— *Durham House.* Uncrowned, 1/2 length bust with MDXLVIII at end of *obv.* legend; *mm.* bow; SCVTVM etc.	*Extremely rare*	
2437	— Normal, uncrowned bust. LVCERNA, etc., on *obv.; mm.* bow	*Extremely rare*	
2438	Crowned bust. *London.* EDWARD VI, etc. R. SCVTVM, etc.; *mm.* 52, 122, 111/52, 111, Y, 94	340	775
2439	— *Durham House.* Crowned, half-length bust; *mm.* bow	*Unique*	
2440	— — King's name on *obv.* and *rev.; mm.* bow (mule of 2439/37)	4000	7500

2441   2444

Small denominations often occur creased or straightened.

		F	VF
		£	£
2441	**Crown.** Uncrowned bust, as 2435; *mm.* 6, Y, 52/-, Y/-............................	700	1300
2442	Crowned bust, as 2438; *mm.* 52, 122, 111, Y (usually *obv.* only)............	475	1000
2443	**Halfcrown.** Uncrowned bust; R. As 2441, *mm.* arrow, Y, Y/-, 52/-	550	1100
2444	Crowned bust, as illus. above; *mm.* 52, 52/111, 111, 122, Y, Y/-	450	900
2445	Similar, but king's name on *rev., mm.* 52, 122	550	1000

Third period, 1550-3

2446	**'Fine' sovereign** (=30s.). King on throne; *mm.* 97, 123	8000	20,000
2447	**Double sovereign.** From the same dies, *mm.* 97	\multicolumn{2}{c}{*Extremely rare*}

2448   2451

2448	**Angel** (=10s.). As illustration; *mm.* 97, 123..	3500	7000
2449	**Half-angel.** Similar, *mm.* 97		*Unique*
2450	**Sovereign.** (=20s.). Half-length figure of king r., crowned and holding		
	sword and orb. R. Crowned shield with supporters; *mm.* y, tun	700	1750
2451	**Half-sovereign.** As illustration above; *mm.* y, tun	425	950
2452	**Crown.** Similar, but *rev.* SCVTVM etc., *mm.* y, tun...............................	675	1750
2453	**Halfcrown.** Similar, *mm.* tun, y...	675	1750

SILVER

2459   2460

First period, Apr. 1547-Jan. 1549

		F	VF
		£	£
2454	**Groat.** Cr. bust r. *Tower*. R. Shield over cross, POSVI, etc.; *mm.* arrow.	250	650
2455	— As last, but EDOARD 6, *mm.* arrow	Extremely rare	
2456	— *Southwark*. *Obv.* as 2454. R. CIVITAS LONDON; *mm.*-/E or none, S in forks	300	700
2457	**Halfgroat.** *Tower*. *Obv.* as 2454; *mm.* arrow	350	750
2458	*Southwark*. As 2456; *mm.* arrow, E	350	750
2459	*Canterbury*. Similar. No *mm.*, also reads EDOARD (as ill.)	200	500
2460	**Penny.** *Tower*. As halfgroat, but E.D.G. etc. R. CIVITAS LONDON; *mm.* arrow	225	700
2461	— *Southwark*. As last, but *mm.* -/E.	250	750
2462	*Bristol*. Similar, but reads ED6DG or E6DG no *mm.*	200	575
2463	**Halfpenny.** *Tower*. O. As 2460, *mm.* E (?). R. Cross and pellets	350	800
2464	— *Bristol*. Similar, no *mm.* but reads E6DG or EDG	275	600

Second period, Jan. 1549-Apr. 1550
At all mints except Bristol, the earliest shillings of 1549 were issued at only 60 grains wt., but of 8 oz. standard. This weight and size were soon increased to 80 grains wt., (S.2466 onwards), but the fineness was reduced to 6 oz. so the silver content remained the same.

2465   2467

60 grains; 8oz

2465	**Shilling.** *Tower*. Broad bust with large crown. *Obv.* TIMOR etc. MDXLIX. R. Small, oval garnished shield dividing ER. EDWARD VI etc., *mm.* 52, -/52, no *mm.*	100	300
2465A	*Southwark*. As last, *mm.* Y, EY/Y	125	350
2465B	*Canterbury*. As last, *mm.* -/rose	Rare	

80 grains; 6oz

2466	*Tower*. Tall, narrow bust with small crown. *Obv.* EDWARD VI etc. MDXLIX or MDL. R. As 2465 but TIMOR etc., *mm.* 52-91a (frequently muled)	75	225

	Fine	VF
	£	£

2466A— *Obv.* as last, MDXLIX. R. Heavily garnis hed shield, Durham House
     style. *mm.* 122 .... *Rare*

2466B *Southwark.* As 2466, *mm.* Y, Y/swan 85   250

2466C — — — R. as 2466A. *mm.* Y 100   325

2467 *Bristol. Obv.* similar to 2466. R. Shield with heavy curved garniture or as
    2466, *mm.* TC/rose TC, rose TC 600   1250

2468 *Canterbury.* As 2466, *mm.* T, t, t/T 90   275

2469 *Durham House.* Bust with elaborate tunic and collar TIMOR etc.
    MDXLIX. R. Oval shield, very heavily garnished in different style.
    EDWARD VI etc., *mm.* bow... 250   500

2468   2470

2470 — Bust as last. INIMICOS etc., no date. R. EDWARD etc. 175   450

2471 — — As last, but legends transposed 250   600

2472 — Bust similar to 2466. EDWARD VI etc. R. INIMICOS etc. 150   400

2472A As last but legends transposed 225   500

2472B *Tower.* Elegant bust with extremely thin neck. R. As 2466, *mm.* 94........ 125   350

2472C *Southwark.* As last, *mm.* Y 125   350

For coins of Edward VI countermarked, see p. 171

2472   2472c

Third period, 1550-3

Very base issue 1550-1 (250 fine)

| | 2473 | | | 2475 | | | 2477 |

		F	VF
		£	£
2473	**Shilling**, *Tower*. As 2472B. MDL or MDLI, *mm.* lion, rose, lion/rose ...	150	300
2473A	*Southwark*. As last, *mm.* lis/Y, Y/lis, lis	150	350
2474	**Penny**. *London*. O. Rose. R. Shield; *mm.* escallop (*obv.*)........................	50	120
2475	— — *York*. *Mm.* mullet (*obv.*) as illustration...	45	90
2476	**Halfpenny**. As penny, but single rose	200	400
2477	**Farthing**. O. Portcullis, R. Cross and pellets	*Extremely rare*	

Fine silver issue, (1551-3)

2478	**Crown**. King on horseback with date below horse. R. Shield on cross;		
	mm. y. 1551; tun, 1551-3 (1553, wire line inner circle may be missing)	200	450
2479	**Halfcrown**. Walking horse with plume; *mm.* y, 1551	150	350
2480	Galloping horse without plume; *mm.* tun, 1551-3	175	450
2481	Large walking horse without plume; *mm.* tun, 1553..............................	375	1000
2482	**Shilling**. Facing bust, rose l., value XII r. *mm.* y, tun (bust varieties).....	40	110

2478

2479

2482   2483   2486

		F £	VF £
2483	**Sixpence**. *London*. Similar, as illustration; *mm*. y/-, -/y, y, tun (bust varieties)	40	125
2484	*York*. As last, but CIVITAS Є BORACI; *mm*. mullet	100	250
2485	**Threepence**. *London*. As sixpence, but III; *mm*. tun	125	300
2486	*York*. As 2484, but III by bust	175	500
2487	**Penny**. 'Sovereign' type; *mm*. tun	—	1400

All Mary's gold coin was struck in 23 carat 3 ½ grain gold, the 'crown' gold denominations being temporarily discontinued. The mintmarks appear at the end of the first or second word of the legends.

Pomegranate   Half-rose (or half-rose and castle)

GOLD

2488

		F £	VF £
2488	**'Fine' Sovereign** (=30s.). Queen enthroned. R. Shield on rose, MDLIII, MDLIIII and undated, *mm.* pomegranate, half-rose (or mule)	1400	3000
2489	**Ryal** (=15s.). As illus, MDLIII. R. As 1950 but ADNO etc. *mm.* pomegranate/-..	*Extremely rare*	
	A very fine specimen sold at auction in November 1985 for £13,000.		
2490	**Angel** (=10s.). Usual type; *mm.* pomegranate, half-rose, none? (Known with rose and M transposed)	450	900
2491	**Half-angel.** Similar; *mm.* pomegranate, pomegranate/-	1750	4500

2489   2492

2492	**Groat.** Crowned bust l. R. VERITAS, etc.; *mm.* pomegranate, pomegranate/-	45	130
2493	**Halfgroat.** Similar	*Extremely rare*	
2494	**Penny.** Similar, but M. D. G. ROSA, etc.	300	750
2495	— As last. R. CIVITAS LONDON; no *mm.*	300	750
2495A	— Base penny. Similar to 2474 but M.D.G. etc.......................*All late 19th cent. fabrications*		

The groats and smaller silver coins of this period have Mary's portrait only, but the shillings and sixpences show the bust of the queen's husband, Philip of Spain.

Mintmarks

Lis (105)　　　　　Half-rose and castle

GOLD

2496A

		F	*VF*
		£	£
2496	**Angel**. As illustration; wire line inner circles, calm sea, *mm.* lis..............	1000	1900
2496A	— — New-style, large wings, wire line i.c..	1100	2000
2496B	— — As above but beaded i.c.	1100	2000
2497	**Half-angel**. Similar to 2496..	*Extremely rare*	

SILVER

2505　　　　　2506　　　　　2510

2498	**Shilling**. Busts face-to-face, full titles, undated, no *mm*............................	145	350
2499	— — — also without mark of value...	170	500
2500	— — 1554..	135	325
2501	— English titles only 1554, 1555...	120	400
2501A	— — undated	*Rare*	
2502	— — without mark of value, 1554, 1555 (rare)	175	550
		Fair	
2503	— — date below bust, 1554, 1555...	£150	
2504	— — As last, but without ANG., 1555..	£200	
2505	**Sixpence**. Similar. Full titles, 1554...	110	350
2506	— English titles only, 1555 (no *mm*., rare), 1557 (*mm*. lis, 1557 only)....	125	375
2506A	— As last but heavy beaded i.c. on obv. 1555. (Irish 4d. obv. mule).......	—	700
2507	— — date below bust, 1554, 1557 (very rare)...	*Fair £175*	
2508	**Groat**. Crowned bust of Mary 1. R. POSIMVS etc.; *mm.* lis...................	45	130
2509	**Halfgroat**. Similar, but POSIM, *mm.* lis	250	700
2510	**Penny**. Similar to 2495, but P. Z. M. etc.; *mm.* lis	250	650
2510A	**Base penny**. Similar to 2495A, but P. Z. M . etc.; *mm.* halved rose and H (or castle)/-	65	175

Similar pence of the York mint were made for currency in Ireland

Elizabeth's coinage is particularly interesting on account of the large number of different denominations issued. `Crown' gold coins were again issued as well as the `fine' gold denominations. In 1559 the base shillings of Edward VI's second and third coinages were called in and countermarked for recirculation at reduced values. The normal silver coinage was initially struck at .916 fineness as in the previous reign but between 1560 and 1577 and after 1582 the old sterling standard of .925 was restored. Between 1578 and 1582 the standard was slightly reduced and the weights were reduced by 1/32nd in 1601. Gold was similarly reduced slightly in quality 1578-82, and there was a slight weight reduction in 1601.

To help alleviate the shortage of small change, and to avoid the expense of minting an impossibly small silver farthing, a threefarthing piece was introduced to provide change if a penny was tendered for a farthing purchase. The sixpence, threepence, threehalfpence and threefarthings were markedwith a rose behind the queen's head to distinguish them from the shilling, groat, half-groat and penny.

Coins of exceedingly fine workmanship were produced in a screw press introduced by Eloye Mestrelle, a French moneyer, in 1561. With parts of the machinery powered by a horse-drawn mill, the coins produced came to be known as 'mill money'. Despite the superior quality of the coins produced, the machinery was slow and inefficient compared to striking by hand. Mestrelle's dismissal was engineered in 1572 and six years later he was hanged for counterfeiting.

Mintmarks

106	21	94	23	53	33	107	92
74	71	26	77	65b	27	7	14
113	60	54	79	72b	86	123	124
90	57	0	1	2			

1558-60	Lis (106)	1578-9	Greek cross (7)
1560-1	Cross crosslet (21)	1580-1	Latin cross (14)
	Martlet (94)	1582	Sword (113)
1560-6	Star (23, milled)	1582-3	Bell (60)
1561-5	Pheon (53)	1582-4	A (54)
1565	Rose (33)	1584-6	Escallop (79)
1566	Portcullis (107)	1587-9	Crescent (72b)
1566-7	Lion (92)	1590-2	Hand (86)
1567-70	Coronet (74)	1591-5	Tun (123)
	Lis (105, milled)	1594-6	Woolpack (124)
1569-71	Castle (71)	1595-8	Key (90)
1570	Pierced mullet (26, milled)	1597-1600	Anchor (57)
1572-3	Ermine (77)	1600	**0**
1573-4	Acorn (65b)	1601-2	**1**
1573-7	Eglantine (27)	1602	**2**

N.B. *The dates for* mms *sometimes overlap. This is a result of using up old dies, onto which the new mark was punched.*

GOLD

Hammered Coinage
First to Third issues, 1559-78. (`Fine' gold of .979. `Crown' gold of .916 fineness. Sovereigns of 240 grs. wt .). Mintmarks; lis to eglantine.

2512

		F	VF
		£	£
2511	`Fine' Sovereign of 30 sh. Queen enthroned, tressure broken by throne, reads Z not ET, no chains to portcullis. R. Arms on rose; *mm*. lis.	1500	3250
2512	—— Similar but ET, chains on portcullis; *mm*. crosslet	1400	3000
2513	**Angel**. St. Michael. R. Ship. Wire line inner circles; *mm*. lis.	300	600
2513A	— Similar, but beaded i.c. on *obv*., *mm*. lis	300	600
2514	—— Similar, but beaded inner circles; ship to r.; *mm*. 106, 21, 74, 77-27	250	450
2515	——— Similar, but ship to l.; *mm*. 77-27	275	500
2516	**Half Angel**. As 2513, wire line inner circles; *mm*. lis	*Extremely rare*	
2516A	— As last, but beaded i.c.s, legend ends. Z.HIB	—	1500
2517	— As 2514, beaded inner circles; *mm*. 106, 21, 74, 77-27	180	400
2518	**Quarter Angel**. Similar; *mm*. 74, 77-27	175	400

2513   2520A

2519	**Half Pound** of 10 sh. Young crowned bust l. R. Arms. Wire line inner circles; *mm*. lis	400	900
2520	— Similar, but beaded inner circles; *mm*. 21, 33-107	300	600
2520A	—— Smaller bust; *mm*. 92	350	700
2520B	—— Broad bust, ear visible; *mm*. 92, 74, 71	350	700
2521	**Crown**. As 2519; *mm*. lis	*Extremely rare*	
2522	— Similar to 2520; *mm*. 21, 33-107	250	575
2522A	— Similar to 2520B; *mm*. 74, 71, 92	275	650
2523	**Half Crown**. As 2519; *mm*. lis		2250
2524	— Similar to 2520; *mm*. 21, 33-107 (2 busts)	275	650
2524A	— Similar to 2520B; *mm*. 107-71	300	700

	F	VF
	£	£

Fourth Issue, 1578-82 (`Fine' gold only of .976). *Mms* Greek cross, Latin cross and sword.

2525	**Angel**. As 2514; *mm*. 7, 14, 113	250	475
2526	**Half Angel**. As 2517; *mm*. 7, 14, 113	180	425
2527	— Similar, but without E and rose above ship; *mm*. 14	375	800
2528	**Quarter Angel**. As last; *mm*. 7, 14, 113	175	350

Fifth Issue, 1583-1600 (`Fine' gold of .979, `crown' gold of .916; pound of 174.5 grs. wt.). Mintmarks: bell to **O**.

2529

2530   2534

2529	**Sovereign** (30 sh.). As 2512, but tressure not normally broken by back of throne; *mm*. 54-123	1350	2500
2530	**Ryal** (15 sh.). Queen in ship. R. Similar to 1950; *mm*. 54-86 (*rev*. only)	2250	6000
2531	**Angel**. As 2514; *mm*. 60-123, 90-**O**	250	450
2532	**Half Angel**. As 2517; *mm*. 60-86, 90-57	200	425
2533	**Quarter Angel**. As 2518; *mm*. 60-123, 90-57	165	350
2534	**Pound** (20 sh.). Old bust l., with elaborate dress and profusion of hair; *mm*., lion and tun/tun, 123-**O**	550	1100
2535	**Half Pound**. Similar; *mm*. 123	450	750
2535A	— Similar but smaller bust with less hair; *mm*. 123-**O**	450	750
2536	**Crown**. Similar to 2534; *mm*. 123-90. *O*	275	600
2537	**Half Crown**. Similar; *mm*. -/123, 123-90, *O*	250	550

Sixth Issue, 1601-3 (`Fine' gold of .979, `crown' gold of .916; Pound of 172 grs. wt.). Mintmarks: **1** and **2**

		F	VF
		£	£
2538	**Angel**. As 2531; *mm.* **1, 2**	300	650
2539	**Pound**. As 2534; *mm.* **1, 2**	600	1300
2540	**Half Pound**. As 2535A; *mm.* **1, 2**	600	1150

2541

2541	**Crown**. As 2536; *mm.* **1, 2**	*Rare*
2542	**Half Crown**. As 2537; *mm.* **1, 2**	*Rare*

Milled Coinage, 1561-70

2543	**Half Pound**. Crowned bust l.; *mm.* star, lis	650	1750
2544	**Crown**. Similar; *mm.* star, lis	800	2000
2545	**Half Crown**. Similar; *mm.* star, lis	1200	2500

For further details on both AV and AR milled coinage, *see* D. G. Borden `An introduction to the milled coinage of Elizabeth I'. BNJ 1983

SILVER

Hammered Coinage
Countermarked Edward VI base shillings(1559)

2546   2547

2546	**Fourpence-halfpenny**. Edward VI 2nd period 6oz shillings countermarked on obverse with a portcullis; *mm.* 66, 52, t, 111, Y and 122	*Extremely rare*
2547	**Twopence-farthing**. Edward VI 3rd period 3 oz shillings countermarked on obverse with a seated greyhound; *mm.* 92. 105, 35 and 87	*Extremely rare*
N.B.	*Occasionally the wrong countermark was used*	

First Issue, 1559-60 (.916 fine, shillings of 96 grs.)

2548   2549

		F	VF
		£	£
2548	**Shilling**. Without rose or date. ELIZABET(H), wire line inner circles, pearls on bodice (three similar busts); *mm*. lis.	175	500
2549	— Similar, ELIZABETH, wire line and beaded inner circles, no pearls on bodice (several busts); *mm*. lis..	100	350

2551   2555

2550	**Groat**. Without rose or date, wire line or no inner circles (two busts); *mm*. lis	100	250
2551	— Similar, wire line and beaded inner circles, large bust; circles *mm*. lis	50	125
2551A	— — Small bust and shield (from halfgroat punch); *mm*. lis	125	300
2552	**Halfgroat**. With out rose or date, wire line inner circles; *mm*. lis	150	350
2553	**Penny**. Without rose or date, wire line inner circles; *mm*. lis	125	300
2554	— Similar but dated 1558 on *obv*.; *mm*. lis	—	1500

Second Issue, 1560-1 (.925 fineness, shilling of 96 grs.)

2555	**Shilling**. Without rose or date, beaded inner circles. ET instead of Z (several bust varieties); *mm*. 21, 94	50	160
2555A	— large bust with pearls on bodice as 2548; *mm*. 21, 94	60	200
2556	**Groat**. Without rose or date, bust as 2551; *mm*. 21, 94	25	65
2557	**Halfgroat**. Without rose or date; *mm*. 21, 94..	25	60
2558	**Penny**. Without rose or date (three bust varieties); *mm*. 21, 94	15	40

Third Issue, 1561-77 (Same fineness and weight as last)

2561   2562   2567   2571

	V £	VF £
2559 **Sixpence**. With rose and date, large flan (27 *mm.* or more), large bust with hair swept back, 1561; *mm.* pheon	150	325
2560 — Similar, small bust, 1561; *mm.* pheon	50	150
2561 — Smaller flan (26.5 *mm.*). Small regular bust, 1561-6; *mm.* 53-107	20	60
2561A— Similar, without rose, 1561; *mm.* pheon	*Extremely rare*	
2561B— Similar, very large bust, with rose, 1563-5; *mm.* pheon	65	175
2562 — Intermediate bust, ear shows, 1566-74; *mm.* 92-65b (also 1567 *mm.* 71/74)	20	60
2562A— Similar, without date; *mm.* lion, coronet, ermine	*Extremely rare*	
2563 — Larger bust, 1573-7; *mm.* 77-27	20	60
2564 **Threepence**. With rose and date 1561, large flan (21 *mm.*); *mm.* pheon .	30	85
2565 — smaller flan (19 *mm.*). Regular bust, 1561-7; *mm.* 53-92	15	45
2566 — taller bust, ear shows, 1566-77; *mm.* 92-27, 27/-, 27/65b	15	45
2566A— Similar, without rose, 1568; *mm.* coronet		*Unique*
2567 **Halfgroat**. Without rose or date; *mm.* 107-71	35	85
2568 **Threehalfpence**. With rose and date 1561, large flan (17 *mm.*) *mm.* pheon	35	90
2569 — — Smaller flan (16 *mm.*); 1561-2, 1564-70, 1572-7; *mm.* 53-107, 74-27	20	55
2570 **Penny**. Without rose or date; *mm.* 33-71, 65b-27, 33/107, 92/107, 74/107	20	50
2571 **Threefarthings**. With rose and date 1561-2, 1568, 1572-7; *mm.* 53, 74, 77-27	40	135

Fourth Issue, 1578-82 (.921 fineness, shilling of 95.6 grs.)

	V £	VF £
2572 **Sixpence**. As 2563, 1578-82; *mm.* 7-113, 14/113, 14/7	20	60
2573 **Threepence**. As 2566, 1578-82; *mm.* 7-113	15	50

2573   2573

		F	VF
		£	£
2574	**Threehalfpence.** As 2569, 1578-9, 1581-2; *mm*. 7-113	25	60
2575	**Penny.** As 2570; *mm*. 7-113, 7/14, 14/7	20	50
2576	**Threefarthings.** As 2571, 1578-9, 1581-2; *mm*. 7-113	50	150

Fifth Issue, 1582-1600 (.925 fineness, shilling of 96 grs.)

		F	VF
2577	**Shilling.** Without rose or date, ELIZAB; ear concealed (two busts) *mm*. 60-72b, ear shows. *mm*. 79-**0** (mules occur)	30	95
2578	**Sixpence.** As 2572, ELIZABETH, 1582; *mm*. bell	30	75
2578A	— Similar, ELIZAB, 1582-1600; *mm*. 60-**0**, also 1583 *mm*. 79/54	25	60
2579	**Halfgroat.** Without rose or date, two pellets behind bust. R. CIVITAS LONDON; *mm*. 60-**0** (*mm*. bell sometimes without pellets)	12	45
2580	**Penny.** Without rose or date. R. CIVITAS LONDON; *mm*. 60-57, 90/-, 57/-, **0**/-	10	40
2581	**Halfpenny.** Portcullis. R. Cross and pellets; *mm*. none, 54-**0**	25	70

2577   2578A   2581

2582   2583

Sixth Issue, 1601-2 (.925 fineness, shilling of 93 grs.)

		F	VF
2582	**Crown.** Similar to illustration of 2583; *mm*. **1, 2**	325	700
2583	**Halfcrown.** As illustration, *mm*. **1, 2**	200	450
2584	**Shilling.** As 2577; *mm*. **1, 2**	35	120
2585	**Sixpence.** As 2578A, 1601-2; *mm*. **1, 2**	30	90
2586	**Halfgroat.** As 2579, *mm*. **1, 2**, 2/-	15	50
2587	**Penny.** As 2580, *mm*. **1, 2**, 2/-	15	45
2588	**Halfpenny.** As 2581, *mm*. **1, 2**	30	80

Milled coinage

2584   2592

		F £	VF £
2589	**Shilling**. Without rose or date; *mm*. star. Plain dress, large size (over 31 *mm*.)	325	800
2590	— decorated dress, large size..	130	400
2591	— — intermediate size (30-31 *mm*.)...	90	285
2592	— — small size (under 30 *mm*.)	80	250
2593	**Sixpence**. Small bust, large rose. R. Cross fourchee, 1561 *mm*. star........	30	90

2593   2594   2596/7   2597

2594	Tall narrow bust with plain dress, large rose, 1561-2; *mm*. star ....*from*	30	90
2595	— similar, but decorated dress, 1562..	30	90
2596	Large broad bust, elaborately decorated dress, small rose, 1562; *mm*. star	25	85
2597	— — cross pattée on *rev*., 1562, 64 *mm*. star	35	95
2598	— similar, pellet border, 1563-4..	50	150
2598A	Bust with low ruff, raised rim, 1564, 1566 (both overdates)....................	70	140
2599	Small bust, 1567-8, R. As 2593; *mm*. lis...	40	110
2600	Large crude bust breaking legend; 1570, *mm*. lis; 1571/0, *mm*. castle (over lis)...	90	250
2601	**Groat**. As illustration..	75	275

2599   2601

		F	VF
		£	£
2602	**Threepence**. With rose, small bust with plain dress, 1561	65	190
2603	Tall narrow decorated bust with medium rose, 1562................................	60	165
2604	Broad bust with very small rose, 1562...	80	210
2605	Cross pattee on *rev.*, 1564/3...	150	400
2606	**Halfgroat**. As groat	75	250
2607	**Threefarthings**. E . D . G . ROSA, etc., with rose. R. CIVITAS LONDON,		
	shield with 1563 above	*Extremely rare*	

Portcullis money
Trade coins of 8, 4, 2, and 1 Testerns were coined at the Tower Mint in 1600/1 for the first voyage of the incorporated 'Company of Merchants of London Trading into the East Indies'. The coins bear the royal arms on the obverse and a portcullis on the reverse and have the *mm.* **O**. They were struck to the weights of the equivalent Spanish silver 8, 4, 2 and 1 reales.

		£	£
2607A	Eight testerns	650	1400
2607B	Four testerns	350	725
2607C	Two testerns..	375	800
2607D	One testern	275	700

2607A

THE HOUSE OF STUART
AND THE COMMONWEALTH

JAMES I, 1603-25

With the accession of James VI of Scotland to the English throne, the royal titles and coat of arms are altered on the coinage; on the latter the Scottish rampant lion and the Irish harp now appear in the second and third quarters. In 1604 the weight of the gold pound was reduced and the new coin became known as the `Unite'. Fine gold coins of 23 1/2 carat and crown gold of 22 carat were both issued, and a gold four-shilling piece was struck 1604-19. In 1612 all the gold coins had their values raised by 10%; but in 1619 the Unite was replaced by a new, lighter 20s. piece, the `Laurel', and a lighter rose-ryal, spur-ryal and angel were minted.

In 1613 the King granted Lord Harrington a licence to coin farthings of copper as a result of repeated public demands for a low value coinage; this was later taken over by the Duke of Lennox. Towards the end of the reign coins made from silver sent to the mint from the Welsh mines had the Prince of Wales's plumes inserted over the royal arms.

Mintmarks

125	105	33	79	84	74	90

60	25	71	45	32	123	132

72b	7a	16	24	125	105	46

First coinage		1613-15	Cinquefoil (32)
1603-4	Thistle (125)	1615-16	Tun (123)
1604-5	Lis (105)	1616-17	Closed book (132)
Second coinage		1617-18	Crescent (72b, gold)
1604-5	Lis (105)	1618-19	Plain cross (7a)
1605-6	Rose (33)	1619	Saltire cross (16, gold)
1606-7	Escallop (79)		
1607	Grapes (84)	Third coinage	
1607-9	Coronet (74)	1619-20	Spur rowel (24)
1609-10	Key (90)	1620-1	Rose (33)
1610-11	Bell (60)	1621-3	Thistle (125)
1611-12	Mullet (25)	1623-4	Lis (105)
1612-13	Tower (71)	1624	Trefoil (46)
1613	Trefoil (45)		

2610   2612

GOLD

First coinage, 1603-4 (Obverse legend reads D' . G' . ANG : SCO : etc.)

		F	VF
		£	£
2608	**Sovereign** (=20s.). King crowned r., half-length, first bust with plain armour. R. EXVRGAT, etc.; *mm.* thistle	600	1250
2609	— second bust with decorated armour; *mm.* 125, 105	650	1400
2610	**Half-sovereign**. Crowned bust r. R. EXVRGAT, etc.; *mm.* thistle	1500	3500
2611	**Crown**. Similar. R. TVEATVR, etc.; *mm.* 125, 105/125	700	2000
2612	**Halfcrown**. Similar; *mm.* thistle, lis	175	500

N.B. *The Quarter-Angel of this coinage is considered to be a pattern (possibly a later strike), having the reverse of the half-crown although coin weights are known.*

2613   2614

Second coinage, 1604-19 (Obverse legend reads D' G' MAG : BRIT : etc.)

2613	**Rose-ryal** (=30s., 33s. from 1612). King enthroned. R. Shield on rose; *mm.* 33-90, 25-132	700	1400
2614	**Spur ryal** (=15s., 16s. 6d. from 1612). King in ship; *mm.* 33, 79, 74, 25-32, 132	1500	3000
2615	**Angel** (=10s., 11s. from 1612). Old type but larger shield; *mm.* 33-74, 60-16	350	650
2616	—— pierced for use as touch-piece	150	350
2617	**Half-angel** (=5s., 5s. 6d. from 1612). Similar; *mm.* 71-132, 7a, 16	1300	3000

Second coinage gold

2620

2622   2627

		F	VF
		£	£
2618	**Unite** (=20s., 22s. from 1612). Half-length second bust r. R. FACIAM etc.; *mm*. lis or rose	225	425
2619	— fourth bust; *mm*. rose to cinquefoil	200	375
2620	— fifth bust; *mm*. cinquefoil to saltire	175	350
2621	**Double-crown**. Third bust r. R. HENRICVS, etc.; *mm*. lis or rose	135	325
2622	Fourth bust; *mm*. rose to bell	135	325
2623	Fifth bust; *mm*. key, mullet to saltire	125	300
2624	**Britain crown**. First bust r.; *mm*. lis to coronet	110	225
2625	Third bust; *mm*. key to cinquefoil	110	225
2626	Fifth bust; *mm*. cinquefoil to saltire	100	215
2627	**Thistle crown** (=4s.). As illus.; *mm*. lis to plain cross	125	250
2628	— IR on only one side or absent both sides; *mm*. 79, 74, 71-123	150	275
2629	**Halfcrown**. I' D' G' ROSA SINE SPINA. First bust; *mm*. lis to key	115	210
2630	Third bust; *mm*. key to trefoil, 45/71	120	225
2631	Fifth bust; *mm*. cinquefoil to plain cross	110	185

Third coinage, 1619-25

		F	VF
2632	**Rose-ryal** (=30s.; 196 1/2 grs.). King enthroned. R. XXX above shield; lis, lion and rose emblems around; *mm*. 24, 125, 105	1000	1900
2633	Similar but plain back to throne; *mm*. 46	1100	2500
2634	**Spur-ryal** (=15s.). As illus. R. Somewhat like 2530, but lis are also crowned. *mm*. 24-125, 46	1600	3250
2635	**Angel** (=10s.) of new type; *mm*. 24-46	450	950
2636	— pierced for use as touch-piece	200	400

2635

2638c   2640

	F	VF
	£	£
2637 **Laurel** (=20s.; 140 1/2 grs.). First (large) laur, bust l.; *mm.* 24, 24/-	225	485
2638 Second, medium, square headed bust, `SS' tie ends; *mm.* 24, 33	200	350
2638A Third, small rounded head, ties wider apart; *mm.* 33, 125	200	350
2638B Fourth head, very small ties; *mm.* 105, 46	200	350
2638C Fourth head variety, tie ends form a bracket to value; *mm.* lis	210	370

2641   2642

2639 Fifth, small rather crude bust; *mm.* trefoil	650	1750
2640 **Half-laurel**. First bust; *mm.* spur rowel	185	375
2641 — As 2638A; *mm.* rose	165	350
2641A — As 2638B; *mm.* 33-46, 105/-	150	315
2642 **Quarter-laurel**. Bust with two loose tie ends; *mm.* 24-105	120	175
2642A Bust as 2638C; *mm.* 105, 46, 105/46	120	175
2642B As last but beaded, i.c. on *rev.* or both sides; *mm.* 105, 46	140	225

Rev. mm. on 1/2 *and* 1/4 *laurels normally follows REGNA.*

2643

		F £	*VF* £

First coinage, 1603-4

2643 **Crown**. King on horseback. R. EXVRGAT, etc., shield; *mm.* thistle, lis — 275 | 700

2644 **Halfcrown**. Similar.. 325 | 900

2645 **Shilling**. First bust, square-cut beard. R. EXVRGAT, etc.; *mm.* thistle ... 40 | 140

2646 — Second bust, beard merges with collar; *mm.* thistle, lis .... 30 | 100

2646

2647   2648

2647 **Sixpence**. First bust; 1603; *mm.* thistle...................................... 30 | 120

2648 Second bust; 1603-4; *mm.* thistle, lis .... 25 | 110

2649 **Halfgroat**. As illustration 2650 but II; *mm.* thistle, lis .... 20 | 65

	F	VF
	£	£
2650 **Penny**. First bust I behind head; *mm*. thistle, lis ?	50	125
2650A— Second bust; *mm*. thistle, lis	40	100
2651 **Halfpenny**. As illustration; *mm*. thistle, lis	20	50

2650   2651

Second coinage, 1604-19

	F	VF
2652 **Crown**. King on horseback. R. QVAE DEVS, etc. *rev.* stops; *mm*. 105-84	250	550
2653 **Halfcrown**. Similar; *mm*. 105-79	350	950
2654 **Shilling**. Third bust, beard cut square and stands out (*cf*. illus.: 2657); *mm*. lis, rose	25	90
2655 — Fourth bust, armour plainer (*cf*. 2658); *mm*. 33-74, 60 over 74	20	80
2656 — Fifth bust, similar, but hair longer; *mm*. 74-7a (several bust varieties)	20	85

2657   2658

	F	VF
2657 **Sixpence**. Third bust; 1604-6; *mm*. lis, rose	25	85
2658 — Fourth bust; 1605-15; *mm*. rose to tun, 90/60, 25/60	20	90
2658A— Fifth bust, 1618; *mm*. plain cross		*Unique*

2660   2663

		F	VF
		£	£
2659	**Halfgroat**. As illus. but larger crown on *obv.*; *mm.* lis to coronet............	12	30
2660	—— Similar, but smaller crown on *obv.*; *mm.* coronet to plain cross	15	40
2660A	As before, but TVEATVR legend both sides; *mm.* 7a............................	40	75
2661	**Penny**. As halfgroat but no crowns; *mm.* 105-32,7a and none, -/84, 32/-	12	30
2662	— As before but TVEATVR legend both sides; *mm.* mullet	100	—
2663	**Halfpenny**. As illus.; *mm.* 105- 25 (except 90), 32; all *mms* on *rev.* only	15	30

Third coinage, 1619-25

2664	**Crown**. As 2652, with plain or grass ground line, colon stops on *obv.*, no		
	stops on *rev.*; *mm.* 33-46	160	360
2665	—— plume over shield; *mm.* 125-46..	180	400

2665

2666   2667

2666	**Halfcrown**. As 2664 but normally plain ground line only; all have bird-		
	headed harp; *mm.* 33-46	100	250
2666A	— — Similar but no ground line; *mm.* rose..	150	325
2667	— — Plume over shield; groundline *mm.* 125-46	125	350
2668	**Shilling**. Sixth (large) bust, hair longer and very curly; *mm.* 24-46	25	80
2669	— — plume over shield; *mm.* 125-46..	40	105
2670	**Sixpence**. Sixth bust; 1621-4; *mm.* 33-46; 1621/0, *mm.* rose	25	100
2671	**Halfgroat**. As 2660 but no stops on *rev.*; *mm.* 24-46 and none, 105 and 46,		
	46/- *mm.* 24 with *rev.* stops known	12	25
2671A	Similar but no inner circles; *mm.* lis, trefoil..	30	90
2672	**Penny**. As illus.; *mm.* 24, 105, two pellets, none, trefoil, many mule *mms*.	12	25
2672A	— Similar but without inner circles on one or both sides; *mm.* lis, two		
	pellets	12	25
2673	**Halfpenny**. As 2663, but no *mm.*	15	25

2670   2672

COPPER

For mintmarks see C. Wilson Peck, *English Copper, Tin and Bronze Coins in the British Museum, 1558-1958.*

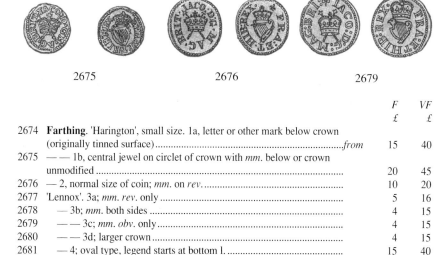

2675   2676   2679

		F £	VF £
2674	**Farthing**. 'Harington', small size. 1a, letter or other mark below crown (originally tinned surface) ....*from*	15	40
2675	— — 1b, central jewel on circlet of crown with *mm.* below or crown unmodified	20	45
2676	— 2, normal size of coin; *mm.* on *rev.*	10	20
2677	'Lennox'. 3a; *mm. rev.* only	5	16
2678	— 3b; *mm.* both sides	4	15
2679	— — 3c; *mm. obv.* only	4	15
2680	— — 3d; larger crown	4	15
2681	— 4; oval type, legend starts at bottom l.	15	40

Numismatically, this reign is one of the most interesting of all the English monarchs. Some outstanding machine-made coins were produced by Nicholas Briot, a French die-sinker, but theycould not be struck at sufficient speed to supplant hand-hammering methods. In 1637 a branch mint was set up at Aberystwyth to coin silver extracted from the Welsh mines. After the king's final breach with Parliament the parliamentary government continued to issue coins at London with Charles's name and portrait until the king's trial and execution. The coinage of copper farthings continued to be manufactured privately under licences held first by the Duchess of Richmond, then by Lord Maltravers and later by various other persons. The licence was finally revoked by Parliament in 1644.

During the Civil War coins were struck at a number of towns to supply coinage for those areas of the country under Royalist control. Many of these coins have an abbreviated form of the 'Declaration' made at Wellington, Shropshire, Sept., 1642, in which Charles promised to uphold the Protestant Religion, the Laws of England and the Liberty of Parliament. Amongst the more spectacular pieces are the gold triple unites and the silver pounds and half-pounds struck at Shrewsbury and Oxford, and the emergency coins made from odd-shaped pieces of silver plate during the sieges of Newark, Scarborough, Carlisle and Pontefract.

105	10	96	71	57	88	101	35

87	107	60	75	123	57	119a	23

119b	98	112	81	120	109

Mintmarks

Tower Mint under Charles I		1635-6	Crown (75)
1625	Lis (105)	1636-8	Tun (123)
1625-6	Cross Calvary (10)	1638-9	Anchor (57)
1626-7	Negro's head (96)	1639-40	Triangle (119a)
1627-8	Castle (71)	1640-1	Star (23)
1628-9	Anchor (57)	1641-3	Triangle in circle (119b)
1629-30	Heart (88)	**Tower Mint under Parliament**	
1630-1	Plume (101)	1643-4	P in brackets (98)
1631-2	Rose (35)	1644-5	R in brackets (112)
1632-3	Harp (87)	1645	Eye (81)
1633-4	Portcullis (107)	1645-6	Sun (120)
1634-5	Bell (60)	1646-8	Sceptre (109)

Mint mark no. 57 is often horizontal to left or right.

59	B	58 *var*	58

Briot's Mint

1631-2	Flower and B (59)	1638-9	Anchor and B (58)
1632	B		Anchor and mullet

On mint mark no. 58 the `B' below the anchor is sometimes shown as ʙ

61   104   35   92   103   6   65b   71

89   91 *var*   131   84   94 *var*   64   93   34

102   67   127   128   129   25   83   100

134   71   A   B   75

Provincial Mints

1638-42	Book (61, *Aberystwyth*)
1642	Plume (104, *Shrewsbury*)
	Pellets or pellet (*Shrewsbury*)
1642-3	Rose (35, *Truro*)
	Bugle (134, *Truro?*)
1642-4	Lion (92, *York*)
1642-6	Plume (103, *Oxford*)
	Pellet or pellets (*Oxford*)
	Lis (105, *Oxford*)
1643	Cross pattee (6, *Bristol*)
	Acorn (65b, *Bristol*)
	Castle (71, *Worcester* or *Shrewsbury*)
	Helmet (89, *Worcester* and *Shrewsbury*)
1643-4	Leopard's head (91 *var. Worcester*)
	Two lions (131, *Worcester*)
	Lis (105, *Worcs.* or *Shrews.*)
	Bunch of grapes (84, *Worcs.* or *Shrews.*)
	Bird (94 var., *Worcs.* or *Shrews.*)

1643-4	Boar's head (*Worcs.* or *Shrews.*)
	Lion rampant (93, *Worcs.* or *Shrews.*)
	Rosette (34, *Worcs.* or *Shrews.*)
1643-5	Plume (102, *Bristol*)
	Br. (67, *Bristol*)
	Pellets (*Bristol*)
	Rose (35, *Exeter*)
	Rosette (34, *Oxford*)
1643-6	Floriated cross (127, *Oxford*)
1644	Cross pattee (6, *Oxford*)
	Lozenge (128, *Oxford*)
	Billet (129, *Oxford*)
	Mullet (25, *Oxford*)
1644-5	Gerb (83, *Chester*)
	Pear (100, *Worcester*)
	Lis (105, *Hereford?*)
	Castle (71, *Exeter*)
1645-6	Plume (102, *Ashby, Bridgnorth*)
1645	A (*Ashby*)
1646	B (*Bridgnorth*)
1648-9	Crown (75, *Aberystwyth Furnace*)

GOLD

Tower mint, under the King, 1625-42

2687

Tower Gold

		F	VF
		£	£

2682 **Angel**. As for James I last issue, but *rev.* reads AMOR POPULI etc;
     without mark of value; *mm.* lis and cross calvary .... 525 | 1300

2683 — — pierced for use as touch-piece .... 200 | 350

2684 — X in field to r.; *mm.* 96-88, 71 and 96/71, 57 and 71/57 .... 425 | 1100

2685 — — — pierced for use as touch-piece .... 200 | 350

2686 — X in field to l.; *mm.* 96, 88, 35-119b .... 400 | 1000

2687 — — — pierced for use as touch-piece .... 200 | 350

2688   2697

2688 **Unite** (=20s.). First bust with ruff and collar of order, high double-crown.
     R. Square-topped shield; *mm.* 105. .... 200 | 350

2688A— Similar, but extra garnishing to shield; *mm.* lis.................................... 225 | 425

2689 — Similar, but flat single-arched crown; *mm.* 105, 10............................ 200 | 375

2689AR. As 2688A. *mm.* 105 .... 225 | 450

2690 Second bust with ruff and armour nearly concealed with scarf; R. Square-
     topped shield with slight garnishing *mm.* 10-88 .... 175 | 350

2690A Similar but more elongated bust, usually dividing legend. *mm.* 57-101,
     88/101.. 175 | 350

2691 — As 2690A but *mm.* anchor below bust .... 275 | 550

2691A*Obv.* as 2690A. R. As next: *mm.* plume.. 200 | 375

2692 Third bust, more armour visible. R. Oval shield with CR at sides; *mm.* 101, 35. 185 | 375

2692A*Obv.* as next. R. As last, *mm.* plume .... 185 | 400

2693 Fourth bust, small lace collar with large high crown usually breaking i.c.,
     long hair. Garter ribbon on breast. R. Oval shield with crowned CR at
     sides; *mm.* 87, 107.. 200 | 400

2693A Similar, but unjewelled crown, within or touching i.c.; *mm.* 107-23........ 200 | 350

2694 Sixth (Briot's) bust, large lace collar. R. Similar; *mm.* 119a-119b.......... 225 | 425

2695 Briot's hammered issue, (square-topped shield); *mm.* 57......................... — | 3000

2696 **Double-crown**. First bust. As 2688. R. Square-topped shield; *mm.* 105.. 150 | 340

2696A Similar to last but wider flatter double-arched crown; *mm.* 105, 10......... 150 | 340

*2697 Second bust. R. Similar to 2690; *mm.* 10-57 .... 145 | 320

*2697A Similar to 2690A: *mm.* 57-101 .... 150 | 330

2697B *Obv.* as last. R. As next: *mm.* plume .... 160 | 350

*For these coins inner circles are sometimes omitted on *obv.*, *rev.*, or both. *See also 2704, 2704A and 2707.*

Tower Gold   *F*   *VF*
                                                                                  £   £

2698 **Double-crown.** Third bust. Flat or domed crown. R. Oval shield with CR at
    sides; *mm.* 101, 35.. 185   400
2699 Fourth bust, large head, high wide crown. R. Oval shield with crowned CR
    at sides; *mm.* 87... 175   350
2699A Similar to last, but flat crown, jewelled outer arch: *mm.* 87-123............. 150   320
2699B Similar, but smaller head, unjewelled crown: *mm.* 60-57....................... 150   320
2699C Sim. to 2699, but bust within i.c.; *mm.* 60 .... *Extremely rare*
2700 Fifth bust (Early Aberystwyth style). R. Similar; *mm.* 57 .... *Extremely rare*
2700A — (Late Aberystwyth style). R. *mm.* 57, 119a 200   400
2701 Sixth bust. R. Normal; *mm.* 119a-119b.............................. .,,,................ 200   400
2702 — R. Briot's square-topped shield; *mm.* 57.. *Extremely rare*
2703 **Crown.** First bust with small round crown. R. Square-topped shield; *mm.*
    105, 10... 115   175
2703A As 2696A. *mm.* cross calvary... 115   175
*2704 Second bust as 2690. R. Similar; *mm.* 10-71 105   175
*2704A As 2690A. *mm.* 57-101, 88/-, 57/-, 101/- 105   175
2704B As 2691. Wire line i.c.s on *rev.*... *Rare*
2705 *Obv.* as 2690A. R. As next; 101, 35, 101/- 135   250
2706 Third bust. R. Oval shield with CR at sides; *mm.* 101 250   500
*2707 Fourth bust. R. Oval shield with crowned CR at sides; *mm.* -/87, 87-119b,
    23/119a, 107/60... 125   190
2708 Fifth (Aberystwyth style) bust. R. Similar; *mm.* anchor 165   350
2709 Sixth (Briot's) bust. R. Similar; *mm.* anchor.. *Unique*

          2703   2714

Tower mint, under Parliament, 1642-9. All Charles I types
2710 **Unite.** Fourth bust, as 2693A; *mm.* (P), (P)/-.. 200   500
2711 Sixth bust, as 2694 but crude style; *mm.* (P), (R), 119b.......................... 325   700
2712 Seventh bust, crude r style; *mm.* eye, sun, sceptre 335   725
2713 **Double-crown.** Fourth bust, as 2699B; *mm.* eye.. *Extremely rare*
2714 Fifth bust, as 2700A; *mm.* sun, sceptre 325   750
2715 Sixth bust, as 2701; *mm.* (P) 400   925
2716 Eighth, dumpy bust with single flat-arched crown; *mm.* sun................... *Unique*
2717 **Crown.** Fourth bust, as 2707 jewelled crown; *mm.* -/98 , 98/-, 98-120.... 150   325
2717A Sim. but unjewelled crown. R. Small crude shield; *mm.* 81-109 150   325

Nicholas Briot's coinage, 1631-2
2718 **Angel.** Type somewhat as Tower but smaller and neater; *mm.* -/B .... *Extremely rare*
2719 **Unite.** As illustration. R. FLORENT etc.; *mm.* flower and B/B............... —   1750
2720 **Double-crown.** Similar but X. R. CVLTORES, etc. *mm.* flower and B/B 450   1100
2720A Similar but King's crown unjewelled: *mm.* flower and B/B, B 500   1200
2721 **Crown.** Similar; *mm.* B... *Extremely rare*
Inner circles sometimes omitted on obv. *or* rev. *or both.*
BRIOTS HAMMERED GOLD: See No. 2695.

2707   2719

| Provincial issues, 1638-49 | F | VF |
| Chester mint | £ | £ |

2722 **Unite**. As Tower. Somewhat like a crude Tower sixth bust. R. Crowned,
       oval shield, crowned CR, *mm.* plume .... *Extremely rare*

  Shrewsbury mint, 1642 (See also 2749)

2723 **Triple unite**, 1642. Half-length figure l holding sword and olive-branch;
       mm.: R. EXVRGAT, etc., around RELIG PROT, etc., in two wavy lines.
       III and three plumes above, date below .... *Extremely rare*

Oxford mint, 1642-6

2724

		F	VF
2724	**Triple unite**. As last, but *mm.* plume, tall narrow bust, 1642	1750	3500
2725	Similar, but 'Declaration' on continuous scroll, 1642-3	1850	4000
2725A	Large bust of fine style. King holds short olive branch; *mm.* small lis.....	*Extremely rare*	
	A good EF specimen fetched £48,000 in auction in May, 1989		
2726	As last, but taller bust, with scarf behind shoulder, 1643, *mm.* plume	2050	4000
2727	Similar, but without scarf, longer olive branch, 1643...............................	1750	3400
2728	Similar, but OXON below 1643, rosette stops...	*Extremely rare*	
2729	Smaller size, olive branch varies, bust size varies, 1644 OXON..............	1850	3850
2730	— Obv. as 2729, 1644 / OX..	2050	4000

2731

		F	VF
		£	£
2731	**Unite.** Tall thin bust. R. 'Declaration' in two wavy lines, 1642; *no mm.* ...	400	950
2732	— R. 'Declaration' in three lines on continuous scroll, 1642-3	400	950
2733	Tall, well-proportioned bust. R. Similar, 1643, no *mm.*	500	1100
2734	Shorter bust, king's elbow not visible. R. Similar, 1643; *mm.* plume/-....	400	825
2735	Similar but longer olive branch curving to l. 1644 / OX; *mm.* plume	400	900
2735A	Similar, but dumpy bust breaking lower i.c., small flan	400	950
2736	Tall bust to edge of coin. R. Similar, 1643	550	1300
2737	As 2734. R. 'Declaration' in three straight lines, 1644 / OX.....................	*Extremely rare*	
2738	Similar to 2734, but smaller size; small bust, low olive branch. 1645	450	1250
2739	— R. Single plume above 'Declaration', 1645-6 / OX; *mm.* plume, rosette, none	500	1100
2740	**Half-unite.** 'Declaration' in three straight lines, 1642	*Extremely rare*	
2741	'Declaration' on scroll; *mm.* plume; 1642-3	500	1100
2742	Bust to bottom of coin, 1643; Oxford plumes	400	850
2743	— 1644 / OX. Three Shrewsbury plumes (neater work)	*Extremely rare*	

Bristol mint, 1645
*2744	**Unite.** Somewhat as 2734; Two busts known. *mm.* Br. or Br/ plumelet.; 1645...	*Extremely rare*	
2745	**Half-unite.** Similar 1645	*Unique?*	

A nearly EF specimen fetched £16,500 in auction Mar. 1988.

Truro mint, 1642-3
2746	**Unite.** *obv.* sim. to Tower 4th bust. R. FLORENT, etc., crowned oval shield between crowned CR, *mm.* rose	*Unique*	
2747	— R. CVLTORES, etc., similar but no CR	*Extremely rare*	

Worcester mint, 1643-4
2748	**Unite.** Crude bust R. FLORENT, etc., double annulet stops, crowned oval shield, lion's paws on either side of garniture, no *mm.*.............................	12500	

Salopia (Shrewsbury) mint, 1644
2749	**Unite.** *Obv.* bust in armour. R. Cr. shield, crowned CR. *mm.* lis/-...........	*Unique?*	

Colchester besieged, 1648
2750	**Ten shillings.** Gateway of castle between CR; below OBS CO L 16 S/X 48. Uniface	*Extremely rare*	

Pontefract besieged, 1648-9. After the death of Charles I, in the name of Charles II
2751	**Unite.** DVM : SPIRO : SPERO around CR crowned. CAROLVS : SECVNDVS : 16 48, castle, OBS on l., PC above.	*Extremely rare*	

A specimen fetched £29,000 in auction in April, 1989.
2752	**Unite.** CAROL : II, etc., around HANC : DEVS, etc. R. POST : MORTEM, etc., around castle. *Octagonal*..	*Extremely rare*	

SILVER

Tower mint, under the King, 1625-42

2759

		F £	VF £
2753	**Crown.** King on horseback with raised sword. 1a. Horse caparisoned with plume on head and crupper. R. Square-topped shield over long cross fourchee; *mm.* 105, 10	150	450
2754	— 1b. Similar, but plume over shield, no cross; *mm.* 105, 10, 71	400	900
2755	— 2a. Smaller horse, plume on hd. only, cross on housings, king holds sword on shoulder. R. Oval garnished shield over cross fourchee, CR above; *mm.* harp	150	400
2756	— 2b^1. — — plume divides CR, no cross; *mm.* 101, 35	175	450
2757	— 2b^2. — — with cross; *mm.* harp	250	650
2758	— 3a. Horse without caparisons. R. Oval shield without CR; *mm.* 60-23	140	330
2759	— 3b. — — plume over shield; *mm.* 107, 75, 123	185	450
2760	'Briot' horse with ground-line; *mm.* 119b	*Three known?*	

2762

		F £	VF £
2761	**Halfcrown.** As 2753. 1a^1. Rose on housings, ground-line; *mm.* lis	90	260
2761A	— Similar, but no rose on housings; *mm.* lis	*Very rare*	
2762	— 1a^2. Similar, but no rose or ground-line; *mm.* 105 (10 over 105)	90	275
2763	1a^3. As last but clumsier horse and shield not over cross; *mm.* 10-96, 10 over lis	60	160
2763A	— Similar but only slight garnishing to shield; *mm.* 10, 71	60	160
2764	— 1a^4. — — with ground-line; *mm.* lis	400	900

		F	VF
2765	— 1b. —— plume over shield; *mm*. 105, 10	350	850
2765A	Similar but only slight garnishing; *mm*. 96-57	350	850
2766	— 2/1b. As 2755 but rose on housings. R. As last; *mm*. heart, plume	*Extremely rare*	
2767	— 2a. As 2755. R. Flattened oval garnished shield without cross; *mm*. 101/ 35 plume, rose, (CR above, divided by rose (rare), lis over rose lis)........	60	125
2768	— 2b. Similar, but large plume between the CR; *mm*. 101, 35	125	300
2769	— 2c. As 2a, but differently garnished oval shield with CR at sides; *mm*. harp, portcullis, 107/87	40	110
2770	— 2d. Similar, but with plume over shield; *mm*. harp	250	600
2770A	3/2 mule, *mm*. portcullis	*Extremely rare*	

2771   2775

2771	— 3a¹. No caparisons on horse, upright sword, scarf flies out from waist. R. Round garnished shield, no CR; *mm*. 60-119a, 60/75	30	90
2772	— 3b. —— plume over shield; *mm*. 107-123	70	175
2773	— 3a². — cloak flies from king's shoulder; R. Shields vary; *mm*. 123-23, 119b, 119b over 119a	30	90
2774	———— rough ground beneath horse; R. Shields vary; *mm*. 119a, 23, 119b	30	100
2775	— 4. Foreshortened horse, mane before chest, tail between legs; *mm*. 23, 119b	25	100

2776   2776A

Most late Tower halfcrowns have irregular flans.

2776	**Shilling**. l. Bust in ruff, high crown, jewelled arches. R. Square-topped shield over cross fourchee; *mm*. lis, (normal weight 92 3/4 grs, 10)	45	125
2776A	Similar but larger crown, plain inner arch; *mm*. 105, 10	40	115
2777	Similar but light weight (81 33/47 grs.); *mm*. 10	75	200
2778	— 1b¹. As 2776A, but plume over shield, no cross; *mm*. 105, 10	125	300
2779	— 1a. Bust in ruff and armour concealed by scarf. R. As 2776; 10-71	30	90
2780	———— light weight; *mm*. cross Calvary (often extremely small XII)	75	200
2781	— 1b². As 2779, but plume over shield, no cross; *mm*. 10-101 (five bust varieties)	50	150
2781A	—— light weight 1b² *mm*. 10	100	250

		F	VF
		£	£
2782	— 1b³, — — — cross; *mm.* negro's head..	350	750
2783	— 2a. More armour visible. R. Oval shield, CR above; *mm.* 88, 101, over 88/101	25	80
2784	— 2b. — — plume over shield; *mm.* 101, 35, 101 over 88/101	100	300
2785	— 3¹. Bust with lace collar, (six bust varieties). R. Flattish oval shield, CR at sides; *mm.* harp, portcullis..	25	75
2786	— 3². — — plume over shield; *mm.* harp (three bust varieties)..............	200	450
2787	— 3a. — no inner circles, rounder shield without CR; *mm.* 60-123 (five bust varieties)..	20	70
2788	— 3b. — — plume over shield; *mm.* 60-123..	50	115

| 2787 | 2791 | 2793 |

2789	— 4¹. Large Aberystwyth bust, medium or small XII. R. Square-topped shield over cross fleury; *mm.* tun, 51 over 123 (obv.) small neat cross ends	50	125
2790	— 4¹. var. Similar, but rounder shoulders, large XII; *mm.* 57, 119a, (cross ends vary)..	20	65
2791	— 4². Smaller Aberystwyth bust with small double-arched crown, small XII; *mm.* tun, small neat cross ends, large XII (with 57).........................	20	65
2792	— 4³. — single-arches, large XII; *mm.* 123, 57, 119a, 119b (cross ends vary)	20	65
2793	— 4⁴. Older (Briot's style) bust, very pointed beard; *mm.* 119a-119b	20	60
2793A	— *Obv.* as last. R. As Briots hammered issue; lozenge stops; *mm.* Δ		*Rare*

| 2797 | 2799 | 2802 |

2794	**Sixpence**. 1. As 2776, but dated 1625-6; *mm.* 105, 10 (large bust *mm.* 10 noted, lightweight?)	45	150
2795	— 1a¹. As 2779, but dated 1625-9; *mm.* 10-88 (busts vary)....................	50	175
2796	— 1a². — no cross, 1630; *mm.* 88, 101	75	250
2797	— 2a. As 2783, no date; *mm.* plume, rose	40	135
2798	— 2b. — plume dividing CR; *mm.* plume, rose, plume/rose....................	60	175
2799	— 3. As 2785; *mm.* harp, portcullis (busts and crowns vary).................	35	135
2799A	— 3. As above but no CR *mm.* portcullis		*Rare*

	F	VF
	£	£

2800	**Sixpence.** — 3a. — no inner circles; *mm.* 60-123 (busts and crowns vary)	25	100
2801	— 4[1]. As first Aberystwyth sixpence, double-arch crown, small VI. R. Square-topped shield over cross; *mm.* tun	25	90
2801A	— 4[1.] Similar but lyre cross ends on *rev*, *mm.* tun	50	75
2802	— 4[1]. var. — similar, but large VI; *mm.* tun, anchor................................	30	100
2803	— 4[2]. Second Aberystwyth bust, single-arched crown; *mm.* 57, 119a.....	20	85
2804	— 4[2]. larger bust, *mm.* 119a..	45	125
2805	— 4[3]. Older (Briot's style) bust; *mm.* 119a-119b (moline cross ends).....	20	95

2806   2808   2818

2806	**Halfgroat**. 1. Crowned rose type; *mm.* 105-96, 105/-	25	85
2807	— 1a. —— without inner circles on one or both sides; *mm.* 96-101, 105, 105/-	10	30
2808	— 2a. King's 2nd bust in ruff and mantle. R. Oval shield; *mm.* plume, rose	10	30
2809	— 2b. Similar, but with plume over shield; *mm.* plume, rose, plume/-	22	55
2809A	—— 2a Var. 3rd bust, with more armour. R. As last; *mm.* plume, rose..	10	25
2809B	—— Sim. but plume over shield; *mm.* 101...	25	50
2810	— 3[1]. Bust with lace collar. R. Oval shield between CR; no inner circles; *mm.* rose harp, crown, portcullis	10	35
2811	— 3[2]-4. —— inner circles sometimes only on one side; *mm.* harp, portcullis	10	35
2814	— 3[5]. —— no CR, inner circles; *mm.* portcullis	10	35
2815	— 3[6]. —— inner circles on *obv.*; *mm.* portcullis....................................	10	35
2816	— 3a[1]. — R. Rounder shield, different garniture, no i.cs.; *mm.* 60-119a.	10	35
2817	— 3a[2]. —— inner circles on *obv.*; *mm.* triangle	10	35
2818	— 3a[3]. —— inner circles both sides; *mm.* 119a-119b..........................	10	35
2819	— 3a[4]. Aberystwyth bust, no inner circles; *mm.* anchor......................	15	40
2820	— 3a[5]. — inner circle on *rev.*; *mm.* anchor	15	40
2821	— 3a[6]. Very small bust, no inner circles; *mm.* anchor...........................	15	40

2822   2828   2837

2822	**Penny**. 1. Rose each side; i.cs.; *mm.* 96, :/lis, lis/:, one or two pellets, lis	10	30
2823	— 1a. — no i.cs.; *mm.* lis, one or two pellets, anchor	10	30
2824	— 1b. — i.c. on *rev.*; *mm.* negro's head/two pellets............................	12	35
2825	— 2. Bust in ruff and mantle. R. Oval shield; i.cs.; *mm.* plume, plume/rose, rose	12	35
2826	— 2[1]. —— no i.cs.; *mm.* plume, rose	15	40
2827	— 2a[1]. More armour visible; no i.cs.; *mm.* plume, rose, plume/rose.......	12	30
2828	— 2a[2]. — i.c. on *obv.*; *mm.* plume, rose, plume over rose	15	40
2829	— 2a[3]. — i.cs. both sides; *mm.* plume, rose	12	35
2830	— 2a[4]. — i.c. on *rev.*; *mm.* rose over plume....................................	20	55

	F	VF
	£	£

2831	— 3¹. Bust in lace collar. R. CR at sides of shield; no i.cs.; *mm.* harp, one or two pellets. ··/harp (also *obv.* i.c. *mm.* harp)	12	30
2832	— 3². — similar but no CR; *mm.* 87, 107, 107/··, none	12	35
2833	— 3³. — — i.c. on *obv.*; *mm.* harp,··,	12	35
2834	— 3⁴. — — i.c. on *rev.*; *mm.* harp	12	35
2835	— 3a¹. — similar, but shield almost round and with scroll garniture; no i.cs.; *mm.* bell, triangle, one to four pellets, none, bell/··	10	25
2835A	— 3a¹ variety — i.c. on *obv.*, *rev.* or both sides; *mm.* triangle/two pellets, Δ,··,	15	35
2836	— 3a³. Aberystwyth bust; i.c. on *obv.* or none; *mm.* one or two pellets or none, or mule of these *mms.*	13	25
2837	**Halfpenny**. Rose each side; no legend or *mm.*	10	30

Many small denominations have uneven irregular flans.

Tower mint, under Parliament, 1642-8. All Charles I type

2838	**Crown**. 4. Foreshortened horse; *mm.* (P) to sun	180	400
2839	— 5. Tall spirited horse; *mm.* sun	200	500
2840	**Halfcrown**. 3a³. As 2773, but coarse work; *mm.* (P) to sun, 81/120	25	85
2841	— 4. Foreshortened horse; *mm.* (P)	125	275
2842	— 5. Tall horse; *mm.* sun, sceptre	40	125
2843	**Shilling**. 4⁴. Briot style bust, *mm,* (P) (R), coarse work; *mm.* eye, sun	30	100

2844   2845A

2844	— 4⁵. Long narrow coarse bust; *mm.* sun, sceptre	35	100
2845	— 4⁶. Short bust with narrow crown; *mm.* sceptre	35	120
2845A	— — Short broad bust, as illus., broader crown; *mm.* sceptre	35	120
2846	**Sixpence**. 4³. Briot style bust; *mm.* (P) to sun	50	125
2847	— 4⁴. Late Aberystwyth bust modified; *mm.* (R) to sceptre	45	115
2848	— 4⁵. Squat bust of crude style; *mm.* sun over eye	120	275
2849	**Halfgroat**. 3a³. Sim. to 2818; *mm.* (P) to eye, sceptre, 98/119b	20	55
2850	— 3a⁷. Older, shorter bust, pointed beard; *mm.* eye to sceptre	18	45
2851	**Penny**. 3a². Older bust; *mm.* pellets, i.c. on *obv.* only	18	50

Nicholas Briot's coinage, 1631-9
  First milled issue, 1631-2

2852	**Crown**. King on horseback. R. Crowned shield between CR crowned; *mm.* flower and B / B	250	600

		F	*VF*
		£	£
2853	**Halfcrown**. Similar...	175	425
2854	**Shilling**. Briot's early bust with falling lace collar. R. Square-topped shield over long cross fourchee; R. Legend starts at top or bottom *mm.* flower and B/B, B...	100	275
2855	**Sixpence**. Similar, but VI behind bust; *mm.* flower and B/B, flower and B/-	55	140

2847   2855   2856

2856	**Halfgroat**. Briot's bust, B below, II behind. R. IVSTITIA, etc., square-topped shield over long cross fourchee...	30	60
2856A	Pattern halfgroat. Uncrowned bust in ruff r. R. crowned, interlocked Cs. (North 2687). (Included because of its relatively regular appearance.)....	35	65
2857	**Penny**. Similar, but I behind bust, no B; position of legend may vary....	30	65

Second milled issue, 1638-9

2858   2859

2858	**Halfcrown**. As 2853, but *mm.* anchor and B...	150	375
2859	**Shilling**. Briot's late bust, the falling lace collar is plain with broad lace border, no scarf. R. As 2854 but cross only to inner circle; *mm.* anchor and B, anchor or muled...	50	130
2860	**Sixpence**. Similar, but VI; *mm.* 57, anchor and mullet/anchor................	30	75

The two last often exhibit flan reduction marks.

Briot's hammered issue, 1638-9

| 2861 | **Halfcrown**. King on Briot's style horse with ground line. R. Square-topped shield; *mm.* anchor, triangle over anchor, also muled with Tower *rev.*.... | 450 | 1050 |
| 2862 | **Shilling**. Sim. to 2859; R. Square-topped shield over short cross fleury; usually *mm.* triangle, over anchor. Each *mm.* alone is very rare, also muled with Tower *obv.* or *rev.* .... | 325 | 750 |

Provincial and Civil War issues, 1638-49

York mint, 1643-4. *Mm.* lion

		F £	VF £
2863	**Halfcrown**. 1. Ground-line below horse. R. Square-topped shield between CR	150	450
2864	— 2. — R. Oval shield as Tower 3a, groundline grass or dotted	135	375
2865	— 3. No ground-line. R. Similar	125	350
2866	*— 4. As last, but EBOR below horse with head held low. Base metal, often very base	110	300
2867	— 5. Tall horse, mane in front of chest, EBOR below. R. Crowned square-topped shield between CR, floral spray in legend	90	250
2868	— 6. As last, but shield is oval, garnished (*rev.* detail variations)	80	210

2868   2870/2

		F £	VF £
2869	— 7. Similar, but horse's tail shows between legs. R. Shield as last, but with lion's skin garniture, no CR or floral spray	70	190
2870	**Shilling**. 1. Bust in scalloped lace collar 3¹. R. EBOR above square-topped shield over cross fleury	60	140
2871	— 2. Similar, but bust in plain armour, mantle; coarse work	70	175
2872	— 3. *Obv.* as 2870. — R. EBOR below oval shield	70	175
2873	— 4. — Similar, but crowned oval shield (*obv.* finer style)	60	140
2874	— 5. — As last, but lion's skin garniture	60	140

2876   2877

		F £	VF £
2875	**Sixpence**. *Obv.* Sim. to 2870. Crowned oval shield	160	425
2876	— —CR at sides	135	325
2877	**Threepence**. As type 4 shilling, but III behind bust. R. As 2870	30	70

These pieces are contemporary forgeries (BNJ1984).

Aberystwyth mint, 1638/9-42. *Mm.* book.
Plume 1=with coronet and band. Plume 2=with coronet only

		F £	*VF* £
2878	**Halfcrown**. Horseman similar to 2773, but plume 2 behind. R. Oval garnished shield with large plume above. *Obv.* plume 2, *rev.* plume 1....	300	750
2879	— Similar to 2774, plume 1 behind King, ground below horse. *Obv.* squat plume 1, *rev.* plume 1.................	350	850
2880	As 2773 but more spirited horse, no ground. FRAN ET HIB, plume 2/1	375	900
2881	**Shilling**. Bust with large square lace collar, plume 2 before, small XII. R. As before. No inner circles	150	425
2882	— inner circle on *rev.*	125	375
2883	As 2881, but large plume 1 or 2, large XII, inner circles..........	125	375
2884	As last, but small narrow head, square lace collar, large or square plume	135	400
2885	Small Briot style face, small crown, plume 2	175	500

2882   2884

2886

2885A	**Sixpence**. *Obv.* as Tower bust 3a, plume before. R. as 2889; *mm.* book (*obv.* only)		*Rare*
2886	Somewhat as 2881, but double-arched crown, small VI; no inner circles, or with rev. inner circle as 2889	130	325
2887	Similar to 2886, but single arched crown, plume 2, inner circle *obv.* Large VI	165	375
2888	Similar, but with inner circles both sides.......	130	325
2889	— — *Rev.* with small squat-shaped plume above, sometimes no *rev. mm.*	135	325
2890	Bust as the first Oxford sixpence; with crown cutting inner circle..........	190	410

2891   2894   2895-9

2891	**Groat**. Large bust, lace collar, no armour on shoulder. Crown breaks or touches inner circle. R. Shield, plume 1 or 2	20	45
2892	— Similar, armour on shoulder, shorter collar. R. Similar......	30	60
2893	— Smaller, neater bust well within circle. R. Similar	20	45

Aberystwyth, *continued*   F   VF
                                                                    £   £

2894	**Threepence**. Small bust, large or small plume 2 before. R. Shield, plume 1 or 2 above, *obv.* legend variations	20	45
2895-9	— Similar, but squat pl. on *obv.*, crown cuts i.c. R. Pl. 2, *Obv.* legend variations	25	55
2900	**Halfgroat**. Bust as Tower type 3. R. Large plume. No inner circles, *mm.* pellet/book,book	55	115
2900A	Bust as 2886. R. As last, no inner circle	45	135
2901	Bust with round lace collar; single arch crown, inner circles, colon stops	35	85
2902	After Briot's bust, square lace collar: inner circles	40	100

2900A   2905   2907

2903	**Penny**. As 2901; CARO; no inner circles	65	145
2904	As 2901; CARO; inner circles	65	145
2905	As last but reads CAROLVS; inner circles	60	135
2906	*Obv.* similar to 2890, tall narrow bust, crown touches inner circle	70	175
2907	**Halfpenny**. No legend. O. Rose. R. Plume	100	250

Aberystwyth-Furnace mint, 1648/9. *Mm.* crown

2908	**Halfcrown**. King on horseback. R. Sim. to 2878	1000	2000
2909	**Shilling**. Aberystwyth type, but *mm.* crown	*Extremely rare*	
2910	**Sixpence**. Similar	*Extremely rare*	

2911   2913

2911	**Groat**. Similar	125	250
2912	**Threepence**. Similar	160	325
2913	**Halfgroat**. Similar. R. Large plume	185	425
2914	**Penny**. Similar	450	900

Uncertain mint (? Hereford)

2915   2930/1

	Fair	Fine
2915 **Halfcrown**. As illustration, dated 1645 or undated	600	1500
2915A— Scarf with long sash ends. CH below horse. R. Oval shield 1644		Rare
2915B— R. Crowned oval shield, lion paws		Rare

Shrewsbury mint, 1642. Plume without band used as *mm.* or in field.

	F £	VF £
2917 **Pound**. King on horseback, plume behind, similar to Tower grp. 3 crowns. R. Declaration between two straight lines, XX and three Shrewsbury plumes above, 1642 below; *mm.* pellets, pellets/-	800	2250
2918 Similar, but Shrewsbury horse walking over pile of arms; no *mm.*, pellets	750	1750
2919 As last, but cannon amongst arms and only single plume and XX above Declaration, no *mm.*	1050	2600
2920 **Half-pound**. As 2917, but X; *mm.* pellets	350	850
2921 Similar, but only two plumes on *rev.*; *mm.*, pellets	400	900
2922 Shrewsbury horseman with ground-line, three plumes on *rev.*; *mm.*, none, pellets/-	325	850
2923 — with cannon and arms or arms below horse; *mm.* pellets/-	300	800
2924 — no cannon in arms, no plume in *obv.* field; *mm.* plume/pellets, plume/-	250	600

2926

2925 **Crown**. Aberystwyth horseman, no ground line	Extremely rare	
2926 Shrewsbury horseman with ground-line; *mm.* -/pellets, pellets/-, none	250	550
2927 **Halfcrown**. *O*. From Aberystwyth die; (S2880); *mm.* book. R. Single plume above Declaration, 1642	Extremely rare	

	F	VF
	£	£

2928 Sim. to Aberystwyth die, fat plume behind. R. Three plumes above
Declaration; *mm.* pellets, pellets/- 165 400
2929 Shrewsbury horseman. R. As 2927, single plume, no *mm* 210 525
2930 — R. 2: plume; 6, above Declaration.. 500 1100
2931 — with ground-line. R. Similar 450 1000
2932 — — R. As 2927, single plume 200 500
2933 — — R. Three plumes above Declaration; *mm.* none or pellets 135 300
2933A *Obv.* as last. R. Aberystwyth die, plume over shield; *mm.* -/book............ *Rare*
2934 — — — no plume behind king; *mm.* plume/pellets 150 325
2935 **Shilling**. *O*. From Aberystwyth die; S2885 *mm.* book. R. Declaration type 400 950
2936 *O*. From Shrewsbury die. R. Similar.. 450 1050

Oxford mint, 1642/3-6. *Mm.* usually plume with band, except on the smaller denominations when
it is lis or pellets. There were so many dies used at this mint that we can give only a selection of the
more easily identifiable varieties.

2937 **Pound**. Large horseman over arms, no exergual line, fine workmanship. R.
Three Shrewsbury plumes and XX above Declaration, 1642 below; *mm.*
plume/pellets 1050 2850

2937

2938 — Similar, but three Oxford plumes, 1643; *mm.* as last 1050 2900
2939 Shrewsbury horseman trampling on arms, exergual line. R. As last, 1642 650 2350
2940 — — cannon amongst arms, 1642-3; *mm.* similar 600 1750
2941 — as last but exergue is chequered, 1642; *mm.* similar 750 2350
2942 Briot's horseman, 1643; *mm.* similar 1500 4500
2943 *O*. As 2937. R. Declaration in cartouche, single large plume above, 1644
OX below 1500 4500
2944 **Half-pound**. As next. R. Shrewsbury die, 1642; *mm.* plume/- 225 500
2945 Oxford dies both sides, 1642-3; *mm.* plume/pellets 200 400
2946 **Crown**. *O*. Shrewsbury die with ground-line. R. As last but V, 1642-3 .. 225 550
2947 Oxford horseman with grass below, 1643 .... 325 800
2948 By Rawlins. King riding over a view of the city. R. Floral scrolls above and
below Declaration, 1644 / OXON below (Beware forgeries!) .... *Extremely rare*
An extremely fine specimen sold at auction in May, 1989 for £24,750.

Oxford Silver, *continued*

		F £	VF £
2949	**Halfcrown**. *O*. From Shrewsbury die S2931 or 2934. R. 3 Ox plumes over `Dec' 1642	135	375
2950	Ox plume, Shrewsbury horse. R. From Shrewsbury die, 1642	105	275
2951	Both Oxford dies, but Shrewsbury type horse, ground-line, 1642	70	200
2952	—— without ground-line, 1642	90	250
2953	Oxford type horse, ground-line, 1643	75	215

2951   2954

2954	— without ground-line, 1643	70	190
2954A	—— R. 3 Shrewsbury plumes, 1642	100	300
2955	Briot's horse, grass below, 1643, 1643 / OX below date	80	225
2956	—— large central plume, 1643, 16 43 / OX, 1644 / OX	90	275
2957	— lumpy ground, 1643, 1643 / OX	80	210
2958	—— large central plume, 1643-4 / OX	80	225
2959	— plain ground, 1644- 5 / OX	80	225
2960	—— large central plume, 1644 / OX	80	225
2960A	Similar. but 2 very small Shrewsbury plumes at sides	100	300
2961	——— Similar, but large date in script	105	325
2962	Rocky ground, two small plumes at date, 1644 / OX	225	500
2963	Large horse (as Briot's, but clumsier), plain ground, 1644-5 / OX	90	275
2964	— lumpy ground, 1644-5 / OX	90	275
2965	—— large central plume, 1644 / OX	90	275
2966	— pebbly ground, 1645-6 / OX	90	275
2967	—— pellets or annulets by plumes and at date, 1645-6 / OX	90	275
2968	— grass below, 1645-6 / OX	90	300
2969	—— rosettes by plumes and at date, 1645 / OX	110	400
2970	**Shilling**. *O*. From Shrewsbury die. R. Declaration type, 1642	100	275
2971	Both Oxford dies. Small bust, 1642-3	60	150
2972	Similar, but coarser work, 1643	60	150
2973	Large bust of fine work, 1643	60	150
2974	— 1644-6 / OX	75	200
2974A	—— 1644 OX. Large date in script	80	175
2975	Bust with bent crown, 1643	90	250
2976	— 1644 / OX	90	250
2977	Rawlins' dies. Fine bust with R on truncation, 1644	135	350
2978	—— 1644 / OX	150	375
2979	Small size, 1646, annulets or pellets at date	105	275

2961   2974

	F	VF
	£	£

2980 **Sixpence**. *O*. Aberystwyth die S2890. R. With three Oxford plumes, 1642-
3; *mm*. book/- 110 250
2981 — R. With three Shrewsbury plumes, 1643; *mm*. book/- 110 240
2982 — R. With Shrewsbury plume and two lis, 1644 / OX; *mm*. book/ - .... *Extremely rare*

2980   2985

2983 **Groat**. *O*. Aberystwyth die S2892. R. As 2985.................................... 40 110
2984 As last but three plumes above Declaration... 75 200
2985 As illustration, with lion's head on shoulder 35 100
2885A *Obv*. as last R. 3 Shrewsbury plumes, 1644 / OX 75 170
2986 Large bust reaching to top of coin. R. As 2985 .... 60 150
2987 Large bust to bottom of coin, lion's head on shoulder, legend starts at
bottom l. R. As last... 70 160
2988 Rawlins' die; similar, but no i.c., and with R on shoulder. R. As last 70 160
2989 *O*. As 2985. R. Large single plume and scroll above Declaration, 1645.. 60 140
2990 *O*. As 2987. R. As last... 60 140
2991 *O*. As 2988. R. Large single plume above Declaration, which is in
cartouche, 1645-6 (over 5) 80 200
2992 **Threepence**. *O*. Aberystwyth die; *mm*. book R. Declaration type,
1644 / OX... 50 125
2993 Rawlins' die, R below shoulder; *mm*. lis. R. Aberystwyth die with oval
shield; *mm*. book 45 125
2994 — R. Declaration type, three lis above, 1644 below; *mm*. lis/- 30 90
2995 — Similar, without the R, 1646 (over 1644); no *mm*. 30 100
2996 **Halfgroat**. R. Aberystwyth type with large plume.................................. 75 175
2997 — R. Declaration type, 1644 / OX; *mm*. cross 110 200

2991   2995   2999

Oxford Silver, *continued.*

		F	VF
		£	£
2998	**Penny**. *O*. Aberystwyth die S2904; *mm.* book. R. Type, small plume	85	200
2999	As 2906 R. Type, large plume	85	200
3000	— Rawlins' die with R. R. Type, small plume	85	200
3001	— Wider bust similar to the halfgroat. R. Similar	100	275
3002	— — R. Declaration type, 1644	350	800

Bristol mint, 1643-5. Mm. usually plume or Br., except on small denominations

		F	VF
3003	**Halfcrown**. *O*. Oxford die with or without ground-line. R. Declaration, three Bristol plumes above, 1643 below....................................	80	250
3004	— Obv. as above. R as above, but *mm.* Br. 1643	70	240
3005	King wears unusual flat crown, *obv. mm.* acorn? between four pellets. R. As 3003, 1643	85	260
3006	— Obv. as above. R as 3004 but 1643-4	85	225
3007	Shrewsbury plume behind king. R. As last..	65	165
3008	— Obv. as above. R as 3004 but Br below date instead of as *mm* . 1644	70	220
3009	— Obv. as 3007 but Br below horse. R as above but 1644-5 75	175	
3010	— Obv. as above. R as 3004 but Br. as *mm.* as well as 1644-5	75	210

3009   3024

3012   3014   3015   3017

		F	VF
3011	**Shilling**. *O*. Oxford die. R. Declaration, 1643, 3 crude plumes above, no *mm.*	80	225
3012	— — R Similar, but *mm.* Br., 1643-4, less crude plumes.........................	80	225
3013	—Obv. Coarse bust. R. As 3011, no *mm.*	90	275
3014	— — Coarse bust, R. as 3012, *mm.* Br, but 1644	80	225
3015	Obv. Bust of good style, plumelet before face. R. As 3012 *mm.* Br. but 1644-5	80	225
3016	— — R.as 3012, 1644, but Br below date instead of *mm*..........................	75	215
3016A	—Obv. as 3015. R as 3012, 1644 but plume and plumelet either side	90	225
3017	—Obv. Taller bust with high crown, no plumelets before, *mm.* Br. on its side. R As 3016 but 3 even plumes, Br.below 1644-5	90	275
3018	—Obv. As 3017 but no *mm.* R as above but *mm..* no Br. below 1644-5..	80	215
3018A	—Obv. As 3018. R as above but plume and plumelets, 1645	90	250

		F	VF
		£	£
3019	**Sixpence.** Small bust, nothing before. R. Declaration, 1643; *mm.* ./Br,...	140	500
3020	Fine style bust. Plumelet before face, 1644; *mm.* ./Br. (on its side)	125	325
3021	**Groat.** Bust l. R. Declaration, 1644...	120	275
3022	— Plumelet before face, 1644..	100	250
3023	— Br. below date, 1644	90	225
3024	**Threepence.** *O.* As 2992. Aberystwyth die; *mm.* book. R. Declaration, 1644	110	325
3025	Bristol die, plume before face, no *mm.*, 1644	125	400
3026	**Halfgroat.** Br. in place of date below Declaration	200	425
3027	**Penny.** Similar bust, I behind. R. Large plume with bands.....................	250	600

Late `Declaration' issues, 1645-6

(Previously given as Lundy Island and/or Appledore and Barnstaple/Bideford, it seems likely that coins marked A, 1645 may be Ashby de la Zouch and the coins marked B or with plumes may be Bridgnorth on Severn.)

		F	VF
3028	**Halfcrown.** A below horse and date and as *rev. mm.* 1645.....................	700	2000
3029	Similar but *rev.* from altered Bristol die (i.e. the A's are over Br.)	525	1500
3030	As 3028 but without A below date 1645...	475	1450
3031	A below horse and as *rev. mm.* Scroll above Declaration, B below 1646	*Extremely rare*	
3032	Plumelet below horse struck over A. R. *Mm.* Shrewsbury plumes; scroll above Declaration, 1646	300	850
3033	— Similar, but plumelet below date	350	1000
3034	**Shilling.** Crowned bust l., *mm.* plume. R. Declaration type; *mm.* A and A below 1645..	350	850
3035	— Similar, but plumelet before face	350	850
3036	Bristol Obv. die, no plumelet, similar to 3016B, *mm.* Br. R Scroll over 'Declaration' 1646, *mm.* plume	*Extremely rare*	
3036A	—. O. as above but *mm.* plume over Br., plume before face. R as above, *mm.* plume or	150	325
3037	Shrewsbury plume before face. R. As last but *mm.* pellet 1646.	135	325

3033   3039

		F	VF
3038	**Sixpence.** *O.* Plumelet before face; *mm.* A; R. 1645, 3 plumelets over 'Dec'	175	400
3039	*O.* Large Shrewsbury plume before face; *mm.* B. R. Scroll above Declaration, 1646, Shrewsbury plume and two plume plumelets	65	140
3040	**Groat.** As 3038	*Extremely rare*	
3041	Somewhat similar, but *obv. mm.* plumelet; 1646......................................	75	165
3042	**Threepence.** Somewhat as last but only single plumelet above Declaration, no line below, 1645; no *mm.*...	100	275
3043	— Scroll in place of line above, 1646 below	65	150
3044	**Halfgroat.** Bust l., II behind. R. Large plume with bands dividing 1646; no *mm.*..	250	600

The penny listed under Bristol may belong to this series. It has the same reverse plume punch.

Truro mint, 1642-3. *Mm.* rose

		F	VF
		£	£

3045 **Half-pound**. King on horseback, face turned frontwards, sash in large bow.
R. CHRISTO, etc., round garnished shield. Struck from crown dies on
thick flan .... *Extremely rare*

3046 **Crown**. Similar type 135   325

3047 — Shield garnished with twelve even scrolls 160   375

3048 King's face in pro file, sash flies out in 2 ends, well-shaped flan, finer
workmanship 135   325

3044   3049

3049 **Halfcrown**. King on spirited horse galloping over arms. R. Oval garnished
shield, 1642 in cartouche below 900   3000

3050 Similar, but no arms. R. Oblong shield, CR at sides 700   2500

3051 Galloping horse, king holds sword. R. Similar 650   2300

3052 — R. Similar, but CR above 600   1900

3053 Trotting horse. R. Similar, but CR at sides 300   750

3054 Walking horse, king's head in profile. R. Similar 275   725

3055 — R. Similar, but CR above 325   850

3055A Similar, but groundline below horse. R. Similar, *mm.* bugle/- .... *Extremely rare*

3056 **Shilling**. Small bust of good style. R. Oblong shield .... *Extremely rare*

3057 Larger bust with longer hair. R. Round shield with eight even scrolls..... 600   1500

3058 — R. Oval shield with CR at sides 550   1400

3059 Normal bust with lank hair. R. As last... 500   1100

3060 — R. As 3057.. 600   1500

3061 — R. Round shield with six scrolls... 350   850

Truro or Exeter mint. *Mm.* rose

3064   3067-9

		F £	VF £
3062	**Halfcrown**. King on horseback, sash tied in bow. R. Oblong shield with CR at sides	110	300
3063	— R. Round shield with eight even scrolls	80	200
3064	— R. Round shield with six scrolls	70	175
3064A	— Angular garnish of triple lines to oblong shield	*Extremely rare*	
3065	—King's sash flies out behind. horse with twisted tail as 3080 R.. As 3063	105	275
3066	— R. As 3064A	*Extremely rare*	
3067	Briot's horse with ground-line. as 3079 R. As 3063	105	275
3068	— R. As 3066		*Unique*
3069	— R. As 3064	105	275

Exeter mint, 1643-6. *Mm.* rose except where stated

3070	**Crown**. As 3046, but 1644 divided by *rev. mm.*	125	275
3071	Similar, but 1644 to l. of *mm.*	110	240
3072	Similar, but 1645 and *rev. mm.* EX	125	275
3073	King's sash in two loose ends; *mm.* castle/rose, 1645		*rare*
3074	— *mm.* castle/EX, 1645	150	325
3075	— *mm.* castle, 1645	100	225
3076	**Halfcrown**. As 3049, but 1644-5 in legend	*Extremely rare*	
3077	Similar, but *rev. mm.* castle, 1645		*Unique*
3078	Short portly figure, leaning backwards on ill-proportioned horse, 1644, 16 rose 44	175	450
3079	Briot's horse and lumpy ground as 3067-9; illustration 1644	125	350

3080   3085/6

3080	Horse with twisted tail, obv. as 3065; 1644-5	120	325
3081	— R. *Mm.* castle, 1645	160	450
3082	— R. *Mm.* EX, 1645	160	450
3083	— R. Declaration type; *mm.* EX. 1644-5	1000	2100
3084	— — — EX also below 1644	900	1750

Larger denominations often have irregular flans.

3085	**Shilling**. As 3061. 1644, 1645, *mm.* rose (may be before, after or middle of date)	125	265
3086	— R. Declaration type, 1645	400	1250
3087	**Sixpence**. Sim. to 3085, 1644, 16 rose 44	135	375
3088	**Groat**. Somewhat similar but 1644 at beginning of *obv.* legend	55	125
3089	**Threepence**. As illustration, 1644	60	140
3090	**Halfgroat**. Similar, but II. R. Oval shield, 1644	80	275
3091	— R. Large rose, 1644	100	300
3092	**Penny**. As last but I behind head	175	425

208 CHARLES 1

3089 3091

Worcester mint, 1643-4

3096

		F	VF
		£	£

3093 **Halfcrown**. King on horseback l., W below; *mm.* two lions. R. Declaration
type 1644; *mm.* pellets 350 900
3094 — R. Square-topped shield; *mm.* helmet, castle 225 850
3095 — R. Oval shield; *mm.* helmet.. 275 825
3096 Similar but grass indicated; *mm.* castle. R. Square-topped shield; *mm.*
helmet or pellets. (Illustrated above).. 225 700
3097 — R. Oval draped shield, lis or lions in legend 250 775
3098 — R. Oval shield CR at sides, roses in legend 275 850
3099 — R. FLORENT etc., oval garnished shield with lion's paws each side . 350 950
3100 Tall king, no W or *mm.* R. Oval shield, lis, roses, lions or stars in legend 250 700
3101 — R. Square-topped shield; *mm.* helmet 275 900
3102 — R. FLORENT, etc., oval shield; no *mm.*.. 350 950
3103 Briot type horse, sword slopes forward, ground-line. R. Oval shield, roses
in legend; *mm.* 91v, 105, none (combinations) 250 850
3104 — Similar, but CR at sides, 91v/- 275 850
3105 Dumpy, portly king, crude horse. R. As 3100; *mm.* 91v, 105, none........ 225 700

3106

3106 Thin king and horse. R. Oval shield, stars in legend; *mm.* 91v, none...... 225 700

Worcester or Salopia (Shrewsbury)

	F	VF
	£	£
3107 **Shilling**. Bust of king l., adequately rendered. R. Square-topped shield; mm. castle	400	1250
3108 — R. CR above shield; mm. helmet and lion	400	1250
3109 — R. Oval shield; mm. lion, pear	375	1250

3111   3117

		F	VF
3110	**Shilling**. Bust a somewhat crude copy of last (two varieties); mm. bird, lis. R. Square-topped shield with lion's paws above and at sides; mm. boar's head, helmet	500	1400
3111	— — CR above	500	1400
3112	— R. Oval shield, lis in legend; mm. lis	475	1300
3113	— R. Round shield; mm. lis, 3 lis	525	1350
3114	Bust r.; mm. pear/-, pear/lis. R. Dr., oval shield with or without CR. (Halfcrown reverse dies)	*Extremely rare*	
3115	**Sixpence**. As 3110; mm. castle, castle/boar's hd	500	1250
3116	**Groat**. As 3112; mm. lis/helmet, rose/helmet	375	750
3117	**Threepence**. Similar; mm. lis obv.	200	425
3118	**Halfgroat**. Similar; mm. lis (O.) various (R.)	350	750

Salopia (Shrewsbury) mint, 1644

		F	VF
3119	**Halfcrown**. King on horseback l. SA below; mm. lis. R. (mm.s lis, helmet, lion rampant, none). Cr. oval shield; mm. helmet	*Extremely rare*	
3120	— R. FLORENT, etc., crowned oval shield, no mm.	*Extremely rare*	
3121	— SA erased or replaced by large pellet or cannon ball; mm. lis in legend, helmet. R. As last	1200	2750
3122	Tall horse and king, no thing below; mm. lis. R. Large round shield with crude garniture; mm. helmet	475	1100
3123	— R. Uncrowned square-topped shield with lion's paw above and at sides; mm. helmet	575	1400
3124	— R. Small crowned oval shield; mm. various	475	1100
3125	— R. As 3120	550	1300
3126	Finer work with little or no mane before horse. R. Cr. round or oval shield	500	1150
3127	Grass beneath horse. R. Similar; mm. lis or rose	650	1400
3128	Ground below horse. R. As 3120	575	1400

Hartlebury Castle (Worcs.) mint, 1646

3129

	F £	VF £

3129 **Halfcrown**. *O. Mm.* pear. R. HC (Hartlebury Castle) in garniture below shield; *mm.* three pears... 950   2250

Chester mint, 1644

3130

	F	VF
3130 **Halfcrown**. As illus. R. Oval shield; *mm.* three gerbs and sword............	375	850
3131 — Similar, but without plume or CHST; R. Cr. oval shield with lion skin; *mm.* prostrate gerb; -/cinquefoil, ˉ/.∴..	450	900
3132 — R. Crowned square-topped shield with CR at sides both crowned *rev.*; *mm.* cinquefoil......................................	500	1300
3133 As 3130, but without plume or CHST. R. Declaration type, 1644 *rev.*; *mm.* plume................................	450	1150
3133A**Shilling**. Bust l. R. Oval garnished shield; *mm.* ∴ (obv. only)	*Extremely rare*	
3133B — R. Square-topped shield; *mm.* as last	*Extremely rare*	
3133C — R . Shield over long cross	*Extremely rare*	
3134 **Threepence**. R. Square-topped shield; *mm.*-/ prostrate gerb..................	300	650

Welsh Marches mint? 1644

3135 **Halfcrown**. Crude horseman, l. R. Declaration of Bristol style divided by dotted lines, 3 plumes above, 1644 below 250   425

Carlisle besieged, 1644-5

3136 **Three shillings**. Large crown above C. R /.III. S. R. OBS . CARL / . 1645.. 1500   3200

3137 Similar but : OBS :/-: CARL :./.1645 1500   3700

3138

		F	VF
		£	£
3138	**Shilling**. As illustration..	950	2500
3139	R. Legend and date in two lines...	1000	2750

Note. *(3136-39) Round or Octagonal pieces exist.*

Newark besieged, several times 1645-6, surrendered May 1646

3140   3144

3140	**Halfcrown**. Large crown between CR ; below, XXX. R. OBS / NEWARK / 1645 or 1646	225	450
3141	**Shilling**. Similar but curious flat shaped crown, NEWARKE, 1645	200	375
3142	Similar but high arched crown, 1645	175	325
3143	— NEWARK, 1645 or 1646...	165	310
3144	**Ninepence**. As halfcrown but IX, 1645 or 1646....................................	175	380
3145	— NEWARKE, 1645..	165	350
3146	**Sixpence**. As halfcrown but VI, 1646...	150	375

Pontefract besieged, June 1648-March 1648-9

3147	**Two shillings** (lozenge shaped). DVM : SPIRO : SPERO around CR crowned. R. Castle surrounded by OBS, PC, sword and 1648.................	*Extremely rare*	
3148	**Shilling** (lozenge shaped, octagonal or round). Similar	325	775
3149	— Similar but XII or r. dividing PC	325	750

After the death of Charles I (30 Jan. 1648/9), in the name of Charles II

3149   3150

	F	VF
	£	£
3150 **Shilling** (octagonal). *O*. As last. R. CAROLVS : SECVNDVS : 1648, castle gateway with flag dividing PC, OBS on l., cannon protrudes on r..........	325	775
3151 CAROL : II : etc., around HANC : DE / VS : DEDIT 1648. R. POST : MORTEM : PATRIS : PRO : FILIO around gateway etc. as last............	325	775

Scarborough besieged, July 1644-July 1645

3165   3168

                                                     £

Type I. Castle with gateway to left, value punched below or to side

3152	**Five shillings and eightpence**	*Extremely rare*
3153	**Crown**. Similar but SC also punched..	*Extremely rare*
3154	**Three shillings and fourpence**. As 3152	*Extremely rare*
3155	**Three shillings**. Similar	*Extremely rare*
3156	**Two shillings and tenpence**. Similar...	5500

£

3157	**Halfcrown**. Similar	4750
3158	**Two shillings and fourpence**. Similar................................	*Extremely rare*
3159	**Two shillings and twopence**. Similar................................	*Extremely rare*
3160	**Two shillings**. Similar	*Extremely rare*
3161	**One shilling and ninepence**. Similar.................................	*Extremely rare*
3162	**One shilling and sixpence**. Similar	*Extremely rare*
3163	**One shilling and fourpence**. Similar.................................	*Extremely rare*
3164	**One shilling and threepence**. Similar	4000
3165	**Shilling**. As illustration...	*Extremely rare*
3166	**Sixpence**. Similar..	*Extremely rare*
3167	**Groat**. Similar	*Extremely rare*

Type II. Castle with two turrets, value punched below

3168	**Two shillings**. Two castles...	*Extremely rare*
3170	**One shilling and sixpence**. Single castle...........................	*Extremely rare*
3171	**One shilling and fourpence**. Similar.................................	4000
3172	**One shilling and threepence**. Similar	*Extremely rare*
3173	**One shilling and twopence**. Similar..................................	*Extremely rare*
3174	**One shilling and one penny**. Similar	*Extremely rare*
3175	**Shilling**. Similar...	4500
3176	**Elevenpence**. Similar	*Extremely rare*
3177	**Tenpence**. Similar	*Extremely rare*
3178	**Ninepence**. Similar..	*Extremely rare*
3179	**Sevenpence**. Similar	*Extremely rare*
3180	**Sixpence**. Similar..	*Extremely rare*

COPPER

For mintmarks see C. Wilson Peck, *English Copper, Tin and Bronze Coins in the British Museum, 1558-1958.*

3185   3191   3194

		F	VF
		£	£
3181	**Royal farthing**. 'Richmond' round, colon stops, 1a. CARO over IACO;		
	mm. on *obv*.	6	18
3182	— — 1b. CARA; *mm*. on *obv*..	60	125
3183	— — 1c. CARO; *mm*. on *obv*..	4	12
3184	— apostrophe stops. 1d. Eagle-headed harp...........................	6	18
3185	— 1e. Beaded harp..	5	15
3186	— 1f. Scroll-fronted harp, 5 jewels on circlet	10	30
3187	— 1g. — — 7 jewels on circlet	5	15
3188	Transitional issue, double-arched crowns..............................	15	45
3189	'Maltravers' round, 3a; *mm*. on *obv. only*	8	20
3190	— 3b. *Mm*. both sides..	4	12

		F	VF
		£	£
3191	— 3c. Different *mm.* either side	5	16
3192	'Richmond' oval. 4a. CARO over IACO; *mm.* both sides	15	40
3193	— — — *mm.* on *obv.*	15	40
3194	— 4b. CARO, colon stops; *mm.* on *obv.*	12	35
3195	— — — — *mm.* on *rev.*	12	35
3196	— — — — *mm.* both sides	12	35
3197	**Royal farthing.** — 4c. apostrophe stops; *mm.* rose on *obv.*	15	40
3198	— — — — *mm.* rose both sides	15	40
3199	— — — — *mm.* rose (*obv.*); scroll (*rev.*)	15	40
3200	'Maltravers' oval. 5. CAROLVS; *mm.* lis both sides	22	45

3201   3207

3201	**Rose farthing.** 1a. Double-arched crowns; double rose; sceptres within inner circle, BRIT; *mm.* on *obv.* or *rev.* or both sides, or different each side	7	20
3202	— 1b. — — sceptres just break circle, BRIT; *mm.* on *obv.* or both sides or no *mm.*	6	18
3203	— 1c. — — sceptres almost to outer circle, BRIT; *mm.*s as 3201	4	15
3204	— 1d. — — — BRI; *mm.* on *obv.* or both sides, or different each side ..4	15	
3205	Transitional mules of types 1d/2, with double and single arched crowns; *mm.* as 3204	7	20
3206	— 2. Single-arched crowns; single rose; *mm.* as 3204	3	9
3207	— 3. Sceptres below crown; *mm.* mullet	10	30

The coins struck during the Commonwealth have inscriptions in English instead of Latin which was considered to savour too much of papacy. St. George's cross and the Irish harp take the place of the royal arms. The silver halfpenny was issued for the last time.

Coins with *mm.* anchor were struck during the protectorship of Richard Cromwell.

Mintmarks

1649-57 Sun   1658-60 Anchor

GOLD

3208   3213

	F	VF
	£	£
3208 **Unite.** As illustration; *mm.* sun, 1649-57	375	700
3209 Similar, *mm.* anchor, 1658, 1660	1000	3000
3210 **Double-crown.** As illus., but X; *mm.* sun, 1649-57	300	575
3211 Similar, *mm.* anchor, 1660	1100	2500
3212 **Crown.** Similar, but V; *mm.* sun, 1649-57	250	400
3213 As illus., *mm.* anchor, 1658, 60..	900	2000

SILVER

		F	VF
3214 **Crown.** Same type; *mm.* sun, 1649, 51-4, 56		200	450
3215 **Halfcrown.** Similar; *mm.* sun, 1649, 1651-6..		100	225
3216 — *mm.* anchor, 1658-1660..	*Fair* 125	350	750
3217 **Shilling.** Similar; *mm.* sun, 1649, 1651-7..		60	125
3218 — *mm.* anchor, 1658-60..	*Fair* 100	275	550
3219 **Sixpence.** Similar; *mm.* sun, 1649, 1651-7..		60	130
3220 — *mm.* anchor, 1658-60	*Fair* 75	200	450

3221   3223

	F	VF
3221 **Halfgroat.** As illustration..	20	50
3222 **Penny.** Similar, but I above shields..	15	40
3223 **Halfpenny.** As illustration..	15	35

Patterns. All said to be only patterns, but some circulated, especially the 1656 halfcrown and the shillings. Half broads exist, but are not contemporary.

GOLD

	F £	VF £	EF £
3224 **Fifty shillings**. Head l. R. Shield, 1656. Inscribed edge			15000

3225

3225 **Broad.** (=20s.). Similar, but grained edge		1600	3750

SILVER

3227

3226 **Crown.** Bust l. R. Shield, 1658. Inscribed edge	475	900	1650
3227 **Halfcrown.** Similar, 1656	600	—	—
3227A — 1658	225	450	850
3228 **Shilling.** Similar, but grained edge, 1658	200	400	700
3229 **Sixpence.** Similar...		*Extremely rare*	

COPPER

3230

3230 **Farthing.** Dr. bust l. R. CHARITIE AND CHANGE, shield	1200	2250	—

There are also other reverses.

As there was no authorized copper coinage under the Commonwealth, towns and traders took it into their own hands to issue small change. Between 1648 and 1672 there was an enormous and very varied issue of these tokens. They were mostly farthings and halfpennies, but there were also some pennies. No collection is truly representative unless it contains at least a few. Many collectors äspecialize in those of their own town or county.

	F
	£
Price of commoner pennies	30
— — — heart shaped pennies	175
— — — round halfpennies	8
— — — octagonal halfpennies	20
— — — heart-shaped halfpennies	110
— — — square or lozenge-shaped halfpennies	125
— — — round farthings	5
— — — square farthings	75
— — — octagonal farthings	30

For further details of seventeenth-century tokens, see Trade Tokens issued in the Seventeenth Century *by* G. C. Williamson, also Seaby's British Tokens and their Values, *and* Seventeenth Century Tokens of the British Isles and their Values by Michael Dickinson, 1986.

For the first two years after the Restoration the same denominations, apart from the silver crown, were struck as were issued during the Commonwealth. In 1662 the hand hammering of coins was abandoned in favour of manufacture by the Roettiers improved mill and screw presses. As a prevention against clipping the larger coins were made with the edge inscribed DECVS ET TVTAMEN and the regnal year and the medium-sized coins were given a grained edge.

The new gold coins were current for 100s., 20s. and 10s., and they came to be called 'guineas' as the gold from which some of them were made was imported from Guinea by the Africa Company (whose badge was the Elephant and Castle). It was not until some years later that the guinea increased in value to 21s. and more. The Africa Co. badge is also found on some silver and so is the plume symbol indicating silver from the Welsh mines. The four smallest silver denominations, though known today as 'Maundy Money', were actually issued for general circulation: at this period the silver penny was probably the only coin distributed at the royal Maundy ceremonies. The smaller 'machine'-made, coins were perhaps minted later than 1662.

A good regal copper coinage was issued for the first time in 1672, but later in the reign, farthings were struck in tin (with a copper plug) in order to help the Cornish tin industry.

For the emergency issues struck in the name of Charles II in 1648/9, see the siege pieces of Pontefract listed under Charles I, nos. 3150-1.

Mintmark: Crown.

GOLD

Hammered coinage, 1660-2
  First issue. Without mark of value

3302   3305

		F	VF
		£	£
3301	**Unite** (=20s.). Type as illustration	450	1050
3302	**Double-crown.** As illustration	500	1100
3303	**Crown.** Similar	450	900

Second issue. With mark of value
3304	**Unite.** Type as illustration	400	900
3305	**Double-crown.** As illustration	400	800
3306	**Crown.** Similar	550	800

SILVER
First issue. Without inner circles or mark of value
3307	**Halfcrown.** Crowned bust, as 3308	400	900
3308	**Shilling.** Similar	125	275
3309	**Sixpence.** Similar	110	250
3310	**Twopence.** Similar	20	50
3311	**Penny.** Similar	20	50
3312	As last, but without mintmark	20	50

3308   3313

3309   3322

	F £	VF £
Second issue. Without inner circles, but with mark of value		
3313 **Halfcrown**. Crowned bust	550	1500
3314 **Shilling**. Similar	250	650
3315 **Sixpence**. Similar	500	1350
3316 **Twopence**. Similar, but mm. on obv. only	135	300
3317 Similar, but mm. both sides (machine made)	15	30
3318 Bust to edge of coin, legend starts at bottom l. (machine made, single arch crown)	15	30
3319 **Penny**. As 3317	15	30
3320 As 3318 (single arch crown)	15	30

3310   3317   3326

	F	VF
Third issue. With inner circles and mark of value		
3321 **Halfcrown**. Crowned bust to i.c. (and rarely to edge of coin)	80	250
3322 **Shilling**. Similar	50	160
3323 **Sixpence**. Similar	50	150
3324 **Fourpence**. Similar	15	35
3325 **Threepence**. Similar	20	40
3326 **Twopence**. Similar	10	25
3327 **Penny**. Similar	25	50

GOLD

Milled coinage

3328

3334   3335

3328   Five guineas. First bust, pointed truncation

	F	VF	EF		F	VF	EF
	£	£	£		£	£	£
1668	700	1300	3600	1674	800	1400	3750
1669	750	1300	3600	1675	750	1250	3500
1670	700	1200	3400	1676	800	1400	3750
1671	800	1450	3750	1677	750	1300	3600
1672	700	1300	3600	1678	700	1300	3600
1673	700	1300	3600				

3329 — with elephant below bust

	F	VF	EF		F	VF	EF
1668	700	1200	3400	1675	950	1800	4500
1669	950	1800	4500	1677/5		*Extremely rare*	

3330 — with elephant and castle below

	F	VF	EF		F	VF	EF
1675		*Extremely rare*		1677	800	1400	3750
1676	750	1300	3600	1678	850	1500	4000

3331 Second bust, rounded truncation

	F	VF	EF		F	VF	EF
1678/7	850	1500	4000	1682	700	1200	3400
1679	700	1200	3400	1683	700	1300	3600
1680	750	1300	3600	1684	700	1200	3400
1681	700	1200	3400				

3332 — with elephant and castle below

	F	VF	EF		F	VF	EF
1680		*Extremely rare*		1683	850	1500	4000
1681	850	1500	4000	1684	700	1200	3400
1682	750	1300	3600				

3333 Two guineas. First bust, pointed truncation

	F	VF	EF		F	VF	EF
	£	£	£		£	£	£
1664	350	800	3250	1669		*Extremely rare*	
1665		*Extremely rare*		1671	400	900	3500

3334 — with elephant below

	F	VF	EF
1664	275	650	2750

3335 Second bust, rounded truncation

	F	VF	EF		F	VF	EF
1675	375	700	3250	1680	400	800	3500
1676	300	550	2750	1681	250	550	2750
1677	250	550	2750	1682	250	550	2750
1678/7	250	500	2500	1683	250	500	2500
1679	300	550	2750	1684	375	650	3000

3336 — with elephant and castle below

	F	VF	EF		F	VF	EF
1676	275	550	2750	1682	250	500	2500
1677		*Extremely rare*		1683	400	800	3500
1678	300	550	2750	1684	400	800	3500

3337 — with elephant only below, 1678 .... *Extremely rare*

Overstruck dates are listed only if commoner than the normal date or if no normal date is known.

3343   3345

		F	VF	EF
3338	**Guinea.** First bust, 1663	500	1450	3250
3339	— with elephant below, 1663	400	1150	3000
3340	Second bust, 1664	350	950	2500
3341	— with elephant below, 1664		*Extremely rare*	

3342 Third bust, normal portrait

	F	VF	EF		F	VF	EF
1664	200	600	1750	1669	250	750	2000
1665	200	600	1750	1670	200	600	1750
1666	200	600	1750	1671	200	600	1750
1667	200	600	1750	1672	250	750	2000
1668	200	600	1750	1673	350	950	2250

3343 — with elephant below

	F	VF	EF		
1664	250	750	2000	1668	....*Extremely rare*
1665	250	750	2000		

3344 Fourth bust, rounded truncation

	F	VF	EF		F	VF	EF
1672	175	500	1550	1679	150	450	1450
1673	175	500	1550	1680	150	450	1450
1674	250	750	2000	1681	175	500	1550
1675	200	600	1750	1682	175	500	1550
1676	150	450	1450	1683	150	450	1450
1677	150	450	1450	1684	175	500	1550
1678	150	450	1450				

	F £	VF £	EF £		F £	VF £	EF £

3345 — with elephant and castle below

1674		*Extremely rare*		1680 400		1200	3000
1675 250		750	2000	1681 250		750	2000
1676 175		500	1550	1682 275		800	2000
1677 175		500	1550	1683 400		1200	3000
1678 350		950	2250	1684 275		800	2000
1679 250		750	2000				

3346 Guinea. Fourth bust, with elephant below

1677		*Extremely rare*		1678		*Extremely rare*	

3347 Half-guinea. First bust, pointed truncation

1669 175		500	1800	1671 225		650	2000
1670 150		350	1500	1672 200		650	2000

3348 Second bust, rounded truncation

1672 175		400	1600	1679 135		350	1500
1673 300		750	2250	1680 300		750	2250
1674 300		750	2250	1681 300		750	2250
1675		*Extremely rare*		1682 200		600	2000
1676 175		375	1500	1683 175		400	1600
1677 175		400	1600	1684 135		325	1500
1678 175		400	1600				

3349 — with elephant and castle below

1676 350		850	—	1682 300		800	2400
1677 300		800	2400	1683		*Extremely rare*	
1678/7 225		650	2000	1684 175		400	1600
1680		*Extremely rare*					

SILVER

3350

3350 Crown. First bust, rose below, edge undated, 1662 40	200	950
3351 — — edge dated, 1662 50	250	1100
3352 — no rose, edge dated, 1662 55	300	1250
3353 — — edge not dated, 1662 50	250	1100
3354 — — new reverse, shields altered, 1663, regnal year on edge in Roman figures ANNO REGNI XV 45	225	1100

3355

	F £	VF £	EF £		F £	VF £	EF £
3355 Second bust, regnal year on edge in Roman figures							
1664	50	225	1100	1666	50	275	1200
1665	150	600	—				

	F £	VF £	EF £		F £	VF £	EF £
3356 — — elephant below bust, 1666					130	500	—
3357 — regnal year on edge in words (e.g. 1667= DECIMO NONO)							
1667	40	180	1000	1670	50	225	1100
1668	40	180	1000	1671	40	180	1000
1669	100	400	—				

	F £	VF £	EF £		F £	VF £	EF £
3358 Third bust							
1671	40	180	1000	1676	40	180	1000
1672	40	180	1000	1677	40	180	1000
1673	40	180	1000	1678/7	100	400	—
1674		*Extremely rare*		1679	40	180	1000
1675/3	165	600	—	1680/79	55	225	1100

	F £	VF £	EF £		F £	VF £	EF £
3359 Fourth bust							
1679	40	180	1000	1682/1	50	225	1100
1680	40	180	1000	1683	110	500	—
1681	45	225	1100	1684	70	350	—
3360 — elephant and castle below bust, 1681					950	2250	—

3367   3369   3370

	F £	VF £	EF £		F £	VF £	EF £

3361 Halfcrown. First bust, regnal year on edge in Roman figures 1663 40   175   800
3362 Second bust, 1664 60   275   1000
3363 Third bust, 1666 500   1750   —
3364 — elephant below bust, 1666..250   550   —
3365 — regnal date on edge in words

  1667/4 .... *Extremely rare*   1669/4 110   350   —
  1668/4 90   300   —   1670 30   125   750

3366 Third bust variety

  1671 30   100   650
  1672 35   125   750

  1672 40   150   700   1679 30   100   650
  1673 30   100   650   1680 100   300   —
  1674 75   250   1000   1681 40   175   800
  1675 40   175   800   1682 50   225   900
  1676 30   90   550   1683 35   125   750
  1677 30   100   650   1684/3 90   350   —
  1678 100   300   —

3367 Fourth bust

  1673 1000   —   —   1683 ....   *Extremely rare*
3368 — plume below bust
3369 — plume below bust and in centre of *rev.*, 1673 ....   *Extremely rare*
3370 — elephant and castle below bust, 1681 ....fair 350   —   —   —   —
3371 Shilling. First bust, 1663..20   75   275

  1663 20   75   275   1668 160   400   —
  1666 ....   *Extremely rare*   1669/6 ....   *Extremely rare*

3372 First bust variety
3373 — elephant below bust, 1666..140   500   —
3374 Guinea head, elephant below bust, 1666...350   1000   —

3371   3376   3380

	F	VF	EF		F	VF	EF
	£	£	£		£	£	£

3375 Second bust

1666	....	*Extremely rare*		1676	30	90	450
1668	20	60	275	1677	30	90	450
1669	....	*Extremely rare*		1678	45	175	650
1670	45	175	650	1679	30	100	450
1671	60	275	750	1680	....	*Extremely rare*	
1672	30	120	500	1681	60	275	750
1673	45	175	750	1682/1	225	500	—
1674	45	175	750	1683	....	*Extremely rare*	
1675	90	300	—				

3376 — plume below bust and in centre of *rev.*

1671	80	350	—	1676	80	350	—
1673	80	400	—	1679	100	450	—
1674	80	350	—	1680	150	550	—
1675	80	400	—				

3377 — plume *rev.* only, 1674...125   450   —
3378 — plume *obv. only*

1677	125	500	—	1679	90	400	—

3379 — elephant and castle below bust, 1681/0..750   —   —
3380 Third (large) bust

1674	125	475	—	1675	75	275	1000

3381 Fourth (large) bust, older features

1683	75	200	850	1684	60	175	750

3382 Sixpence

1674	15	45	150	1680	25	90	300
1675	15	45	150	1681	15	45	150
1676	20	90	300	1682/1	18	65	200
1677	15	45	150	1683	15	45	150
1678/7	18	65	200	1684	15	50	180
1679	18	65	200				

3383 Fourpence. Undated. Crowned bust l. to edge of coin, value
behind. R. Shield 7   15   30
3384 Dated. *O.* As illustration on p.226. Four Cs

1670	4	10	30	1678	4	9	27
1671	4	10	30	1679	3	9	27
1672/1	4	10	30	1680	3	9	27
1673	4	10	30	1681	3	9	27
1674	4	10	30	1682	4	9	27
1675	4	10	30	1683	3	9	27
1676	4	10	30	1684	3	9	27
1677	4	9	27				

3385 Threepence. Undated. As 3383 8   18   40

	3384				3386	3388	3390

	F	VF	EF			F	VF	EF
	£	£	£			£	£	£

3386 Threepence. Dated. As illustration

Date	F	VF	EF	Date	F	VF	EF
1670	4	9	27	1678	4	8	25
1671	4	8	25	1679	4	7	25
1672/1	4	8	25	1680	4	9	27
1673	4	8	25	1681	4	9	27
1674	4	8	25	1682	4	9	27
1675	4	9	27	1683	4	9	27
1676	4	8	25	1684	4	9	27
1677	4	8	25				

3387 Twopence. Undated. As 3383 (double arch crown) 6   12   25

3388 Dated. As illustration

Date	F	VF	EF	Date	F	VF	EF
1668	4	8	25	1677	4	8	25
1670	4	8	25	1678	4	8	25
1671	4	8	25	1679	4	8	25
1672/1	4	8	25	1680	4	8	25
1673	4	8	25	1681	4	8	25
1674	4	8	25	1682	4	8	25
1675	4	8	25	1683	4	8	25
1676	4	8	25	1684	4	8	25

3389 Penny. Undated. As 3383 (double arch crown) 8   17   40

3390 Dated. As illustration

Date	F	VF	EF	Date	F	VF	EF
1670	7	16	35	1678	7	16	35
1671	7	16	35	1679	13	25	45
1672/1	7	16	35	1680	7	16	35
1673	7	16	35	1681	8	18	40
1674	7	16	35	1682	8	17	38
1675	7	16	35	1683	7	16	35
1676	8	17	38	1684	8	17	38
1677	7	16	35				

3391 Maundy Set. Undated. The four coins 45   100   150

3392 Dated. The four coins. Uniform dates

Date	F	VF	EF	Date	F	VF	EF
1670	32	65	175	1678	35	70	180
1671	30	60	165	1679	32	65	175
1672	32	65	175	1680	30	60	165
1673	30	60	165	1681	35	70	180
1674	30	60	165	1682	32	65	175
1675	30	60	165	1683	30	60	165
1676	30	60	165	1684	32	65	175
1677	30	60	165				

3393   3394

3393 Copper **halfpenny**

	F	VF	EF		F	VF	EF
	£	£	£		£	£	£
1672	20	60	225	1675	20	60	225
1673	20	60	225				

3394 Copper **farthing.** As illustration

	F	VF	EF		F	VF	EF
1672	12	30	175	1675	18	40	175
1673	12	30	175	1679	20	50	225
1674	15	35	175				

3395

3395 Tin **farthing.** Somewhat similar, but with copper plug, edge inscribed NUMMORVM
FAMVLVS, and date on edge only

	Fair	F	VF	EF
	£	£	£	£
1684	20	45	150	500
1685			*Extremely rare*	

Tin halfpence and farthings provided the only base metal coinage during this short reign. All genuine tin coins of this period have a copper plug.

GOLD

	F £	VF £	EF £		F £	VF £	EF £
3396 Five guineas. First bust l., sceptres misplaced, 1686 950		1600	3800				
3397 — sceptres normal.							
1687..........900	1500	3600		1688..........850	1450	3600	
3397a Second bust							
1687..........900	1500	3600		1688..........850	1450	3600	
3398 First bust. Elephant and castle below bust							
1687..........1000	1650	4000		1688..........1000	1650	4000	
3399 Two guineas. Similar							
1687..........450	1300	3000		1688/7 500	1400	3250	

3403   3404

	F £	VF £	EF £		F £	VF £	EF £
3400 Guinea. First bust							
1685..........180	450	1250		1686..........225	600	1900	
3401 — elephant and castle below							
1685 225	650	2150		1686	*Extremely rare*		
3402 Second bust							
1686..........180	450	1250		1688..........180	450	1250	
1687..........180	450	1250					
3403 — elephant and castle below							
1686..........300	950	—		1688..........200	500	1700	
1687..........200	500	1700					
3404 Half-guinea							
1686..........150	375	1350		1688..........175	425	1500	
1687..........225	525	1800					
3405 Elephant and castle below, 1686..........450		1500	—				

SILVER

	F £	VF £	EF £		F £	VF £	EF £
3406 Crown. First bust, 1686..........60		250	600				
3407 Second bust							
1687..........45	175	450		1688..........55	225	550	

3406

	F £	VF £	EF £			F £	VF £	EF £
					1st bust		2nd bust	
3408 Halfcrown. First bust								
1685	40	135	500		1687	40	135	500
1686	40	135	500					
3409 Second bust								
1687	50	200	600		1688	45	155	550
3410 Shilling								
1685	35	135	375		1687/6	40	155	450
1686	35	135	375		1688	40	155	450

3408 .... 1st bust .... 2nd bust

3411   Plume in centre of *rev.*, 1685 .... *Extremely rare*

3410   3412

3412 Sixpence. Early type shields								
1686	25	80	250		1687	30	90	275
3413 Late type shields								
1687	25	80	250		1688	30	90	275

	3414		3415	3416	3417		
	F	*VF*	*EF*		*F*	*VF*	*EF*
	£	£	£		£	£	£

3414 Fourpence. *O.* As illus. R. IIII crowned

1686.............................5	14	30		1688...............................5	14	30
1687/6........................5	13	28				

3415 Threepence. As illustration

1685.............................5	13	27	1687/6.........................5	13	27
1686.............................5	13	27	1688............................5	13	27

3416 Twopence. As illustration

1686 5	13	25	1688 5	13	25
1687 5	13	25			

3417 Penny. As illustration

1685.............................9	20	30	1687 9	20	30
1686.............................9	20	30	1688 9	20	30

3418 Maundy Set. As last four. Uniform dates

1686..........................35	70	150	1688............................35	70	150
1687..........................35	70	150			

TIN

		3419				3420		
					Fair	*F*	*VF*	*EF*
					£	£	£	£
3419	**Halfpenny**							
	1685...				20	40	150	550
	1686...				22	45	175	600
	1687...				20	40	150	550
3420	**Farthing.** Cuirassed bust							
	1684...					*Extremely rare*		
	1685...				20	40	150	550
	1686...				22	45	175	600
	1687...					*Extremely rare*		
3421	Draped bust, 1687				30	55	200	650

Due to the poor state of the silver coinage, much of it worn hammered coin, the guinea, which wasvalued at 21s. 6d. at the beginning of the reign, circulated for as much as 30s. by 1694. The tin halfpennies and farthings were replaced by copper coins in 1694. The rampant lion of Orange is now placed as an inescutcheon on the centre of the royal arms.

GOLD

3422   Five guineas. Conjoined heads r.

	F	VF	EF		F	VF	EF
	£	£	£		£	£	£
1691	750	1500	3250	1693	750	1500	3250
1692	750	1500	3250	1694	800	1600	3500

3422

3423   — elephant and castle below

	F	VF	EF		F	VF	EF
1691	850	1800	4000	1693	1100	2100	4500
1692	900	1800	4000	1694	1000	2000	4250

3424   Two guineas. Conjoined heads r.

	F	VF	EF		F	VF	EF
1693	400	900	3000	1694/3	400	900	3000

3425   — elephant and castle below

	F	VF	EF		F	VF	EF
1691		*Extremely rare*		1694/3	650	1400	4000
1693	650	1400	4000				

3427

3426   Guinea. Conjoined heads r.

	F	VF	EF		F	VF	EF
1689	180	450	1250	1692	225	650	1700
1690	200	550	1450	1693	225	600	1450
1691	225	600	1450	1694	180	500	1350

3427   — elephant and castle below

	F	VF	EF		F	VF	EF
1689	200	500	1350	1692	250	600	1450
1690	270	750	1950	1693		*Extremely rare*	
1691	225	550	1450	1694	250	600	1600

3428   — elephant only below

	F	VF	EF		F	VF	EF
1692	270	750	1950	1693		*Extremely rare*	

Overstruck dates are listed only if commoner than the normal date or if no normal date is known.

| | 3429 | | | | 3430 | | |

	F	VF	EF		F	VF	EF
	£	£	£		£	£	£
3429 **Half-guinea.** First heads, 1689			175			450	1200
3430 — Second head, normal portraits							
1690	180	450	1300	1693		*Extremely rare*	
1691	225	550	1500	1694	125	350	1000
1692	180	450	1300				
3431 — — elephant and castle below							
1691	155	450	1100	1692	125	350	1000
3432 — — elephant only below, 1692						*Extremely rare*	

SILVER

3433

3433 **Crown.** Conjoined busts							
1691	120	300	1000	1692	120	300	1000

| | 3434 | | | | 3435 | | |

3434 **Halfcrown.** First busts and first shields, 1689			25			70	300
3435 — and second shield							
1689	30	80	375	1690	35	120	450

	F £	VF £	EF £		F £	VF £	EF £

3436 Second busts. R. As illustration below

	F £	VF £	EF £		F £	VF £	EF £
1691............32	110	400		1693............30	90	375
1692............35	120	450				

3436   3438

3437 Shilling. Similar

	F	VF	EF		F	VF	EF
1692............30	120	500		1693............25	110	450

3438 Sixpence. Similar

	F	VF	EF		F	VF	EF
1693............20	65	250		1694............40	140	400

3439 Fourpence. First busts, no tie to wreath

	F	VF	EF		F	VF	EF
1689............5	14	30		1691............7	19	40
1690............6	16	35		1694............7	17	38

3440 Second busts, tie to wreath

	F	VF	EF		F	VF	EF
1692............7	18	40		1694............9	21	45
1693............9	21	45				

3441 Threepence. First busts, no tie

	F	VF	EF		F	VF	EF
1689............5	12	28		1691............12	28	45
1690............5	14	30				

3442 Second busts, tie to wreath

	F	VF	EF		F	VF	EF
1691............7	19	40		1693............6	17	38
1692............7	19	40		1694............6	16	37

3443 Twopence

	F	VF	EF		F	VF	EF
1689............4	11	30		1693............5	14	35
1691............5	14	35		1694............6	15	38
1692............5	14	35				

3444 Penny. Legend continuous over heads, 1689 ....90 200 375

3445 Legend broken by heads

	F	VF	EF		F	VF	EF
1690............10	23	50		1693............10	23	50
1691............10	23	50		1694............10	23	50
1692............10	23	50				

3446

	F £	VF £	EF £		F £	VF £	EF £
3446 Maundy Set. As last pieces. Uniform dates							
1689 130	275	500		1693 60	120	210	
1691 50	110	200		1694 50	110	200	
1692 50	110	200					

TIN AND COPPER

3448   3451

	Fair £			
3447 Tin **Halfpenny.** Small draped busts, 1689 175	350	900	—
3448 Large cuirassed busts; date only on edge			
1690..20	40	115	450
3449 — date in exergue and on edge			
1691..20	40	115	450
1692..20	40	115	450
3450 Tin **Farthing.** Small draped busts			
1689..90	175	500	—
1689, edge 1690	*Extremely rare*		
3451 Large cuirassed busts			
1690, edge 1689	*Extremely rare*		
1690..20	50	120	475
1691..20	50	120	475
1692..22	55	125	525

3452   3453

3452 Copper **Halfpenny,** 1694	15	35	300
3453 Copper **Farthing,** 1694	20	40	350

In 1696 a great re-coinage was undertaken to replace the hammered silver that made up most of the coinage in circulation, much of it being clipped and badly worn. Branch mints were set up at Bristol, Chester, Exeter, Norwich and York to help with the re-coinage. For a short time before they were finally demonetized, unclipped hammered coins were allowed to circulate freely provided they were officially pierced in the centre. Silver coins with roses between the coats of arms were made from silver obtained from the West of England mines.

GOLD

3454   3457

3454 Five guineas. First bust

	F £	VF £	EF £		F £	VF £	EF £
1699	850	1450	3000	1700	850	1450	3250

3455 — elephant and castle below, 1699				1000	1700	3500	
3456 Second bust ('fine work'), 1701. Plain or ornamental sceptres				850	1450	3250	
3457 **Two guineas** ('fine work'), 1701				900	1550	3600	

3458   3460   3466

3458 Guinea. First bust

	F	VF	EF		F	VF	EF
1695	150	375	900	1697	180	450	1100
1696	180	450	1100				

3459 — elephant and castle below

1695	200	500	1300	1696		*Extremely rare*	

3460 Second bust, human-headed harp

1697	180	450	1000	1700	150	325	750
1698	150	325	750	1701	150	325	750
1699	200	500	1300				

3461 — elephant and castle below

1697	350	1000	—	1699		*Extremely rare*	
1698	225	600	1450	1700	400	1100	—

		F	VF	EF
		£	£	£
3462	**Guinea.** Second bust. R. Human headed harp. Large lettering and large date, 1698 150		350	900
3463	— R. Scrolled harp, 1701 150		350	900
3464	— — elephant and castle, 1701		*Extremely rare*	
3465	Third bust ('fine work'), 1701 300		700	2500
3466	**Half-guinea.** R. With early harp, 1695 100		250	650
3467	**Half-guinea.** Elephant and castle. R. With early harp			

	F	VF	EF				
	£	£	£				
1695 225	550	1500	1696 115		300	850

3468	R. With late harp						
1697 160	400	1300	1700 110		250	600
1698 110	250	600	1701 110		250	600
1699	*Extremely rare*					

3469	— elephant and castle, 1698 180		450	1300

SILVER

3470 Crown. First bust, first harp

1695 25	95	300	1696 25		95	275

3471	Second bust (hair across breast), 1696			*Unique*
3472	Third bust, first harp, 1696 30		100	300
3473	— second harp, 1697 250		800	—
3474	Third bust variety, third harp, 1700 30		115	325

3490

3475	**Halfcrown.** Small shields, 1696 15		50	175
3476	— B (*Bristol*) below bust, 1696 20		70	225
3477	— C (*Chester*) below bust, 1696 30		125	375
3478	— E (*Exeter*) below bust, 1696 45		175	500
3479	— N (*Norwich*) below bust, 1696 25		90	275
3480	— y (*York*) below bust, 1696 30		125	375
3481	Large shield, early harp, 1696 15		50	175
3482	— — B (*Bristol*) below bust, 1696 20		70	225
3483	— — C (*Chester*) below bust, 1696 25		90	275
3484	— — E (*Exeter*) below bust, 1696 30		125	375
3485	— — N (*Norwich*) below bust, 1696 45		175	500
3486	— — y (*York*) below bust, 1696 25		90	275
3487	Large shields, ordinary harp			

1696 35	135	400	1697 15		50	175

3488	— — B (*Bristol*) below bust, 1697 20		80	250

	F	VF	EF		F	VF	EF
	£	£	£		£	£	£

3489 — — C *(Chester)* below bust

| 1696 | 35 | 135 | 400 | 1697 | 20 | 70 | 225 |

3490 — — E *(Exeter)* below bust

| 1696 | 35 | 135 | 400 | 1697 | 20 | 55 | 195 |

3491 —— N *(Norwich)* below bust

| 1696 | 45 | 175 | 500 | 1697 | 20 | 70 | 225 |

3492 — — y *(York)* below bust, 1697 20   55   195

3493 Second bust (hair across breast), 1696 .... *Unique*

3494 Halfcrown. Modified large shields

| 1698 | 15 | 55 | 200 | 1700 | 20 | 60 | 225 |
| 1699 | 30 | 90 | 300 | 1701 | 25 | 65 | 250 |

3495 Elephant and castle below bust, 1701 .... *Fair* 250

3496 Plumes in angles on *rev.*, 1701 30   100   300

1st bust   2nd bust   3rd bust   3507

3rd bust var.   4th bust   5th bust

3497 Shilling. First bust

| 1695 | 18 | 50 | 150 | 1697 | 9 | 25 | 80 |
| 1696 | 9 | 25 | 80 | | | | |

3498 — B *(Bristol)* below bust

| 1696 | 18 | 45 | 135 | 1697 | 20 | 50 | 150 |

3499 — C *(Chester)* below bust

| 1696 | 20 | 50 | 150 | 1697 | 20 | 50 | 150 |

3500 — E *(Exeter)* below bust

| 1696 | 20 | 50 | 150 | 1697 | 20 | 50 | 150 |

3501 — N *(Norwich)* below bust

| 1696 | 20 | 50 | 150 | 1697 | 20 | 50 | 150 |

3502 — y *(York)* below bust

| 1696 | 20 | 50 | 150 | 1697 | 20 | 50 | 150 |

3503 — Y *(York)* below bust

| 1696 | 22 | 60 | 175 | 1697 | 22 | 60 | 175 |

		F	VF	EF
		£	£	£
3504	**Shilling.** Second bust (hair across breast), 1696			*Unique*
3505	Third bust, 1697	9	25	80
3506	— B (*Bristol*) below bust, 1697	22	60	175
3507	— C (*Chester*) below bust			

	F	VF	EF			VF	EF
	£	£	£			£	£
1696	45	150	450	1697	20	50	150

		F	VF	EF
3508	— E (*Exeter*) below bust, 1697	22	60	175
3509	— N (*Norwich*) below bust, 1697	20	60	175
3510	— y (*York*) below bust			

						VF	EF
1696		*Extremely rare*		1697	22	60	175

		F	VF	EF
3511	Third bust variety			

	F	VF	EF			VF	EF
1697	9	25	85	1698	18	50	150

		F	VF	EF
3512	— B (*Bristol*) below bust, 1697	22	60	175
3513	Third bust variety C (*Chester*) below bust, 1697	50	150	450
3514	— R. Plumes in angles, 1698	55	175	525
3515	Fourth bust ('flaming hair')			

	F	VF	EF			VF	EF
1698	30	70	250	1699	30	70	250

3516	Fifth bust (hair high)			

	F	VF	EF			VF	EF
1699	22	60	200	1701	22	60	200
1700	15	35	100				

3517	— R. Plumes in angles			

	F	VF	EF			VF	EF
1699	40	115	350	1701	40	115	350

		F	VF	EF
3518	— R. Roses in angles, 1699	55	150	450
3519	— plume below bust, 1700	750	—	—

3520

3542

		F	VF	EF
3520	**Sixpence.** First bust, early harp			

	F	VF	EF			VF	EF
1695	20	60	175	1696	5	18	50

		F	VF	EF
3521	— — B below bust, 1696	8	22	65
3522	— — C below bust, 1696	15	45	135
3523	— — E below bust, 1696	20	60	175
3524	— — N below bust, 1696	12	40	120
3525	— — y below bust, 1696	10	30	90
3526	— — Y below bust, 1696	20	60	175
3527	— later harp, large crowns, 1696	25	75	225
3528	— — — B below bust			

	F	VF	EF			VF	EF
1696	25	75	225	1697	20	60	175

		F	VF	EF
3529	— — — C below bust, 1697	25	75	225
3530	— — — E below bust, 1697	22	70	225
3531	— — small crowns			

	F	VF	EF			VF	EF
1696	20	65	190	1697	8	22	65

3532	— — — B below bust			

	F	VF	EF			VF	EF
1696	18	55	160	1697	12	40	120

	F £	VF £	EF £		F £	VF £	EF £
3533 — — — C below bust							
1696 35	10	300		1697 12	40	120	
3534 — — — E below bust, 1697 15					45	135	
3535 — — — N below bust							
1696..........................30	90	275		1697..........................10	30	90	
3536 — — — y below bust, 1697...25					75	225	
3537 Second bust							
1696 150	300	—		1697 35	120	350	
3538 Third bust, large crowns							
1697 5	18	50		1700 8	22	65	
1698 8	22	65		1701 11	35	90	
1699 27	80	240					
3539 — — B below bust, 1697..15					45	135	
3540 — — C below bust, 1697..25					70	200	
3541 — — E below bust, 1697..30					90	275	
3542 Third bust small crowns, 1697 10					30	90	
3543 — — C below bust, 1697..22					65	180	
3544 — — E below bust, 1697...16					50	150	
3545 — — Y below bust, 1697..25					80	240	
3546 — R. Plumes in angles							
1698..........................10	30	90		1699..........................14	40	120	
3547 — R. Roses in angles, 1699 25					75	225	
3548* — plume below bust, 1700..					*Extremely rare*		

3549	3550	3551	3552

	F £	VF £	EF £		F £	VF £	EF £
3549 Fourpence. R. 4 crowned							
1697..........................		Unique		1700 9	20	45	
1698 10	22	50		1701 10	24	55	
1699 9	22	50		1702 9	20	45	
3550 Threepence. R. 3 crowned							
1698 9	20	45		1700 9	20	45	
1699 10	22	48		1701 9	20	45	
3551 Twopence. R. Crown to edge of coin, large figure 2							
1698..........................9	19	38		1700..........................9	19	38	
1699..........................9	18	36		1701..........................9	18	38	
3551A R Crown within inner circle of legend, smaller figure 2							
1699 9	18	36		1701 9	18	38	
1700 9	19	38					

An extremely fine specimen sold at auction in October 1985 for £3500.

	F	VF	EF			F	VF	EF
	£	£	£			£	£	£

3552 Penny. R. 1 crowned

1698	9	19	38	1700	10	20	40
1699	10	20	40	1701	9	19	38

3553 Maundy Set. As last four. Uniform dates

1698	50	105	180	1700	55	115	190
1699	55	115	190	1701	50	105	180

COPPER

3554 Halfpenny. First issue. Britannia with r. hand raised

1695	8	30	175	1697	7	25	175
1696	7	25	175	1698	9	40	200

3554

3555 Second issue. R. Date in legend

1698	8	30	175	1699	7	25	175

3556 Third issue. R. Britannia with r. hand on knee

1699	7	25	175	1701	8	30	175
1700	7	25	175				

3557   3558

3557 Farthing. First issue

1695	10	35	225	1698	60	175	
1696	9	30	200	1699	9	30	200
1697	9	30	200	1700	9	30	200

3558 Second issue. R. Date at end of legend

1698	25	75	400	1699	14	45	275

The Act of Union of 1707, which effected the unification of the ancient kingdoms of England and Scotland into a single realm, resulted in a change in the royal arms—on the after-Union coinage the English lions and Scottish lion are emblazoned per pale on the top and bottom shields. After the Union the rose in the centre of the reverse of the gold coins is replaced by the Garter star.

Following a successful Anglo-Dutch expedition against Spain, bullion seized in Vigo Bay was sent to be minted into coin, and the coins made from this metal had the word VIGO placed below the queen's bust.

GOLD

Before Union with Scotland
3560   Five guineas

	F	VF	EF		F	VF	EF
	£	£	£		£	£	£
1705	1000	2250	6000	1706	950	2000	5500

3561   VIGO below bust, 1703 6000   15,000   43,000

3562   3564

3562   Guinea

1702	175	550	1750	1706	275	700	2250
1705	275	675	2150	1707	325	800	2500

3563   VIGO below bust, 1703 3000   7000   —
3564   Half-guinea

1702	225	550	1750	1705	225	550	1750

3565   VIGO below bust, 1703 2250   5000   —

After Union with Scotland. The shields on the reverse are changed

3566

3566	**Five guineas.** Ordinary bust, 1706	850	1900	5000
3567	Narrower shields, tall narrow crowns, larger rev. letters, 1709	950	2000	5500
3568	Broader shields			

1711	850	1900	5000	1714/3	850	1900	5000
1713	950	2000	5500				

	F £	VF £	EF £		F £	VF £	EF £
3569 Two guineas							
1709	350	800	2200	1713	350	800	2200
1711	350	800	2200	1714	400	900	2750

3569   3574

3570 Guinea. First bust

	F	VF	EF		F	VF	EF
1707	200	400	1100	1708			*Extremely rare*
3571 — elephant and castle below, 1707					400	950	2500
3572 Second bust							
1707		*Extremely rare*		1709	200	425	1200
1708	180	375	1000				
3573 — elephant and castle below							
1708	350	900	2500	1709	325	800	2250
3574 Third bust							
1710	150	300	700	1713	150	275	650
1711	150	300	700	1714	150	275	650
1712	200	400	1100				
3575 Half-guinea							
1707	160	325	900	1711	135	260	700
1708	200	450	1200	1712	160	325	900
1709	135	275	750	1713	135	275	750
1710	120	260	700	1714	135	275	750

ANNE

SILVER

243

Before Union with Scotland

3576

	F £	VF £	EF £		F £	VF £	EF £
3576	**Crown.** VIGO below bust, 1703		...90			275	750
3577	R. Plumes in angles, 1705		...150			450	1350
3578	R. Roses and plumes in angles						
	1706...70	225	600	1707...65		200	600
3579	**Halfcrown.** No marks below bust or on *rev.* (i.e. plain), 1703...275				750	—	
3580	VIGO below bust, 1703		...25			80	275
3581	R. Plumes in angles						
	1704...45	150	400	1705...30		95	275
3582	R. Roses and plumes in angles						
	1706...25	80	250	1707...20		70	200

3583   3589

	F	VF	EF
3583	**Shilling.** First bust, 1702 ...30	90	225
3584	— R. Plumes in angles, 1702 ...30	100	275
3585	— VIGO below bust, 1702 ...30	100	275
3586	Second bust, VIGO below, 1703 ...20	60	150
3587	— plain		
	1704...165 400 — 1705...40	100	275
3588	— R. Plumes in angles		
	1704...40 120 300 1705...30	90	250
3589	— R. Roses and plumes in angles		
	1705...25 75 200 1707...30	85	225

| 3593 | | | | 3594 | | Early Shield | Late Shield |

		F £	VF £	EF £		F £	VF £	EF £
3590	**Sixpence.** VIGO below bust, 1703					12	35	95
3591	Plain, 1705					20	70	200
3592	R. Early shields, plumes in angles, 1705					16	50	150
3593	R. Late shields, plumes in angles, 1705					20	60	175
3594	R. Roses and plumes in angles							
	1705	18	60	200	1707	16	45	125

3595 **Fourpence.** First bust, small face, curls at back of head point downwards. R Small crown above the figure 4

	F	VF	EF		F	VF	EF
1703	5	15	30	1704	5	14	28

3595A Second bust, larger face, curls at back of head point upwards

1705	5	15	30	1709	5	14	28
1706	5	14	28	1710	5	14	28
1708	5	14	28				

3595B R Large crown with pearls on arch, larger serifs on the figure 4

1710	5	14	28	1713	5	14	28

3595C Second bust, but with re-engraved hair.

1710	5	14	28	1713	5	14	28

3596 **Threepence.** First head, broad bust, tie riband pointing outwards. R. Crowned 3

1703					7	15	35

3596A Second head, taller and narrow bust, tie riband pointing inwards

1704	5	12	26	1706	5	14	28
1705	5	12	26				

3596B Third Head, similar to first bust but larger and hair more finely engraved

1707	5	14	28	1710	5	14	28
1708	5	14	28	1713	5	14	28
1709	5	14	28				

3597 **Twopence.** First bust, as fourpence R. Crown to edge of coin, small figure 2

1703	5	13	27	1706	5	13	27
1708	5	12	26	1707	5	13	27
1704	5	12	26				

3597A Second bust, as fourpence R Crown within inner circle of legend, large figure 2.

1708	5	12	26	1710	5	12	26
1709	5	13	27	1713	5	12	26

3598 **Penny. R.** Crowned 1

1703	9	20	35	1709	8	18	32
1705	8	18	32	1710	12	25	35
1706	8	18	32	1713	9	20	35
1708	9	20	40				

3599 Maundy Set. As last four. Uniform dates

1703	40	75	175	1709	40	75	175
1705	40	75	175	1710	45	80	180
1706	35	70	165	1713	40	75	125
1708	40	75	175				

3599

After Union with Scotland

The shields on reverse are changed. The Edinburgh coins have been included here as they are now coins of Great Britain.

3600

	F £	VF £	EF £		F £	VF £	EF £
3600 Crown. Second bust, E (Edinburgh) below							
1707	50	150	450	1708	50	165	500
3601 — plain							
1707	50	150	450	1708	50	150	450
3602 R. Plumes in angles, 1708					55	225	675
3603 Third bust. R. Roses and plumes, 1713					50	150	450

3604   3609

	F	VF	EF		F	VF	EF
3604 Halfcrown. R. Plain							
1707	17	50	150	1709	18	55	165
1708	15	45	135	1713	20	60	180
3605 — E below bust							
1707	18	55	150	1709	65	225	675
1708	18	55	150				
3606 R. Plumes in angles, 1708					30	90	250
3607 R. Roses and plumes in angles							
1710	25	80	225	1713	25	80	225
1712	22	70	200	1714	22	70	200
3608 Shilling. Second bust, E below							
1707	18	50	150	1708	30	95	300
3609 — E* below							
1707	35	110	350	1708	20	60	175

Overstruck dates are listed only if commoner than normal date or if no normal date is known.

		F	VF	EF		F	VF	EF
		£	£	£		£	£	£

3610 Shilling. R. Third bust. Plain.

1707............12	35	90	1709............12	35	90
1708............8	25	75	1711............40	150	450

3611 — R. Plumes in angles

1707............22	60	175	1708............15	45	135

3612 — E below

1707............15	40	120	1708............25	80	250

3613 Second bust. R. Roses and plumes, 1708 50   150   450

3614 Third bust. R. Roses and plumes

1708............25	70	200	1710............12	35	90

3615 — 'Edinburgh' bust, E* below

1707............................	*Extremely rare*		1709............30	95	275
1708............25	80	250			

3616 — E below, 1709 ....   *Extremely rare*

3617 Fourth bust. R. Roses and plumes

1710............25	90	250	1713/2 15	50	150
1712............12	35	90	1714............12	35	90

3618 — plain, 1711 8   20   60

3620   3623

3619 Sixpence. Normal bust. R. Plain

1707............9	22	65	1711............5	15	45
1708............10	30	90			

3620 — E below bust

1707............10	30	90	1708............12	40	120

3621 — E* below bust, 1708 12   50   150
3622 'Edinburgh' bust, E* below, 1708 15   55   165
3623 Normal bust. R. Plumes in angles

1707............11	35	95	1708............12	40	120

3624 — R. Roses and plumes in angles, 1710 15   50   150

COPPER

3625

3625 Farthing, 1714 75   150   350

THE HOUSE OF HANOVER
GEORGE I, 1714-27

The coins of the first of the Hanoverian kings have the arms of the Duchy of Brunswick and Luneberg on one of the four shields, the object in the centre of the shield being the crown of Charlemagne. The king's German titles also appear, in abbreviated form, and name him 'Duke of Brunswick and Luneberg. Arch-treasurer of the Holy Roman Empire, and Elector', and on the guinea of 1714, 'Prince Elector'. A quarter-guinea was struck for the first time in 1718, but it was an inconvenient size and the issue was discontinued.

Silver coined from bullion supplied to the mint by the South Sea Company in 1723 shows the company's initials S.S.C.; similarly Welsh Copper Company bullion has the letters W.C.C. below the king's bust and plumes and an interlinked CC on the reverse. Roses and plumes together on the reverse indicate silver supplied by the Company for Smelting Pit Coale and Sea Coale.

GOLD

3626 Five guineas

	F	VF	EF		F	VF	EF
	£	£	£		£	£	£
1716	1000	2100	4750	1720	1250	2250	5000
1717	1250	2250	5000	1726	1000	2250	4750

3626

3627 Two guineas

	F	VF	EF		F	VF	EF
1717	500	900	3000	1726	425	850	2800
1720	500	900	3000				

3627   3628

		F	VF	EF
3628	**Guinea.** First head. R. Legend ends ET PR . EL (Prince Elector),			
	1714	300	750	2000
3629	Second head, tie with two ends, 1715	175	375	900
3630	Third head, no hair below truncation			
	1715......150 300 850 1716	200	450	1000

3633   3638

	F	VF	EF		F	VF	EF
	£	£	£		£	£	£

3631 Guinea. Fourth head, tie with loop at one end

1716	150	300	850	1720	150	300	850
1717	175	350	1000	1721	175	400	1000
1718		*Extremely rare*		1722	150	300	850
1719	150	300	850	1723	175	400	1000

3632 — elephant and castle below

1721		*Extremely rare*		1722		*Extremely rare*	

3633 Fifth (older) head, tie with two ends

1723	200	400	1000	1726	150	350	800
1724	200	400	1000	1727	225	500	1350
1725	200	400	1000				

3634 — elephant and castle below, 1726 500   1100   —

3635 Half-guinea. First head

1715	150	250	650	1721		*Extremely rare*	
1717	125	250	650	1722	125	250	650
1718	100	200	600	1723		*Extremely rare*	
1719	100	200	600	1724	150	300	700
1720	175	375	800				

3636 — elephant and castle below, 1721 .... *Extremely rare*

3637 Second (older) bust

1725	90	225	500	1727	100	250	650
1726	100	250	650				

3638 Quarter-guinea, 1718 35   85   165

SILVER

3639 Crown. R. Roses and plumes in angles

1716	115	250	850	1720/18	175	350	1100
1718/6	175	350	1100	1726	125	300	950

3639

	F £	VF £	EF £		F £	VF £	EF £
3640 R. SSC (South Sea Company) in angles, 1723...................................	125	300	950				
3641 Halfcrown. Plain (proof only), 1715 *FDC* £4000							
3642 R. Roses and plumes in angles							
1715...........................45		150	500	1720/17 45		150	500
1717...........................45		150	500				

3643

3647

	F £	VF £	EF £		F £	VF £	EF £
3643 R. SSC in angles, 1723..	45	140	450				
3644 R. Small roses and plumes, 1726	600	1400	—				
3645 Shilling. First bust. R. Roses and plumes							
1715...........................15		45	140	1720...........................15		45	140
1716...........................30		120	350	1721/0 18		55	175
1717...........................15		45	140	1722...........................15		45	140
1718...........................15		40	135	1723...........................15		45	140
1719...........................30		120	325				
3646 — plain (i.e. no marks either side)							
1720...........................15		45	140	1721...........................55		200	500
3647 R. SSC in angles, 1723..	9	25	75				
3648 Second bust, bow to tie. R. Similar, 1723	15	45	135				

3650

3652

	F £	VF £	EF £		F £	VF £	EF £
3649 — R. Roses and plumes							
1723 18		50	150	1726 110		350	1100
1724 18		50	150	1727 90		300	850
1725 18		50	150				
3650 — W.C.C. (Welsh Copper Company) below							
1723...........................90		300	850	1725...........................90		325	900
1724...........................90		325	900	1726...........................90		325	900
3651 Sixpence. R. Roses and plumes in angles							
1717...........................25		75	175	1720/17 25		75	175
3652 R. SSC in angles, 1723..	5	20	65				
3653 R. Small roses and plumes, 1726	20	50	150				

	3654		3655			3656		3657	

	F £	VF £	EF £			F £	VF £	EF £
3654 Fourpence								
1717 7	18	36			1723 7	18	36
1721 7	18	36			1727 8	19	38
3655 Threepence								
1717 7	19	33			1723 8	20	35
1721 8	20	35			1727 8	20	35
3656 Twopence								
1717.................4	10	22			1726...................4	9	20
1721.................4	9	20			1727...................4	10	22
1723.................4	10	22					
3657 Penny								
1716 3	7	16			1725 3	7	16
1718 3	7	16			1726 4	10	20
1720 3	7	16			1727 4	10	20
1723 3	7	16					

3658 Maundy Set. As last four. Uniform dates

1723.................35	80	175			1727.................35	80	175

COPPER

	3661			3662	

	F £	VF £	EF £		F £	VF £	EF £
3659 Halfpenny. 'Dump' issue							
1717 8	35	150		1718 8	35	150
3660 Second issue							
1719.................5	35	175		1722.................5	35	175
1720.................5	35	175		1723.................5	35	175
1721.................5	35	175		1724.................5	35	175
3661 Farthing. 'Dump' issue, 1717 60	150	400				
3662 Second issue							
1719 5	30	175		1722 6	35	190
1720 5	30	175		1723 6	35	190
1721 5	30	175		1724 6	35	190

Silver was coined only spasmodically by the Mint during this reign and no copper was struck after 1754. Gold coins made from bullion supplied by the East India Company bear the company's initials. Some of the treasure seized by Admiral Anson during his circumnavigation of the globe, 1740-4, and by other privateers, was made into coin which had the word LIMA below the king's bust to celebrate the expedition's successful harassment of the Spanish colonies in the New World. Hammered gold was finally demonetized in 1733.

GOLD

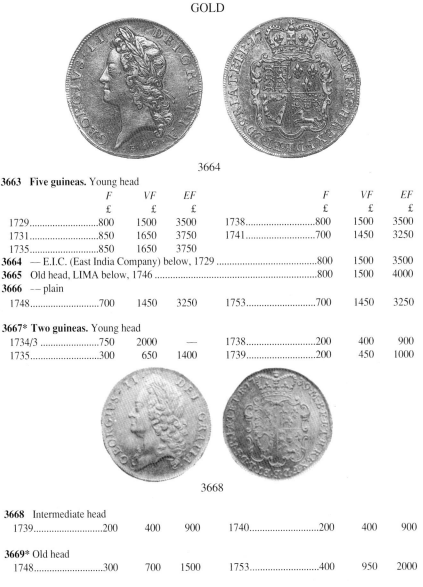

3664

3663 Five guineas. Young head

	F	VF	EF		F	VF	EF
	£	£	£		£	£	£
1729	800	1500	3500	1738	800	1500	3500
1731	850	1650	3750	1741	700	1450	3250
1735	850	1650	3750				

3664 — E.I.C. (East India Company) below, 1729 ...... 800 1500 3500
3665 Old head, LIMA below, 1746 ...... 800 1500 4000
3666 -- plain

1748	700	1450	3250	1753	700	1450	3250

3667* Two guineas. Young head

1734/3	750	2000	—	1738	200	400	900
1735	300	650	1400	1739	200	450	1000

3668

3668 Intermediate head

1739	200	400	900	1740	200	400	900

3669* Old head

1748	300	700	1500	1753	400	950	2000

*Beware recent forgeries.
Overstruck dates are listed only if commoner than normal date or if no normal date is known.

3671   3674

	F £	VF £	EF £		F £	VF £	EF £
3670 Guinea. First young head, small lettering, 1727	350	1000	2200				
3671 — larger lettering, smaller shield							
1727	250	650	1500	1728	300	700	1650
3672 Second (narrower) young head							
1729 *proof only FDC £3600*				1731	160	400	1250
1730	200	400	1500	1732	200	500	1500
3673 — E.I.C. below							
1729	350	900	2500	1732	250	600	1650
1731	250	600	1650				
3674 — larger lettering on *obv.*							
1732	225	500	1450	1736	180	450	1250
1733	150	375	950	1737	200	500	1450
1734	150	375	950	1738	180	450	1250
1735	160	350	1100				
3675 — — E.I.C. below, 1732					300	700	1750
3676 Intermediate head							
1739	150	375	900	1741/39		*Extremely rare*	
1740	160	450	1250	1743*		*Extremely rare*	
3677 — E.I.C. below, 1739					300	700	1750
3678 — larger lettering on *obv.*							
1745	225	500	1450	1746	200	450	1000
3679 — LIMA below, 1745					275	500	1300
3680 Old head							
1747	150	350	800	1753	125	300	700
1748	125	300	700	1755	175	375	850
1749	125	300	700	1756	125	275	650
1750	150	350	700	1758	115	250	600
1751	125	300	650	1759	115	250	600
1752	125	300	650	1760	120	275	650

3681   3679   3685

A very fine specimen sold at auction in March 1990 for £3300 plus 10% buyer's premium.

	F £	VF £	EF £		F £	VF £	EF £
3681 Half-guinea. Young head							
1728	150	375	900	1734	120	350	800
1729	120	400	1000	1735			*?exists*
1730		*Extremely rare*		1736	120	400	1000
1731	200	600	1500	1737		*Extremely rare*	
1732	150	425	1100	1738	110	325	800
1733			*?exists*	1739	110	325	800
3682 — E.I.C. below							
1729	250	500	1500	1732		*Extremely rare*	
1730	300	1000	—	1739		*Extremely rare*	
1731		*Extremely rare*					
3683 Intermediate head							
1740	200	600	1500	1745	200	600	1500
1743			*?Unique*	1746	120	350	750
3684 — LIMA below, 1745					350	900	1850
3685 Old head							
1747	160	500	1200	1753	100	250	500
1748	130	300	625	1755	100	250	450
1749		*Extremely rare*		1756	90	225	450
1750	110	275	550	1758	90	225	450
1751	120	325	700	1759..,	80	175	400
1752	120	325	700	1760	80	175	400

SILVER

3686 Crown. Young bust. R. Roses and plumes in angles

1732	90	250	600	1735	90	250	600
1734	110	275	750	1736	90	250	650

3686

3687 — R. Roses in angles

1739	80	200	500	1741	80	200	500

3688 Old head. R. Roses in angles, 1743 ... 80 200 500

3689 — LIMA below, 1746 ... 80 200 500

3690 — Plain (i.e. no marks either side)

1746 *proof only FDC* £1750

1750	100	275	650	1751	135	325	750

3692

	F £	VF £	EF £		F £	VF £	EF £
3691 Halfcrown. Young bust R. plain (proof only), 1731 *FDC* £1800							
3692 — R. Roses and plumes							
1731............................25	80	300		1735............................30	90	350	
1732............................25	80	300		1736............................35	125	450	
1734............................30	90	350					
3693 — R. Roses							
1739..........................22	70	225		1741............................22	75	300	
3694 Old bust. R. Roses							
1743............................20	65	200		1745............................20	65	200	
3695 — LIMA below							
1745............................18	45	135		1746............................18	45	135	
3696 — R. Plain							
1746 *proof only FDC* £700							
1750............................35	130	350		1751............................50	175	500	
3697 Shilling. Young bust. R. Plumes							
1727............................35	100	300		1731 50	175	450	
3698 — R. Roses and plumes							
1727............................20	50	135		1731............................20	50	135	
1728............................30	75	175		1732............................30	75	175	
1729............................30	75	175					
3699 — larger lettering. R. Roses and plumes							
1734............................12	35	110		1736............................12	35	110	
1735............................12	35	110		1737............................12	35	110	
3700 — R. plain, 1728 40	150	400					
3701 — R. Roses							
1739............................10	35	85		1741............................12	35	95	
3702 Old bust. R. Roses							
1743............................10	30	75		1747............................12	35	100	
1745............................20	55	150					

3701   3702

	F £	VF £	EF £		F £	VF £	EF £
3703 — LIMA below							
1745	10	30	75	1746	30	90	250
3704 — R. plain							
1746 *proof only FDC £450*				1751	30	90	200
1750	20	55	125	1758	4	12	35

3708   3710

	F £	VF £	EF £		F £	VF £	EF £
3705 Sixpence. Young bust. R. Plain, 1728					30	90	250
3706 — R. Plumes, 1728					25	70	175
3707 — R. Roses and plumes							
1728	12	32	90	1734	25	50	135
1731	12	32	90	1735	25	50	135
1732	12	32	90	1736	20	45	125
3708 — R. Roses							
1739	12	32	90	1741	12	32	90
3709 Old bust. R. Roses							
1743	12	32	90	1745	15	35	100
3710 — LIMA below							
1745	10	30	75	1746	7	20	50
3711 — plain							
1746 *proof only FDC £325*							
1750	20	50	145	1757	3	8	22
1751	25	75	200	1758	3	8	22
3712 Fourpence. Young head. R. Small dome-shaped crown without pearls on arch, figure 4							
1729	4	9	18	1731	4	9	18
3712A R.Double domed crown with pearls, large figure 4							
1732	4	9	18	1740	4	9	18
1735	4	9	18	1743	4	9	18
1737	4	9	18	1746	4	9	18
1739	4	9	18	1760	4	9	18
3713 Threepence. Young head. R. Crowned 3, pearls on arch							
1729					4	9	18
3713A R Ornate arch							
1731	4	9	18	1732	4	9	18
3713B R. Double domed crown with pearls							
1735	4	9	18	1743	4	9	18
1737	4	9	18	1746	4	9	18
1739	4	9	18	1760	4	9	18
1740	4	9	18				

	F £	VF £	EF £		F £	VF £	EF £

3714 Twopence. Young head. R. Small crown and figure 2

1729	3	7	14	1731	3	7	14

3714A R. Large crown

1732	3	7	14	1743	3	7	14
1735	3	7	14	1746	3	7	14
1737	3	7	14	1756	3	7	14
1739	4	8	16	1759	3	7	14
1740	4	9	18	1760	3	7	14

3715 Penny. Young head. R. Date over small crown and figure 1

1729	3	5	10	1731	3	5	10

3715A R. Large crown dividing date

1732	3	5	10	1753	3	5	10
1735	3	5	10	1754	3	5	10
1737	3	5	10	1755	3	5	10
1739	3	5	10	1756	3	5	10
1740	3	5	10	1757	3	5	10
1743	3	5	10	1758	3	5	10
1746	3	5	10	1759	3	5	10
1750	3	5	10	1760	3	5	10
1752	3	5	10				

3716

3716 Maundy Set. As last four. Uniform dates

1729	27	50	110	1739	25	50	90
1731	27	50	110	1740	25	50	100
1732	27	55	110	1743	25	50	100
1735	25	55	100	1746	25	50	100
1737	25	55	100	1760	27	55	110

3717

	F £	VF £	EF £		F £	VF £	EF £
3717 Halfpenny. Young bust							
1729 5	25	95		1735 5	25	95
1730 5	25	95		1736.........................5	25	95
1731 5	25	95		1737.........................5	25	95
1732 5	25	95		1738.........................4	22	85
1733 5	25	95		1739.........................5	25	95
1734 5	25	95				
3718 Old bust, GEORGIUS							
1740 4	20	80		1744 4	18	70
1742 4	20	80		1745 4	18	70
1743 4	18	70				
3719 — GEORGIVS							
1746.........................4	20	80		1751.........................4	18	70
1747.........................4	20	80		1752.........................4	18	70
1748.........................4	18	70		1753.........................4	18	70
1749.........................4	18	70		1754.........................4	18	70
1750.........................4	18	70				

3720   3722

3720 Farthing. Young bust							
1730.........................5	25	85		1735.........................4	20	75
1731.........................5	25	85		1736.........................5	25	85
1732.........................6	30	90		1737.........................4	20	75
1733.........................5	25	85		1739.........................4	20	75
1734.........................6	30	90				
3721 Old bust. GEORGIUS							
1741.........................5	30	100		1744.........................5	30	100
3722 — GEORGIVS							
1746.........................4	18	65		1750.........................5	25	85
1749.........................5	22	70		1754.........................1	10	35

During the second half of the 18th century very little silver or copper was minted. In 1797 Matthew Boulton's 'cartwheels', the first copper pennies and twopences, demonstrated the improvement from the application of steam power to the coining press.

During the Napoleonic Wars bank notes came into general use when the issue of guineas was stopped between 1797 and 1813, but gold 7s. pieces were minted to relieve the shortage of smaller money. As an emergency measure Spanish 'dollars' were put into circulation for a short period after being countermarked, and in 1804 Spanish dollars were overstruck and issued as Bank of England dollars.

The transition to a 'token' silver coinage began in 1811 when the Bank of England had 3s and 1s. 6d. tokens made for general circulation. Private issues of token money in the years 1788-95 and 1811-15 helped to alleviate the shortage of regal coinage. A change over to a gold standard and a regular 'token' silver coinage came in 1816 when the Mint, which was moved from its old quarters in the Tower of London to a new site on Tower Hill, began a complete re-coinage. The guinea was replaced by a 20s. sovereign, and silver coins were made which had an intrinsic value lower than their face value. The St. George design used on the sovereign and crown was the work of Benedetto Pistrucci.

Early coinages

GOLD

3724

3723 Five guineas. Pattern only
  1770 *FDC* £62,000   1777 *FDC* £62,000
  1773 *FDC* £62,000
3724 Two guineas. Pattern only
  1768 *FDC* £22,000   1777 *FDC* £22,000
  1773 *FDC* £22,000
There are different bust varieties for 3723 and 3724, for further details see Douglas-Morris, November 1974, lots 127-132.

	F	VF	EF
	£	£	£
3725 Guinea. First head, 1761 (also with three leaves at top of wreath)	375	850	2500

3725   3726   3727

3726 Second head
  1763...........................250   500   1250   1764...........................200   400   1000

	F £	VF £	EF £		F £	VF £	EF £
3727 Third head							
1765	110	200	450	1770	120	225	475
1766	85	150	325	1771	100	175	425
1767	125	225	525	1772	85	150	325
1768	100	175	400	1773	85	150	325
1769	100	175	400				

3728 Fourth head

	F £	VF £	EF £		F £	VF £	EF £
1774	75	135	300	1781	85	160	350
1775	75	135	300	1782	85	160	350
1776	75	135	300	1783	85	160	350
1777	75	135	300	1784	85	160	350
1778	95	175	375	1785	75	135	300
1779	85	160	350	1786	75	135	300

3728   3729

3729 Fifth head. R. 'Spade'-shaped shield

	F £	VF £	EF £		F £	VF £	EF £
1787	75	130	250	1794	75	130	250
1788	75	130	250	1795	100	175	400
1789	75	135	275	1796	100	175	400
1790	75	130	250	1797	80	140	275
1791	75	130	250	1798*	75	130	250
1792	75	135	250	1799	90	150	350
1793	75	130	250	*Beware counterfeits*			

3730 Sixth head. R. Shield in Garter, known as the Military guinea, 1813.......   350   600

3730

3731 **Half-guinea**. First head

	F £	VF £	EF £		F £	VF £	EF £
1762	150	400	1200	1763	200	600	1350

3732 Second head

	F £	VF £	EF £		F £	VF £	EF £
1764	90	225	475	1772		*Extremely rare*	
1765/4	250	600	—	1773	90	250	550
1766	90	250	500	1774	150	300	1000
1768	90	250	550	1775	150	300	1000
1769	90	250	500				

3733   3734   3737

	F	VF	EF		F	VF	EF
	£	£	£		£	£	£

3733 Half-guinea Third head (less fine style)

1774		*Extremely rare*		1775	175	450	1250

3734 Fourth head

1775	70	135	275	1781	80	140	300
1776	70	135	275	1783	300	800	—
1777	65	120	250	1784	70	135	275
1778	80	140	300	1785	65	120	250
1779	95	200	500	1786	65	120	250

3735 Fifth head. R. 'Spade' type

1787	60	115	225	1794	60	125	250
1788	60	115	225	1795	80	175	300
1789	65	125	250	1796	65	125	250
1790	60	115	225	1797	60	115	225
1791	65	125	250	1798	60	115	225
1792	350	850	—	1800	125	350	—
1793	60	115	225				

3736 Sixth head. R. Shield in Garter

1801	45	60	125	1803	45	65	135
1802	45	65	135				

3737 Seventh head. with short hair. R. As last

1804	45	60	125	1809	45	65	135
1805		*Extremely rare*		1810	45	65	135
1806	45	65	135	1811	75	150	350
1808	45	65	135	1813	65	135	275

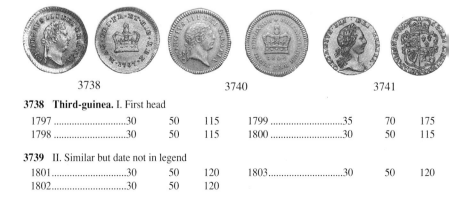

3738   3740   3741

3738 Third-guinea. I. First head

1797	30	50	115	1799	35	70	175
1798	30	50	115	1800	30	50	115

3739 II. Similar but date not in legend

1801	30	50	120	1803	30	50	120
1802	30	50	120				

	F £	VF £	EF £		F £	VF £	EF £
3740 III. Second head with short hair							
1804	30	50	120	1810	30	50	120
1806	30	50	120	1811	125	300	650
1808	30	50	120	1813	75	150	300
1809	30	50	120				
3741 Quarter-guinea, 1762			35	75	150		

For gold of the 'new coinage', 1817-20, see page 268.

SILVER

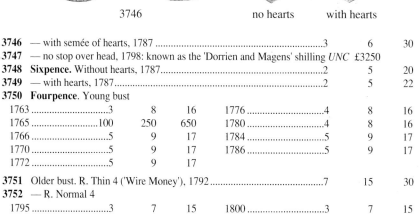

3742

	F	VF	EF
3742 **Shilling.** Young bust, known as the 'Northumberland' shilling, 1763	100	175	350
3743 Older bust, no semée of hearts in the Hanoverian shield, 1787	3	6	30
3744 — — no stop over head, 1787	5	10	40
3745 — — no stops at date, 1787	5	10	45
3745A — — no stops on *obv.*, 1787	30	100	250

3746   no hearts   with hearts

	F	VF	EF
3746 — with semée of hearts, 1787	3	6	30
3747 — no stop over head, 1798: known as the 'Dorrien and Magens' shilling *UNC* £3250			
3748 **Sixpence.** Without hearts, 1787	2	5	20
3749 — with hearts, 1787	2	5	22
3750 **Fourpence.** Young bust			
1763 ... 3	8	16	1776 ... 4 ... 8 ... 16
1765 ... 100	250	650	1780 ... 4 ... 8 ... 16
1766 ... 5	9	17	1784 ... 5 ... 9 ... 17
1770 ... 5	9	17	1786 ... 5 ... 9 ... 17
1772 ... 5	9	17	
3751 Older bust. R. Thin 4 ('Wire Money'), 1792	7	15	30
3752 — R. Normal 4			
1795 ... 3	7	15	1800 ... 3 ... 7 ... 15

3750   3751   3755

3753 Threepence. Young bust

	F £	VF £	EF £		F £	VF £	EF £
1762	2	9		1772	3	6	14
1763	2	5	9	1780	3	6	14
1765	100	250	500	1784	3	7	15
1766	3	6	14	1786	3	6	14
1770	3	6	14				

3754   Older bust. R. Thin 3 ('Wire Money'), 1792 7   15   30
3755   — R. Normal 3

1795	3	7	14	1800	3	7	14

3756 Twopence. Young bust

1763	2	5	11	1776	2	5	11
1765	75	175	450	1780	2	5	11
1766	2	5	11	1784	2	5	11
1772	2	5	11	1786	2	5	11

3757   Older bust. R. Thin 2 ('Wire Money'), 1792...5   12   25
3758   — R. Normal 2

1795	2	4	7	1800	2	4	7

3759 Penny. Young bust

1763	2	5	11	1779	2	5	10
1766	2	5	10	1780	2	5	11
1770	2	5	10	1781	2	5	10
1772	2	5	10	1784	2	5	10
1776	2	5	11	1786	2	5	10

3760   Older bust. R. Thin 1 ('Wire Money'), 1792...2   5   8
3761   — R. Normal 1

1795	1	2	6	1800	1	2	6

3762 Maundy Set. Uniform dates
3763   — Older bust. R. Thin numerals ('Wire Money'), 1792 50   80   175

1763	26	45	115	1780	26	45	115
1766	26	45	115	1784	26	45	115
1772	26	45	115	1786	26	45	115

3764   — R. Normal numerals. Uniform dates

1795	20	35	80	1800	20	35	75

Emergency issue
3765   Dollar (current for 4s. 9d.). Spanish American 8 *reales* counter -
marked with head of George III in oval 50   125   250
3766   — octagonal countermark 75   150   350
3767   Half-dollar with similar oval countermark...60   135   300

3765 3767 3766

Bank of England issue

3768

	F £	VF £	EF £

3768 Dollar (current for 5s.). Laureate bust of king. R. Britannia seated
  l., 1804 ....35 70 175
*These dollars were re-struck from Spanish-American 8 reales until at least 1811. Dollars that show
dates of original coin are worth rather more.*

3769 3770

3769 Three shillings. Draped bust in armour. R. BANK / TOKEN / 3 SHILL / date (in oak wreath)

	F £	VF £	EF £		F	VF	EF
1811..........................8		15	45	1812..........................9	16	50

	F £	VF £	EF £		F £	VF £	EF £

3770 Three shillings. Laureate head r. R. As before but wreath of oak and laurel

1812	8	15	45	1815	8	15	45
1813	8	15	45	1816	90	175	450
1814	8	15	45				

3771   3771

3771 Eighteen pence. Draped bust in armour

1811	5	12	35	1812	5	12	35

3772 — Laureate head

1812	4	11	30	1815	4	11	30
1813	4	11	30	1816	4	11	30
1814	4	11	30				

3773 Ninepence. Similar, 1812 (pattern only) *FDC* £900

For the last or 'new coinage', 1816-20, see page 268.

COPPER

First issue — London

3774

3774 Halfpenny. Cuirassed bust r. R. Britannia

1770	3	12	60	1773	2	10	55
1771	2	10	55	1774	3	12	60
1772	2	10	55	1775	3	15	65

3775

3775 Farthing

1771	15	35	110	1774	3	12	65
1773	2	8	50	1775	4	15	70

Second issue—Soho mint. 'Cartwheel' coinage

3776

	F	VF	EF		F	VF	EF
	£	£	£		£	£	£

3776 Twopence. Legends incuse on raised rim, 1797 7   18   90
3777 Penny, 1797. Similar 6   15   55
Halfpence and farthings of this issue are patterns.

Third issue—Soho mint

3778

3778 Halfpenny. Draped bust r., 1799..   3   30
3779 Farthing, 1799..   3   30

Fourth issue—Soho mint

3780   3782

3780 Penny. Different bust

1806..........................1   4   50   1807............................1   6   55

3781 Halfpenny

1806..........................   2   30   1807   3   40

3782 Farthing

1806..........................   2   30   1807..........................   3   40

In 1787 the regal copper coinage was very scanty, and so pennies and halfpennies were struck by the Anglesey Copper Mining Company and a fresh token epoch began. They present an immense variety of types, persons, buildings, coats of arms, local legends, political events, etc., all drawn upon for subjects of design. They were struck by many firms in most cities and towns in the country and are to be found in good condition. Circulated specimens are so common that they have little value.

    For further details of 18th-century tokens see *The Provincial Token-Coinage of the Eighteenth Century,* by Dalton and Hamer, and Seaby's *British Tokens and Their Values.*

	VF	EF
	£	£
Price of commoner pennies..	5	14
— — — halfpennies	4	11
— — — farthings..	3	9

Bury St. Edmunds penny

Anglesey penny   Coventry halfpenny

Isaac Newton Farthing

With the issue of the copper coinage of 1797 tokens were made illegal, but the dearth of silver currency was still felt. During the Napoleonic wars, a small wave of prosperity in the industrial districts brought the inevitable need for small change, so in 1811 tokens again made their appearance. On this occasion silver ones were made as well as copper. These, with two exceptions were suppressed before the last coinage of George III.

For further details of 19th-century silver tokens see *The Nineteenth Century Token Coinage* by W. J. Davis and *Silver Token-Coinage 1811-1812*, by R. Dalton, also Seaby's *British Tokens and Their Values.*

	VF £	EF £
Price of the commoner five shillings	350	700
— — — four shillings	125	250
— — — three shillings	135	275
— — — halfcrowns	60	120
— — — two shillings	55	110
— — — eighteen pence	20	40
— — — shillings	11	22
— — — sixpences	10	20

Sheffield Shilling   Charing Cross Sixpence

	VF £	EF £
Price of the commoner threepences	25	125
— — — twopences	12	50
— — — pennies	3	13
— — — halfpennies	2	8
— — — farthings	2	9

Withymoor Scythe Works Penny, 1813

Last or new coinage, 1816-20

The year 1816 is a landmark in the history of our coinage. For some years at the beginning of the 19th century Mint production was virtually confined to small gold denominations, regular full production being resumed only after the Mint had been moved from the Tower of London to a new site on Tower Hill. Steam powered minting machinery made by Boulton and Watt replaced the old hand-operated presses and these produced coins which were technically much superior to the older milled coins.

In 1816 for the first time British silver coins were produced with an intrinsic value substantially below their face value, the first official token coinage.

Our present 'silver' coins are made to the same weight standard and are still legal tender from 1816 with the exception of the halfcrown. The old guinea was replaced by a sovereign of twenty shillings in 1817, the standard of 22 carat (.916) fineness still being retained.

Engraver's and/or designer's initials:
 B.P. (Benedetto Pistrucci)

GOLD

3783

3783* Five pounds, 1820 (Pattern only) *FDC*. . . . . *Extremely rare*
A Brilliant mint-state specimen sold at auction in November 1989 for £47,500 plus 10% buyer's premium.
*Beware counterfeits
3784 Two pounds, 1820 (Pattern only) *FDC*. £12,000
3785 Sovereign. Coarse hair, legend type A (Descending colon after BRITANNIAR, no space between REX and F:D:). R. St. George

	F	VF	EF		F	VF	EF
	£	£	£		£	£	£
1817	75	125	375	1819*		*Extremely rare*	
1818	85	150	450				

An almost VF specimen sold at auction in March 1992 for £15,500 plus 10% buyer's premium.
3785A— legend type B (Ascending colon after BRITANNIAR, space between REX and F:D:)
 1818 ....85 150 450
3785B Wiry curls, legend type A.
 1818 .... *Extremely Rare*
3785C— legend type B.
 1818 .... *Extremely rare* 1820..........................75 125 375

3785 3785A 3786

	F	VF	EF		F	VF	EF
	£	£	£		£	£	£

3786 Half-sovereign. R. Crowned shield

| 1817 | 50 | 85 | 175 | 1820 | 55 | 90 | 200 |
| 1818 | 55 | 90 | 200 | | | | |

SILVER

3787

3787 Crown. Laureate head r. R. Pistrucci's St. George and dragon within Garter

		F	VF	EF
		£	£	£
1818, edge	LVIII	9	25	115
— —	LIX	10	30	120
1819 —	LIX	9	25	115
— —	LX	10	30	120
1820 —	LX	9	25	115

3788

3788 Halfcrown. Large or 'bull' head

| 1816 | 6 | 18 | 80 | 1817 | 6 | 18 | 80 |

3789

	F £	VF £	EF £		F £	VF £	EF £

3789 Halfcrown. Small head

	F	VF	EF		F	VF	EF
1817..........................6	18	80		1819..........................7	20	90	
1818..........................7	20	90		1820..........................9	28	130	

3790   3791

3790 Shilling. R. Shield in Garter

	F	VF	EF		F	VF	EF
1816..........................2	6	25		1819..........................3	7	30	
1817..........................3	7	30		1820..........................3	7	30	
1818..........................7	20	85					

3791 Sixpence. R. Shield in Garter

	F	VF	EF		F	VF	EF
1816..........................2	5	22		1819..........................3	7	30	
1817..........................2	6	25		1820..........................3	7	30	
1818..........................3	7	30					

3792

3792 Maundy Set (4d., 3d., 2d. and 1d.)

	EF £	FDC £		EF £	FDC £
1817..........................	80	150	1820..........................	80	150
1818..........................	80	150			

		EF	FDC
3793	**— fourpence,** 1817, 1818, 1820..*from*	14	30
3794	**— threepence,** 1817, 1818, 1820 ....*from*	14	30
3795	**— twopence,** 1817, 1818, 1820 ....*from*	8	13
3796	**— penny,** 1817, 1818, 1820...*from*	7	11

The Mint resumed the coinage of copper farthings in 1821, and pennies and halfpennies in 1825. A gold two pound piece was first issued for general circulation in 1823.

Engraver's and/or designer's initials:
B. P. (Benedetto Pistrucci)
J. B. M. (Jean Baptiste Merlen)

GOLD

3797

3797   Five pounds, 1826 (proof only). R. Shield............................*FDC* £8000

3798

	VF £	EF £
3798 Two pounds, 1823. Large bare head. R. St. George.................................	275	550
3799 1826. Type as 3797 (proof only) ....*FDC* 2750		

3800

3800   Sovereign. Laureate head. R. St. George

	F £	VF £	EF £		F £	VF £	EF £
1821............................	75	125	375	1824............................	75	130	400
1822*..........................	75	130	400	1825............................	100	275	1000
1823............................	110	300	1100				

Beware counterfeits.

3801

	F £	VF £	EF £		F £	VF £	EF £

3801 Sovereign. Bare head. R. Crowned shield

1825	75	135	350	1828*	500	1250	2750
1826	75	135	350	1829	85	140	375
— Proof *FDC* £1500				1830	85	140	375
1827*	85	140	375				

      3802   3803   3804

3802 Half-sovereign. Laureate head. R. Ornately garnished shield.

1821					175	375	1000

3803 — R. Plain shield

| 1823 | 65 | 125 | 350 | 1825 | 60 | 110 | 300 |
| 1824 | 60 | 120 | 325 | | | | |

3804 — Bare head. R. Garnished shield

| 1826 | 60 | 110 | 300 | 1827 | 60 | 110 | 300 |
| — Proof *FDC* £875 | | | | 1828 | 55 | 100 | 250 |

*Beware counterfeits

SILVER

3805

3805 Crown. Laureate head. R. St. George

1821, edge SECUNDO	12	40	250
1822 — SECUNDO	15	50	325
— — TERTIO	14	45	275

3806

3806 Crown. Bare head. R. Shield with crest (proof only), 1826 *FDC* £2250

3807 3808

3807 Halfcrown. Laureate head. R. Garnished shield

	F	VF	EF		F	VF	EF
	£	£	£		£	£	£
1820	7	25	95	1823	225	650	1950
1821	7	25	95				

3808 — R. Shield in Garter and collar

	F	VF	EF		F	VF	EF
1823	7	30	110	1824	10	40	150

3809

3809 Bare head. R. Shield with crest

1824		*Extremely rare*		1826 Proof *FDC* £400			
1825	7	25	85	1828	12	40	175
1826	6	22	80	1829	10	35	150

3810   3811   3812

	F £	VF £	EF £		F £	VF £	EF £

3810   Shilling. Laureate head. R. Garnished shield

1821 5   15   60

3811   — R. Shield in Garter

1823 12   40   150   1825 5   18   75
1824 5   18   75

3812   Bare head R. Lion crown

1825 3   9   40   1827 8   30   110
1826 3   8   35   1829 6   20   80
— Proof *FDC £175*

3813   3814   3815

3813   Sixpence. Laureate head. R. Garnished shield

1821 3   10   45

3814   — R. Shield in Garter

1824.............................3   10   45   1826.........................15   40   140
1825.............................3   10   45

3815   Bare head. R. Lion on crown

1826.............................3   8   30   1828.............................4   15   60
— Proof *FDC £110*   1829.............................3   10   45
1827.............................8   30   100

3816

3816   Maundy Set (4d., 3d., 2d. and 1d.)

	EF £	FDC £		EF £	FDC £
1822..........................	65	125	1827..........................	55	105
1823..........................	55	105	1828..........................	55	105
1824..........................	60	115	1829..........................	55	105
1825..........................	55	105	1830..........................	55	105
1826..........................	55	105			

	EF	FDC
	£	£
3817 **Maundy fourpence,** 1822-30 ....*from*	11	18
3818 — **threepence**, small head, 1822...	20	35
3819 — — normal head, 1823-30 ....*from*	10	17
3820 — **twopence,** 1822-30 ....*from*	8	10
3821 — **penny,** 1822-30 ....*from*	5	8

COPPER

First issue, 1821-6

3822

	F	VF	EF		F	VF	EF
	£	£	£		£	£	£

3822 Farthing. Laureate bust, draped

1821		4	20	1825		4	18
1822		4	18	1826 1		6	30
1823		4	22				

Second issue, 1825-30

3823

3827

3823 Penny. Laureate head. R. Britannia

1825..........................4	12	50	1826 Proof *FDC £200*			
1826..........................4	10	40	1827..........................25	80	900	

3824 Halfpenny. Similar

1825..........................9	25	90	1826 Proof *FDC £100*			
1826..........................	5	24	1827..........................3	8	40	

3825 Farthing. Similar

1826..........................	3	15	1828..........................		4	20
— Proof *FDC £100*			1829..........................		6	35
1827..........................	5	25	1830..........................		4	20

3826 Half-farthing (for use in Ceylon). Similar

1828..........................4	12	45	1830..........................4		12	45

3827 Third-farthing (for use in Malta). Similar

1827..	3	15

In order to prevent confusion between the sixpence and half-sovereign the size of the latter was reduced in 1834, but the smaller gold piece was not acceptable to the public and in the following year it was made to the normal size. In 1836 the silver groat was again issued for general circulation: it is the only British silver coin which has a seated Britannia as the type. Crowns were not struck during this reign for general circulation; but proofs or patterns of this denomination were made and are greatly sought after. Silver threepences and three-halfpence were minted for use in the Colonies.

Engraver's and/or designer's initials:
    W. W. (William Wyon)

GOLD

3828

3828   Two pounds, 1831 (proof only) ....*FDC*   £5000

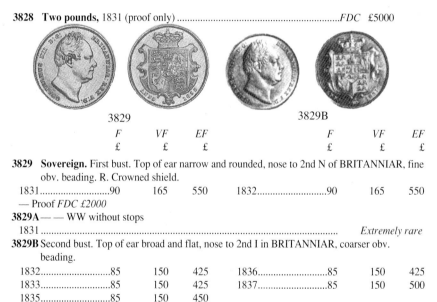

3829   3829B

	F	*VF*	*EF*			*F*	*VF*	*EF*
	£	£	£			£	£	£

3829   Sovereign. First bust. Top of ear narrow and rounded, nose to 2nd N of BRITANNIAR, fine obv. beading. R. Crowned shield.

1831	90	165	550		1832	90	165	550

— Proof *FDC £2000*

3829A — — WW without stops

1831 .... *Extremely rare*

3829B Second bust. Top of ear broad and flat, nose to 2nd I in BRITANNIAR, coarser obv. beading.

1832	85	150	425		1836	85	150	425
1833	85	150	425		1837	85	150	500
1835	85	150	450					

3830   3831

3830   Half-sovereign. Small size

1831 Proof *FDC* £1250				1834	90	150	400

	F £	VF £	EF £		F £	VF £	EF £
3831 Large size							
1835	75	150	400	1837	90	165	450
1836	100	225	500				
3832 *Obv.* struck from 6d. die, 1836					500	950	2000

SILVER

3833

3833 Crown. R. Shield on mantle, 1831 (proof only) ....*FDC* £3500

3834

3834 Halfcrown. R. Shield on mantle

	F	VF	EF		F	VF	EF
1831 Proof *FDC* £400				1836	9	30	125
1834	8	25	95	1837	12	50	200
1835	12	50	175				

3835   3836

3835 Shilling. R. Value in wreath

	F	VF	EF		F	VF	EF
1831 Proof *FDC* £225				1836	5	18	80
1834	5	18	80	1837	7	30	125
1835	6	22	95				

3836 Sixpence. R. Value in wreath

	F	VF	EF		F	VF	EF
1831	3	9	40	1835	3	9	40
— Proof *FDC* £150				1836	6	20	90
1834	3	10	40	1837	4	18	80

3837

	F £	VF £	EF £		F £	VF £	EF £
3837 Groat. R. Britannia seated							
1836		3	16	1837		3	16
3838 Threepence (for use in the West Indies). As Maundy threepence but with a dull surface							
1834	1	6	30	1836	1	5	28
1835	1	5	28	1837	2	7	36

3839

3839 Three-halfpence (for Colonial use). R. Value

	F	VF	EF		F	VF	EF
1834		3	16	1836		4	20
1835		3	18	1837	5	20	75

3840

3840 Maundy Set (4d., 3d., 2d. and 1d.).

	EF £	FDC £		EF £	FDC £
1831	80	150	1834	75	140
— Proof *FDC £250*			1835	75	140
1832	75	140	1836	75	140
1833	75	140	1837	75	140

3841 — **fourpence**, 1831-7 ...... *from*	11	20
3842 — **threepence**, 1831-7 ...... *from*	20	30
3843 — **twopence**, 1831-7 ...... *from*	7	13
3844 — **penny**, 1831-7 ...... *from*	7	12

COPPER

3845

	F £	VF £	EF £		F £	VF £	EF £
3845 Penny. No initials on truncation							
1831...........................6	25	90		1834...........................7	30	100	
— Proof *FDC £225*				1837...........................9	40	150	
3846 WW on truncation, 1831 8					35	125	
3847 Halfpenny. As penny							
1831...........................2	7	30		1834...........................2	7	35	
— Proof *FDC £125*				1837...........................1	6	25	
3848 Farthing. Similar							
1831...........................	3	16		1835...........................	3	16	
— Proof *FDC £120*				1836...........................	4	20	
1834...........................	3	16		1837...........................	3	16	

3847   3848

3849 Half-farthing (for use in Ceylon). Similar

1837 12   40   175

3850 Third-farthing (for use in Malta). Similar

1835   3   15

3849   3850

In 1849, as a first step towards decimalization, a silver florin ($^1/_{10}$th pound) was introduced, but the coins of 1849 omitted the usual *Dei Gratia* and these so-called 'Godless' florins were replaced in 1851 by the 'Gothic' issue. The halfcrown was temporarily discontinued but was minted again from 1874 onwards. Between 1863 and 1880 reverse dies of the gold and silver coins were numbered in the course of Mint experiments into the wear of dies. The exception was the florin where the die number is on the obverse below the bust.

The gold and silver coins were redesigned for the Queen's Golden Jubilee in 1887. The double-florin which was then issued was abandoned after only four years; the Jubilee sixpence of 1887, known as the 'withdrawn' type, was changed to avoid confusion with the half-sovereign. Gold and silver were again redesigned in 1893 with an older portrait of the Queen, but the 'old head' was not used on the bronze coinage until 1895. The heavy copper penny had been replaced by the lighter bronze 'bun' penny in 1860. In 1874-6 and 1881-2 some of the bronze was made by Heaton in Birmingham, and these have a letter H below the date. From 1897 farthings were issued with a dark surface.

Early sovereigns had a shield-type reverse, but Pistrucci's St. George design was used again from 1871. In order to increase the output of gold coinage, branches of the Royal Mint were set up in Australia at Sydney and Melbourne and, later, at Perth for coining gold of imperial type.

Engraver's and/or designer's initials:

    W. W. (William Wyon)   J. E. B. (Joseph Boehm)

    L. C. W. (Leonard Charles Wyon)   T. B. (Thomas Brock)

GOLD

Young head coinage, 1838-87

3851

3851   **Five pounds.** 1839. R. 'Una and the lion' (proof only)..............................   *FDC*   £18,500

3852   3852C   3852D

	F	VF	EF		VF	EF
	£	£	£		£	£

3852 Sovereign. Type I, first (small) young head. R. First shield. London mint

1838	70	90	300	1844		60	140
1839	100	200	800	1845		60	150
— Proof FDC £2500				1846		60	150
1841	400	800	2500	1847		60	140
1842		60	140	1848		Extremely rare	
1843		60	140				

3852A— narrower shield. Considerably modified floral emblems

1843 ....Extremely rare

A practically EF specimen was sold at auction in March 1992 for £2500 plus 10% buyers premium.

3852B Type I, second (large) head. W W still in relief. R. Shield with repositioned legend

1848		60	140	1853		60	120
1849		60	140	1854		60	130
1850		60	160	1855		60	120
1851		60	130	1872		60	120
1852		60	120				

3852C— — WW incuse

1853		60	120	1858		60	175
— Proof FDC £4500				1859		60	130
1854		60	130	1860		60	120
1855		60	120	1861		60	120
1856		60	130	1862		60	120
1857		60	130	1863		60	120

3852D— — As 3852C 'Ansell' ribbon. Additional raised line on the lower part of the ribbon

1859 150   350   1100

3852E— — As 3852C with 827 on truncation

1863 ....Extremely rare

* A *VF* specimen sold at auction in March 1992 for £1750 plus buyer's premium.

3852B   3853

3853 — — As 3852C die number below wreath

1863		60	120	1868		60	120
1864		60	110	1869		60	110
1865		60	130	1870		70	160
1866		60	110				

3853A— — As 3853 with 827 on truncation (Always die no 22)

1863 ....Extremely rare

3853B — — WW in relief die number below wreath

1870		60	120	1873		60	120
1871		60	110	1874		1100	—
1872		60	110				

3854   3855

	VF £	EF £		F £	VF £	EF £

3854 — — As 3853B but with M below wreath for Melbourne

1872 M	65	175	1882 M		65	175
1873 M	*Extremely rare*		1883 M		200	600
1874 M	65	175	1884 M		65	175
1879 M	*Extremely rare*		1885 M		65	175
1880 M	900	2750	1886 M		1400	3250
1881 M	70	225	1887 M		700	2000

3854A — — As 3853 W W incuse but with S below wreath for Sydney

1871 S	60	90	200

3855 — — As 3854 but with S below wreath for Sydney

1871 S	60	130	1881 S	60	110
1872 S	60	130	1882 S	60	110
1873 S	60	130	1883 S	60	110
1875 S	60	110	1884 S	60	110
1877 S	60	110	1885 S	60	130
1878 S	60	110	1886 S	60	130
1879 S	60	110	1887 S	60	130
1880 S	60	110			

3856A

3856 Sovereign, type II, first young head. WW buried in narrow truncation. R. St. George. London mint. Horse with short tail. Large BP

1871	110

3856A — — As 3856 R. Horse with long tail. Small BP

1871	90	1876		90
1872	90	1878		100
1873	100	1879	150	500
1874	110	1880		90

3856B — — As 3856 but with small BP

1880	90	1885	110
1884	100		

3856C — — As 3856 but no BP

1880	90

	VF £	EF £		VF £	EF £

3856D — — Second head. WW on broad truncation. R. Horse with long tail, small BP

1880.. 110

3856E — — As 3856D but horse with short tail. No BP

1880.. 90

3856F — — As 3856E but small BP

1884... 100   1885... 110

3857   3858

3857 — — First head. WW buried in truncation, M below head for Melbourne mint. R. Horse with long tail, small BP

1872 M	90	270	1877 M		95
1873 M		160	1878 M		95
1874 M		160	1879 M		115
1875 M		115	1880 M		95
1876 M		115	1881 M		95

3857A — — As 3857 but horse with short tail, no BP

1881 M		95	1882 M		95

3857B — — As 3857A but with small BP

1882 M		95	1884 M		95
1883 M		95	1885 M		95

3857C — — Second head. WW on broad truncation. R. Horse with short tail, small BP

1882 M		95	1885 M		95
1883 M		95	1886 M		95
1884 M		95	1887 M		95

3858 — — First head. WW buried in narrow truncation, S below head for Sydney mint. #R. Horse with short tail, large BP

1871 S 90   200

3858A — — As 3858 but horse with lo ng tail, small BP

1871 S	80	180	1876 S		90
1872 S	60	160	1877 S		*Extremely rare*
1873 S		140	1879 S	60	160
1874 S		90	1880 S		95
1875 S		90			

3858B — — As 3858 but with no BP

1880 S		95	1881 S		95

	EF		EF
	£		£

3858C Sovereign. Second head. WW on broad truncation. R. Horse with long tail, small BP

1880 S 110

3858D — — As 3858C but horse with short tail, no BP

| 1881 S .... | 95 | 1882 S .... | 95 |

3858E — — As 3858D but small BP

1882 S	95	1885 S	95
1883 S	95	1886 S	95
1884 S	95	1887 S	95

3859

3860

3859 Half-sovereign. R. Sheild. London mint

	VF	EF		VF	EF
	£	£		£	£
1838	75	200	1852	80	175
1839 Proof only *FDC £1000*			1853	60	135
1841	90	250	— Proof *FDC £2750*		
1842	60	135	1854	*Extremely rare*	
1843	90	250	1855	65	140
1844	70	200	1856	65	140
1845	250	800	1857	80	175
1846	75	200	1858	60	140
1847	75	200	1859	60	140
1848	75	200	1860	60	135
1849	65	175	1861	60	150
1850	200	500	1862	750	—
1851	65	150	1863	65	135

	VF £	EF £		VF £	EF £
3860 — — die number below shield					
1863	80	200	1873	55	150
1864	60	135	1874	65	150
1865	60	135	1875	55	135
1866	60	135	1876	55	130
1867	60	135	1877	55	130
1869	60	135	1878	55	130
1870	70	135	1879	75	250
1871	60	135	1880	55	130
1872	60	135			
3861 — — As 3859 (no die number) but head in slightly lower relief					
1880	60	135	1884	55	115
1883	55	115	1885	55	115

3862

3863

	VF	EF		VF	EF
3862 — — S below shield for Sydney mint					
1871 S	85	475	1881 S	150	650
1872 S	95	500	1882 S	175	1250
1875 S	90	400	1883 S	95	350
1879 S	95	450	1886 S	95	450
1880 S	95	475	1887 S	95	450
3863 — — M below shield for Melbourne mint					
1873 M	100	450	1884 M	200	1000
1877 M	125	500	1885 M	300	1500
1881 M	200	700	1886 M	125	550
1882 M	125	500	1887 M	250	1250

Jubilee coinage, 1887-93

3864

3864 Five pounds. R. St. George

1887	400	600

— Proof *FDC £2100*

	VF £	EF £		VF £	EF £

3865 Two pounds. Similar

1887 .... 160 350
— Proof *FDC £850*

3866 Sovereign. R. St. George. London mint

1887 80   1890 80
— Proof *FDC £500*   1891 80
1888 80   1892 80
1889 80

3866   3867   3869

3867 — Sovereign. M on ground for Melbourne mint

1887 M 80   1891 M 80
1888 M 80   1892 M 80
1889 M 80   1893 M 80
1890 M 80

3868 — — S on ground for Sydney mint

1887 S .... 125 325   1891 S 80
1888 S 110   1892 S 85
1889 S 80   1893 S 85
1890 S 80

3869 Half-sovereign. R. Shield. London mint

1887 70   1891 80
— Proof *FDC £300*   1892 75
1890 70   1893 80

3870 — — M below shield for Melbourne mint

1887 M .... 95 275   1893 M 110 350

3871 — — S below shield for Sydney mint

1887 S .... 90 250   1891 S 90 250
1889 S 110 350

Old head coinage, 1893-1901

3872 Five pounds. R. St. George

1893 .... 500 950
— Proof *FDC £2250*

3873

	VF £	EF £

3873 Two pounds. Similar

1893... 250 450

— Proof *FDC £1000*

3874 Sovereign. R. St. George, London mint

1893	BV	1898	BV
— Proof *FDC £550*		1899	BV
1894	BV	1900	BV
1895	BV	1901	BV
1896	BV		

3876   3877

3875 — R. St. George. M on ground for Melbourne mint

1893 M	BV	1898 M	BV
1894 M	BV	1899 M	BV
1895 M	BV	1900 M	BV
1896 M	BV	1901 M	BV
1897 M	BV		

3876 — — P on ground for Perth mint

1899 P	95	1901 P	BV
1900 P	BV		

3877 — — S on ground for Sydney mint

1893 S	BV	1898 S	BV
1894 S	BV	1899 S	BV
1895 S	BV	1900 S	BV
1896 S	BV	1901 S	BV
1897 S	BV		

NB   BV stands for Bullion value.

3878

	F £	VF £	EF £		F £	VF £	EF £

3878 Half-sovereign. R. St. George. London mint

1893			60	1897			60
— Proof *FDC £350*				1898			60
1894			60	1899			60
1895			60	1900			60
1896			60	1901			60

3879 — — M on ground for Melbourne mint

1893 M			*Extremely rare*	1899 M		75	200
1896 M		75	200	1900 M		75	200

3880 — — P on ground for Perth mint

1899 P			Proof *unique*	1900 P		90	300

3881 — — S on ground for Sydney mint

1893 S		70	200	1900 S		60	150
1897 S		70	200				

SILVER

Young head coinage

3882

3882 Crown. Young head. R. Crowned shield

	F	VF	EF		F	VF	EF
1839 Proof only *FDC £2500*				1845	16	45	375
1844	16	55	400	1847	18	60	500

	VF £	EF £	FDC £
3883*'Gothic' type, as illustration; inscribed edge, mdcccxlvii=1847	275	450	850
— Proof, Plain edge *FDC £950*			

*Beware of recent forgeries.

3884 — — mdcccliii=1853. Proof *FDC £3000*

3883

3888

	F £	VF £	EF £		F £	VF £	EF £

3885 Halfcrown. Type A¹. Young head with one ornate and one plain fillet binding hair. WW in relief on truncation, 1839 ....250 600 2000

3886 — Proof *FDC £650*

3887 Type A³. Two plain fillets. WW incuse

| 1839 | ....250 | 600 | 2000 | 1840 | ....12 | 40 | 175 |

3888 Type A⁴. Similar but no initials on truncation

1841	30	100	400	1846	9	35	130
1842	10	35	150	1848/6	30	100	550
1843	18	60	275	1849	15	60	225
1844	9	35	130	1850	12	45	200
1845	9	35	130	1853 Proof *FDC £1000*			

3889 Type A⁵. As last but inferior workmanship

1874	7	18	75	1881	7	18	75
1875	7	22	80	1882	7	22	80
1876	7	22	85	1883	7	18	75
1877	7	22	80	1884	7	18	75
1878	7	22	80	1885	7	18	75
1879	8	30	110	1886	7	18	75
1880	7	22	80	1887	7	18	80

	3890				3892	
	F	VF	EF		F	VF	EF
	£	£	£		£	£	£

3890 Florin, 'Godless' type (i.e. without D.G.), 1849......................................5   20   65

3891 'Gothic' type B[1], reads brit:, WW below bust, date at end of obverse legend in gothic numerals (1851 to 1863)

	F	VF	EF		F	VF	EF
mdcccli........................	?	*Proof only*		mdccclvii....................6	25	100
mdccclii....................5	20	85		mdccclviii.................6	25	100
mdcccliii....................5	22	95		mdccclix 6	25	100
— Proof *FDC £1100*				mdccclx 7	30	135
mdcccliv 200	500	1750		mdccclxii 20	100	300
mdccclv 6	25	100		mdccclxiii................50	175	650
mdccclvi 6	27	120				

3892 — type B[2]; as last but die number below bust (1864 to 1867)

mdccclxiv 6	25	100		mdccclxvi 7	30	130
mdccclxv 6	27	110		mdccclxvii 14	60	175

3893 — type B[3], reads britt:, die number (1868 to 1879)

mdccclxviii.............6	27	120		mdccclxxiv 6	25	100
mdccclxix 6	25	100		mdccclxxv 6	25	100
mdccclxx 6	25	100		mdccclxxvi 6	25	110
mdccclxxi 6	25	100		mdccclxxvii 6	25	110
mdccclxxii................5	20	80		mdccclxxix	*Extremely rare*	
mdccclxxiii...............5	20	80				

3894 — type B[4]. As last but with border of 48 arcs and no WW

1877 mdccclxxvii.. *Extremely rare*

3895 — type B[5]. Similar but 42 arcs (1867, 1877 and 1878)

mdccclxvii	*Extremely rare*			mdccclxxviii.............6	25	100
mdccclxxvii 6	25	110				

3896 — type B[5/6]. As last but no die number (1877, 1879)

mdccclxxvii	*Extremely rare*			mdccclxxix	*Extremely rare*	

3897 — type B[6], reads britt:, WW; 48 arcs (1879)

mdccclxxix 6   25   100

3898 — type B[7]. As last but no WW, 38 arcs (1879)

mdccclxxix 6   25   100

3899 — type B[3/8]. As next but younger portrait (1880)

mdccclxxx .... *Extremely rare*

3900 — type B[8]. Similar but 34 arcs (1880 to 1887)

mdccclxxx 6	25	100		mdccclxxxv 5	20	90
mdccclxxxi...............5	20	90		mdccclxxxvi.............5	22	95
mdccclxxxiii.............5	20	90		mdccclxxxvii..............	*? exists*	
mdccclxxxiv..............5	20	90				

	F £	VF £	EF £		F £	VF £	EF £

3901 — type B[9]. Similar but 46 arcs

1887 mdccclxxxvii 8 30 140

3906

3902 Shilling. Type A[1]. First head, WW on truncation

| 1838 | ......4 | 15 | 60 | 1839 | ......5 | 15 | 65 |

3903 Type A[2]. Second head, WW (proof only), 1839 *FDC £225*

3904 Type A[3]. Second head, no initials on truncation

1839	4	13	50	1853	4	14	50
1840	8	30	130	— Proof *FDC £400*			
1841	8	30	130	1854	30	110	400
1842	7	15	55	1855	4	13	50
1843	4	20	85	1856	4	13	50
1844	6	14	55	1857	4	13	50
1845	4	15	65	1858	4	13	50
1846	4	15	55	1859	4	13	50
1848 over 6	24	70	350	1860	6	22	80
1849	4	20	70	1861	6	22	80
1850	90	300	800	1862	10	35	110
1851	20	60	200	1863	10	55	175
1852	4	14	55				

3905 Type A[4]. As before but die number above date

| 1864 | ......4 | 13 | 50 | 1866 | ......4 | 13 | 50 |
| 1865 | ......4 | 13 | 50 | 1867 | ......4 | 14 | 55 |

3906 Type A[6]. Third head, die number above date

1867	20	65	225	1874	3	9	35
1868	4	13	50	1875	3	9	35
1869	4	16	70	1876	3	13	55
1870	4	16	70	1877	3	9	35
1871	3	9	35	1878	3	9	35
1872	3	9	35	1879	7	30	150
1873	3	9	35				

3907 Type A[7]. Fourth head; no die number

1879	4	14	50				
1880	3	8	27	1884	3	8	27
1881	3	8	27	1885	2	5	20
1882	7	28	80	1886	2	5	20
1883	3	8	27	1887	5	15	60

	F £	VF £	EF £		F £	VF £	EF £

3908 Sixpence. Type A. First head

Date	F £	VF £	EF £	Date	F £	VF £	EF £
1838	2	9	35	1852	3	10	40
1839	2	9	35	1853	2	9	35
— Proof *FDC £150*				— Proof *FDC £250*			
1840	3	10	40	1854	30	100	350
1841	4	15	50	1855	2	9	35
1842	3	10	40	1856	3	10	40
1843	3	11	40	1857	3	10	40
1844	2	9	35	1858	3	10	40
1845	3	10	40	1859	2	9	35
1846	2	9	35	1860	3	10	40
1848	20	65	250	1862	15	60	250
1850	3	10	40	1863	8	35	150
1851	3	10	40	1866			*Extremely rare*

3909   3912

3909 Type A^2. First head; die number above date

Date	F £	VF £	EF £	Date	F £	VF £	EF £
1864	3	8	40	1866	3	8	40
1865	4	12	50				

3910 Type A^3. Second head; die number above date

Date	F £	VF £	EF £	Date	F £	VF £	EF £
1867	4	14	55	1874	2	7	35
1868	4	14	55	1875	2	7	35
1869	4	20	80	1876	4	14	60
1870	4	20	80	1877	2	7	35
1871	3	8	40	1878	2	7	35
1872	3	8	40	1879	4	16	60
1873	2	7	35				

3911 Type A^4. Second head; no die number

Date	F £	VF £	EF £	Date	F £	VF £	EF £
1871	4	12	50	1879	3	8	40
1877	3	8	40	1880	4	12	50

3912 Type A^5. Third head

Date	F £	VF £	EF £	Date	F £	VF £	EF £
1880	1	5	22	1884	1	5	20
1881	1	5	20	1885	1	5	20
1882	4	16	60	1886	1	5	20
1883	1	5	20	1887	1	4	18

3913 Groat (4d.). R. Britannia

Date	F £	VF £	EF £	Date	F £	VF £	EF £
1838		4	20	1847/6 (or 8)	12	40	135
1839		5	25	1848		4	22
— Proof *FDC £110*				1849		4	22
1840		5	22	1851	15	50	150
1841		6	32	1852	22	75	225
1842		5	30	1853	30	90	275
1843		5	30	— Proof *FDC £275*			
1844		5	30	1854		4	22
1845		5	30	1855		4	22
1846		5	30				

3914   3914A   3914C   3914D

Threepence. R. Crowned 3; as Maundy threepence but with a less prooflike surface

3914   Type A^1. First bust, young head, high relief, ear fully visible.
R Tie ribbon closer to tooth border, cross on crown further from tooth border, figure 3

	VF £	EF £		VF £	EF £
1838*	4	30	1851	4	35
1839*	5	40	1852*	Extremely rare	
— Proof (see Maundy)			1853	6	60
1840*	5	45	1854	4	35
1841*	5	50	1855	5	50
1842*	5	50	1856	5	45
1843*	4	30	1857	5	45
1844*	5	45	1858	4	35
1845	4	22	1859	3	20
1846	6	60	1860	5	45
1849	5	45	1861	3	25
1850	3	25			

3914A Type A^2. First bust variety, slightly older portrait with acquiline nose

	VF	EF		VF	EF
1859	3	20	1864	4	30
1860	4	30	1865	5	45
1861	3	25	1866	4	30
1862	4	35	1867	4	35
1863	5	45	1868	3	25

3914B Type A^3. Second Bust, slightly larger, lower relief, mouth fuller, nose more pronounced, rounded truncation

1867	5	45

3914C Obv. as last. R. Tie ribbon further from tooth border, cross on crown nearer to tooth border

	VF	EF		VF	EF
1867	4	35	1874	3	18
1869	5	55	1875	3	18
1870	3	22	1876	3	18
1871	4	30	1877	3	18
1872	3	25	1878	3	18
1873	3	18	1879	3	18

3914D Type A^4. Third bust, older features, mouth closed, hair strands leading from 'bun' vary

	VF	EF		VF	EF
1880	3	20	1884	3	15
1881	3	20	1885	3	15
1882	4	35	1886	3	15
1883	3	15	1887	3	15

Issued for Colonial use only.

3915 Three-halfpence (for Colonial use). R. Value, etc.

1838	3	18	1842	3	25
1839	3	16	1843	2	14
1840	4	35	1860	4	40
1841	3	16	1862	4	35

3916

3916 Maundy Set (4d., 3d., 2d. and 1.)

	EF £	FDC £		EF £	FDC £
1838	35	60	1862	35	55
1839	35	60	1863	35	55
— Proof FDC £200			1864	35	55
1840	35	60	1865	35	55
1841	40	60	1866	35	55
1842	35	60	1867	35	55
1843	35	60	1868	35	55
1844	35	60	1869	35	55
1845	35	60	1870	35	55
1846	35	60	1871	35	55
1847	35	60	1872	35	55
1848	35	60	1873	35	55
1849	40	70	1874	35	55
1850	35	60	1875	35	55
1851	35	60	1876	35	55
1852	35	60	1877	35	55
1853	35	60	1878	35	55
— Proof FDC £300			1879	35	55
1854	35	60	1880	35	55
1855	40	70	1881	35	55
1856	35	60	1882	35	55
1857	35	60	1883	35	55
1858	35	60	1884	35	55
1859	35	60	1885	35	55
1860	35	60	1886	35	55
1861	35	60	1887	35	55

		EF	FDC
3917 — fourpence, 1838-87	from	6	10
3918 — threepence, 1838-87	from	12	20
3919 — twopence, 1838-87	from	4	7
3920 — penny, 1838-87	from	3	6

Maundy Sets in the original dated cases are worth approximately £5 more than the prices quoted.

Jubilee Coinage

3921

3921 Crown. R. St. George

	F £	VF £	EF £		F £	VF £	EF £
1887	6	15	30	1890	8	22	55
— Proof *FDC £375*				1891	8	24	65
1888	9	22	50	1892	10	25	80
1889	6	15	30				

3922

3922 Double-florin (4s.). R. Cruciform shields. Roman I in date

1887	5	8	25

3923 Similar but Arabic 1 in date

	F	VF	EF		F	VF	EF
1887	5	8	25	1889	6	10	30
— Proof *FDC £175*				1890	6	12	35
1888	6	12	35				

3924   3925

3924 Halfcrown. R. Shield in collar

	F	VF	EF		F	VF	EF
1887	3	4	16	1890	3	12	45
— Proof *FDC £115*				1891	3	12	45
1888	3	7	30	1892	3	12	45
1889	3	7	30				

	F	VF	EF		F	VF	EF
	£	£	£		£	£	£

3925 Florin. R. Cruciform shields

1887	3	3	14	1890	5	20	60
— Proof *FDC* £75				1891	8	35	125
1888	3	5	20	1892	8	30	110
1889	3	6	24				

3926   3927

3926 Shilling. Small head. R. Shield in Garter

1887		2	9	1888	1	4	15
— Proof *FDC* £55				1889	12	50	200

3927 Large head. R. As before

1889	1	4	20	1891	1	4	30
1890	1	4	25	1892	1	4	30

3928   3929   3930

3928 Sixpence. R. Shield in Garter (withdrawn type)

1887						2	8

—Proof *FDC* £40

3929 R. Value in wreath

1887		2	8	1891		3	18
1888		3	15	1892		3	18
1889		3	15	1893	80	300	850
1890		3	16				

3930 Groat (for use in British Guiana). R. Britannia

1888					3	10	25

3931 Threepence. As Maundy but less prooflike surface

1887		1	4	1890		2	7
— Proof *FDC* £27				1891		2	7
1888		3	9	1892		3	10
1889		2	7	1893	4	22	90

3932 Maundy Set (4d., 3d., 2d. and 1d.)

	EF	FDC		EF	FDC
	£	£		£	£
1888	35	55	1891	35	55
1889	35	55	1892	35	55
1890	35	55			

Maundy Sets in the original dated cases are worth approximately £5 more than the prices quoted.

3932

	EF £	FDC £
3933 — fourpence, 1888-92 ....*from*	9	13
3934 — threepence, 1888-92 ....*from*	11	21
3935 — twopence, 1888-92 ....*from*	5	10
3936 — penny, 1888-92 ....*from*	5	10

Old head coinage

3937

3937 Crown. R. St. George. Regnal date on edge

	F £	VF £	EF £
1893 — LVI 6		20	95
— — Proof *FDC £400*			
— — LVII12 12		35	150
1894 — LVII6 6		25	110
— — LVIII6 6		25	110
1895 — LVIII6 6		22	100
— — LIX 6 6		22	100
1896 — LIX 9 9		30	135
— — LX 6 6		22	100
1897 — LX 6 6		22	100
— — LXI 6 6		20	95
1898 — LXI12 12		35	150
— — LXII6 6		25	110
1899 — LXII6 6		25	110
— — LXIII6 6		25	110
1900 — LXIII6 6		20	95
— — LXIV 6		20	95

3938

	F £	VF £	EF £		F £	VF £	EF £

3938 Halfcrown. R. Shield in collar

1893 3	6	25		1897 3	6	25
— Proof *FDC £150*				1898 3	6	30
1894 3	8	45		1899 3	6	30
1895 3	6	30		1900 3	6	25
1896 3	6	30		1901 3	6	25

3939 Florin. R. Three shields within Garter

1893 3	5	25		1897 3	5	25
— Proof *FDC £95*				1898 3	5	30
1894 3	8	40		1899 3	5	25
1895 3	6	35		1900 3	5	25
1896 3	5	30		1901 3	5	25

3939   3940

3940 Shilling. R. Three shields within Garter

1893..................................	3	12		1897..................................	3	12
— Proof *FDC £60*				1898..................................	3	12
1894..................................	4	18		1899..................................	3	14
1895..................................	3	14		1900..................................	3	12
1896..................................	3	12		1901..................................	3	12

3941 Sixpence. R. Value in wreath

1893	3	10		1897	3	12
— Proof *FDC £40*				1898	3	12
1894	4	16		1899	3	12
1895	3	12		1900	3	10
1896	3	12		1901	3	10

3941

	EF £		EF £

3942 Threepence. R. Crowned 3. As Maundy but less prooflike surface

1893	3	1897	4
— Proof *FDC £30*		1898	4
1894	6	1899	3
1895	6	1900	3
1896	4	1901	3

3943

	EF £	FDC £		EF £	FDC £
3943 Maundy Set (4d., 3d., 2d. and 1d.)					
1893	30	45	1898	30	45
1894	30	45	1899	30	45
1895	30	45	1900	30	45
1896	30	45	1901	30	45
1897	30	45			
3944 — **fourpence**, 1893-1901 ...*from*				5	8
3945 — **threepence**, 1893-1901 ...*from*				10	17
3946 — **twopence**, 1893-1901 ...*from*				5	6
3947 — **penny**, 1893-1901 ...*from*				5	6

Maundy Sets in the original dated cases are worth approximately £5 more than the prices quoted.

COPPER AND BRONZE
Young head copper coinage, 1838-60

3948

	F £	VF £	EF £		F £	VF £	EF £
3948 Penny. R. Britannia							
1839 Bronzed proof *FDC £225*				1853		3	16
1841		4	25	Proof *FDC £225*			
1843	20	75	300	1854		3	16
1844	2	5	35	1855		3	16
1845	3	12	60	1856	5	20	90
1846	2	8	45	1857		3	20
1847	2	6	35	1858		3	18
1848/7	2	6	30	1859		4	22
1849	20	75	300	1860*		225	400
1851	2	8	45				

3949

	F	VF	EF		F	VF	EF
3949 Halfpenny. R. Britannia							
1838		2	16	1852		3	24
1839 Bronzed proof *FDC £90*				1853		2	9
1841		2	14	— Proof *FDC £125*			
1843	1	8	40	1854		2	9
1844		3	20	1855		2	9
1845	15	45	150	1856		3	22
1846		4	25	1857		3	14
1847		4	25	1858		2	16
1848		5	30	1859		3	18
1851		3	22	1860*			2750

Overstruck dates are listed only if commoner than normal date, or if no normal date is known.

Copper

3950

	F £	VF £	EF £		F £	VF £	EF £

3950 Farthing. R. Britannia

	F	VF	EF		F	VF	EF
1838		4	20	1850		4	22
1839		3	18	1851	3	10	45
— Bronzed proof FDC £110				1852	3	11	45
1840		3	18	1853		3	22
1841		3	18	— Proof FDC £250			
1842		7	45	1854		4	22
1843		3	18	1855		5	25
1844	15	40	150	1856	2	7	40
1845		4	22	1857		3	22
1846		7	35	1858		3	22
1847		4	22	1859	5	15	45
1848		4	22	1860*	—	—	3000
1849	7	30	110				

These 1860 large copper pieces not to be confused with the smaller and commoner bronze issue with date on reverse (nos. 3954, 3956 and 3958).

3951   3952   3953

3951 Half-farthing. R. Value

1839	1	3	16	1852	1	4	18
1842	1	3	16	1853	2	7	32
1843			5	— Proof FDC £200			
1844			5	1854	3	15	45
1847	1	3	12	1856	3	15	45
1851	1	4	18				

3952 Third-farthing (for use in Malta). R. Britannia

1844		6	18	60

3953 Quarter-farthing (for use in Ceylon). R. Value

1839	4	12	27	1853	5	14	30
1851	5	14	30	— Proof FDC £250			
1852	4	12	27				

Bronze coinage, 'bun head' issue, 1860-95

3954   3955

	F £	VF £	EF £		F £	VF £	EF £
3954*Penny. R. Britannia							
1860		5	24	1878		6	35
1861		5	24	1879		3	18
1862		4	22	1880		6	35
1863		4	22	1881		6	40
1864	3	25	150	1882*		*Extremely rare*	
1865		6	40	1883		5	27
1866		5	27	1884		3	15
1867		6	45	1885		3	15
1868	2	10	75	1886		3	18
1869	20	75	300	1887		3	15
1870	2	10	60	1888		3	18
1871	6	25	150	1889		2	14
1872		5	27	1890		2	14
1873		5	27	1891		2	12
1874		6	40	1892		2	14
1875		4	20	1893		2	14
1877		4	20	1894		4	25

3955 — H (Ralph Heaton & Sons, Birmingham) below date

	F	VF	EF		F	VF	EF
1874 H		7	35	1881 H		5	26
1875 H	8	50	175	1882 H		3	18
1876 H		4	20				

*1882 without `H' was sold in auction condition extremely fine for £1700, March 1988.

3956

	F £	VF £	EF £		F £	VF £	EF £

3956 Halfpenny. R. Britannia

	F	VF	EF		F	VF	EF
1860		3	15	1878	2	6	40
1861		3	15	1879		3	15
1862		3	13	1880		4	25
1863		5	25	1881		4	25
1864		5	30	1883		3	22
1865	2	6	40	1884		2	12
1866		5	30	1885		2	12
1867	2	6	40	1886		2	12
1868		5	32	1887		2	10
1869	3	25	90	1888		2	12
1870		5	26	1889		2	12
1871	6	30	100	1890		2	10
1872		4	24	1891		2	10
1873		5	30	1892		2	20
1874	2	8	60	1893		2	12
1875		3	20	1894		3	22
1877		3	20				

3957 — H below date

	F	VF	EF		F	VF	EF
1874 H		3	22	1881 H		2	20
1875 H		5	28	1882 H		2	20
1876 H		2	20				

3958

3960

3958 Farthing. R. Britannia

	F	VF	EF		F	VF	EF
1860		2	10	1880		2	14
1861		2	12	1881		1	8
1862		2	12	1883		4	20
1863	10	30	90	1884			5
1864		2	18	1885			5
1865		2	12	1886			5
1866		2	10	1887			8
1867		3	16	1888			7
1868		3	16	1890			7
1869		5	22	1891			5
1872		2	12	1892	2	6	20
1873		1	9	1893			5
1875	4	10	35	1894			7
1878			7	1895	3	8	30
1879			7				

	F	VF	EF		VF	EF
	£	£	£		£	£

3959 Farthing R. Britannia. H below date

1874 H			14	1881 H		12
1875 H			6	1882 H		12
1876 H	4	10	30			

3960 Third-farthing (for use in Malta). R. Value

1866	8	1881	10
1868	9	1884	9
1876	10	1885	9
1878	9		

Old head issue, 1985-1901

3961

3961 Penny. R. Britannia

1895	6	1899	5
1896	5	1900	3
1897	5	1901	2
1898	10		

3961 'High Tide'   3961A 'Low Tide'

3961A As last but 'Low tide', 1895.. 18   75

3962

3962 Halfpenny. Type as Penny. R. Britannia

1895	6	1899	4
1896	5	1900	3
1897	5	1901	2
1898	5		

	EF £		EF £

3963 Farthing. R. Britannia. Bright finish

| 1895 .... | 4 | 1897 .... | 5 |
| 1896 .... | 4 | | |

3964

3964 — Dark finish

1897	4	1900	3
1898	4	1901	2
1899	4		

THE HOUSE OF SAXE-COBURG GOTHA

EDWARD VII, 1901-10

Five pound pieces, two pound pieces and crowns were only issued in 1902. A branch of the Royal Mint was opened at Ottawa and coined sovereigns of imperial type from 1908.

Unlike the coins in most other proof sets, the proofs issued for the Coronation in 1902 have a matt surface in place of the more usual brilliant finish.

Designer's initials:
De S. (G. W. de Saulles)

GOLD

3965

	VF £	EF £	UNC £
3965 Five pounds. 1902. R. St. George	450	650	800
3966 — Proof. 1902. *Matt surface FDC £750*			
3967 Two pounds. 1902. Similar	200	350	500
3968 — Proof. 1902. *Matt surface FDC £425*			

3967   3969

	EF £	UNC £		EF £	UNC £
3969 Sovereign. R . St. George. London mint					
1902 Matt proof *FDC £140*			1906		BV
1902		BV	1907		BV
1903		BV	1908		BV
1904		BV	1909		BV
1905		BV	1910		BV
3970 — C on ground for Ottawa mint					
1908 C (Satin proof only) *FDC £2750*			1910 C	200	300
1909 C	200	300			

	VF	EF	UNC		VF	EF	UNC
	£	£	£		£	£	£

3971 — M on ground for Melbourne mint

1902 M			BV	1907 M			BV
1903 M			BV	1908 M			BV
1904 M			BV	1909 M			BV
1905 M			BV	1910 M			BV
1906 M			BV				

3972 — P on ground for Perth mint

1902 P			BV	1907 P			BV
1903 P			BV	1908 P			BV
1904 P			BV	1909 P			BV
1905 P			BV	1910 P			BV
1906 P			BV				

3973 — S on ground for Sydney mint

1902 S			BV	1907 S			BV
1903 S			BV	1908 S			BV
1904 S			BV	1909 S			BV
1905 S			BV	1910 S			BV
1906 S			BV				

BV *Stands for bullian value*

3974

3974 Half-sovereign. R. St. George. London mint

1902 Matt proof *FDC £100*			1906		45	50
1902	45	50	1907		45	50
1903	45	50	1908		45	50
1904	45	50	1909		45	50
1905	45	50	1910		45	50

3975 — M on ground for Melbourne mint

1906 M	55	80	175	1908 M	55	80	200
1907 M	55	80	175	1909 M	55	80	175

3976 — P on ground for Perth mint

1904 P	175	550	—	1909 P	140	400	—
1908 P	175	600	—				

3977 — S on ground for Sydney mint

1902 S	60	125	250	1908 S	55	110	175
1903 S	55	110	175	1910 S	55	110	175
1906 S	55	110	175				

SILVER

3978

	F	VF	EF	UNC
	£	£	£	£

3978 Crown. R. St. George
1902 20   35   70   130
3979 — but *matt proof FDC £100*

3980

	F	VF	EF	UNC		F	VF	EF	UNC
	£	£	£	£		£	£	£	£
3980 Halfcrown. R. Shield in Garter									
1902 3	8	30	55		1906 4	10	70	110
— Matt proof *FDC £55*					1907 4	12	75	120
1903 25	90	350	550		1908 5	14	100	150
1904 15	55	250	400		1909 4	12	80	130
1905* 70	250	750	975		1910 4	10	55	90
3981 Florin. R. Britannia standing									
1902 2	6	30	50		1906 3	9	50	75
— Matt proof *FDC £40*					1907 4	12	60	90
1903 3	9	50	75		1908 4	14	80	120
1904 4	12	60	90		1909 4	13	75	110
1905* 10	30	175	300		1910 2	7	40	65

*Beware of forgeries.

3981	3982	3983

	F	VF	EF	UNC		F	VF	EF	UNC
	£	£	£	£		£	£	£	£

3982 Shilling. R. Lion on crown

	F	VF	EF	UNC		F	VF	EF	UNC
1902		2	15	25	1906		2	20	35
— Matt proof *FDC £25*					1907		4	25	40
1903	1	5	50	90	1908	1	6	60	90
1904	1	5	40	65	1909	1	5	50	85
1905*	25	85	300	475	1910		2	15	25

Beware of recent forgeries.

3983 Sixpence. R. Value in wreath

	F	VF	EF	UNC		F	VF	EF	UNC
1902		1	15	25	1906		2	20	35
— Matt proof *FDC £20*					1907		2	25	40
1903		2	20	35	1908		3	30	50
1904	1	4	35	55	1909		2	25	40
1905		2	25	40	1910		1	15	25

3984 Threepence. As Maundy but dull finish

	F	VF	EF	UNC		F	VF	EF	UNC
1902			3	5	1907			8	14
1903			8	14	1908			8	14
1904		3	30	45	1909			8	14
1905		2	20	35	1910			6	10
1906		1	20	35					

3985

	EF	FDC		EF	FDC
	£	£		£	£

3985 Maundy Set (4d., 3d., 2d. and 1d.)

	EF	FDC		EF	FDC
1902	25	40	1906	25	40
— Matt proof *FDC £40*			1907	25	40
1903	25	40	1908	25	40
1904	25	40	1909	30	50
1905	25	40	1910	35	55

	EF £	FDC £
3986 — **fourpence,** 1902-10 ....*from*	5	9
3987 — **threepence,** 1902-10 ....*from*	5	11
3988 — **twopence,** 1902-10 ....*from*	5	8
3989 — **penny,** 1902-10 ....*from*	5	8

Maundy sets in the original dated cases are worth approximately £5 more than the prices quoted.

BRONZE

3990

3990 'High Tide'   3990A 'Low Tide'

3990 Penny. R. Britannia

	EF £	UNC £		VF £	EF £	UNC £
1902	4	8	1907		8	20
1903	8	20	1908		8	20
1904	12	25	1909		8	20
1905	10	22	1910		7	14
1906	8	20				

3990A As last but 'Low tide', 1902 3   20   40

3991

	EF £	UNC £		VF £	EF £	UNC £
3991 Halfpenny. R. Britannia						
1902	4	8	1907		5	12
1903	6	14	1908		5	12
1904	8	20	1909		8	20
1905	8	20	1910		7	15
1906	7	15				
3991A As last but 'Low tide', 1902				10	25	45

3992   3993

3992 Farthing. Britannia. Dark finish					
1902	3	6	1907	5	10
1903	5	10	1908	5	10
1904	7	14	1909	5	10
1905	5	10	1910	7	14
1906	5	10			

3993 Third-farthing (for use in Malta)		
1902 R. Value	3	6

No proofs of the bronze coins were issued in 1902

THE HOUSE OF WINDSOR
GEORGE V, 1910-36

Paper money issued by the Treasury during the First World War replaced gold for internal use after 1915 but the branch mints in Australia and South Africa (the main Commonwealth gold producing countries) continued striking sovereigns until 1930-2. Owing to the steep rise in the price of silver in 1919/20 the issue of standard (.925) silver was discontinued and coins of .500 silver were minted.

In 1912, 1918 and 1919 some pennies were made under contract by private mints in Birmingham. In 1918, as half-sovereigns were no longer being minted, farthings were again issued with the ordinary bright bronze finish. Crown pieces had not been issued for general circulation but they were struck in small numbers about Christmas time for people to give as presents in the years 1927-36, and in 1935 a special commemorative crown was issued in celebration of the Silver Jubilee.

As George V died in January, it is likely that all coins dated 1936 were struck during the reign of Edward VIII.

Designer's initials:
  B. M. (Bertram Mackennal)   P. M. (Percy Metcalfe)   K. G. (Kruger Gray)

GOLD

3994

FDC
£

3994 Five pounds. R. St. George, 1911 (Proof only) 1300
3995 Two pounds. R. St. George, 1911 (Proof only) 625
Forgeries exist.

3996

	VF	EF	UNC
	£	£	£

3996 Sovereign. R. St. George. London mint

	VF	EF	UNC		VF	EF	UNC
1911			BV	1915			BV
— Proof FDC £275				1916			90
1912			BV	1917*	1800	3500	—
1913			BV	1925			BV
1914			BV				

Forgeries exist of these and of most other dates and mints.
BV *stands for bullion value*

312

	VF £	EF £	UNC £		VF £	EF £	UNC £

3997 — C on ground for the Ottawa mint

1911 C		95	110	1917 C		95	110
1913 C	175	350	—	1918 C		95	110
1914 C	90	200	—	1919 C		95	110
1916 C		7500	—				

3997

3998

4004

3998 — I on ground for India (Bombay) mint, 1918 100

3999 — M on ground for Melbourne mint

1911 M			BV	1920 M	800	1700	—
1912 M			BV	1921 M		3750	—
1913 M			BV	1922 M	1200	3500	—
1914 M			BV	1923 M			BV
1915 M			BV	1924 M			BV
1916 M			BV	1925 M			BV
1917 M			BV	1926 M			BV
1918 M			BV	1928 M	550	1350	—
1919 M			100				

4000 — small head

1929 M	250	950	—	1931 M	75	125	250
1930 M		90	150				

4001

4002

4001 — P on ground for Perth mint

1911 P			BV	1920 P			BV
1912 P			BV	1921 P			BV
1913 P			BV	1922 P			BV
1914 P			BV	1923 P			BV
1915 P			BV	1924 P			BV
1916 P			BV	1925 P			BV
1917 P			BV	1926 P			BV
1918 P			BV	1927 P			BV
1919 P			BV	1928 P			BV

	VF £	EF £	UNC £		VF £	EF £	UNC £
4002 Sovereign. — — small head							
1929 P			BV	1931 P			BV
1930 P			BV				
4003 — S on ground for Sydney mint							
1911 S			BV	1919 S			BV
1912 S			BV	1920 S*			*Extremely rare*
1913 S			BV	1921 S	500	1200	—
1914 S			BV	1922 S**			*Extremely rare*
1915 S			BV	1923 S***			*Extremely rare*
1916 S			BV	1924 S	300	600	1000
1917 S			BV	1925 S			BV
1918 S			BV	1926 S****			*Extremely rare*
4004 — SA on ground for Pretoria mint							
1923 SA		1200	2500	1926 SA			BV
1923 SA Proof *FDC £750*				1927 SA			BV
1924 SA		2650	—	1928 SA			BV
1925 SA			BV				
4005 — — small head							
1929 SA			BV	1931 SA			BV
1930 SA			BV	1932 SA			100

*   A good EF specimen sold at auction in March 1992 for £104,000 plus buyer's premium.
**   An EF specimen sold at auction in March 1992 for £11,000 plus buyer's premium.
***   An EF Speciem sold at auction in March 1992 for £5,800 plus buyer's premium.
****   An EF Specimen sold at auction in March 1992 for £16,000 plus buyer's premium.

4006

4006 Half-sovereign. R. St. George. London mint							
1911		45	50	1913		45	50
— Proof *FDC £200*				1914		45	50
1912		45	50	1915		45	50
4007 — M on ground for Melbourne mint							
1915 M					55	80	125
4008 — P on ground for Perth mint							
1911 P	55	70	80	1918 P	200	350	500
1915 P	55	70	80	1919 P, 1920 P (*Not circulated*)			
4009 — S on ground for Sydney mint							
1911 S	50	70	90	1915 S	45	50	60
1912 S	50	70	90	1916 S	45	50	60
1914 S	50	60	75				
4010 — SA on ground for Pretoria mint							
1923 SA Proof *FDC £475*				1926 SA		45	50
1925 SA		45	50				

SILVER

First coinage. Sterling silver (.925 fine)

4011

	EF £	UNC £		EF £	UNC £
4011 Halfcrown. R. Crowned shield in Garter					
1911	25	50	1915	12	25
— Proof *FDC £70*			1916	12	25
1912	30	55	1917	18	35
1913	35	70	1918	12	25
1914	12	30	1919	18	35

4012

	EF	UNC		EF	UNC
4012 Florin. R. Cruciform shields					
1911	20	40	1915	12	25
— Proof *FDC £50*			1916	12	25
1912	25	45	1917	18	35
1913	35	65	1918	12	25
1914	12	25	1919	18	35
4013 Shilling. R. Lion on crown, inner circles					
1911	8	18	1915	8	18
— Proof *FDC £35*			1916	8	18
1912	18	35	1917	10	20
1913	25	50	1918	8	18
1914	8	18	1919	12	25

4013

4014

	EF £	UNC £		EF £	UNC £
4014 Sixpence. R. Similar					
1911..............................	8	15	1916..............................	8	18
— Proof *FDC £30*			1917..............................	14	40
1912..............................	12	25	1918..............................	8	18
1913..............................	16	30	1919..............................	10	20
1914..............................	8	18	1920..............................	12	25
1915..............................	8	18			
4015 Threepences. As Maundy but dull finish					
1911..............................	3	5	1916..............................	3	5
1912..............................	3	5	1917..............................	3	5
1913..............................	3	5	1918..............................	3	5
1914..............................	3	5	1919..............................	3	5
1915..............................	3	5	1920..............................	4	6

4016

	EF £	FDC £		EF £	FDC £
4016 Maundy Set (4d., 3d., 2d. and 1d.)					
1911..............................	25	45	1916..............................	25	40
— Proof *FDC £60*			1917..............................	25	40
1912..............................	25	40	1918..............................	25	40
1913..............................	25	40	1919..............................	25	40
1914..............................	25	40	1920..............................	25	40
1915..............................	25	40			
4017 — **fourpence,** 1911-20 ....*from*				5	8
4018 — **threepence,** 1911-20...*from*				8	12
4019 — **twopence,** 1911-20 ....*from*				5	8
4020 — **penny,** 1911-20...*from*				7	10

Second coinage. Debased silver (.500 fine). Types as before.

	EF	UNC		VF	EF	UNC
	£	£		£	£	£
4021 Halfcrown						
1920	20	40	1924		30	50
1921	25	50	1925	15	100	175
1922	20	40	1926		30	55
1923	12	20				
4022 Florin						
1920	20	35	1924		30	50
1921	20	35	1925	8	75	135
1922	16	30	1926		30	50
1923	14	25				
4023 Shilling						
1920	16	30	1924		20	35
1921	20	50	1925		35	55
1922	16	30	1926		12	27
1923	14	25				
4024 Sixpence						
1920	10	18	1923		16	30
1921	10	18	1924		10	18
1922	11	20	1925		12	20

4025   4026

4025— new beading and broader rim						
	EF	UNC			EF	UNC
1925	10	18	1926		12	20
4026 Threepence						
1920	3	5	1925		10	20
1921	3	5	1926		10	20
1922	4	6				

	EF	FDC		EF	FDC
	£	£		£	£
4027 Maundy Set (4d., 3d., 2d. and 1d.)					
1921	25	40	1925	25	40
1922	25	40	1926	25	40
1923	25	40	1927	25	40
1924	25	40			
4028 — **fourpence**, 1921-7 ....*from*			6	9	
4029 — **threepence**, 1921-7 ....*from*			8	12	
4030 — **twopence**, 1921-7 ....*from*			6	10	
4031 — **penny**, 1921-7 ....*from*			7	11	

2nd coinage   3rd coinage

Third coinage. As before but modified effigy, with details of head more clearly defined. The BM on truncation is nearer to the back of the neck and without stops; beading is more pronounced.

	VF £	EF £	UNC £		VF £	EF £	UNC £
4032 Halfcrown							
1926	4	30	50	1927		18	30
4033 Shilling							
1926		12	20	1927		18	30
4034 Sixpence							
1926		6	14	1927		10	18
4035 Threepence							
1926						3	5

Fourth coinage. New types, 1927-36

4036

4036 Crown. R. Crown in wreath
1927 Proof only *FDC £110*

1928	35	80	135
1929	40	95	150
1930	40	95	150
1931	45	110	175
1932	65	140	200
1933	40	95	150
1934	400	600	950
1936	65	140	200

4037   4038

	VF £	EF £	UNC £		VF £	EF £	UNC £

4037 Halfcrown. R. Shield

	VF £	EF £	UNC £		VF £	EF £	UNC £
1927 Proof only *FDC £30*				1932		10	30
1928		8	14	1933		9	16
1929		8	14	1934		25	40
1930	10	75	130	1935		6	12
1931		9	16	1936		5	10

4038 Florin. R. Cruciform sceptres, shield in each angle

	VF £	EF £	UNC £		VF £	EF £	UNC £
1927 Proof only *FDC £35*				1932	9	70	125
1928		7	12	1933		9	16
1929		7	12	1935		7	12
1930		11	18	1936		6	10
1931		8	18				

4039   4040

4039 Shilling. R. Lion on crown, no inner circles

	EF	UNC		EF	UNC
1927	12	20	1932	8	14
— Proof *FDC £20*			1933	7	12
1928	7	12	1934	14	25
1929	7	12	1935	7	12
1930	18	30	1936	6	10
1931	8	14			

4040 Sixpence. R. Three oak sprigs with six acorns

	EF	UNC		EF	UNC
1927 Proof only *FDC £18*			1929	3	6
1928	3	6	1930	4	6

4041 — closer milling

	EF	UNC		EF	UNC
1931	7	14	1934	8	16
1932	12	20	1935	5	10
1933	6	12	1936	3	6

4042

4042 Threepence. R. Three oak sprigs with three acorns

	EF £	UNC £		EF £	UNC £
1927 Proof only *FDC £30*			1933	1	2
1928	10	18	1934	1	2
1930	8	14	1935	1	2
1931	1	2	1936	1	2
1932	1	2			

	EF £	FDC £		EF £	FDC £
4043 Maundy Set. As earlier sets					
1928	30	45	1933	30	45
1929	30	45	1934	30	45
1930	30	45	1935	30	45
1931	30	45	1936	35	50
1932	30	45			

		EF	UNC
4044 — fourpence, 1928-36	*from*	6	10
4045 — threepence, 1928-36	*from*	7	12
4046 — twopence, 1928-36	*from*	6	9
4047 — penny, 1928-36	*from*	8	13

Silver Jubilee Commemorative issue

4048

	VF £	EF £	UNC £
4048 Crown, 1935. R. St. George, incuse lettering on edge	3	8	15
4049 — Specimen striking issued in box			30
4050 — raised lettering on edge .Proof (.925 Æ) *FDC £200*			

BRONZE

4051

	F £	VF £	EF £	UNC £		F £	VF £	EF £	UNC £
4051 Penny. R. Britannia									
1911			4	10	1918			4	10
1912			4	10	1919			3	8
1913			4	10	1920			3	8
1914			5	14	1921			3	8
1915			5	14	1922			12	25
1916			4	10	1926			15	35
1917			3	8					

4052 — H (The Mint, Birmingham, Ltd.) to l. of date

	F	VF	EF	UNC		F	VF	EF	UNC
1912 H		1	20	45	1919 H		7	65	125
1918 H		8	75	135					

4053 — KN (King's Norton Metal Co.) to l. of date

	F	VF	EF	UNC		F	VF	EF	UNC
1918 KN	2	10	90	175	1919 KN	2	12	110	200

4054 — modified effigy

	F	VF	EF	UNC		F	VF	EF	UNC
1926	3	25	250	500	1927			3	5

4055 — small head

	EF	UNC		EF	UNC
1928	3	5	1933*	*Extremely rare*	
1929	3	5	1934	10	18
1930	4	6	1935	2	4
1931	5	9	1936	1	2
1932	12	20			

4056 Halfpenny. R. Britannia

	EF	UNC		EF	UNC
1911	4	9	1919	4	9
1912	4	9	1920	4	9
1913	4	9	1921	4	9
1914	4	9	1922	7	15
1915	4	9	1923	5	11
1916	4	9	1924	4	9
1917	4	9	1925	5	11
1918	4	9			

4057 — modified effigy

	EF	UNC		EF	UNC
1925	7	15	1927	4	9
1926	6	14			

*An extremely fine specimen sold at auction for £15,000 in November 1985.

4056　　　　　　　　　　　4058

	EF £	UNC £		EF £	UNC £
4058 — small head					
1928	2	5	1933	2	5
1929	2	5	1934	4	9
1930	2	5	1935	2	5
1931	2	5	1936	1	2
1932	2	5			

4059　　　　　　　　　　4062

	EF	UNC		EF	UNC
4059 Farthing. R. Britannia. Dark finish					
1911	3	6	1915	4	8
1912	2	4	1916	2	4
1913	2	4	1917	1	2
1914	2	4	1918	9	18
4060 — Bright finish, 1918-25				1	2
4061 — Modified effigy					
1926	1	2	1932	0.50	1
1927	1	2	1933	1	2
1928	1	2	1934	2	4
1929	1	2	1935	2	4
1930	1	2	1936	0.75	2
1931	1	2			
4062 Third-farthing (for use in Malta). R. Value					
1913				3	5

Abdicated 10 December. Created Duke of Windsor (1936-72)

No coins of Edward VIII were issued for currency within the United Kingdom bearing his name and portrait. The mint had commenced work on a new coinage prior to the Abdication, and various patterns were made. No proof sets were issued for sale and only a small number of sets were struck.

 Coins bearing Edward's name, but not his portrait, were issued for the colonial territories of British East Africa, British West Africa, Fiji and New Guinea. The projected U.K. coins were to include a shilling of essentially `Scottish' type and a nickel brass threepence with twelve sides which might supplement and possibly supersede the inconveniently small silver threepence.

Designer's initials:
 H. P. (T. Humphrey Paget)
 K. G. (Kruger Gray)
 W. P. (Wilson Parker)

4063

4063* Proof Set
 Gold, £5, £2 and £1, 1937 .... *not issued*

Silver Crown, Halfcrown, Florin, Scottish shilling, sixpence and threepence, 1937   *not issued*

The following coins were sold at auction in December 1984 and October 1985.

	£
Sovereign, brilliant, with some hair lines in field	40,000
Halfcrown, brilliant mint state	16,000
Shilling, pattern	20,000
Sixpence, brilliant mint state	9,500

Nickel brass. Threepence, 1937	*not issued*
Bronze. Penny. Halfpenny and Farthing, 1937	*not issued*

Pattern

4064 Nickel brass dodecagonal threepence, 1937. R. Thrift plant of more
naturalistic style than the modified proof coin. A small number of these
coins were produced for experimental purposes and a few did get into
circulation   24,750

Colonial issues

            4068   4071

	UNC £
4065 British East Africa. Bronze 10 cents, 1936	4
4066 — — 5 cents, 1936	3
4067 British West Africa. Cupro-nickel penny, 1936	2
4068 — — Halfpenny, 1936	2
4069 — — One-tenth penny, 1936	1
4070 Fiji. Cupro-nickel penny, 1936	4
4071 New Guinea. Bronze penny, 1936	3

The coins of East Africa and West Africa occur without mm. (London) and with H (Heaton) Birmingham and KN (King's Norton) Birmingham. The prices quoted are for the commonest of each type, regardless of mm.

Though they were at first issued concurrently, the twelve-sided nickel-brass threepence superseded the small silver threepence in 1942. Those dated 1943-4 were not issued for circulation in the U.K. In addition to the usual English 'lion' shilling, a shilling, of Scottish type was issued concurrently. This depicts the Scottish lion and crown flanked by the shield of St. Andrew and a thistle. In 1947, as silver was needed to repay the bullion lent by the U.S.A. during the war, silver coins were replaced by coins of the same type and weight made of cupro-nickel. In 1949, after India had attained independence, the title *Indiae Imperator* was dropped from the coinage. Commemorative crown pieces were issued for the Coronation and the 1951 Festival of Britain.

Designer's initials:
K. G. (Kruger Gray)
H. P. (T. Humphrey Paget)
W. P. (Wilson Parker)

GOLD

4074

		FDC
		£
4074 Five pounds. R. St. George, 1937. Proof		650
4075 Two pounds. Similar, 1937. Proof		375
4076 Sovereign. Similar, 1937. Proof		350
4077 Half-sovereign. Similar, 1937. Proof		125

SILVER

First coinage. Silver, .500 fine, with title IND:IMP

4078

	VF £	EF £	UNC £
4078 Crown. Coronation commemorative, 1937. R. Arms and supporters	4	10	18

4079 — — Proof *FDC* £35

4080   4081

	EF £	UNC £		UNC £
4080 Halfcrown. R. Shield				
1937		6	1942	5
— Proof *FDC* £10			1943	6
1938	3	16	1944	4
1939		6	1945	4
1940		6	1946	4
1941		6		
4081 Florin. R. Crowned rose, etc.				
1937		6	1942	4
— Proof *FDC* £8			1943	4
1938	3	15	1944	4
1939		5	1945	4
1940		5	1946	4
1941		4		

4082   4083

4082 Shilling. 'English'. R. Lion on large crown

		UNC			UNC
1937		5	1942		4
— Proof *FDC* £6			1943		4
1938	2	15	1944		4
1939		5	1945		3
1940		5	1946		3
1941		5			

	EF £	UNC £		VF £	EF £	UNC £

4083 Shilling. 'Scottish'. R. Lion seated facing on crown, etc.

1937		5	1942			5
— Proof *FDC* £7			1943			5
1938	2	15	1944			5
1939		5	1945			3
1940		6	1946			3
1941		6				

4084

4085

4084 Sixpence. R. GRI crowned

1937		3	1942			2
— Proof *FDC* £4			1943			2
1938	1	6	1944			2
1939		4	1945			2
1940		4	1946			2
1941		4				

4085 Threepence. R. Shield on rose

1937		2	1941		1	3
— Proof *FDC* £4			1942*	1	5	12
1938		2	1943*	2	8	15
1939	3	8	1944*	3	12	25
1940		3				

For colonial use only.

4086

	FDC £		FDC £

4086 Maundy Set. Silver, .500 fine. Uniform dates

1937	45	1942	45
— Proof *FDC* £50		1943	45
1938	45	1944	45
1939	45	1945	45
1940	45	1946	45
1941	45		

	FDC		*FDC*
	£		£

4087 — **fourpence**, 1937-46 .... from 9
4088 — **threepence**, 1937-46...from 9
4089 — **twopence**, 1937-46 .... from 9
4090 — **penny**, 1937-46.. from 12

Second coinage. Silver, .925 fine, with title IND.IMP (Maundy only)
4091 Maundy Set (4d., 3d., 2d. and 1d.). Uniform dates

1947	45	1948	45

4092 — **fourpence**, 1947-8.. 9
4093 — **threepence**, 1947-8 10
4094 — **twopence**, 1947-8.. 9
4095 — **penny**, 1947-8 12

Third coinage. Silver, .925 fine, but omitting IND.IMP. (Maundy only)
4096 Maundy Set (4d., 3d., 2d. and 1d.). Uniform dates

1949	45	1951	45
1950	45	1952	45

The 1952 Maundy was distributed by Queen Elizabeth II.

4097 — **fourpence**, 1949-52 ....from 9
4098 — **threepence**, 1949-52 ....from 9
4099 — **twopence**, 1949-52 ....from 9
4100 — **penny**, 1949-52 .... from 12

CUPRO-NICKEL

Second coinage. Types as first (silver) coinage, IND.IMP.
4101 Halfcrown. R. Shield

	UNC		*UNC*
	£		£
1947	4	1948	4

4102 Florin. R. Crowned rose
1947	4	1948	3

4103 Shilling. 'English' type
1947	5	1948	3

4104 'Scottish' type
1947	4	1948	3

4105 Sixpence. GRI crowned
1947	3	1948	2

Third coinage. Types as before but title IND.IMP. omitted

               4106   4110

	UNC		VF	EF	UNC
	£		£	£	£
4106 Halfcrown			— Proof *FDC* £9		
1949	5		1951		7
1950	6		1952		*Extremely rare*
— Proof *FDC* £9					
4107 Florin					
1949	7		1951		7
1950	7		— Proof *FDC* £8		
— Proof *FDC* £8					
4108 Shilling. 'English' type					
1949	6		1951		6
1950	6		— Proof *FDC* £6		
— Proof *FDC* £6					
4109 'Scottish' type					
1949	8		1951		7
1950	7		— Proof *FDC* £6		
— Proof *FDC* £6					
Cupro-nickel					
4110 Sixpence. As illustration			1951		4
1949	4		— Proof *FDC* £4		
1950	4		1952	1	10	30
— Proof *FDC* £4					

Festival of Britain issue

4111

	EF	UNC
	£	£
4111 Crown. R. St. G eorge, 1951. *Proof-like*	2	5

NICKEL BRASS

4112   4113

First issue, with title IND.IMP.
4112 Threepence (dodecagonal). R. Thrift

	VF	EF	UNC		VF	EF	UNC
	£	£	£		£	£	£
1937......................................			2	1942......................................			2
—Proof *FDC* £4				1943......................................			2
1938...............................		2	6	1944......................................			3
1939...............................		3	15	1945......................................			5
1940......................................			5	1946......................	3	30	110
1941......................................			3	1948...............................		3	15

Second issue, omitting IND.IMP.
4113

	VF	EF	UNC		VF	EF	UNC
1949.........................	4	35	120	1951................................		8	30
1950...............................		8	25	— Proof *FDC* £25			
— Proof *FDC* £25				1952......................................			3

BRONZE

First issue, with title IND.IMP.

4114

	UNC £		UNC £
4114 Penny. R. Britannia			
1937	2	1944	7
— Proof *FDC* £6		1945	5
1938	2	1946	2
1939	5	1947	2
1940	6	1948	2

4115 Halfpenny. R. Ship

4115   4116

1937	2	1943	2
— Proof *FDC* £4		1944	2
1938	3	1945	3
1939	4	1946	6
1940	6	1947	3
1941	5	1948	2
1942	2		
4116 Farthing. R. Wren			
1937	1	1943	0.65
— Proof *FDC* £4		1944	0.65
1938	2	1945	0.65
1939	0.65	1946	0.65
1940	1	1947	0.65
1941	0.75	1948	0.75
1942	0.75		

Bronze
Second issue, without IND.IMP. Types as before
4117 Penny

	VF	EF	UNC		VF	EF	UNC
	£	£	£		£	£	£
1949			2	1951	6	12	18
1950	4	10	20	— Proof *FDC* £16			
— Proof *FDC* £16							

4118   4119

4118 Halfpenny

1949	5	1951	5
1950	4	— Proof *FDC* £4	
— Proof *FDC* £4		1952	3

4119 Farthing

1949	1	1951	0.70
1950	0.70	— Proof *FDC* £3	
— Proof *FDC* £4		1952	0.80

The coins dated 1952 were issued during the reign of Elizabeth II.

The earliest coins of this reign have the title BRITT.OMN, but in 1954 this was omitted from the Queen's titles owing to the changing status of so many Commonwealth territories. The minting of 'English' and 'Scottish' shillings was continued. A Coronation commemorative crown was issued in 1953, another crown was struck on the occasion of the 1960 British Exhibition in New York and a third was issued in honour of Sir Winston Churchill in 1965. A very small number of proof gold coins were struck in 1953 for the national museum collections, but between 1957 and 1968 gold sovereigns were minted again in quantity for sale in the international bullion market and to counteract the activities of counterfeiters.

Owing to inflation the farthing had now become practically valueless; production of these coins ceased after 1956 and the coins were demonetized at the end of 1960. In 1965 it was decided to change to a decimal system of coinage in the year 1971. As part of the transition to decimal coinage the halfpenny was demonetized in August 1969 and the halfcrown in January 1970. (See also introduction to Decimal Coinage on p. 340.)

Designer's initials:
  G. L. (Gilbert Ledward)
  W. P. (Wilson Parker)
  M. G. (Mary Gillick)
  W. G. (William Gardner)
  E. F. (Edgar Fuller)
  C. T. (Cecil Thomas)
  P. N. (Philip Nathan)
  R. D. M. (Raphael David Maklouf)
  N. S. (Norman Sillman)

Other designers whose initials do not appear on the coins:
  Christopher Ironside
  Arnold Machin
  David Wynne
  Professor Richard Guyatt
  Eric Sewel
  Leslie Durbin
  Derek Gorringe

PRE-DECIMAL ISSUES

GOLD

First coinage, with title BRITT.OMN, 1953. *Proof only*
4120　Five pounds. R. St. George .... *None issued for collectors*
4121　Two pounds. Similar .... *None issued for collectors*
4122* Sovereign. Similar .... *None issued for collectors*

*A brilliant mint state specimen sold at auction for £24,000 in June 1985.

4123 Half-sovereign. Similar .... *None issued for collectors*

Second issue, BRITT.OMN omitted

4125

4124 Sovereign. R. St. George
1957 .... BV

4125 Similar, but coarser graining on edge

1958	BV	1965	BV
1959	BV	1966	BV
1962	BV	1967	BV
1963	BV	1968	BV
1964	BV		

BV *Stands for bullian value*

SILVER

The Queen's Maundy are now the only coins struck regularly in silver.
The location of the Maundy ceremony is given for each year.

First issue, with title BRITT.OMN.   FDC
£

4126 Maundy Set (4d., 3d., 2d. and 1d.), 1953. St Paul's	225
4127 — fourpence, 1953	40
4128 — threepence, 1953	40
4129 — twopence, 1953	40
4130 — penny, 1953	50

Second issue, with BRITT.OMN omitted

4131

FDC
£

4131 Maundy Set (4d., 3d., 2d. and 1d.). Uniform dates

1954 *Westminster*	50	1963 *Chelmsford*	50
1955 *Southwark*	50	1964 *Westminster*	50
1956 *Westminster*	50	1965 *Canterbury*	50
1957 *St. Albans*	50	1966 *Westminster*	50
1958 *Westminster*	50	1967 *Durham*	50
1959 *Windsor*	50	1968 *Westminster*	50
1960 *Westminster*	50	1969 *Selby*	50
1961 *Rochester*	50	1970 *Westminster*	50
1962 *Westminster*	50	*See also p. 343*	

4132 — fourpence, 1954-70	*from*	10
4133 — threepence, 1954-70	*from*	10
4134 — twopence, 1954-70	*from*	10
4135 — penny, 1954-70	*from*	11

CUPRO-NICKEL

First issue, 1953, with title BRITT.OMN.

4136

	EF £	UNC £	PROOF FDC £
4136 Crown. Queen on horseback. R. Crown in centre of cross, shield in each angle, 1953	1	3	25

4137   4138

	EF	UNC
4137 Halfcrown, with title BRITT.OMN. R. Arms, 1953	3	8
4138 Florin. R. Double rose, 1953	3	6

4139   4140   4141

	EF	UNC
4139 Shilling. 'English'. R. Three lions, 1953	1	4
4140 'Scottish'. R. Lion rampant in shield, 1953	1	4
4141 Sixpence. R. Interlaced rose, thistle, shamrock and leek, 1953	0.70	3
4142 Set of 9 uncirculated cu-ni, ni-br and Æ coins (2/6 to 1/4d.) in Royal Mint plastic envelope	8	

ELIZABETH II 337

Cupro-nickel
Second issue, similar types but omitting BRITT.OMN.

4143   4144

	EF	UNC
	£	£
4143 Crown, 1960. Bust r. R. As 4136	2	5
— — Similar, from polished dies (New York Exhibition issue)	4	18
4144 Churchill commemorative, 1965. As illustration. R. Bust of Winston Churchill r.		0.75
— — Similar, satin- finish. *Specimen*		250

4145 Halfcrown. R. As 4137

	EF	UNC			
	£	£			
1954	2	15	1961		1
1955		4	1962		1
1956		5	1963		1
1957		2	1964		3
1958	2	12	1965		1
1959	2	15	1966		0.60
1960		3	1967		0.60

4146

4146 Florin. R. As 4138

1954	3	30	1961		2
1955		3	1962		1
1956		3	1963		0.75
1957	2	20	1964		0.60
1958	1	10	1965		0.50
1959	2	25	1966		0.45
1960		2	1967		0.40

	EF	UNC			UNC
	£	£			£

4147 Shilling. 'English' type. R. As 4139

	EF	UNC		UNC
1954		2	1961	0.75
1955		2	1962	0.50
1956		7	1963	0.25
1957		1	1964	0.30
1958	2	15	1965	0.30
1959		1	1966	0.30
1960		1		

4148 'Scottish' type. R. As 4140

	EF	UNC		UNC
1954		2	1961	5
1955		3	1962	1
1956		7	1963	0.25
1957	2	15	1964	0.50
1958		1	1965	0.50
1959	2	15	1966	0.30
1960		1		

4149 Sixpence. R. As 4141

	UNC		UNC
1954	3	1961	3
1955	1	1962	0.30
1956	1	1963	0.25
1957	0.65	1964	0.20
1958	4	1965	0.15
1959	0.35	1966	0.15
1960	4	1967	0.15

NICKEL BRASS

4152   4153

First issue, with title BRITT.OMN.
4152 Threepence (dodecagonal). R. Crowned portcullis, 1953 1
— Proof *FDC* £4
Second issue (omitting BRIT.OMN)
4153 Similar type

	UNC		UNC
1954	4	1961	0.35
1955	5	1962	0.30
1956	5	1963	0.20
1957	3	1964	0.20
1958	6	1965	0.20
1959	3	1966	0.15
1960	3	1967	0.15

BRONZE

First issue, with title BRITT.OMN.

	4154				4158

	VF	EF	UNC	PROOF FDC
	£	£	£	£
4154 Penny. R. Britannia (only issued with Royal Mint set in plastic envelope), 1953	0.60	2	5	6
4155 Halfpenny. R. Ship, 1953			2	4
4156 Farthing. R. Wren, 1953			0.75	3

Second issue, omitting BRITT.OMN.

	UNC		UNC
	£		£
4157 Penny. R. Britannia (1954-60 *not issued*)			
1954	*Extremely rare*	1964	0.10
1961	0.50	1965	0.10
1962	0.15	1966	0.10
1963	0.15	1967	0.10
4158 Halfpenny. R. Ship (1961 *not issued*)			
1954	4	1962	0.10
1955	4	1963	0.10
1956	4	1964	0.10
1957	0.60	1965	0.10
1958	0.35	1966	0.10
1959	0.20	1967	0.10
1960	0.10		

	4156		4159

	EF	UNC
	£	£
4159 Farthing. R. Wren		
1954	0.80	1956 ... 0.55	2
1955	0.75		

A decision to adopt decimal currency was announced in February 1968 following the appointment of a Committee of Enquiry in 1961. This would require a major re-coinage but a decision had already been made to build a new mint at Llantrisant in South Wales The first phase was completed by December 1968 when HM The Queen struck the first coins at the official opening. The second phase was completed during late 1975 at which time all coin production at Tower Hill ceased.

Though the official change-over to a decimal currency did not take place until 15 February 1971, three decimal denominations were circulated prior to this date. The 10 and 5 *new pence,* equivalent to the former florin and shilling, were introduced in 1968 and the seven-sided 50 *new pence* (equal to ten shillings) was issued during October 1969. Two coins which were not required in the decimal system were withdrawn and demonetized; the halfpenny on 1 August 1969 and the halfcrown on 1 January 1970.

To familiarize the public with the decimal coins a small pack was issued during 1968 comprising the 10 and 5 *new pence* coins dated 1968, and the bronze 2, 1 and $1/2$ *new pence* dated 1971 although the bronze coins were not legalized for current use until 'Decimal Day'.

In 1982 the word 'new' was omitted from the reverse design which now bore the denomination in words and figures. The first ever 20 pence coin was also issued in 1982, and the following year saw the first circulating non-precious metal £1 coin. The reverse design of the £1 coin was changed each year from 1984 to 1988, and from 1989 the designs repeat again from the 1984 variation onwards. The $1/2$ (new) pence was demonetized in December 1984, and coins dated that year were only issued in sets.

The first of a number of changes to the coinage took place in 1990. A smaller 5p was introduced thus bringing to an end a specification for the 5p and its 1/- equivalent first introduced in 1816. A smaller size 10p was issued in 1992, and plans are being made to replace the 1p and 2p bronze coins with pieces made of copper plated steel. All pre-decimal 1/- coins plus the same size 5p coins ceased to be legal tender on 31 December 1990. The pre-decimal 2/- coins plus the same size 10p coins will cease to be legal tender during 1993.

Some base metal coins, from 50p downwards, only appear in Royal Mint specimen sets and these are indicated in the texts by asterisks following the dates.

An interesting error was discovered during 1991 – a 1983 2p with 'new pence' reverse instead of 'two pence'. Three pieces have so far been recorded and as no 2p coins were issued for circulation that year all the error coins must have come from specimen sets.

Several commemorative coins have been issued. In 1973 the UK's admission to the EC was commemorated by a 50p piece. The same denomination is being used for a double commemoration in 1992-93, the UK's Presidency of the EC from July 1992 and the completion of the Single Market from 1 January 1993. Crown size 25 pence (equivalent to 5/-) pieces were issued to celebrate the Silver Wedding of HM The Queen and Prince Philip in 1972, the Queen's Silver Jubilee in 1977, the 80th Birthday of Queen Elizabeth, the Queen Mother in 1980, and for the Royal Wedding in 1981. A further crown-sized coin was issued in 1990 for the 90th Birthday of Queen Elizabeth, the Queen Mother with a face value of £5. The face value of a cupro-nickel crown had been five shillings or 25 pence since 1951 although the equivalent of 5/- in 1951 was £3.27 in 1990. Thus it is hoped that this new £5 face value will stand for many years. A second £5 crown is planned for 1993 to commemorate the 40th Anniversary of the Coronation.

In 1986 the Royal Mint introduced a nickel-brass £2 piece in honour of the XIII

Commonwealth Games in Scotland. Two further pieces were issued in 1989 for the 300th Anniversary of the Bill of Rights (in England and Wales) and the Claim of Right (in Scotland). These coins were not intended to circulate.

All silver (Æ) coins are minted in .925 sterling silver unless otherwise stated.

There have been developments with the gold coinage. In 1979 the first proof sovereign since 1937 was issued, and 1980 saw a proof five pound, two pound and half-sovereign. Annual issues have appeared since. A four coin Britannia series with weights based on one ounce was introduced in 1987.

What of the future? No firm decisions for the further development of the coinage have been announced. The 50 pence coin is now the largest and heaviest in circulation and any further changes may well involve that coin. There is a movement within the EC towards a unified coinage possibly based on the ECU (European Currency Unit) although again no decisions have yet been made. A number of EC countries have issued coins denominated in ECUs (or dual denominated) or have authorized the issue of patterns. No such pieces have either been issued by the British Mint or authorized.

GOLD

4201

4204

	UNC £		UNC £
4201 Five pounds. As illustration			
1980 Proof *FDC* £400		1982 Proof *FDC* £450	
1981 Proof *FDC* £400		1984 Proof *FDC* £400	
4202 As illustration, `U' in a circle to left of date			
1984	350		
4203 Two pounds			
1980 Proof *FDC* £225		1983 Proof *FDC* £175	
1982 Proof *FDC* £225			
4204 Sovereign. As illustration			
1974	BV	1981	BV
1976	BV	— Proof *FDC* £80	
1978	BV	1982	BV
1979	BV	— Proof *FDC* £80	
— Proof *FDC* £80		1983 Proof *FDC* £85	
1980	BV	1984 Proof *FDC* £90	
— Proof *FDC* £80			
4205 Half-sovereign			
1980 Proof *FDC* £50		1983 Proof *FDC* £55	
1982	40	1984 Proof *FDC* £55	
— Proof *FDC* £50			

(For proof sets which include some or all of the above coins, see the list on pages 357-8.)

SILVER

	FDC £		FDC £
4211 Maundy Set (4p, 3p, 2p and 1p). Uniform dates. Types as 4131			
1971 *Tewkesbury Abbey*	55	1982 *St. David's Cathedral*	55
1972 *York Minster*	55	1983 *Exeter Cathedral*	55
1973 *Westminster Abbey*	55	1984 *Southwell Minster*	55
1974 *Salisbury Cathedral*	55	1985 *Ripon Cathedral*	55
1975 *Peterborough Cathedral*	55	1986 *Chichester Cathedral*	55
1976 *Hereford Cathedral*	55	1987 *Ely Cathedral*	75
1977 *Westminster Abbey*	65	1988 *Lichfield Cathedral*	75
1978 *Carlisle Cathedral*	55	1989 *Birmingham Cathedral*	75
1979 *Winchester Cathedral*	55	1990 *Newcastle Cathedral*	75
1980 *Worcester Cathedral*	55	1991 *Westminster Abbey*	75
1981 *Westminster Abbey*	55	1992 *Chester Cathedral*	85

4212 — fourpence, 1971-92	*from*	13
4213 — threepence, 1971-92	*from*	13
4214 — twopence, 1971-92	*from*	13
4215 — penny, 1971-92	*from*	15

*The Queen's Maundy are now the only coins struck regularly in .925 silver. The place of
distribution is shown after each date.*

NICKEL-BRASS

4221   4222

	UNC £
4221 One pound (Royal Arms design). Edge DECUS ET TUTAMEN	
1983	2
— Specimen in presentation folder	3
— Proof in Æ ....*FDC 20*	
— Proof piedfort in Æ.......................*FDC 110*	
4222 One pound (Scottish design). Edge NEMO ME IMPUNE LACESSIT	
1984	2
— Specimen in presentation folder	5
— Proof in Æ *FDC* £20	
— Proof piedfort in Æ *FDC* £60	

CUPRO-NICKEL

4223		4224

	UNC		UNC
	£		£

4223 Fifty new pence (seven-sided). R. Britannia r.

1969	2	1978	2
1970	4	1979	2
1976	2	1980	2
1977	2	1981	2

4224 Accession to European Economic Community. R. Clasped hands, 1973........................... 1.50

— — (Proof in case) *FDC* £2

4225

4225 Fifty (50) pence. 'New' omitted. As illustration

1982	2	1984*	
1983	2		

4226

4226 Twenty-five pence. Silver Wedding Commemorative, 1972... 0.75

— (*R* proof in case) *FDC* £20

— (Cu.-ni. proof.) Issued in 1972 Mint set. See PS22 4

4227

| | UNC |
| | £ |

4227 Twenty-five pence Silver Jubilee Commemorative, 1977.. 0.60

— (Æ proof in case) *FDC* £12

— (Cu.-ni. proof.) Only issued in 1977/Mint set. See PS27 4

— (Cu.-ni. Specimen striking.) Issued in Royal Mint folder 2

4228

4228 Twenty-Five Pence Queen Mother 80th Birthday Commemorative, 1980 .... 0.75

— (Æ proof in case) *FDC* £30

— (Cu.-ni. Specimen striking.) Issued in Royal Mint folder 1

4229

4229 Twenty-five pence. Royal Wedding Commemorative, 1981.. 0.90

— (Æ proof in case) *FDC* £28

— (Cu.-ni. Specimen striking.) Issued in Royal Mint folder 2

4230

4230 Twenty (20) pence. As illustration

1982	0.40	1983	0.40
(*Æ* Proof piedfort) *FDC* £36		1984	0.40

4231

4232

4233

4234

	UNC		UNC
	£		£

4231 Ten new pence. R. Lion passant guardant.

1968	0.30	1975	0.50
1969	0.30	1976	0.50
1970	0.30	1977	0.75
1971	0.40	1979	0.50
1973	0.40	1980	0.75
1974	0.40	1981	0.75

4232 Ten (10) pence. As illustration

1982*		1984*	
1983*			

4233 Five new pence. R. Crowned thistle

1968	0.20	1977...	0.20
1969	0.30	1978	0.20
1970	0.30	1979	0.20
1971	0.20	1980	0.20
1975...	0.20		

4234 Five (5) pence. As illustration

1982*		1984*	
1983*			

DECIMAL COINAGE
BRONZE

4235

4236

	UNC £		UNC £
4235 Two new pence. R. Plumes			
1971	0.10	1978	0.30
1975	0.20	1979	0.15
1976	0.20	1980	0.15
1977	0.10	1981	0.15
4236 Two (2) pence. As illustration			
1982*		1984*	
1983*			
—Error. R as 4235			

4237   4238   4239   4240

	UNC £		UNC £
4237 One new penny. R. Crowned portcullis			
1971	0.10	1977	0.10
1973	0.20	1978	0.20
1974	0.20	1979	0.10
1975	0.20	1980	0.10
1976	0.20	1981	0.20
4238 One (1) penny. As illustration			
1982	0.10	1984*	
1983	0.20		
4239 Half new penny. R. Crown			
1971	0.10	1977	0.10
1973	0.20	1978	0.10
1974	0.20	1979	0.10
1975	0.25	1980	0.10
1976	0.20	1981	0.20
4240 Half (1/2) penny. As illustration			
1982	0.10	1984*	
1983	0.25		
4250 Decimal specimen folder. Contains 1968 10p and 5p and 1971 2p, 1p and 1/2p			0.50

The new effigy is designed by Raphael David Maklouf, FRSA. It is only the third portrait of the Queen to be used on UK coinage, the previous change of portrait being in 1968 with the introduction of decimal coins. The designer's initials R.D.M. appear on the truncation. There is no portrait change on the Maundy coins.

GOLD

4251   4253

UNC

£

4251 Five pounds. R. St. George
1985 Proof *FDC* £400	1991 Proof *FDC* £450
1990 Proof *FDC* £450	1992 Proof *FDC* £500

4252 Five Pounds R. St. George, 'U' in a circle to left of date

1985	350
1986	375
1990	450
1991	450
1992	500

4253 Five Pounds Uncouped portrait of Queen Elizabeth II. As illustration. R. St. George, `U' in a circle to left of date.

1987	400
1988	400

4254 Five Pounds 500th Anniversary of Sovereign

1989	460

1989 Proof *FDC* £470

1985 Proof *FDC* £225	1990 Proof *FDC* £200
1987 Proof *FDC* £180	1991 Proof *FDC* £250
1988 Proof *FDC* £180	1992 Proof *FDC* £300

4262 Two pounds R. St. Andrew's cross surmounted by a thistle of Scotland. Edge XII COMMONWEALTH GAMES SCOTLAND 1986 *(See illus. 4301)*
1986 Proof *FDC* £175

4263 Two pounds 500th Anniversary of Sovereign
1989 Proof *FDC* £250

4271 Sovereign. R. St. George
1985 Proof *FDC* £100	1990 Proof *FDC* £150
1986 Proof *FDC* £100	1991 Proof *FDC* £150
1987 Proof *FDC* £100	1992 Proof *FDC* £150
1988 Proof *FDC* £100	

4272 Sovereign. 500th Anniversary of Sovereign
1989 Proof *FDC* £160

4277

4276 Half-sovereign. R. St. George

1985 Proof *FDC* £60   1990 Proof *FDC* £80
1986 Proof *FDC* £60   1991 Proof *FDC* £80
1987 Proof *FDC* £60   1992 Proof *FDC* £80
1988 Proof *FDC* £60

4277 Half -Sovereign 500th Anniversary of Sovereign
1989 Proof *FDC* £80

4281

UNC
£

4281 Britannia. One hundred pounds. (1oz of fine gold)
R. Britannia standing.

1987... 250
— Proof *FDC* £300
1988... 250
— Proof *FDC* £300
1989... 275
— Proof *FDC* £350
1990... 275
— Proof *FDC* £350
1991... 275
— Proof *FDC* £400
1992... 275
— Proof *FDC* £450

4286

UNC
£

4286 Britannia. Fifty pounds. (1/2oz of fine gold).
R. Britannia standing.

1987 130
— Proof *FDC* £160
1988 130
— Proof *FDC* £160
1989 140
— Proof *FDC* £175
1990 140
— Proof *FDC* £200
1991 140
— Proof *FDC* £200
1992 140
— Proof *FDC* £250

4291

4291 Britannia. Twenty five pounds. (1/4oz of fine gold).
R. Britannia standing.

1987 70
— Proof *FDC* £85
1988 70
— Proof *FDC* £85
1989 75
— Proof *FDC* £100
1990 75
— Proof *FDC* £120
1991 75
— Proof *FDC* £120
1992 75
— Proof *FDC* £135

4296

UNC
£

4296 Britannia. Ten pounds.(1/10oz of fine gold).
R. Britannia standing.
1987.. 30
— Proof *FDC* £50
1988.. 30
— Proof *FDC* £50
1989.. 30
— Proof *FDC* £55
1990.. 35
— Proof *FDC* £65
1991.. 35
— Proof *FDC* £65
1992.. 35
— Proof *FDC* £65
For proof sets which include some or all of the above see the list on page 357

NICKEL-BRASS

4301

4301 Two pounds. R. St. Andrew's cross surmounted by a thistle of Scotland. Edge XIII
COMMONWEALTH GAMES SCOTLAND 1986
1986 3
— Specimen in presentation folder 5
— Struck in .500 silver.. 12
— Proof in *AR FDC* £20
— Specimen in presentation folder 5
— For specimens struck in *AV* see 4262

4302   4303

UNC
£

4302 Two Pounds 300th Anniversary of Bill of Rights. Cypher of William and Mary, House of Commons mace and St. Edward's crown.

1989 3
— Specimen in presentation folder 5
— Proof *Æ* *FDC* £23
— Proof piedfort in *Æ* *FDC* £40

4303 Two Pounds 300th Anniversary of Claim of Right (Scotland). R. As 4302, but with crown of Scotland.

1989 4
— Specimen in presentation folder 6
— Proof in *Æ* *FDC* £23
— Proof piedfort in *Æ* *FDC* £40

4311

4311 One pound (Welsh design). Edge PLEIDIOL WYF I'M GWLAD

1985 2
— Specimen in presentation folder 3
— Proof in *Æ* *FDC* £21
— Proof piedfort in *Æ* *FDC* £55
1990 2
— Proof in *Æ* *FDC* £21

4312

4312 One Pound (Northern Ireland design). Edge DECUS ET TUTAMEN

1986 2
— Specimen in presentation folder 3
— Proof in *Æ* *FDC* £21
— Proof piedfort in *Æ* *FDC* £45
1991 2
— Proof in *Æ* *FDC* £20

4313   4314

4313 One Pound (English design). Edge DECUS ET TUTAMEN

1987 2

— Specimen in presentation folder 3

— Proof in **Æ** *FDC* £21

— Proof piedfort in **Æ** *FDC* £45

1992 2

— Proof in **Æ** *FDC* £21

4314 One Pound (Royal arms). Edge DECUS ET TUTAMEN

1988 2

— Specimen in presentation folder 3

— Proof in **Æ** *FDC* £21

— Proof piedfort **Æ** *FDC* £45

4315 One Pound (Scottish design). Edge NEMO ME IMPUNE LACESSIT (Illus. as 4222)

1989 2

— Proof in **Æ** *FDC* £21

— Proof piedfort in **Æ** *FDC* £60

CUPRO-NICKEL

4331

| | UNC |
| | £ |

4331 Five pounds (crown). Queen Mother 90th birthday commemorative.

—1990 7

Specimen in presentation folder 9

— Proof in Æ **in case** *FDC* £25

— Proof in N **in case** *FDC* £650

4341

4341 Fifty pence. R. Britannia r.

1985 2

1986*...

1987*...

1988*...

1989*...

1990*...

1991*...

1992*...

4342

4342 Fifty pence Presidency of the Council European Community Ministers and completion of the Single Market. R Conference table top and twelve stars

1992-1993 ....

— Proof in Æ in case *FDC* £24

— Proof piedfort in Æ in case *FDC*...   £45

— Proof in Æ in case *FDC* £375

4351

4351 Twenty pence. R. Crowned double rose

1985..

1986*..

1987..

1988..

1989..

1990..

1991..

1992..

4357

4356 Ten pence. R. Lion passant guardant

1985*..

1986*..

1987*..

1988*..

1989*..

1990*..

1991* ....

1992*..

4357 Ten pence R Lion passant Guardant: diam. 24.5mm

1992...

— Proof in *R FDC* £15

— Proof piedfort in *R FDC* £30

4361

4361 Five pence. R. Crowned thistle

1985*...

1986*...

1987..

1988..

1989..

1990*...

— Proof in *R FDC* £12

4362

4362 Five pence. R. Crowned thistle: diam 18mm

1990..

— Proof in *R FDC* £12

— Proof piedfort in *R FDC* £25

1991..

1992..

BRONZE

4366

4366 Two pence. R. Plumes

1985..

1986..

1987..

1988..

1989..

1990..

1991..

1992..

4371

4371 One penny. R. Portcullis with chains

1985...
1986...
1987...
1988...
1989...
1990...
1991...
1992...

Issued by the Royal Mint in official case from 1887 onwards, but earlier sets were issued privately by the engraver.

All pieces have a finish superior to that of the current coins.

		No. of coins	FDC £
PS1	**George IV.** New issue, **1826.** Five pounds to farthing	(11)	18,000
PS2	**William IV.** Coronation, **1831.** Two pounds to farthing	(14)	16,000
PS3	**Victoria,** young head, **1839.** 'Una and the Lion' five pounds, and sovereign to farthing	(15)	27,500
PS4	— **1853.** Sovereign to quarter-farthing, including Gothic type crown	(16)	18,000
PS5	Jubilee head. Golden Jubilee, **1887.** Five pounds to threepence	(11)	4,750
PS6	— — Crown to threepence	(7)	850
PS7	Old head, **1893.** Five pounds to threepence	(10)	5,750
PS8	— — Crown to threepence	(6)	900
PS9	**Edward VII.** Coronation, **1902.** Five pounds to Maundy penny. Matt surface	(13)	1,450
PS10	— — Sovereign to Maundy penny. Matt surface	(11)	375
PS11	**George V.** Coronation, **1911.** Five pounds to Maundy penny	(12)	2,450
PS12	— — Sovereign to Maundy penny	(10)	650
PS13	— — Halfcrown to Maundy penny	(8)	300
PS14	New types, **1927.** Crown to threepence	(6)	200
PS15	**George VI.** Coronation, **1937.** Gold. Five pounds to half-sovereign	(4)	1,450
PS16	— — — Silver, etc. Crown to farthing, including Maundy	(15)	110
PS17	Mid-Century, **1950.** Halfcrown to farthing	(10)	35
PS18	Festival of Britain, **1951.** Crown to farthing	(10)	50
PS19	**Elizabeth II.** Coronation, **1953.** Crown to farthing	(10)	35
PS20	'Last Sterling' set, **1970.** Halfcrown to halfpenny plus medallion	(8)	15
PS21	Decimal coinage set, **1971.** 50 new pence ('Britannia') to 1/2 penny, plus medallion	(6)	6
PS22	— **1972.** As last, but includes the cu.-ni. Silver Wedding crown	(7)	8
PS23	— **1973.** As PS21 but 'EEC' 50p	(6)	5
PS24	— **1974.** As PS21	(6)	5
PS25	— **1975.** As last	(6)	5
PS26	— **1976.** As last	(6)	5
PS27	— **1977.** As PS21 but including the proof Silver Jubilee crown struck in cupro-nickel	(7)	8
PS28	— **1978.** As PS21	(6)	8
PS29	— **1979.** As last	(6)	7
PS30	— **1980.** As last	(6)	6
PS31	— — Five pounds to half-sovereign	(4)	700
PS32	— **1981.** U.K. Proof coin Commemorative collection. (Consists of £5, £1, Royal Wedding crown (25p) in Æ, plus base metal proofs as PS21.)	(9)	500
PS33	— — As PS21	(6)	6
PS34	**Elizabeth II, 1982.** U.K. Uncirculated (specimen) set in Royal Mint folder. New reverse types, including 20 pence	(7)	4
PS35	— — As last but proofs in Royal Mint sealed plastic case, plus medallion	(7)	8
PS36	— Æ Five pounds to half-sovereign	(4)	800
PS37	— **1983.** As PS34, includes 'U.K.' £1	(8)	8
PS38	— — As PS35, includes 'U.K.' £1	(8)	12
PS39	— Æ £2, £1, £1/2 in case	(3)	300
PS40	— **1984.** As PS37 but with 'Scottish' £1	(8)	7
PS41	— — As PS38 but with 'Scottish' £1	(8)	10
PS42	— — Æ £5, £1, £1/2 in case	(3)	525

PS43 — **1985.** As PS37 but with new portrait, also includes 'Welsh' £1. The set does not contain the now discontinued halfpenny	(7)	5
PS44 — — As last but proofs in Royal Mint sealed plastic case, plus medallion	(7)	10
PS45 — — As last but within a deluxe red leather case	(7)	15
PS46 — — *N* £5, £2, £1, £1/2 in case	(4)	750
PS47 — **1986.** As PS43 but with new two pounds and the 'Northern Ireland' £1 (8)		8
PS48 — — As PS44 but with two pounds and 'Northern Ireland' £1	(8)	15
PS49 — — As last but within a deluxe red leather case	(8)	18
PS50 — — *N* £2 (as 4262), £1, £1/2 in a deluxe red leather case	(3)	300
PS51 — **1987.** As PS43 but with 'English' £1	(7)	5
PS52 — — As last but proofs in Royal Mint sealed plastic case, plus medallion	(7)	18
PS53 — — As last but within a deluxe red leather case	(7)	23
PS54 — — *N* £2 (as 4261), £1, £1/2 in a deluxe red leather case	(3)	325
PS55 — — **Britannia** *N* proofs. £100, £50, £25, £10 in a deluxe case	(4)	600
PS56 — — As last but only containing the £25, £10 in a deluxe case	(2)	135
PS57 — **1988.** As PS43 but with 'Arms' £1	(7)	6
PS58 — — As last but proofs in Royal Mint sealed plastic case, plus medal lion	(7)	21
PS59 — — As last but within a deluxe leather case	(7)	27
PS60 — — *N* £2 (as 4261), £1, £1/2 in a deluxe case	(3)	350
PS61 — — **Britannia** proofs. As PS55	(4)	600
PS62 — — As PS56	(2)	135
PS63 — **1989.** As PS43 but with 'Scotland' £1	(7)	9
PS64 — — As last but proofs and with 2 x £2	(9)	23
PS65 — — As last but within red leather case	(9)	30
PS66 — — Sovereign Anniversary *N* £5, £2, £1, £1/2	(4)	1000
PS67 — — As last but only containing £2, £1, £1/2	(3)	450
PS68 — — 2 x £2 in Royal Mint folder	(2)	8
PS69 — — As last but silver piedfort proofs	(2)	95
PS70 — — As last but silver proofs	(2)	42
PS71 — — **Britannia** proofs. As PS55	(4)	700
PS72 — — As PS56	(2)	150
PS73 — **1990.** As PS43 but with 'Welsh' £1 and new 5p	(8)	.9
PS74 — — As last but proofs	(8)	22
PS75 — — As last but within red leather case	(8)	29
PS76 — — *N* £5, £2, £1, £1/2 in case	(4)	850
PS77 — — *N* £2, £1, £1/2 in case	(3)	400
PS78 — — 2 x 5p *R* proofs (as 4306 & 4307)	(2)	35
PS79 — — **Britannia** proofs. As PS55	(4)	800
PS80 — **1991.** As PS43 but with 'Northern Ireland' £1	(7)	8
PS81 — — As last but proofs	(7)	23
PS82 — — As last but within red leather case	(7)	30
PS83 — — *N* £5, £2, £1, £1/2 in case	(4)	950
PS84 — — *N* £2, £1, £1/2 in case	(3)	450
PS85 — — Britannia proofs. As PS55	(4)	850
PS86 — **1992** As PS43 but with 'English £1' and 'European Community' 50p	(9)	.9
PS87 — — As last but proofs	(9)	28
PS88 — — As last but with red leather case	(9)	35
PS89 — — *N* £5, £2, £1, £1/2 in case	(4)	1150
PS90 — — *N* £2, £1, £1/2 in case	(3)	500
PS91 — — 2 x 10p *R* proofs. As 4301, 4302	(2)	36
PS92 — — Britannia proofs. As PS55	(4)	1000

The prices given are for absolutely perfect sets with uncleaned, brilliant or matt surfaces. Sets are often seen with one or more coins showing imperfections such as scratches, bumps on the edge, etc. Any flaws will substantially affect the value of a set.

APPENDIX I

A SELECT NUMISMATIC BIBLIOGRAPHY

Listed below is a selection of general books on British numismatics and other works that the specialist collector will need to consult.

General Books:

NORTH, J. J. *English Hammered Coins,* Vol. I, c. 650-1272; Vol. II, 1272-1662.

BROOKE, G. C. *English Coins.* (3rd Ed., 1951).

SUTHERLAND, C. H. V. *English Coinage, 600-1900.*

KENYON, R. Ll. *Gold Coins of England.*

GRUEBER, H. A. *Handbook of the Coins of Great Britain and Ireland.*

SEABY, P.J. *The Story of British Coinage*

Specialist Works:

MACK, R. P. *The Coinage of Ancient Britain.*

ALLEN, D. *The Origins of Coinage in Britain: A Reappraisal.*

VAN ARSDELL R. *Celtic Coinage of Britain.*

DOLLEY, R. H. M. (ED.). *Anglo-Saxon Coins; studies presented to Sir Frank Stenton.*

KEARY, C. and GREUBER, H. *English Coins in the British Museum: Anglo-Saxon Series.*

BROOKE, G. C. *English Coins in the British Museum: The Norman Kings.*

ALLEN, D. F. *English Coins in the British Museum: The Cross-and-Crosslets ('Tealby') type of Henry II.*

LAWRENCE, L. A. *The Coinage of Edward III from 1351.*

WHITTON, C. A. *The Heavy Coinage of Henry VI.*

BLUNT, C. E. and WHITTON, C. A. *The Coinages of Edward IV and of Henry VI (Restored).*

MORRIESON, LT.-COLl. H. W. *The Coinages of Thomas Bushell, 1636-1648.*

NORTH, J. J. and PRESTON-MORLEY, P. J. *The John G. Brooker Collection: Coins of Charles I.*

SEABY H.A. and RAYNER, P.A. *The English Silver Coinage from 1649.* 5th ed. due 1992.

MARSH, M. A. *The Gold Sovereign and The Gold Half Sovereign.*

SPINK & SON, LTD. *The Milled Coinage of England, 1662-1946.*

PECK, C. W. *English Copper, Tin and Bronze Coins in the British Museum, 1558-1958.*

LINECAR, H. W. A. *British Coin Designs and Designers.*

BESLY, E. *Coins and Medals of the English Civil War*

DICKINSON, M. *Seventeenth Century Tokens of the British Isles*

and other authoritative papers published in the *Numismatic Chronicle* and *British Numismatic Journal.*

APPENDIX II

FOREIGN LEGENDS ON ENGLISH COINS

A DOMIONO FACTUM EST ISTUD ET EST MIRABILE IN OCULIS NOSTRIS. (This is the Lord's doing and it is marvellous in our eyes: *Psalm 118*, 23.) First used on 'fine' sovereign of Mary.

AMOR POPULI PRAESIDIUM REGIS. (The love of the people is the King's protection.) Reverse legend on angels of Charles I.

ANNO REGNI PRIMO, etc. (In the first year of the reign, etc.) Used around the edge of many of the larger milled denominations.

CHRISTO AUSPICE REGNO. (I reign under the auspice of Christ.) Used extensively in the reign of Charles I.

CIVIUM INDUSTRIA FLORET CIVITAS. (By the industry of its people the State) On the 1951 Festival crown of George VI.

CULTORES SUI DEUS PROTEGIT. (God protects His worshippers.) On gold double crowns and crowns of Charles I.

DECUS ET TUTAMEN. (An ornament and a safeguard.) This inscription on the edge of all early large milled silverwas suggested by Evelyn, he having seen it on the vignette in Card. Richelieu's Greek Testament, and of courserefers to the device as a means to prevent clipping. (Virgil, *Aen* v.262.) This legend also appears on the edge of U.K. and Northern Ireland one pound coins.

DIRIGE DEUS GRESSUS MEOS. (May the Lord direct my steps.) On the 'Una' 5 pounds of Queen Victoria.

DOMINE NE IN FURORE TUO ARGUAS ME. (O Lord, rebuke me not in Thine anger: *Psalm 6, 1.)*. First used on the half-florin of Edward III and then on all half-nobles.

D*omiNus Deus Omnipotens REX*. (Lord God, Almighty King.) (Viking coins.)

DUM SPIRO SPERO. (Whilst I live, I hope.) On the coins struck at Pontefract Castle during the Civil War after Charles I had been imprisoned.

EXALABITUR IN GLORIA. (He shall be exalted in glory.) On all quarter-nobles.

EXURGAT DEUS ET DISS IPENTUR INIMICI EIUS. (Let God arise and let His enemies be scattered: *Psalm* 68, 1.) On the Scottish ducat and early English coins of James I (VI) and was chosen by the King himself.

FACIAM EOS IN GENTEM UNAM. (I will make them one nation: *Ezek. 37, 22.)* On unites and laurels of James I.

FLORENT CONCORDIA REGNA. (Through concord kingdoms flourish.) On gold unite of Charles I and broad of Charles II.

HANC DEUS DEDIT. (God has given this, i.e. crown .) On siege-pieces of Pontefract struck in the name of Charles II.

HAS NISI PERITURUS MIHI ADIMAT NEMO. (Let no one remove these [letters] from me under penalty of death.) On the edge of crowns and half-crowns of Cromwell.

HENRICUS ROSAS REGNA JACOBUS. (Henry united the roses, James the kingdoms.) On English and Scottish gold coins of James I (VI).

INIMICOS EJUS INDUAM CONFUSIONE. (As for his enemies I shall clothe them with shame: *Psalm* 132, 18.) On shillings of Edward VI struck at Durham House, Strand.

JESUS AUTEM TRANSIENS PER MEDIUM ILLORUM IBAT. (But Jesus, passing through the midst of them, went His way: *Luke iv. 30.)* The usual reverse legend on English nobles, ryals and hammered sovereigns before James I; also on the very rare Scottish noble of David II of Scotland and the unique Anglo-Gallic noble of Edward the Black Prince.

JUSTITIA THRONUM FIRMAT. (Justice strengthens the throne.) On Charles I half-groats and pennies and Scottish twenty-penny pieces.

LUCERNA PEDIBUS MEIS VERBUM EST. (Thy word is a lamp unto my feet: *Psalm*

119, 105.) Obverse legend on a rare half-sovereign of Edward VI struck at Durham
House, Strand.

MIRABILIA FECIT. (He made marvellously.) On the Viking coins of (?) York.

NEMO ME IMPUNE LACESSIT. (No-one provokes me with impunity.) On the 1984
Scottish one pound.

NUMMORUM FAMULUS. (The servant of the coinage.) The legend on the edge of the
English tin coinage at the end of the seventeenth century.

O CRUX AVE SPES UNICA. (Hail! O Cross, our only hope.) On the reverse of all half-
angels.

PAX MISSA PER ORBEM. (Peace sent throughout the world.) The reverse legend of a
pattern farthing of Anne.

PAX QUÆRITUR BELLO. (Peace is sought by war.) The reverse legend of the
Cromwell broad.

PER CRUCEM TUAM SALVA NOS CHRISTE REDEMPTOR. (By Thy cross, save us,
O Christ, our Redeemer.) The normal reverse of English angels.

PLEIDIOL WYF I'M GWLAD. (True am I to my country.) Taken from the Welsh
National Anthem. Used on the 1985 Welsh one pound.

POST MORTEM PATRIS PROFILIO. (For the son after the death of the father.) On
siege-pieces struck at\Pontefract in 1648 (old style) after the execution of Charles I.

POSUI DEUM ADJUTOREM MEUM. (I have made God my Helper: *comp. Psalm* 54,
4.) Used on many English and Irish silver coins from Edward III until 1603. Altered to
POSUIMUS and NOSTRUM on the coins of Philip and Mary.

PROTECTOR LITERIS LITERÆ NUMMIS CORONA ET SALUS. (A protection to the
letters [on the face of the coin], the letters [on the edge] are a garland and a safeguard to
the coinage.) On the edge of the rare fifty-shilling piece of Cromwell.

QUÆ DEUS CONJUNXIT NEMO SEPARET. (What God hath joined together let no
man put asunder: *Matt. 19, 6.*) On the larger silver English and Scottish coins of James I
after he succeeded to the English throne.

REDDE CUIQUE QUOD SUUM EST. (Render to each that which is his own.) On a
Henry VIII type groat of Edward VI struck by Sir Martin Bowes at Durham House,
Strand.

R ELIGIO PROTESTANTIVM LEGES ANGLIÆ LIBE RTAS PARLIAMENTI. (The
religion of the Protestants, the laws of England, the liberty of the Parliament.) This is
known as the 'Declaration' and refers to Charles I's declaration to the Privy Council at
Wellington, 19th Sept., 1642; it is found on many of his coins struck at the provincial
mints during the Civil War. Usually abbreviated to REL:PROT:LEG:ANG:LIB:PAR:

ROSA SINE SPINA. (A rose without a thorn.) Found on some gold and small coins of
Henry VIII and later reigns.

RUTILANS ROSA SINE SPINA. (A dazzling rose without a thorn.) As last but on small
gold only.

SCUTUM FIDEI PROTEGEN EUM *o EAM.* (The shield of faith shall protect him or
her.) On much of the gold of Edward VI and Elizabeth.

TALI DICATA SIGNO MENS FLUCTUARI NEQUIT. (Consecrated by such a sign the
mind cannot waver: from a hymn by Prudentius written in the fourth century, entitled
'Hymnus ante Somnum'.) Only on the gold 'George noble' of Henry VIII.

TIMOR DOM INI FONS VITÆ. (The fear of the Lord is a fountain of life: *Prov. 14, 27.*)
On many shillings of Edward VI.

TUETUR UNITA DEUS. (May God guard these united, i.e. kingdoms.) On many English
Scottish and Irish coins of James I.

VERIT AS TEMPORIS FILIA. (Truth, the daughter of Time.) On English and Irish coins
of Mary Tudor.

ICH DIEN. (I serve.) Aberystwyth Furnace 2d, and Decimal 2p.

Some Royal Titles:

REX ANGL*orum*—King of the English.

REX SAXONUM OCCIDENTA LIM —King of the West Saxons.

DEI GR*Atia* ANGL*iae* ET FRANC*iae* DomiN*us* HYBerniae ET AQVIT*aniae*—*By the Grace of God, King of* England and France, Lord of Ireland and Aquitaine.

D*ei GRAtia Magnae Britanniae, FRanciae ET Hiberniae REX Fidei Defensor BRunsviciensis ET Luneburgen-sis Dux, Sacri Romani Imperii Archi-THesaurarius ET ELector*=By the Grace of God, King of Great Britain, France and Ireland, Defender of the Faith, Duke of Brunswick and Luneburg, High Treasurer and Elector of the Holy Roman Empire.

BRITANNIARUM REX —King of the Britains (i.e. Britain and British territories overseas).

BRITT:OMN:REX:FID:DEF:IND:IMP: —King of all the Britains, Defender of the Faith, Emperor of India. Although not *Latin* legends, the following Norman-French mottoes might usefully be added here:

DIEU ET MON DROIT. (God and my right.) On halfcrowns of George IV and later monarchs

HONI SOIT QUI MAL Y PENSE. (Evil to him who evil thinks.) The Motto of the Order of the Garter, first used on the Hereford (?) halfcrowns of Charles I. It also occurs on the Garter Star in the centre of the reverse of the silver coins of Charles II, but being so small it is usually illegible; it is more prominent on the coinage of George III.

Numismatic Clubs and Societies, Magazines and Dealers.

Coins News is the major monthly numismatic magazine. Spink's *Numismatic Circular* is long established, its first edition appeared in December 1892. There are many numismatic magazines which carry articles of interest, such as the *CNG Review* and the *S & B Bulletin.*

Many local clubs and societies are affiliated to the British Association of Numismatic Societies, (B.A.N.S) which holds an annual Congress. Details of your nearest numismatic club can be obtained from the Hon. Secretary, Philip Mernick, British Association of Numismatic Societies, c/o Bush, Boake Allen Ltd. Blackhorse Lane, London E17 5QP.

The two principal learned societies are the Royal Numismatic Society, c/o Department of Coins and Medals, the British Museum, Great Russell Street, Bloomsbury, London WC1 3DG, and the British Numismatic Society, c/o Graham Dyer, The Royal Mint, Llantrisant, Pontyclun, mid Glamorgan, Wales. Both these societies publish an annual journal.

A list of dealer members of the British Numismatic Trade Association may be obtained from the Secretary, David Fletcher, PO Box 64, Coventry CV5 6SN.

APPENDIX III

MINTMARKS AND OTHER SYMBOLS ON ENGLISH COINS

A MINTMARK (*mm.*), a term borrowed from Roman and Greek numismatics where it showed the place of mintage, was generally used on English coins to show where the legend began (a religious age preferred a cross for the purpose). Later, this mark, since the dating of coins was not usual, had a periodic significance, changing from time to time. Hence it was of a secret or 'privy' nature; other privy marks on a coin might be the code-mark of a particular workshop or workman. Thus a privy mark (including the *mm.*) might show when a coin was made, or who made it. In the use of precious metals this knowledge was necessary to guard against fraud and counterfeiting.

Mintmarks are sometimes termed 'initial marks' as they are normally placed at the commencement of the inscription. Some of the symbols chosen were personal badges of the ruling monarch, such as the rose and sun of York, the boar's head of Richard III, the dragon of Henry Tudor or the thistle of James I; others are heraldic symbols or may allude to the mint master responsible for the coinage, e.g. the *mm.* bow used on the Durham House coins struck under John Bowes and the WS mark of William Sharrington of Bristol.

A table of mintmarks is given on the next page. Where mintmarks appear in the catalogue they are sometimes referred to only by the reference number, in order to save space, i.e. *mm. 28* (=mintmark Sun), *mm.28/74* (=*mm.* Sun on obverse, mm. Coronet on reverse), *mm. 28/-* (=*mm.* Sun on obverse only).

MINTMARKS AND OTHER SYMBOLS

1	Edward III, Cross 1 (Class B+C).	
2	Edward III, broken Cross 1 (Class D).	
3	Edward III, Cross 2 (Class E)	
4	Edward III, Cross 3 (Class G)	
5	Cross Potent (Edw. III Treaty)	
6	Cross Pattee (Edw. III Post Treaty) Rich. III).	
7	(a) Plain of Greek Cross. (b) Cross Moline.	
8	Cross Patonce.	
9	Cross Fleuree.	
10	Cross Calvary (Cross on steps).	
11	Long Cross Fitchee.	
12	Short Cross Fitchee.	
13	Restoration Cross (Hen. VI).	
14	Latin Cross.	
15	Voided Cross (Henry VI).	
16	Saltire Cross.	
17	Cross and 4 pellets.	
18	Pierced Cross.	
19	Pierced Cross & pellet.	
20	Pierced Cross & central pellet.	
21	Cross Crosslet.	
22	Curved Star (rayant).	
23	Star.	
24	Spur Rowel.	
25	Mullet.	
26	Pierced Mullet.	
27	Eglantine.	
28	Sun (Edw. IV).	
29	Mullet (Henry V).	
30	Pansy.	
31	Heraldic Cinquefoil (Edw. IV).	
32	Heraldic Cinquefoil (James I).	
33	Rose (Edw. IV).	
34	Rosette (Edw. IV).	
35	Rose (Chas. I).	
36	Catherine Wheel.	
37	Cross in circle.	
38	Halved Sun (6 rays) & Rose.	
39	Halved Sun (4 rays) & Rose.	
40	Lis-upon-Half-Rose.	
41	Lis-upon-Sun & Rose.	
42	Lis-Rose dimidiated.	

43	Lis-issuant-from-Rose.
44	Trefoil.
45	Slipped Trefoil, James I (1).
46	Slipped Trefoil, James I (2).
47	Quatrefoil.
48	Saltire.
49	Pinecone.
50	Leaf (-mascle, Hen. VI).
51	Leaf (-trefoil, Hen. VI).
52	Arrow.
53	Pheon.
54	A.
55	Annulet.
56	Annulet-with-pellet.
57	Anchor.
58	Anchor & B.
59	Flower & B.
60	Bell.
61	Book.
62	Boar's Head (early Richard III).
63	Boar's Head (later Richard III).
64	Boar's Head, Charles I.
65	Acorn (a) Hen. VIII (b) Elizabeth.
66	Bow.
67	Br. (Bristol, Chas. I).
68	Cardinal's Hat.
69	Castle (Henry VIII).
70	Castle with H.
71	Castle (Chas. I).
72	Crescent (a) Henry VIII (b) Elizabeth.
73	Pomegranate. (Mary; Henry VIII's is broader).
74	Coronet.
75	Crown.
76	Crozier (a) Edw. III (b) Hen. VIII.
77	Ermine.
78	Escallop (Hen. VII).
79	Escallop (James I).
80	Eye (in legend Edw. IV).
81	Eye (Parliament).
82	Radiate Eye (Hen. VII).
83	Gerb.
84	Grapes.
85	Greyhound's Head.
86	Hand.
87	Harp.

88	Heart.
89	Helmet.
90	Key.
91	Leopard's Head.
91A	Crowned Leopard's Head with collar (Edw. VII).
92	Lion.
93	Lion rampant.
94	Martlet.
95	Mascle.
96	Negro's Head.
97	Ostrich's Head.
98	P in brackets.
99	Pall.
100	Pear.
101	Plume.
102	Plume. Aberystwyth and Bristol.
103	Plume. Oxford.
104	Plume. Shrewsbury.
105	Lis.
106	Lis.
107	Portcullis.
108	Portcullis. Crowned.
109	Sceptre.
110	Sunburst.
111	Swan.
112	R in brackets.
113	Sword.
114	T (Henry VIII).
115	TC monogram.
116	WS monogram.
117	y or Y.
118	Dragon (Henry VII).
119	(a) Triangle (b) Triangle in Circle.
120	Sun (Parliament).
121	Uncertain mark.
122	Grapple.
123	Tun.
124	Woolpack.
125	Thistle.
126	Figure 6 (Edw. VI).
127	Floriated cross.
128	Lozenge.
129	Billet.
130	Plume. Lundy Is.
131	Two lions.
132	Clasped book.
133	Cross pomee.
134	Bugle.

The reign after a mintmark indicates that from which the drawing is taken. A similar mm. may have been used in another reign and will be found in the chronological list at the beginning of each reign..

1	2	3	4	5	6	7a	7b	8 9
10	11	12	13	14	15	16	17	18 19
20	21	22	23	24	25	26	27	28 29
30	31	32	33	34	35	36	37	38 39
40	41	42	43	44	45	46	47	48 49
50	51	52	53	54	55	56	57	58 59
60	61	62	63	64	65a	65b	66	67 68
69	70	71	72a	72b	73	74	75	76 77
78	79	80	81	82	83	84	85	86 87
88	89	90a	90b	90c	91	92	93	94 95
96	97	98	99	100	101	102	103	104 105
106	107	108	109	110	111	112	113	114 115
116	117a	117b	118	119a	119b	120	121	122 123
124	125	126	127	128	129	130	131	132 133
134								